New Perspectives on

MICROSOFT® PROJECT 2000

Introductory

LISA FRIEDRICHSEN

RACHEL BIHELLER BUNIN

APPROVED COURSEWARE

EXPERT

COURSE TECHNOLOGY

Thomson Learning™

ONE MAIN STREET, CAMBRIDGE, MA 02142

Australia • Canada • Denmark • Japan • Mexico • New Zealand • Philippines
Puerto Rico • Singapore • South Africa • Spain • United Kingdom • United States

New Perspectives on Microsoft Project 2000—Introductory is published by Course Technology.

Managing Editor	Greg Donald
Senior Editor	Donna Gridley
Senior Product Manager	Rachel Crapser
Acquisitions Editor	Christine Guivernau
Product Manager	Karen Shortill
Product Manager	Catherine Donaldson
Associate Product Manager	Melissa Dezotell
Editorial Assistant	Jill Kirn
Developmental Editor	Rachel Bunin
Production Editor	Elena Montillo
Manufacturing Coordinator	Denise Sandler
Text Designer	Meral Dabcovich
Cover Art Designer	Douglas Goodman

© 2000 by Course Technology, a division of Thomson Learning

For more information contact:

Course Technology
One Main Street
Cambridge, MA 02142
Or find us on the World Wide Web at: http://www.course.com

For permission to use material from this text or product, contact us by:
Web: *www.thomsonrights.com*
Phone: 1-800-730-2214
Fax: 1-800-730-2215

Trademarks

Disclaimer

ISBN 0-7600-7076-8

Printed in the United States of America

1 2 3 4 5 6 7 8 9 MZR 04 03 02 01 00

PREFACE

The New Perspectives Series

About New Perspectives

Course Technology's **New Perspectives Series** is an integrated system of instruction that combines text and technology products to teach computer concepts, the Internet, and microcomputer applications. Users consistently praise this series for innovative pedagogy, use of interactive technology, creativity, accuracy, and supportive and engaging style.

How is the New Perspectives Series different from other series?

The **New Perspectives Series** distinguishes itself by **innovative technology**, from the renowned Course Labs to the state-of-the-art multimedia that is integrated with our Concepts texts. Other distinguishing features include **sound instructional design**, **proven pedagogy**, and **consistent quality**. Each tutorial has students learn features in the context of solving a realistic case problem rather than simply learning a laundry list of features. With the **New Perspectives Series**, instructors report that students have a complete, integrative learning experience that stays with them. They credit this high retention and competency to the fact that this series incorporates critical thinking and problem solving with computer skills mastery. In addition, we work hard to ensure accuracy by using a multi-step quality assurance process during all stages of development. Instructors focus on teaching and students spend more time learning

Choose the coverage that's right for you

New Perspectives applications books are available in the following categories:

Brief

2-4 tutorials

Brief: approximately 150 pages long, two to four "Level I" tutorials, teaches basic application skills.

Introductory

6 or 7 tutorials, or Brief + 2 or 3 more tutorials

Introductory: approximately 300 pages long, four to seven tutorials, goes beyond the basic skills. These books often build out of the Brief book, adding two or three additional "Level II" tutorials. The book you are holding is an Introductory book.

Comprehensive

Introductory + 4 or 5 more tutorials. Includes Brief Windows tutorials and Additional Cases

Comprehensive: approximately 600 pages long, eight to twelve tutorials, all tutorials included in the Introductory text plus higher-level "Level III" topics. Also includes two Windows tutorials and three or four fully developed Additional Cases.

Advanced

Quick Review of basics + in-depth, high-level coverage

Advanced: approximately 600 pages long, covers topics similar to those in the Comprehensive books, but offers the highest-level coverage in the series. Advanced books assume students already know the basics, and therefore go into more depth at a more accelerated rate than the Comprehensive titles. Advanced books are ideal for a second, more technical course.

Office

Quick Review of basics + in-depth, high-level coverage

Office: approximately 800 pages long, covers all components of the Office suite as well as integrates the individual software packages with one another and the Internet.

Custom Editions

Choose from any of the above to build your own Custom Editions or CourseKits

Custom Books The New Perspectives Series offers you two ways to customize a New Perspectives text to fit your course exactly: *CourseKits*™—two or more texts shrinkwrapped together. We offer significant price discounts on *CourseKits*™. *Custom Editions*® offer you flexibility in designing your concepts, Internet, and applications courses. You can build your own book by ordering a combination of topics bound together to cover only the subjects you want. There is no minimum order, and books are spiral bound. Contact your Course Technology sales representative for more information.

What course is this book appropriate for?

New Perspectives on Microsoft Project 2000—Introductory can be used in any course in which you want students to learn all the most important topics of Project 2000, including planning a project, creating project schedules, communicating project information, using the critical path, assigning resources, tracking progress, and sharing information across applications and the Web. It is particularly recommended for a full-semester course on Project Management using Project 2000. This book assumes that students have learned basic Windows navigation and file management skills from Course Technology's New Perspectives on *Microsoft Windows 98—Brief, New Perspectives on Microsoft Windows NT Workstation 4.0—Introductory*, or an equivalent book.

What is the Microsoft Office User Specialist Program?

The Microsoft Office User Specialist Program provides an industry-recognized standard for measuring an individual's mastery of an Office application. Passing one or more MOUS Program certification exams helps your students demonstrate their proficiency to prospective employers and gives them a competitive edge in the job marketplace. Course Technology offers a growing number of Microsoft-approved products that cover all of the required objectives for the MOUS Program exams. For a complete listing of Course Technology titles that you can use to help your students get certified, visit our Web site at *www.course.com*.

After completing the tutorials and exercises in this book, students will be prepared to take the MOUS exam for Microsoft Project 2000. For more information about certification, please visit the MOUS program site at *www.mous.net*.

Proven Pedagogy

CASE

Tutorial Case Each tutorial begins with a problem presented in a case that is meaningful to students. The case turns the task of learning how to use an application into a problem-solving process.

45-minute Sessions Each tutorial is divided into sessions that can be completed in about 45 minutes to an hour. Sessions allow instructors to more accurately allocate time in their syllabus, and students to better manage their own study time.

1.
2.
3.

Step-by-Step Methodology We make sure students can differentiate between what they are to *do* and what they are to *read*. Through numbered steps—clearly identified by a gray shaded background—students are constantly guided in solving the case problem. In addition, the numerous screen shots with callouts direct students' attention to what they should look at on the screen.

TROUBLE?

TROUBLE? Paragraphs These paragraphs anticipate the mistakes or problems that students may have and help them continue with the tutorial.

"Read This Before You Begin" Page Located opposite the first tutorial's opening page for each level of the text, the Read This Before You Begin Page helps introduce technology into the classroom. Technical considerations and assumptions about software are listed to save time and eliminate unnecessary aggravation. Notes about the Student Disks help instructors and students get the right files in the right places, so students get started on the right foot.

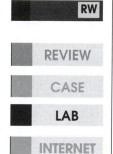

Quick Check Questions Each session concludes with meaningful, conceptual Quick Check questions that test students' understanding of what they learned in the session. Answers to the Quick Check questions are provided at the end of each tutorial.

Reference Windows Reference Windows are succinct summaries of the most important tasks covered in a tutorial and they preview actions students will perform in the steps to follow.

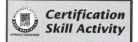

End-of-Tutorial Review Assignments, Case Problems, and Lab Assignments Review Assignments provide students with additional hands-on practice of the skills they learned in the tutorial using the same case presented in the tutorial. These Assignments are followed by three to four Case Problems that have approximately the same scope as the tutorial case but use a different scenario. In addition, some of the Review Assignments or Case Problems may include Exploration Exercises that challenge students and encourage them to explore the capabilities of the program they are using, and/or further extend their knowledge.

File Finder Chart This chart, located in the back of the book, visually explains how students should set up their Data Disk, what files should go in what folders, and how to save the files in the course of their work.

MOUS Certification Chart In the back of the book, you'll find a chart that lists all the skills for the Microsoft Office User Specialist Exam and Expert Exam on Project 2000. With page numbers referencing where these skills are covered in this text and where students get hands-on practice in completing the skill, the chart can be used as an excellent study guide in preparing for the MOUS exams.

Instructor's Resource Kit for this title contains:

- Electronic Instructor's Manual in Word 97 format
- Sample Syllabus
- Data Files
- Solution Files
- Course Test Manager Testbank
- Course Test Manager Engine
- Figure Files

These Teaching Tools come on CD-ROM. If you don't have access to a CD-ROM drive, contact your Course Technology customer service representative for more information.

The New Perspectives Teaching Tools Package

Electronic Instructor's Manual Our Instructor's Manuals include tutorial overviews and outlines, technical notes, lecture notes, solutions, and Extra Case Problems. Many instructors use the Extra Case Problems for performance-based exams or extra credit projects. The Instructor's Manual is available as an electronic file, which you can get from the Instructor Resource Kit (IRK) CD-ROM or download it from **www.course.com**.

Data Files Data Files contain all of the data that students will use to complete the tutorials, Review Assignments, and Case Problems. A Readme file includes instructions for using the files. See the "Read This Before You Begin" page for more information on Student Files.

Solution Files Solution Files contain every file students are asked to create or modify in the tutorials, Review Assignments, Case Problems, and Extra Case Problems. A Help file on the Instructor's Resource Kit includes information for using the Solution files.

Figure Files Many figures in the text are provided on the IRK CD-ROM to help illustrate key topics or concepts. Instructors can create traditional overhead transparencies by printing the figure files. Or they can create electronic slide shows by using the figures in a presentation program such as PowerPoint.

Course Test Manager: Testing and Practice at the Computer or on Paper Course Test Manager is cutting-edge, Windows-based testing software that helps instructors design and administer practice tests and actual examinations. Course Test Manager can automatically grade the tests students take at the computer and can generate statistical information on individual as well as group performance.

Online Companions: Dedicated to Keeping You and Your Students Up-To-Date Visit our faculty sites and student sites on the World Wide Web at www.course.com. Here instructors can browse this text's password-protected Faculty Online Companion to obtain an online Instructor's Manual, Solution Files, Student Files, and more.

More innovative technology
Course CBT

Enhance your students' Office 2000 classroom learning experience with self-paced computer-based training on CD-ROM. Course CBT engages students with interactive multimedia and hands-on simulations that reinforce and complement the concepts and skills covered in the textbook. All the content is aligned with the MOUS (Microsoft Office User Specialist) program, making it a great preparation tool for the certification exams. Course CBT also includes extensive pre- and post-assessments that test students' mastery of skills. These pre- and post-assessments automatically generate a "custom learning path" through the course that highlights only the topics with which students need help.

Skills Assessment Manager

How well do your students *really* know Microsoft Office? Skills Assessment Manager (SAM) is a performance-based testing program that measures students' proficiency in Microsoft Office 2000. SAM is available for Office 2000 in either a live or simulated environment. You can use SAM to place students into or out of courses, monitor their performance throughout a course, and help prepare them for the MOUS certification exams.

CyberClass CyberClass is a Web-based tool designed for on-campus or distance learning. Use it to enhance how you currently run your class by posting assignments and your course syllabus or holding online office hours. Or, use it for your distance learning course, and offer mini-lectures, conduct online discussion groups, or give your mid-term exam. For more information, visit our Web site at: www.course.com/products/cyberclass/index.html.

WebCT

WebCT is a tool used to create Web-based educational environments and also uses WWW browsers as the interface for the course-building environment. The site is hosted on your school campus, allowing complete control over the information, WebCT has its own internal communication system, offering internal e-mail, a Bulletin Board, and a Chat room. Course Technology offers pre-existing supplemental information to help in your WebCT class creation, such as a suggested Syllabus, Lecture Notes, and Practice Tests.

Acknowledgments

Thanks go to Course Technology for giving me the opportunity to write this book with Lisa, my co-author, wonderful friend, and excellent teacher. Special thanks to Donna Gridley for putting it all together, to Karen Shortill for managing the book at Course, to Elena Montillo for her excellent production management, to Nicole Ashton for outstanding work as our validator, and to Adrian Jenkins at Microsoft for all his support during the development and helping us through all the technical issues with Project 2000 and the beta program. I want to thank my husband, David, for his incredible support, and of course, my three wonderful children Jennifer, Emily, and Michael, for keeping me laughing and making it all worthwhile.

Rachel Biheller Bunin

Thank you to the best textbook publishing team in the world at Course Technology, and especially to our daily leaders, Karen Shortill and Melissa Dezotell. Thank you to our outstanding reviewers, Tony Briggs, David Overbye, and Bill Leban, for their meaningful feedback. Thank you to my co-author, developmental editor, and awesome friend, Rachel Bunin. Finally, thanks to my loving husband, Doug.

Lisa Friedrichsen

BRIEF CONTENTS

TABLE OF CONTENTS

Reference Windows

Tutorial Tips

These tutorials will help you learn about Microsoft Project 2000. The tutorials are designed to be worked through at a computer. Each tutorial is divided into sessions. Watch for the session headings, such as Session 1.1 and Session 1.2. Each session is designed to be completed in about 45 minutes, but take as much time as you need. It's also a good idea to take a break between sessions.

Before you begin, read the following questions and answers. They will help you use the tutorials.

Where do I start?

Each tutorial begins with a case, which sets the scene for the tutorial and gives you background information to help you understand what you will be doing. Read the case before you go to the lab. In the lab, begin with the first session of a tutorial.

How do I know what to do on the computer?

Each session contains steps that you will perform on the computer to learn how to use Microsoft Project 2000. Read the text that introduces each series of steps. The steps you need to do at a computer are numbered and are set against a shaded background. Read each step carefully and completely before you try it.

How do I know if I did the step correctly?

As you work, compare your computer screen with the corresponding figure in the tutorial. Don't worry if your screen display is somewhat different from the figure. The important parts of the screen display are labeled in each figure. Check to make sure these parts are on your screen.

What if I make a mistake?

Don't worry about making mistakes—they are part of the learning process. Paragraphs labeled "TROUBLE?" identify common problems and explain how to get back on track. Follow the steps in a TROUBLE? paragraph only if you are having the problem described. If you run into other problems:

- Carefully consider the current state of your system, the position of the pointer, and any messages on the screen.

- Complete the sentence, "Now I want to…" Be specific, because identifying your goal will help you rethink the steps you need to take to reach that goal.

- If you are working on a particular piece of software, consult the Help system.

- If the suggestions above don't solve your problem, consult your technical support person for assistance.

How do I use the Reference Windows?

Reference Windows summarize the procedures you will learn in the tutorial steps. Do not complete the actions in the Reference Windows when you are working through the tutorial. Instead, refer to the Reference Windows while you are working on the assignments at the end of the tutorial.

How can I test my understanding of the material I learned in the tutorial?

At the end of each session, you can answer the Quick Check questions. The answers for the Quick Checks are at the end of that tutorial.

After you have completed the entire tutorial, you should complete the Review Assignments and Case Problems. They are carefully structured so that you will review what you have learned and then apply your knowledge to new situations.

What if I can't remember how to do something?

You should refer to the Task Reference at the end of the book; it summarizes how to accomplish tasks using the most efficient method.

Before you begin the tutorials, you should know the basics about your computer's operating system. You should also know how to use the menus, dialog boxes, Help system, and My Computer.

Now that you've read Tutorial Tips, you are ready to begin.

New Perspectives on

MICROSOFT®
PROJECT 2000

Read This Before You Begin

To the Student

Data Files

To complete the Tutorials, Review Assignments, and Case Problems, you need Data Files. Your instructor may provide the Data Files, or you can download them by going to Course Technology's Web site, *www.course.com*. See the front inside cover of this book for more information on downloading your Data Files.

From Course Technology's Web site, the Data Files will be downloaded to you as a single compressed, executable file (7076-8.exe). After you download the file, double-click it to extract the actual Data Files. The files will be placed on your hard drive using the following general folder structure:

C:\7076-8\Tutorial.01\Tutorial\data files…
C:\7076-8\Tutorial.01\Review\data files…
C:\7076-8\Tutorial.01\Cases\data files…

While it is possible to use floppy disks to complete Tutorials 1 through 5, Tutorial 6 should be completed using a hard drive or large removable storage device such as a zip or jazz drive. Tutorial 6 covers integration features that involve multiple files, and the steps cannot be completed using a single floppy disk.

All of the instructions in this book ask you to open and save files to your Data Disk, but if it is possible to work from your hard drive, we recommend that you create the following folders, copy the corresponding data files into the folders before working on Tutorials, and use the Solution folders on your hard drive as your "Data Disk."

C:\YourName\Tutorial.0x\Tutorial\Solution
C:\YourName\Tutorial.0x\Review\Solution
C:\YourName\Tutorial.0x\Cases\Solution

If you are working with Data Files from other New Perspectives textbooks (and therefore have other Tutorial, Review, and Case folders to manage), you may wish to modify the folder hierarchy to identify the book you are using as well. For example, the following hierarchy allows you to manage the Data Files of multiple New Perspectives books from within the YourName folder:

C:\YourName\Project2000\Tutorial.0x\Tutorial\Solution
C:\YourName\Project2000\Tutorial.0x\Review\Solution
C:\YourName\Project2000\Tutorial.0x\Cases\Solution

If you are working on a hard disk and have to transport your files using floppy disks, we recommend you take advantage of

WinZip™, to compress and archive your files within their folder structure. To find out more about WinZip™ go to the Web site *www.winzip.com* and click the link for Basic Information.

If you use floppy disks as the "Data Disks" for Tutorials 1 through 5, you will need to use more than one floppy disk for each Tutorial. We recommend that you label each disk clearly with both the Tutorial number and whether the files on the disk are for the Tutorial, Review, or Case assignments. The following guidelines will help to determine how many floppy disks you will need for each Tutorial:

Tutorial 1: 1 disk
Tutorial 2: 1 disk
Tutorial 3: 2 disks
    Disk 1: Tutorial and Review
    Disk 2: Cases
Tutorial 4: 3 disks
    Disk 1: Tutorial
    Disk 2: Review
    Disk 3: Cases
Tutorial 5: 3 disks
    Disk 1: Tutorial
    Disk 2: Review
    Disk 3: Cases
Tutorial 6: hard disk required

Using Your Own Computer

If you are going to work through this book using your own computer, you need:

■ **Computer System:** Microsoft Project 2000 and Windows 95 or higher must be installed on your computer. This book assumes a complete installation of Project 2000.

■ **Special Considerations for Tutorial 6:** Tutorial 6 requires installation of Microsoft Excel 2000, Word 2000, Access 2000, and Internet Explorer 5.

Visit Our World Wide Web Site

Additional materials designed especially for you are available on the World Wide Web.
Go to http://www.course.com/NewPerspectives/Project2000

To the Instructor

The Data Files are available on the Instructor's Resource Kit for this title. Follow the instructions in the Help file on the CD-ROM to install the programs to your network or standalone computer. For information on managing Data Files, see the "To the Student" section above.

You are granted a license to copy the Data Files to any computer or computer network used by students who have purchased this book.

In this tutorial you will:

- Learn about project management phases and goals

- Learn project management terminology

- Understand the benefits of project management

- Understand how Project 2000 supports successful project management

- Open and explore an existing project

- Understand and switch between different project views

- Compare the Gantt Chart and Network Diagram views

- Use the project timescale and calendar

- Use Print Preview and the Page Setup dialog box

- Explore the Project 2000 Help system

PLANNING A PROJECT

Preparing for a Local Area Network Installation with Microsoft Project 2000

JLB Partners

As the new Office Manager for JLB Partners, a small accounting firm, you have acquired new office management responsibilities over the past year. The managing Certified Public Accountant (CPA) partner, Emily Kelsey, recently asked you to direct a new and exciting project: managing the firm's local area network (LAN) installation. Although the firm has only six personal computers that support the four CPAs, the receptionist, and you, the installation will still be a challenge. Even with small projects, the details can become overwhelming, deadlines can slip, and communication with management can be difficult.

Although your college degree was in business, you have many friends who took information systems courses. You seek the advice of an old friend, Aaron Michaels. Aaron tells you that a LAN implementation is nothing more than a **project**, a defined sequence of steps that achieve an identified goal, and he offers to help you plan those steps for your LAN installation. He also suggests that you use **Microsoft Project 2000** to document and manage the LAN project because of its ability to help you calculate dates, responsibilities, and costs. Aaron explains that Project 2000 will also help you clearly communicate project information to Emily.

Aaron teaches "Fundamentals of Project Management Using Microsoft Project 2000" at the local community college and invites you to enroll. He explains that all projects can benefit from professional project management but that technical and computer projects are especially good candidates due to their increased complexity, cost, and management expectations. You present the idea to Emily, and she wholeheartedly supports your enrollment in the class.

SESSION 1.1

In this session, you will be introduced to the phases, terminology, and benefits of formal project management, as well as learn how Microsoft Project 2000 supports these benefits.

Introduction to Project Management

Project management is the process of defining, organizing, tracking, and communicating information about a project in order to meet a project goal. The **project goal** is achieved when a series of tasks are completed that produce a desired outcome, at a specified level of quality, and within a given timeframe and budget. Examples of project goals include: install a new computer system, build a house, earn a college degree, and find a job. Microsoft Project 2000 helps you to meet the quality, time frame, and budget goals by analyzing and summarizing information about the project. It also identifies ways to complete project tasks more *efficiently* and *effectively*. Being **efficient** means doing tasks faster, with fewer resources, and with lower costs. Although being efficient is important and leads to greater productivity, being *effective* is much more important, as well as more difficult to achieve. Being **effective** means to meet the actual goals of the project rather than just doing the project tasks quickly. It doesn't matter if a new computer system is installed in the specified time frame and under budget if it doesn't work as intended. Using a tool such as Project 2000 will help you to be both efficient *and* effective by organizing task details as well as how they interrelate, by automatically updating date and cost information, and by providing communication tools used to make informed decisions.

Project Goal

The first step in formally managing a project of any size is to define the project goal. The project goal should be as short and as simple as possible, yet as detailed as necessary to clearly communicate the specific quality, time frame, and budget expectations of management. The project is finished when the project manager—the primary source of information regarding project status—and management agree that the project goal has been met.

In your case, the project goal is to *network six computers to easily share resources within a time frame of three months and within a budget of $50,000*. This goal assumes that some additional project steps will define which resources need to be shared, as well as determine how this is done "easily." Gaining management agreement to a concise project goal that addresses the issues of quality, time frame, and budget is essential in order for both the project manager and management to stay synchronized with appropriate expectations. Figure 1-1 gives some sample project goals.

Figure 1-1	SETTING PROJECT GOALS
VAGUE PROJECT GOALS	**IMPROVED PROJECT GOALS**
Find a job	Secure a local job within the next six months in the area of information systems that pays at least $35,000 annually.
Organize the company retreat	Plan the annual company retreat in the month of January in a warm climate convention center within a budget of $100,000.
Build a house	Build a four-bedroom house in Overland Park within budget for occupancy by July 1.
Run a fundraiser	Hold a fundraising event to finance the new band uniforms by September 1.

Often, during the course of a project, you will need to revise the project goal as unexpected issues alter the original plan. For example, you might have initially underestimated the cost or time required to complete the project. Project 2000 helps both the project manager and management predict and understand project issues and progress so that negative effects on the quality, time frame, or cost of the project can be minimized.

Phases of Project Management

The duration of the project is divided into four distinct phases: defining, creating, tracking, and closing. Each phase requires appropriate communication to management if you hope to stay synchronized with their needs and desires. Figure 1-2 describes the typical tasks and responsibilities that occur within each phase. Microsoft Project 2000 supports each of these phases by providing an integrated database into which you enter the individual pieces of project information (tasks, durations, resources, dates, and costs). It uses the project information to create the screens and reports necessary to communicate project status throughout each phase.

Figure 1-2	PHASES OF PROJECT MANAGEMENT
PHASE	**TYPICAL RESPONSIBILITIES**
Defining	■ Setting the project goal ■ Identifying the necessary project start or finish date limitations ■ Identifying the project manager ■ Identifying project budget and quality considerations
Creating	■ Entering project tasks, durations, and relationships ■ Identifying project subdivisions and milestones ■ Documenting available resources as well as their associated costs ■ Entering applicable resource or task restrictions such as intermediate due dates or not-to-exceed costs ■ Assigning resources to tasks
Tracking	■ Updating project start, finish, and resource usage to completed or partially completed tasks ■ Managing resource and task conflicts ■ Working with the project to meet management timing, resource, and cost objectives ■ Changing the project to meet new or unexpected demands
Closing	■ Entering the final status of the finished project, including task date, resource, and cost information ■ Printing the final reports used to analyze the performance of the project

Project Management Terminology

Understanding key project terminology is fundamental to your success as a project manager.

Task

A **task** is the specific action that needs to be completed in order to achieve the project goal. Examples of tasks within a LAN installation include document current hardware, purchase new equipment, wire the office, and train the users. The specificity of the task depends on its complexity as well as on the needs of the users of the project information. If "train the users" involves learning multiple software applications such as spreadsheets, word processing, and new accounting software, a single training task is probably too broad. If the task is to train the new users on how to create a new LAN password, however, a single task describing this effort is probably sufficient.

Duration

Each task has **duration**, which is how long it takes to complete the task. Some task durations are *not flexible* in that they do not change according to the amount of resources applied. Meetings fall into this category because, for example, it generally doesn't matter if five or six employees attend the orientation meeting—the scheduled duration of the meeting is still two hours. Most tasks, however, have a flexible duration, meaning that if two people of equal qualifications were assigned to the task, the task could be completed in half the time. Wiring the office and unboxing new computers are examples of tasks with *flexible* durations.

In Project 2000, durations can also be *estimated* or *firm*. An **estimated duration** appears with a question mark (?) after the duration. If you do not enter a duration for a new task, it will appear with an estimated default duration of one day, which appears as "1 day?" in the Project 2000 window. By providing for both estimated and firm durations, Project 2000 gives you the ability to quickly find and filter on tasks with durations that are not firm.

Resource

Resources are the people, equipment, or facilities (such as a conference room) that need to be assigned to a task in order to complete it. Some resources have defined hourly costs that will be applied as the task is completed (the software trainer charges $100/hour). Some tasks have per-use costs (the conference room charge is $200/use). Some resource costs are not applied to a particular task but rather to the entire project (a temporary receptionist is hired for the duration of the project to answer telephones while existing employees are being trained). The degree to which you track task and project costs is a function of what management wants. If management is mainly concerned about when a project will be finished, and the project is well within budget, it might be foolish to spend the extra time and energy to track detailed costs. If management needs to track detailed project costs, then resource assignments and their associated costs must be entered and managed.

Project Manager

The **project manager** is the central person to which all of the details of the project converge for entry into the project plan. The project manager often supervises the project's implementation and is the main source of project status information for management. The project manager is also expected to balance conflicting business needs, such as the need to finish a project by July 1, but also to finish it under budget. As such, the project manager must have excellent organizational and communication skills.

Scope

The **scope** is the total amount of products and services that the project is supposed to provide. A clear project goal will help communicate the scope of the project. The more precise the project objectives and deliverables, the clearer the scope becomes. Projects that are not well defined or those that do not have appropriate management involvement and support often suffer from scope creep. **Scope creep** is the condition whereby projects grow and change in unanticipated ways that increase costs, extend deadlines, or otherwise negatively affect the project goal.

Quality

Quality is the degree to which something meets an objective standard. Almost every project and task has implied quality standards. Without effective communication, however, they can be interpreted much differently by the project manager and by the employee or contractor completing the task. The more clearly those standards are defined, the more likely that the task will be completed at a quality level acceptable to the project manager. Both the project manager and the person completing the task must agree on key quality measurements. For example, the task "install computer cabling" involves other issues that determine whether the task will be completed in a high-quality manner. Issues to consider include the following:

- Will the installation be completed in a manner that doesn't interrupt the regular workday?
- How will the office furniture be moved and returned to its original location?
- What cable testing will be conducted?
- What type of cable documentation will be provided?
- When will payment be due?

Risk

Risk is the probability that a task, resource, or cost is miscalculated in a way that creates a negative impact on the project. Obviously, all risk cannot be eliminated. People get sick, accidents happen, and Murphy's Law is alive and well. Later you will learn how to use Microsoft Project to minimize project risk.

Benefits of Project Management

As you have learned, the major benefit of formal project management is to complete a project goal at a specified level of quality within a given time frame and budget. You begin to understand how this can be applied to your project at JLB Partners. Within this broad benefit statement are several subset benefits, as identified in Figure 1-3.

Figure 1-3	BENEFITS OF PROJECT MANAGEMENT
Better understanding of overall project goals
Better understanding of project tasks, durations, schedule dates, and costs
More organized and streamlined way to manage the many details of a project
More accurate and reliable project status information
More efficient use of project resources
Better communication between management, the project manager, and others
Faster response to conflicting project goals
Greater awareness of project progress
Faster project completion
Lower project costs
Fewer project failures

How Microsoft Project 2000 Supports Successful Project Management

Microsoft Project 2000 is software that allows you to enter the details of a project into one organized central repository. It offers an organized, secure, and easy way to manage the many details of the project. In so doing, Project 2000 software exhibits the characteristics of several types of application software, as explained in Figure 1-4.

Figure 1-4	MICROSOFT PROJECT 2000 COMPARED TO OTHER SOFTWARE APPLICATIONS
APPLICATION SOFTWARE	**PROJECT 2000 SIMILARITIES**
Database	Manages lists of tasks, durations, dates, resources, costs, constraints, and notes.
Spreadsheet	Automatically recalculates durations and costs, task start and finish dates, and project start or finish date.
Chart	Provides several graphical views of project information, including the Gantt Chart, Network Diagram, and Calendar views to give you a visual overview of your data.
Report Writer	Includes several predefined reports that provide varying degrees of detail in all areas of the project. Allows the user to customize existing reports to show exactly the amount of detail needed.

With Project 2000, you start a project by entering a few sequential tasks. Project 2000's integrated approach allows you to expand the project as needed. You don't need to use all of the sophisticated features of Project 2000 in order to benefit. As your project information needs evolve, you can always enter and evaluate more information, such as planned, scheduled, and actual time frames, costs, and resource allocations.

Project 2000 Tools

The Gantt Chart and Network Diagram are two important basic communication tools included in Project 2000. As you learn about project management, you will find that these two tools are essential building blocks for your education.

Gantt Chart

The **Gantt Chart**, named for Henry Gantt, a pioneer of project management techniques, provides a graphical visualization of the project that displays each task as a horizontal bar, as illustrated in Figure 1-5. The length of the bar corresponds to the duration of the task. The primary purpose of the Gantt Chart is to graphically display task durations.

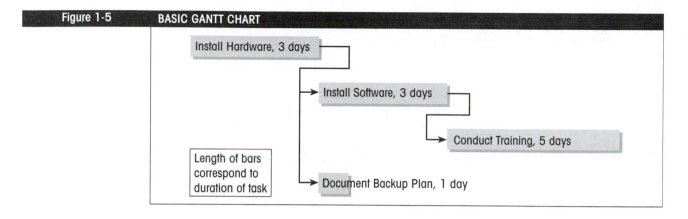

Figure 1-5   BASIC GANTT CHART

Network Diagram

The **Network Diagram**, also called the **PERT Chart** (Program Evaluation Review Technique) and shown in Figure 1-6, graphically highlights the interdependencies of tasks. The Network Diagram displays each task as a box, or node. Dependent tasks are linked together through link lines, thus creating a clear picture of how the tasks will be sequenced. The primary purpose of the Network Diagram is to display the critical path. The **critical path** is the tasks and durations that determine the shortest period to complete the project. Used together, the Network Diagram and the Gantt Chart form a solid foundation for effective and efficient project management.

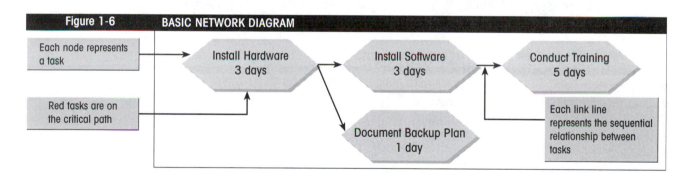

Figure 1-6   BASIC NETWORK DIAGRAM

Project 2000 supports many other features that help you to perform as an effective project manager. You will learn how to take advantage of these tools as you work through this book. Now that you know the benefits of project management and the basic terminology, you can start Project 2000 and begin to plan the LAN installation project for JLB Partners.

Session 1.1 QUICK CHECK

1. What are the four basic activities of project management?

2. When is the project goal achieved?

3. Differentiate "efficient" from "effective."

4. Write an improved project goal for the following: "write a book."

5. Define the following project management terms:
   a. task
   b. duration
   c. resource
   d. project manager

6. Identify several benefits of project management.

7. Describe what a Gantt Chart looks like, and identify its primary purpose.

8. Describe what a Network Diagram looks like, and identify its primary purpose.

SESSION 1.2

In this session, you will start Microsoft Project 2000, explore the Project 2000 window, save a new project, open an existing project, save updates to an existing project, and learn about project views.

Getting Around Project 2000

Before you can create a project, you need to start Project 2000 and learn about the organization of the Project 2000 window.

To start Microsoft Project 2000:

1. Make sure that Windows is running on your computer and that the Windows desktop appears on your screen.

2. Click the **Start** button on the taskbar to display the Start menu, and then point to **Programs** to display the Programs menu.

3. Point to **Microsoft Project** on the Programs menu. See Figure 1-7.

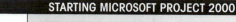

Figure 1-7   **STARTING MICROSOFT PROJECT 2000**

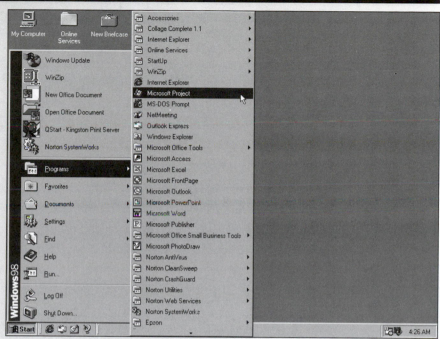

TROUBLE? If you don't see the Microsoft Project option on the Programs menu, look in the Microsoft group folders or ask your instructor or technical support person for help.

TROUBLE? These figures were created while running the default settings for Windows 98 and Project 2000. Other operating systems (for example, Windows NT and Windows 98 Using Web-Style) and different system options (screen resolution and colors, for example) might change the way that the figures appear. You don't need to worry about cosmetic differences or various taskbar options. Focus instead on the key information as identified by the callouts to make sure that you are synchronized with the steps.

4. Click **Microsoft Project**. After a short pause, the Microsoft Project copyright information appears in a message box and remains on the screen until the Project 2000 program window, containing a blank project, appears. See Figure 1-8.

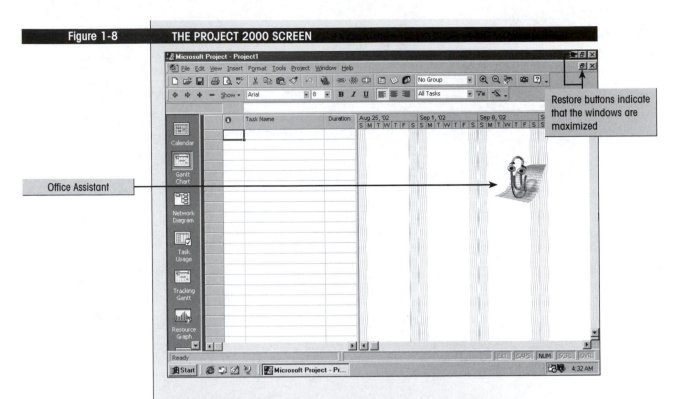

| Figure 1-8 | THE PROJECT 2000 SCREEN |

Office Assistant

Restore buttons indicate that the windows are maximized

TROUBLE? Microsoft Project will prompt you to register the product the first time it is used. If you are working with your own copy of Project, it's a good idea to register the product with Microsoft in order to receive support and future product information.

TROUBLE? If the Help window automatically opens, close it. You will learn more about Help later in the tutorial.

5. If the Microsoft Project 2000 program window does not fill the entire screen as shown in Figure 1-8, click the **Maximize** button ▢ in the upper-right corner of the program window.

TROUBLE? If the Office Assistant (see Figure 1-8) appears on your screen when you start Project 2000, click Help on the menu bar and then click Hide the Office Assistant. You will learn more about the Office Assistant later in this tutorial.

Project 2000 is now running and ready to use.

Checking Default Settings

Project 2000 provides a set of standard settings, called **default settings**, which are appropriate for most projects. The rest of this section explains what your Project 2000 window should look like and how to synchronize it with those in the tutorials.

You can view your project in many ways, called **views**, which display task, resource, and cost information with varying levels of detail. The default view, however, is Gantt Chart view.

To check the Project Start Date and Finish Date:

1. Click the **Gantt Chart** button 📊 on the View Bar if it is not already chosen.

2. Click **Project** on the menu bar, and then click **Project Information** to open the Project Information dialog box.

   Important default settings include those shown in the Project Information dialog box shown in Figure 1-9.

Figure 1-9	PROJECT INFORMATION DIALOG BOX

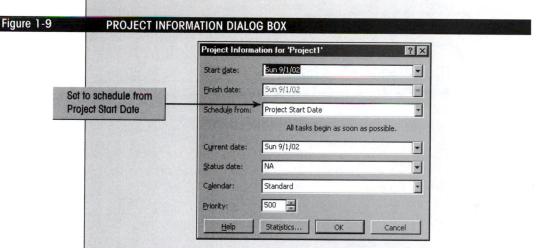

Set to schedule from Project Start Date

The **Start Date** is the date that the project will start. The **Finish Date** is the date that Project 2000 calculates as the date that the project will finish. If you enter a Start Date, Project 2000 will calculate the Finish Date based on the task durations and relationships within the project. If you change the Schedule from option to Project Finish Date, however, you will be able to enter a Finish Date, and Project 2000 will calculate a Start Date. Finish Date scheduling is appropriate for projects such as conventions based on an immovable finish date.

3. Click the **Schedule from** list arrow, and then click **Project Finish Date**.

   Notice that the Start Date list arrow and text box are dimmed. You can set only the Start Date *or* the Finish Date of the project. Project 2000 will calculate the other. When there are no tasks in the project, the Start Date and Finish Date are the same date.

4. Click the **Schedule from** list arrow, and then click **Project Start Date**.

   "Project Start Date" is the default setting for the Schedule from option. As tasks are added, the Finish Date is constantly recalculated based on the durations and relationships of the tasks entered. Another date that you might want to change is the Current date. By default, the **Current date** is today's date (as determined by the battery within your computer or network time server.)

5. Click the **Current date** list arrow. The Calendar appears showing the current month as determined by your computer's clock. Today's date is circled in red. See Figure 1-10.

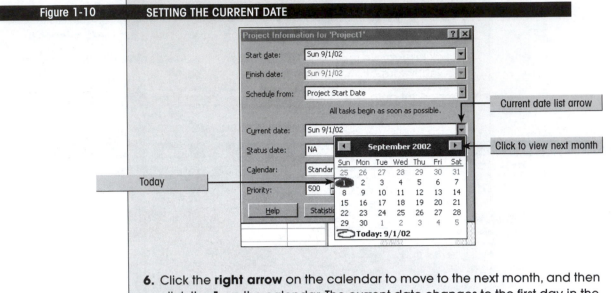

Figure 1-10   **SETTING THE CURRENT DATE**

6. Click the **right arrow** on the calendar to move to the next month, and then click the **1** on the calendar. The current date changes to the first day in the next month.

7. Click **Cancel** in the Project Information dialog box to cancel the changes that you were exploring.

Viewing **the Project 2000 Screen**

The Project 2000 window consists of a number of elements that are common to all Windows applications, such as the menu bar, title bar, and status bar.

Title Bar

The **title bar** is the top bar of any application software running on a Windows computer; see Figure 1-11. It identifies both the project name as well as the application name. When you start a new project, the generic "Project1" filename appears in the title bar. Once you save a new project or if you open an existing project, the project's filename will appear in the title bar.

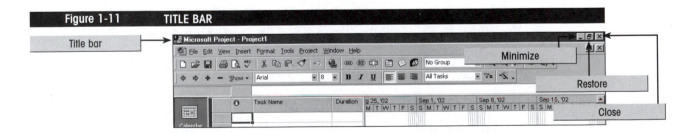

Figure 1-11   **TITLE BAR**

The right corner of the title bar contains three buttons to (from left to right) Minimize, Restore, and Close the Project 2000 application window. These buttons are common to all Windows applications. If the Project application window is not maximized, the middle button is a Maximize rather than a Restore button.

Menu Bar

Although the menu and toolbars can be moved by dragging their left edges, the menu bar is usually located directly below the title bar as shown in Figure 1-12. The **menu bar** contains the File, Edit, View, Insert, Format, Tools, Project, Window, and Help menus, which are used to issue commands in Project 2000. All of Project 2000 commands can be found through the use of the menu system.

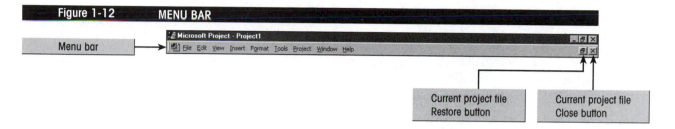

| Figure 1-12 | MENU BAR |

The right corner of the menu bar contains two buttons that are similar to the buttons above them on the title bar. From left to right, these are used to Restore or Maximize and Close the current project window (as opposed to the application window). These buttons are common to all Windows applications.

Toolbars

Toolbars represent the most popular Project 2000 commands as little pictures or icons. Project 2000, like other Windows applications, uses toolbars to represent the most commonly used commands. They shield you from the vast number of options provided in the menu system. As a beginner, you will likely use the toolbars. As you use Project 2000 in more ways, you'll use the vast menu system more and more often.

By default, two toolbars should be on the opening Project 2000 window: Standard and Formatting, as shown in Figure 1-13. The View Bar is on the left side of the window. To determine the name of a button on the Standard or Formatting toolbars, position the mouse pointer over the button without clicking. A **ScreenTip,** a small box with the name of the button, will appear. The View Bar lists the name of the button beneath the icon.

TROUBLE? If your View Bar displays "PERT Chart" instead of "Network Diagram" on the third button down, an older version of Project 2000 probably was installed on your computer and some of its program files are overriding some of the Project 2000 default settings. See your instructor, as this will affect some of the advanced Project 2000 features discussed later in this book.

Figure 1-13   STANDARD AND FORMATTING TOOLBARS

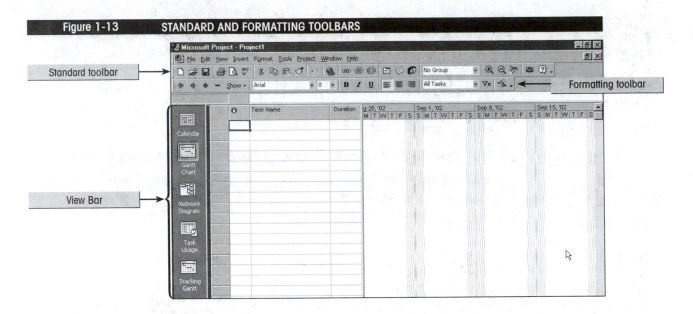

Standard Toolbar

By default, the Standard toolbar is positioned directly under the menu bar. The left side of the **Standard toolbar** contains buttons that are common to almost all Windows applications, such as New, Open, Save, Print, Print Preview, Spell Check, Cut, Copy, and Paste. On the right side of the Standard toolbar, you'll find buttons specific to Project 2000, such as Link Tasks, Unlink Tasks, Split Task, and Assign Resources.

Formatting Toolbar

By default, the Formatting toolbar is positioned directly under the Standard toolbar. As with most Windows applications, the **Formatting toolbar** contains buttons that improve the appearance of the project such as font, bold, italics, and alignment. On the left and right ends of the Formatting toolbar are several buttons to help you organize, outline, and filter tasks.

Entering Your First Tasks

Every project contains tasks. One of the best ways to learn about the window elements that are specific to Project 2000 is to enter a few sample tasks.

To enter your first task and duration:

1. Click the **Task Name cell** in row 1, and type **Document Hardware**. Notice that the text also appears in the **Entry Bar** between the Formatting toolbar and the Task Name column heading. You will learn how the Entry Bar works in the next section. Task names should be as short as possible, and yet long enough to clearly identify the task. Task names generally start with a verb.

2. Press the **right arrow** key. The Duration cell for the first row is now the active cell. The default entry is 1 day?. The default duration for a task is estimated at 1 day, but the duration can be changed at any time.

3. Type **5**, and then press the **Enter** key.

By default, because this project is scheduled from a Start Date and not from a Finish Date, tasks begin on the Current date. If the Current date is a nonworking day, the project starts on the next working day. Your screen should look like Figure 1-14.

Figure 1-14 **FIRST TASK ENTERED**

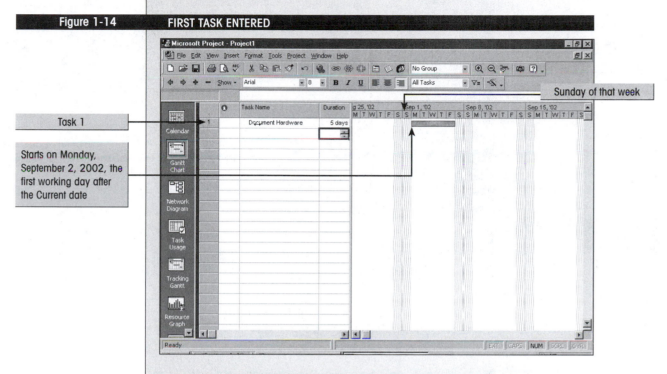

TROUBLE? Your project will start on today's date unless you change the Current date setting in the Project Information dialog box, so your screen will have different dates than those shown in the figures.

Estimated durations are entered and displayed with a question mark. The default unit of measurement is days, and therefore you should enter "d" or "days." You have made the duration for this task 5 days because it will involve researching, inspecting, and documenting each existing piece of equipment. This effort is estimated to take 1 day per computer, and JLB Partners currently has five computers. The second task that you will enter, Document Software, involves finding all existing software licensing agreements, making sure that each user is on the most current level of software possible, and documenting each workstation's software configuration. You estimate that the effort will take two days per computer, and you must research five machines.

To enter your second task and duration:

1. Click the **Task Name cell** in row 2, type **Document Software**, press the **Tab** key, type **10** in the Duration cell, and then press the **Enter** key.

   The corresponding bar in the Gantt Chart ends exactly two weeks, or 10 working days, from today. Your screen should look like Figure 1-15.

Figure 1-15	TWO TASKS ENTERED FOR THE NEW PROJECT

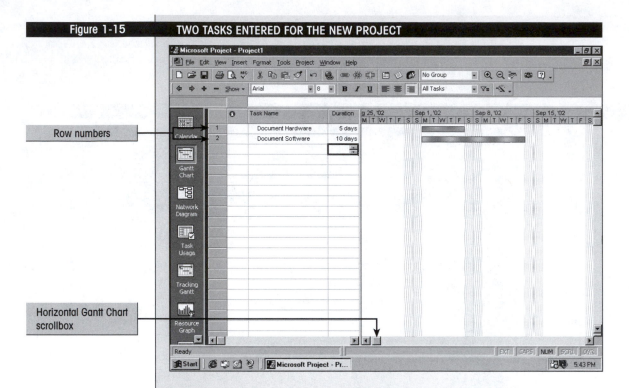

Row numbers

Horizontal Gantt Chart scrollbox

TROUBLE? The bars on the Gantt Chart might or might not be visible, depending on the time period displayed on the timescale. You will learn about the timescale later.

As you enter more tasks in your project, the Gantt Chart will probably become too large to view in its entirety, and you'll need to scroll to different time periods within the chart to focus on specific tasks.

2. Drag the **horizontal Gantt Chart scrollbox** to the right to the middle of the scroll bar. As you drag the scroll box, a date ScreenTip appears to indicate how far you are moving the timescale.

Often, you'll want to return to the first bar in the Gantt Chart.

3. Press and hold the **Alt** key, then press the **Home** key. The Alt+Home keystroke combination always moves the Gantt Chart to the project's Start Date so that the first bar is visible.

Learning how to enter tasks and durations is the beginning of working with the Project 2000 window. Various elements in the window are specific to Project 2000. These elements are identified in the Project 2000 window shown in Figure 1-16.

Figure 1-16	VIEW BAR, ENTRY BAR, AND ENTRY TABLE

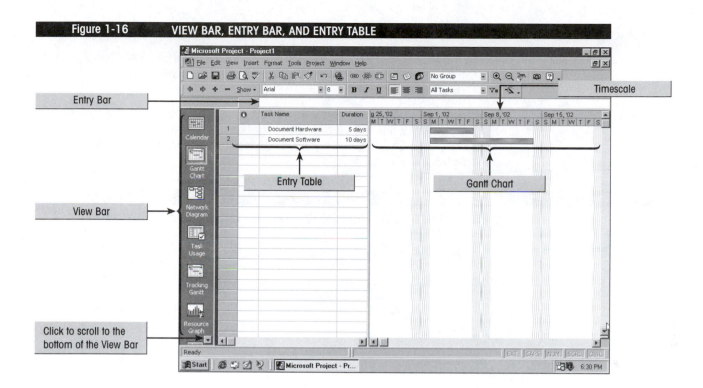

The View Bar

The **View Bar** contains several buttons that you use to switch between project views. The small black triangle that points down at the bottom of the View Bar indicates that more buttons are available.

The Entry Table and the Entry Bar

The default Project 2000 window displays two parts, the Entry Table on the left and the Gantt Chart on the right. The **Entry Table** is a spreadsheet-like display of project information, organized in rows (each task is entered in a new row) and columns (the individual pieces of information about each task comprise the columns). The two most important pieces of information about each task are its Task Name and Duration.

By default, the **Entry Bar** is positioned just below the Formatting toolbar and just above the Project 2000 window. You can use the Entry Bar to enter or edit an existing entry, such as a task name or duration. It works in a manner similar to that of the Edit bar in a spreadsheet product. As you enter tasks in the Entry Table, the text is also entered in the Entry Bar. If you are making an entry that has a limited number of available choices (for example, if you are assigning a resource to a task), the right edge of the Entry Bar will display a list arrow. You can click the list arrow to see a list of available options.

The Entry Table exists of many more columns of information than you see on the window shown in Figure 1-16. These columns include the Finish (date), Predecessors (tasks that must be completed before this task can be started), and Resource Names (resources assigned to this task). The Start Date is assumed to be today's date, unless specified otherwise.

To drag the split bar:

1. Place the mouse pointer on the **split bar** on the right edge of the Duration column. The pointer changes to ◀▮▶. This bar is called the **split bar**, and it vertically separates the table from the chart.

2. Press and hold the **left mouse button**, and then drag the ◀▮▶ pointer to move the right edge of the Entry Table to the right until you see the Resource names column, as shown in Figure 1-17. By dragging the split bar to the right, you can see the additional columns.

Figure 1-17	DRAGGING THE SPLIT BAR

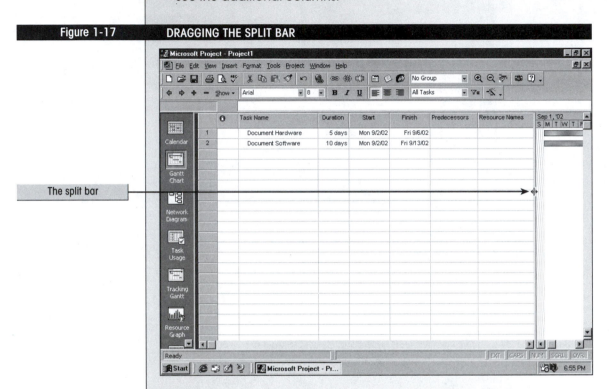

The split bar

3. Press and hold the **left mouse button**, and then drag the **split bar** to the left up to the right edge of the Start column.

Often, the columns in the Entry Table are filled in automatically as you enter information about the task elsewhere in the project. The start date, for example, is automatically the Current date, unless you specify something else. The finish date is automatically calculated as the start date plus the duration. The Predecessors column and Resource Names columns will be automatically filled in as you specify task relationships (which tasks must be completed before others) and assign resources. You may also type directly into the Entry Table, but generally, the Task Name and Duration columns are the only ones that you complete directly from the keyboard.

Gantt Chart

You have already learned that the Gantt Chart is a primary tool used by project managers to graphically communicate information about a project. Each task is identified as a horizontal bar, the length of which corresponds to its duration as measured by the timescale at the top of the chart. The Gantt Chart can be formatted to show many other attributes of the project, including relationships between tasks, resource assignments, and dates. As you enter more information into the project, the default Gantt Chart changes to display the information.

Timescale

The **timescale** is displayed along the top edge of the Gantt Chart, as shown in Figure 1-18. It displays the unit of measure that determines the length of each bar. The timescale has two rows: a major scale (the upper scale) and a minor scale (the lower scale). By default, the **major scale** is measured in weeks and displays the date for the Sunday of that week. By default, the **minor scale** is measured in days and displays the first letter of the day of the week.

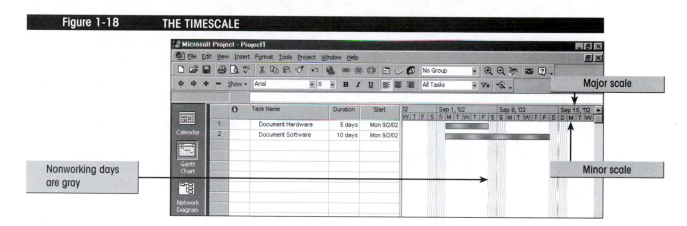

Figure 1-18   THE TIMESCALE

Both the major and minor scales can be modified to display a different unit of measure (minutes, hours, days, weeks, months, quarters, and years), as well as a different label. Weeks can be displayed in different ways, including January 30, 2002; Jan 30, '02; 1/30/02; and Sun 1/30/02. As the scale is changed, the bars on the Gantt Chart automatically adjust to the new scale.

Current Date

By default, the **current date** is today's date and is represented in the Gantt Chart by a dotted vertical line. Unless specified differently, all tasks are scheduled and all progress is measured from the current date. However, you can easily change it. Note that the dotted line is not clearly visible if the current date is Saturday or Sunday or Monday because it appears in or next to the nonworking day line.

Working Days / Nonworking Days

Nonworking days are displayed as light gray vertical bars on the Gantt Chart. By default, Saturday and Sunday are considered nonworking days. Therefore, if a task has a three-day duration and starts on Friday, the bar will stretch through Saturday and Sunday, finishing on the third working day, or Tuesday. For specific holidays or vacation days in which no work should be scheduled, you can enter the project's calendar and specify more nonworking days. Similarly, you can change Saturday or Sunday to be working days if you need to schedule work then. Later, you'll learn that individual resources can be assigned individual calendars to accommodate individual work schedules, vacations, and holidays.

Saving a Project

Saving a project file is very similar to saving a word processing document or spreadsheet. You specify a filename, as well as a location for the file. The filename follows Windows conventions in that it can be several characters long and can include spaces. The location consists of the specified drive and folder/subfolders.

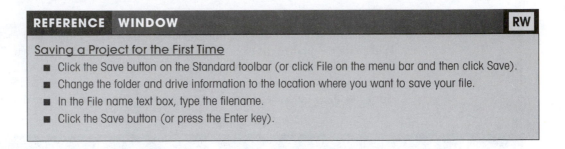

REFERENCE WINDOW RW

<u>Saving a Project for the First Time</u>
- Click the Save button on the Standard toolbar (or click File on the menu bar and then click Save).
- Change the folder and drive information to the location where you want to save your file.
- In the File name text box, type the filename.
- Click the Save button (or press the Enter key).

Project 2000 automatically appends the **.mpp** filename extension to identify the file as a Microsoft Project 2000 file. Depending on how Windows is set up on your computer, however, you might not see the .mpp extension. These tutorials assume that filename extensions are displayed.

To save the project:

1. Place your Student Data Disk in the appropriate disk drive.

   TROUBLE? If you don't have a Student Data Disk, see your instructor or technical support person or follow the instructions on the "Read This Before You Begin" page at the beginning of this book on how to create a Student Data Disk.

2. Click the **Save** button 🖫 on the Standard toolbar. The Save As dialog box opens. See Figure 1-19.

Figure 1-19   SAVE AS DIALOG BOX

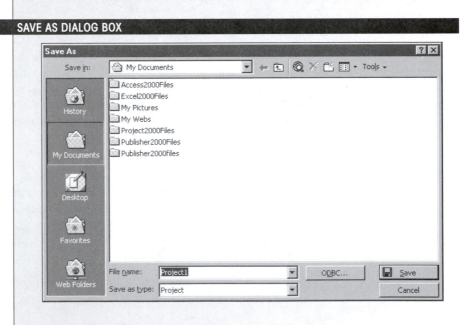

3. Type **LAN** in the File name text box.

4. Click the **Save in** list arrow, click the drive containing your Student Data Disk, double-click the **Tutorial.01** folder, and then double-click the **Tutorial** folder. The Tutorial folder opens, ready for you to save the document. See Figure 1-20.

Figure 1-20   **SAVING THE LAN FILE TO THE STUDENT DATA DISK**

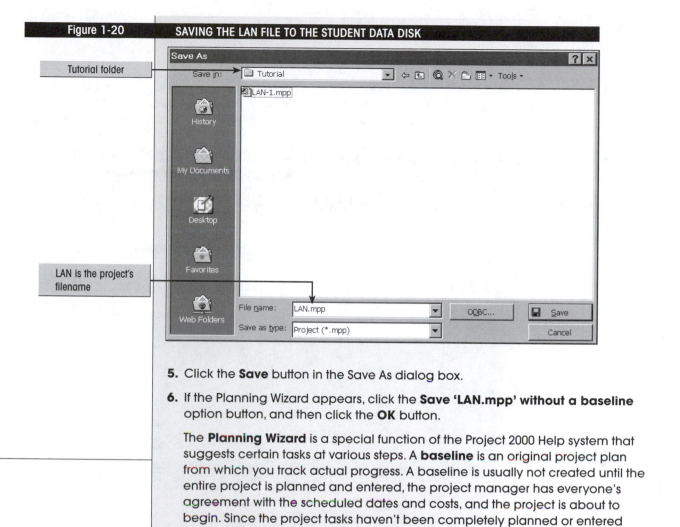

5. Click the **Save** button in the Save As dialog box.

6. If the Planning Wizard appears, click the **Save 'LAN.mpp' without a baseline** option button, and then click the **OK** button.

The **Planning Wizard** is a special function of the Project 2000 Help system that suggests certain tasks at various steps. A **baseline** is an original project plan from which you track actual progress. A baseline is usually not created until the entire project is planned and entered, the project manager has everyone's agreement with the scheduled dates and costs, and the project is about to begin. Since the project tasks haven't been completely planned or entered yet, you do not wish to save the baseline.

The name of your file, LAN.mpp, now appears in the title bar, and the file is saved on your Data Disk.

Closing a Project File

As with other Windows applications, you may have more than one file open (in this case, a project file) and then switch between them using the Window menu options. If, however, you are finished working with the current project, have saved it to a disk, and wish to work on another, you should close the current project to free computer resources for other tasks.

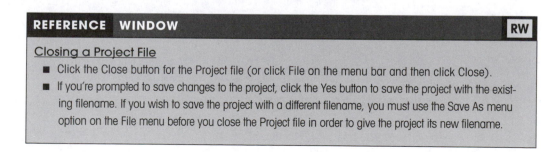

REFERENCE WINDOW   **RW**

Closing a Project File

- Click the Close button for the Project file (or click File on the menu bar and then click Close).
- If you're prompted to save changes to the project, click the Yes button to save the project with the existing filename. If you wish to save the project with a different filename, you must use the Save As menu option on the File menu before you close the Project file in order to give the project its new filename.

You want to close the LAN project file to take a quick break before continuing to add tasks.

To close an existing project:

1. Click the **Close** button for the project file, as shown in Figure 1-21. By clicking the project's Close button, you can close the existing project but not exit Project 2000. At this point, you can start a new project or open an existing project.

Figure 1-21	CLOSING A PROJECT FILE

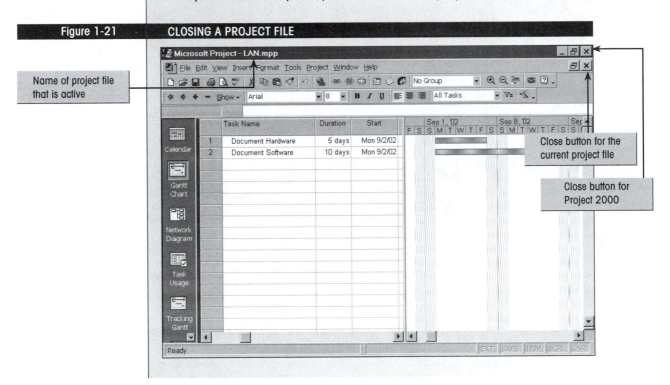

Name of project file that is active

Close button for the current project file

Close button for Project 2000

Opening an Existing Project

Often, you'll use the same project file over a period of several days, weeks, or months as you build, update, and track project progress. Therefore, it is absolutely essential that you are comfortable opening existing project files.

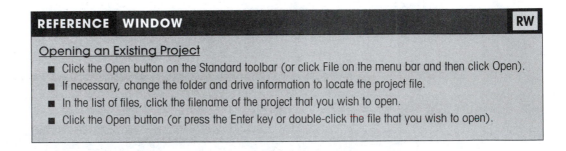

REFERENCE   WINDOW   **RW**

Opening an Existing Project
- Click the Open button on the Standard toolbar (or click File on the menu bar and then click Open).
- If necessary, change the folder and drive information to locate the project file.
- In the list of files, click the filename of the project that you wish to open.
- Click the Open button (or press the Enter key or double-click the file that you wish to open).

To open an existing project:

1. Place your Data Disk in the appropriate disk drive.

2. Click the **Open** button 📂 on the Standard toolbar. The Open dialog box opens.

3. Click the **Look in** list arrow, click the drive containing your Student Data Disk, double-click the **Tutorial.01** folder, and then double-click the **Tutorial** folder. The Tutorial folder is now open, ready for you to choose the project that you wish to open. See Figure 1-22.

Figure 1-22	THE OPEN DIALOG BOX

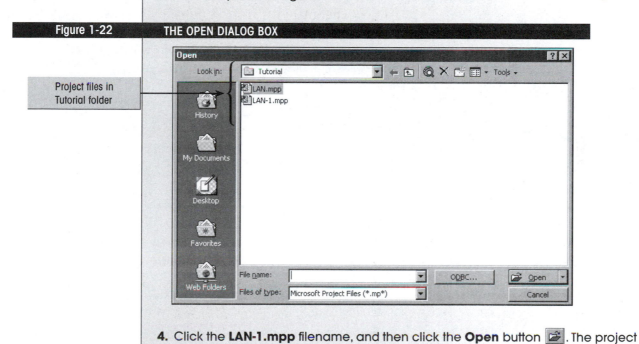

Project files in Tutorial folder

4. Click the **LAN-1.mpp** filename, and then click the **Open** button 📂. The project file **LAN-1.mpp** opens in the Project 2000 window.

The LAN-1 project opens and is ready for you to use. It opens in the view that was last used before the file was closed.

Exiting **Project 2000**

You are now ready to **exit**, or quit, Project 2000.

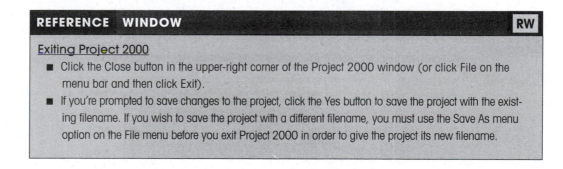

REFERENCE WINDOW **RW**

Exiting Project 2000
- Click the Close button in the upper-right corner of the Project 2000 window (or click File on the menu bar and then click Exit).
- If you're prompted to save changes to the project, click the Yes button to save the project with the existing filename. If you wish to save the project with a different filename, you must use the Save As menu option on the File menu before you exit Project 2000 in order to give the project its new filename.

> *To save the existing project with the same filename and exit Project 2000:*
>
> 1. Click the **Save** button 🖫 on the Standard toolbar, click **Save without a base-line** (if prompted) option button and then click the **OK** button.
> 2. Click the Project 2000 **Close** button ☒ on the title bar to exit Project 2000. You are returned to the Windows desktop.

When you exit Project 2000, it is no longer running on your computer. To work on another Project 2000 file, you must start the program again by clicking Start on the taskbar.

You report your progress to Emily. She is pleased that you have learned so much about Project 2000 in such a short time. She feels that you will soon be ready to tackle the LAN installation project for JLB Partners. However, a project has many views that you still need to explore. You'll learn more about views in Session 1.3.

Session 1.2 QUICK CHECK

1. When entering a new task in Gantt Chart view, two pieces of information are generally entered first. What are they?

2. What are the main features of the Standard toolbar?

3. What are the main features of the Formatting toolbar?

4. By default, what table is shown in the Gantt Chart view?

5. In Gantt Chart view, if you drag the split bar to the right, what is displayed?

6. Describe the components of the default timescale in Gantt Chart view.

7. What is the difference between closing a project file and exiting Project 2000?

SESSION 1.3

In this session, you will explore views, magnification, and timescales and learn how to work with print settings and the Project 2000 Help system.

Understanding Project Views

Project 2000 provides many different views of a project that support the informational needs of different users and purposes. Some views (such as the chart views) present a broad look at the entire project, whereas others (such as the form views) focus on specific pieces of information about each task. Three major categories of views are available.

- **Graphical**: A chart or graphical representation of data using bars, boxes, lines, and images.
- **Sheet**: A spreadsheet-like representation of data in which each task is displayed as a new row and each piece of information (field) about the task is represented by a column. Different **tables** are applied to a sheet to display different fields.

■ **Form**: A specific view of many pieces of information (fields) of *one task*. Forms are used to focus on the details of one task.

Views are further differentiated according to the type of data that they analyze, whether task or resource information. Since tasks and their corresponding durations are the first pieces of data entered into a project, you will focus on the task views now. Later, when resources and their corresponding costs are entered, you can explore resource views.

Figure 1-23 describes some of the predesigned views within each category that Project 2000 provides to help you display the task information that you need.

Figure 1-23	COMMON PROJECT VIEWS (TASK VIEWS)	
CATEGORY	**VIEW**	**PURPOSE**
Graphical	Gantt Chart	Shows each task as a horizontal bar, the length and position of which correspond to a timescale at the top of the chart.
	Network Diagram	Shows each task as a box, with linking lines drawn between related tasks to emphasize task sequence as well as the critical path.
	Calendar	Shows the tasks as bars on a typical desk calendar in a month-at-a-time format.
Task Sheet or Tables	Entry Table	Columns are Task Name, Duration, Start (date), End (date), Predecessors, and Resource Names. The default Gantt Chart view displays the Task Sheet with the Entry Table on the left, with two visible columns (Task Name and Duration).
	Cost Table	Contains task cost information, much of which is calculated when resources are assigned.
	Schedule Table	Presents dates and whether the task is on the critical path.
	Summary Table	Presents what percentage of the task's duration, costs, and assigned hours have been completed.
	Tracking Table	Presents actual and remaining durations and costs.
	Variance Table	Compares actual Start and Finish dates to baseline dates to the dates that the tasks would be completed had the project been executed according to the original plan.
	Work Table	Compares actual and remaining work to be completed to baseline measurements. **Baseline work** is the amount of work (number of hours) required to finish a task if the task is executed according to the original plan.
Form	Task Details Form	Provides all of the information about a single task in one window.
	Task Name Form	Provides limited information about a single task: task name, resources, and predecessors.
Combination	Gantt Chart (top) Task Name Form (bottom)	Provides an overview of many tasks of the project at the top of the screen, and displays the details of the current task at the bottom. Usually a table or chart view on the top and a form view on the bottom of the screen. A common combination view places the Gantt Chart view on the top and the Task Name form on the bottom.

Don't become overwhelmed by trying to learn all of the project views now. As you build the actual project and your information needs grow, studying these views will become more natural and meaningful. Two key points to remember are that several views are available and changes made in one view of the project are automatically updated and displayed in all other views.

To start Microsoft Project 2000 and open the LAN-1.mpp project file:

1. Make sure that Windows is running on your computer and that the Windows desktop shows on your screen.

2. Click the **Start** button on the taskbar to display the Start menu and then point to **Programs** to display the Programs menu.

3. Click **Microsoft Project**. After a short pause, the Microsoft Project copyright information appears in a message box and remains on the screen until the Project 2000 program window, containing a blank project, appears.

   TROUBLE? If the Microsoft Project 2000 program window does not fill the screen, then click the **Maximize** button ▣ in the upper-right corner of the program window.

   TROUBLE? If the Help window automatically opens, close it. You will learn more about Help later in the tutorial.

4. Click the **Open** button 🖼 on the Standard toolbar, click **LAN-1.mpp** in the Tutorial folder on your Data Disk, and then click the **Open** button.

Project 2000 is now running and the file LAN-1 is ready for you to begin working on. The Office Assistant might or might not be open on your screen.

Changing the Project View

As you work with Project 2000, you will find that you need to view the information in the different views. You can easily access the Gantt Chart view (the default Project 2000 view) and other common views by clicking their respective buttons in the View Bar or by choosing options from the View menu.

REFERENCE WINDOW   RW

Changing the Project View
- Click the appropriate view button on the View Bar or choose a view from the View menu.
- To open a split view, choose Split from the Window menu, or drag the horizontal split bar up, or double-click the horizontal split bar.
- To close a split view, choose Remove Split from the Window menu option, or drag the horizontal split bar down, or double-click the horizontal split bar.

To change a project view:

1. Click the **Calendar** button 🔲 on the View Bar.

The project is now displayed as a desk calendar in a month-at-a-time format. Each task is displayed on the calendar as a horizontal bar. The length of each bar represents the duration of the task, placed at the appropriate start and finish dates. The task name and duration appears within the bar. When you need to make changes to tasks in Calendar view, you open the Task Information dialog box for that task.

2. Place the pointer on **Document Current Environment**. The pointer changes to ✥. Double-click ✥ to open the Task Information dialog box for task 1, click the **General tab**, double-click **10d** in the Duration text box, type **5**, and then click the **OK** button.

The change in duration is immediately updated in all views. Note also that the nonworking days of Saturday and Sunday are not used when calculating the task's duration, as shown in Figure 1-24.

Figure 1-24   **CALENDAR VIEW**

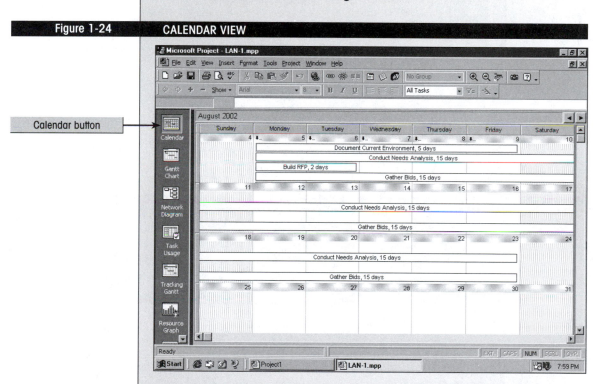

3. Click the **Network Diagram** button 🔳 on the View Bar.

The project is now displayed as a series of boxes, as shown in Figure 1-25. The lines between the boxes represent relationships between the tasks, the sequence of how the tasks must be completed. The box displays the task name in the top line, the task identification number and duration in the middle, and scheduled start and finish dates information at the bottom.

Figure 1-25   **NETWORK DIAGRAM**

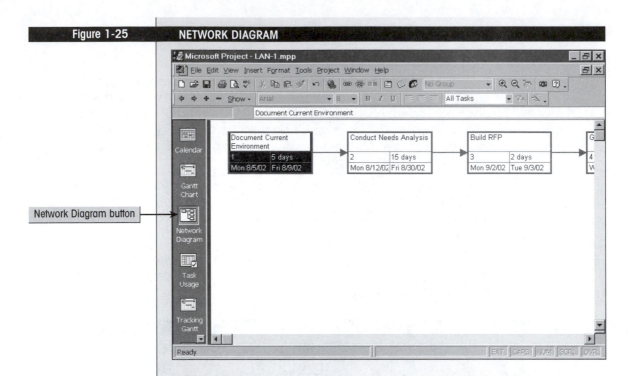

4. Double-click **Conduct Needs Analysis** to open the Task Information dialog box for task 2. Double-clicking the task to display the Task Information dialog box is one way to edit a task in almost any view.

5. Click the **Notes** tab, click in the **Notes** text box, and then type **Ask about current and future application needs**, as shown in Figure 1-26.

Figure 1-26   **NOTES TAB OF THE TASK INFORMATION DIALOG BOX**

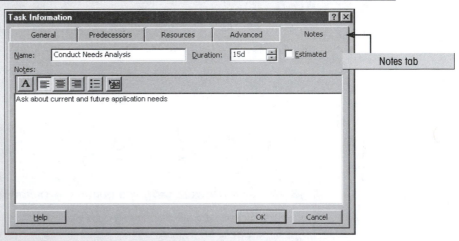

6. Click the **OK** button, and then click the **Gantt Chart** button 📋 on the View Bar. A **note icon** appears in the **Indicator column** to the left of task 2 in the Gantt Chart view to indicate that a note is attached to this task, as shown in Figure 1-27. You could display the note by double-clicking the note icon.

Figure 1-27 NOTE ICON IN GANTT CHART VIEW

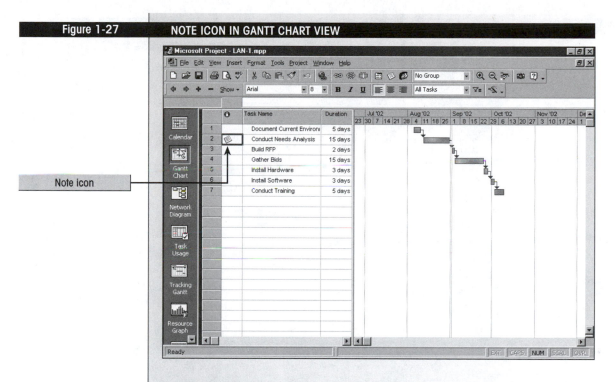

Note icon

Most often, you'll enter data about the project into one of the table views, such as the Entry Table that appears to the left of the Gantt Chart view, but you can edit tasks in any view.

The other buttons on the View Bar are used to display information about task completion information and resource information and will be explored in later tutorials. The View menu also provides a complete list of all views available in Project 2000.

To familiarize yourself with the View menu:

1. Click **View** on the menu bar. The first three options on the View menu correspond to the three graphical views of a project: Calendar, Gantt Chart, and Network Diagram. Other menu options correspond to views that highlight resource or tracking information.

2. Click **More Views**. The More Views dialog box opens, listing all of the available views.

3. Double-click **Relationship Diagram**. The Relationship Diagram chart focuses on only one task, showing both the **predecessors**, tasks that must be completed before that task, and **successors**, tasks that cannot be completed until after that task.

4. Click to the left of the scroll box in the **horizontal scroll bar**, and then click to the right of the scroll box in the **horizontal scroll bar**. Clicking in the horizontal scroll bar moves between tasks in the Relationship Diagram.

5. Click in the **horizontal scroll bar** to position the Relationship Diagram on the fourth task, as shown in Figure 1-28.

Figure 1-28   RELATIONSHIP DIAGRAM

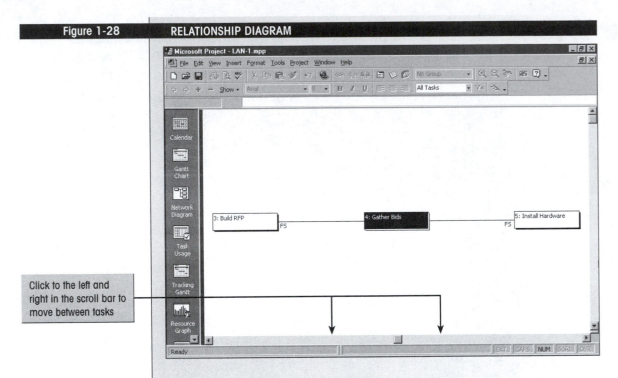

Click to the left and right in the scroll bar to move between tasks

6. Click the **Gantt Chart** button on the View Bar. The Gantt Chart view displays the Task Entry table on the left with the fourth task as the current task.

7. Drag the **split bar** to the right so that all of the columns are displayed, with Task Name on the left and Resource Names on the right, as shown in Figure 1-29.

The dates in the Start and Finish columns are based on the project Start Date, task duration, and task relationships. The Predecessors column indicates which task or tasks need to be finished before that task can start.

Figure 1-29   TASK ENTRY TABLE

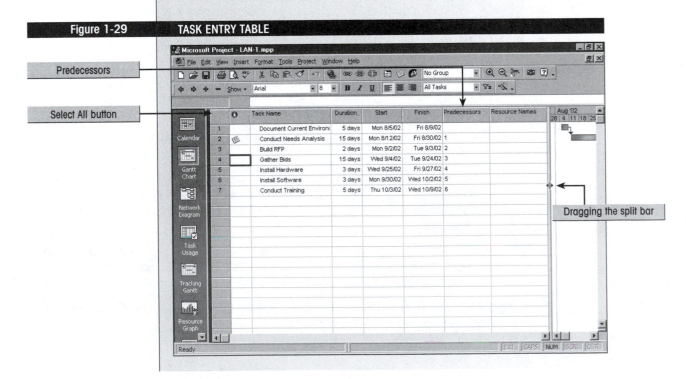

Predecessors

Select All button

Dragging the split bar

8. Right-click the **Select All** button for the Task Entry table, and then click **Schedule** to display the Task Schedule table, as shown in Figure 1-30.

| Figure 1-30 | TASK SCHEDULE TABLE |

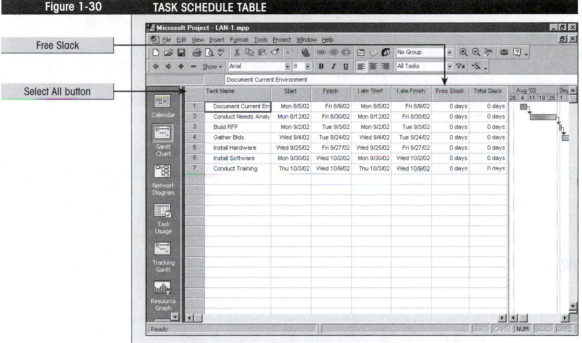

The Task Schedule table displays the scheduled Start and Finish dates as well as the Late Start and Late Finish dates. All of the tasks in this file are completed in sequence, so there is no slack. **Slack** is the amount of time that an activity may be delayed from its scheduled Start date without delaying the entire project. As you complete a project plan, assign resources, and start tracking an actual project, the rest of the tables will become more valuable.

Project 2000 allows you to display more than one view on the screen at one time so that you can view information about many tasks in one area and details about the current task in another. This type of arrangement is called a **split window**.

The top part of a split window is often the Gantt Chart view, and the bottom part is often a form view. **Forms** are intended to display detailed information about one task at a time. You can add, delete, or edit information within a form just as you can within a table or the Task Information dialog box. Many types of forms are available, each focusing on different details of the project.

To work with split windows and forms:

1. Right-click the **Select All** button for the Task Schedule table, and then click **Entry**. The default task table appears.

2. Drag the **split bar** to the left so that Duration is the last visible column in the Entry Table.

3. Click **Window** on the menu bar, and then click **Split**. Your screen should look like Figure 1-31, with the default Gantt Chart view on top and a task form view on the bottom. The Gantt Chart on top shows several tasks and their associated Gantt Chart bars, and the Task Form view at the bottom shows details for just one task.

Figure 1-31   **SPLIT WINDOW**

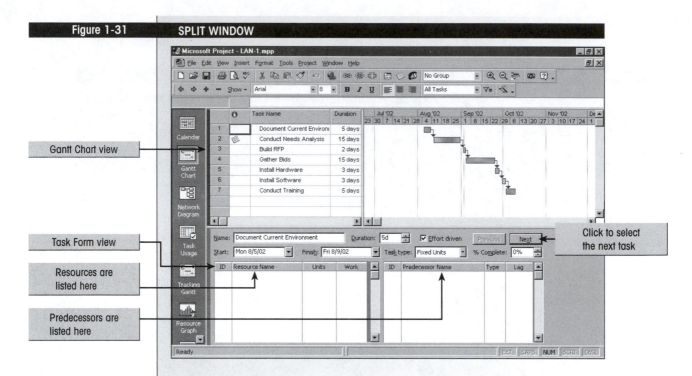

Gantt Chart view

Task Form view

Resources are listed here

Predecessors are listed here

Click to select the next task

4. Click the **Next** button in the form to move to the second task, and then click the **Next** button again. Notice that as you move from task to task in the form, the same task is selected in the Entry Table and you are able to view the details for the selected task in the form. Another way to view the details of a particular task is to click that task in the Entry Table in the upper-left portion of the window.

5. Right-click anywhere inside of the **form**, and then click **Predecessors & Successors**. Now the form displays tasks that precede the third task on the left and tasks that follow the third task on the right, as shown in Figure 1-32.

Figure 1-32   **TASK FORM DISPLAYING PREDECESSORS AND SUCCESSORS**

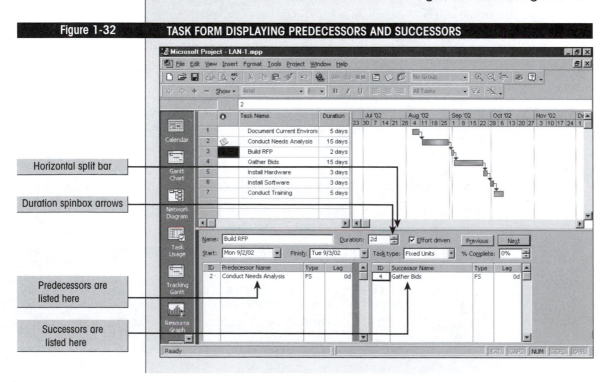

Horizontal split bar

Duration spinbox arrows

Predecessors are listed here

Successors are listed here

6. Right-click anywhere inside of the **form** and then click **Resources & Predecessors**. Resources & Predecessors is the default form that is displayed when you split the screen.

7. Click the **Duration** up spin arrow in the form to increase the duration of the third task, Build RFP, to 3 days, and then click on the form. Changes made in the Form view, or any view, simultaneously update all of the other views.

8. Place the pointer on the **horizontal split bar**, and then double-click ⇕. The form closes, and you are returned to the default Gantt Chart view. You can also close the split by clicking Window on the menu bar, and then clicking Remove Split.

Being able to move quickly from one view to the next is a critical Project 2000 skill. Over time, you'll learn many other views. For now, however, you need to know only that many views exist and how to move among them. The default Gantt Chart view with the Entry Table on the left is the primary view in which you enter project information, so that's the one that you need to focus on as you begin to build a project.

Saving a Project with a New Name

When changes are made to a project, you need to determine whether you want to save the updates to the existing project file or create a new project file with a new project name. Usually, updates to an existing project file should be saved to the existing project name by clicking the Save button on the Standard toolbar. Throughout this book, however, you'll be asked to open a partially completed project from the Data Disk and then save the changes that you made to the project with a new name. Using this technique, you do not modify the original project files on the Data Disk.

REFERENCE WINDOW | **RW**

Saving a Project with a New Name
- Click File on the menu bar, and then click Save As.
- If necessary, change the folder and drive information to the location where you want to save the file.
- In the File name text box, type the filename.
- Click the Save button (or press the Enter key).

Save the LAN-1 project file with the name **LAN-1-Your Initials**. By using your initials as part of the filename, you will be able to recognize your work easily in a classroom setting. The figures in this book are saved using the initials EK, for the JLB Partners managing partner, Emily Kelsey.

To save a project file with a new name:

1. Place your Data Disk in the appropriate disk drive.

2. Click **File** on the menu bar, and then click **Save As**. The Save As dialog box opens.

3. Type **LAN-1-Your Initials** in the File name text box.

TROUBLE? If you are in a large class and want to be sure that your file and print-outs can be distinguished on a large print queue in a lab, use your name as part of the filename.

4. Click the **Save in** list arrow, click the drive containing your Data Disk, double-click the **Tutorial.01** folder, and then double-click the **Tutorial** folder. The Save As dialog box should list the file **LAN.mpp** that you saved earlier in this tutorial as well as the file **LAN-1.mpp** that was provided on your Data Disk.

5. Click the **Save** button in the Save As dialog box.

6. If the Planning Wizard dialog box opens, click the **Save 'LAN-1-Your Initials' without a baseline option** button, and then click the **OK** button. The dialog box closes, and you are returned to the project window. The new name of your file appears in the title bar. If you wanted to repeat this exercise, you could open the **LAN-1.mpp** file from your Data Disk and do it again.

Magnification

As your project grows, seeing all of your project tasks in the chart views becomes more difficult. Being able to magnify and reduce the size of the project on the screen becomes important.

In Gantt Chart view, the timescale determines the length of the bar. Therefore, if the timescale is measured in hours, then the bar for a task that lasts 8 hours will be very long. If the timescale is measured in days, however, then the bar will be quite short. The timescale is composed of both a major scale (the upper scale), and a minor scale (the lower scale). You can modify both the unit of time as well as how the label is displayed, to meet your needs.

Similarly, other views allow you to enlarge and reduce the amount of project information on the screen as well. Changing the magnification of a project is called **zooming in** and **zooming out**.

Zooming In and Zooming Out

The easiest way to adjust the Gantt Chart timescale is to use the **Zoom In** 🔍 and **Zoom Out** 🔍 buttons on the Standard toolbar. Clicking the Zoom In button 🔍 displays smaller units of measure on the Gantt Chart timescale, which in turn expands the size of each bar.

To zoom in on the Gantt Chart:

1. Click the **Zoom In** button 🔍 on the Standard toolbar five times, and then click the **horizontal scroll bar** to display Monday Aug 5. Each time you click the Zoom In button 🔍, the timescale shows smaller and smaller units of measure, until it displays hours as the major scale and 15-minute intervals as the minor scale, as shown in Figure 1-33.

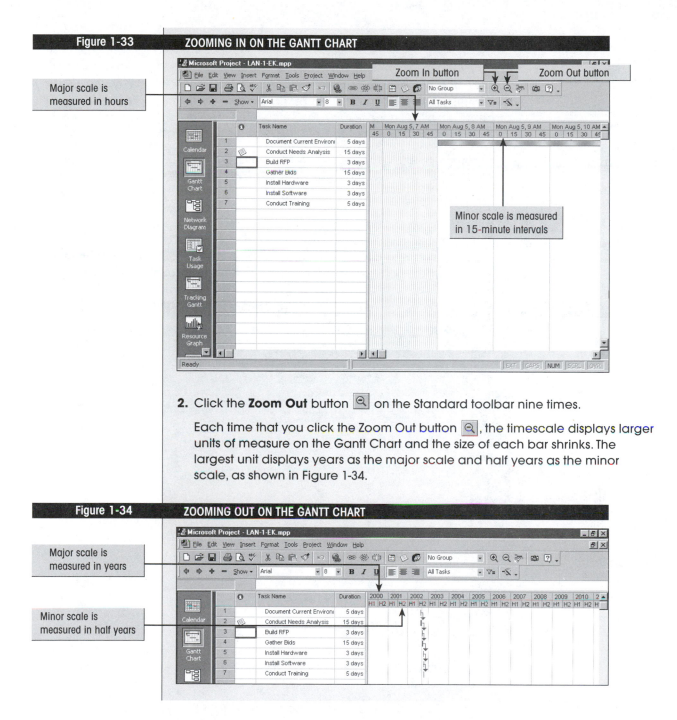

Figure 1-33   ZOOMING IN ON THE GANTT CHART

Major scale is measured in hours

Zoom In button   Zoom Out button

Minor scale is measured in 15-minute intervals

2. Click the **Zoom Out** button on the Standard toolbar nine times.

Each time that you click the Zoom Out button, the timescale displays larger units of measure on the Gantt Chart and the size of each bar shrinks. The largest unit displays years as the major scale and half years as the minor scale, as shown in Figure 1-34.

Figure 1-34   ZOOMING OUT ON THE GANTT CHART

Major scale is measured in years

Minor scale is measured in half years

You can also zoom in and out of the Network Diagram and Calendar views. While neither of these views displays a timescale, the overall effect of zooming is the same. Zooming in shows fewer tasks or days (but allows you to see the details for what *is* displayed much clearer), and zooming out shows more tasks or days (but fewer details).

To zoom in and out of the Network Diagram and Calendar views:

1. Click the **Network Diagram** button 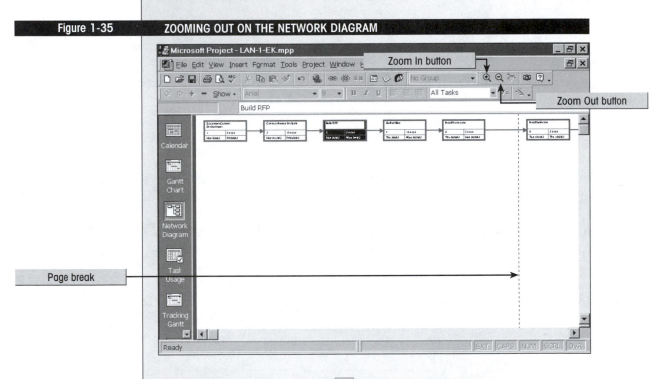 on the View Bar, and then click the **Zoom In** button as many times as possible until there are no more visible changes in the magnification. Zooming in on the Network Diagram increases the size of the boxes, thereby making them easier to read.

   TROUBLE? If the Office Assistant displays a message when you have reached the highest level of magnification, click the **OK** button in the Office Assistant's message box.

2. Click the **Zoom Out** button five times to make your screen look like Figure 1-35. Zooming out on the Network Diagram decreases the size of the boxes, thereby allowing more to appear on the screen at one time. The dotted lines on the screen indicate where page breaks will occur if the Network Diagram is printed.

Figure 1-35	ZOOMING OUT ON THE NETWORK DIAGRAM

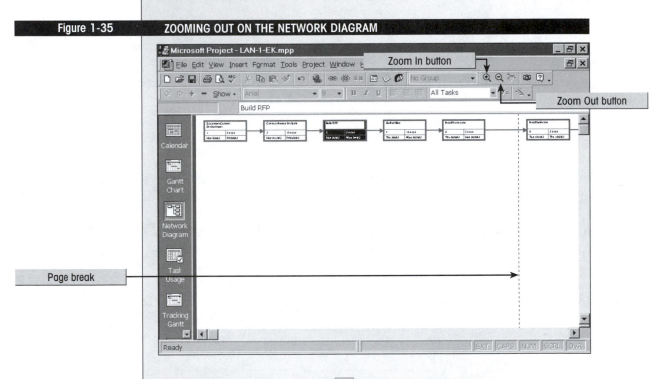

3. Click the **Calendar** button on the View Bar. You can see four weeks on the screen.

4. Click the **Zoom In** button on the View Bar. Your screen displays only two weeks, as shown in Figure 1-36. Zooming in on the Calendar view increases the size of the daily squares, thereby allowing you to see more information in each day.

Figure 1-36

ZOOMING IN ON THE CALENDAR

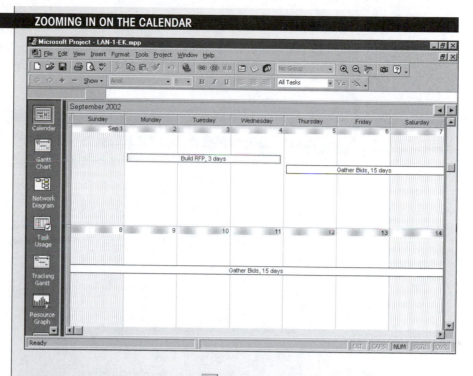

5. Click the **Zoom Out** button  on the View Bar twice. Zooming out on the Calendar decreases the size of the boxes, thereby allowing more days to be displayed on the screen at one time. You should see six weeks in your screen.

6. Click the **Gantt Chart** button on the View Bar to return to Gantt Chart view. Because each view retains the zoom magnification that was last displayed, in that view you see years and half years on the chart.

7. Click the **Zoom** buttons on the View Bar as necessary to display months as the major scale and date numbers as the minor scale.

Modifying the Timescale

If the existing timescales do not meet your needs, you can modify the timescale to represent a custom unit of time and custom label. For example, you might want the major scale to display a two-week increment and the minor scale to display a daily increment with the format 1/30/02, 1/31/02, 2/1/02, and so on.

REFERENCE WINDOW   **RW**

Modifying the Timescale

- Double-click the timescale in the Gantt Chart view.
- Enter changes in the Timescale dialog box.
- Click the OK button.

To modify the timescale:

1. Double-click any month or date on the **timescale** to open the Timescale dialog box, as shown in Figure 1-37. The Major scale and Minor scale reflect the last zoom level that you displayed in the Gantt Chart.

Figure 1-37 | **TIMESCALE DIALOG BOX**

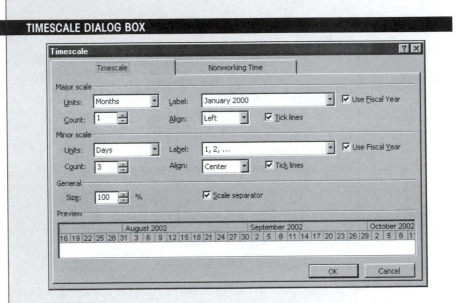

2. Click the **Major scale Units** list arrow, click **Weeks**, click the **Major scale Count** up spin arrow to increment it to **2**, click the **Major scale Label** list arrow, and then click **Jan 30, Feb 6**. These changes expand the major scale to display a two-week increment with the appropriate labels.

3. Click the **Minor scale Units** list arrow, click **Days**, click the **Minor scale Label** list arrow, and then click **1/31/00, 2/1/00**, as shown in Figure 1-38.

Figure 1-38 | **CHANGING THE TIMESCALE**

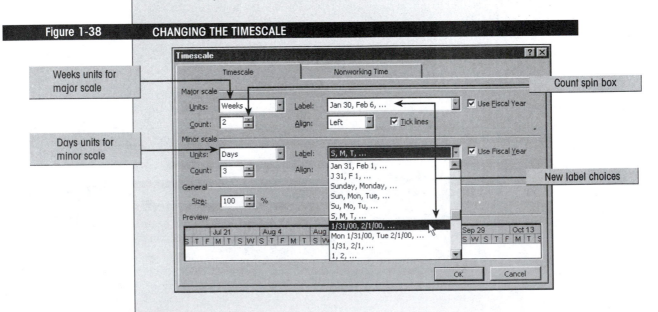

4. Click the **OK** button to apply the timescale changes. You can see the changes in the Gantt Chart view.

The Timescale dialog box also offers options to change the alignment, tick lines, and nonworking times. You will explore these later in the book.

Printing a View

Almost every view of a project, with the exception of form views, can be printed. The chart views of a project can be quite large, so printing involves several extra considerations, most important of which is to make sure that you **preview** the printout on the screen before you print it in order to check the magnification and total number of pages.

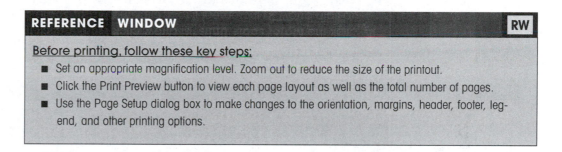

REFERENCE   WINDOW | **RW**

Before printing, follow these key steps:
- Set an appropriate magnification level. Zoom out to reduce the size of the printout.
- Click the Print Preview button to view each page layout as well as the total number of pages.
- Use the Page Setup dialog box to make changes to the orientation, margins, header, footer, legend, and other printing options.

To print the Gantt Chart:

1. Click the **Print Preview** button 🔍 on the Standard toolbar. The project appears in Print Preview, as shown in Figure 1-39. The Zoom In pointer 🔍 enables you to get a close look at any part of the screen.

Figure 1-39 | **THE GANTT CHART IN PRINT PREVIEW**

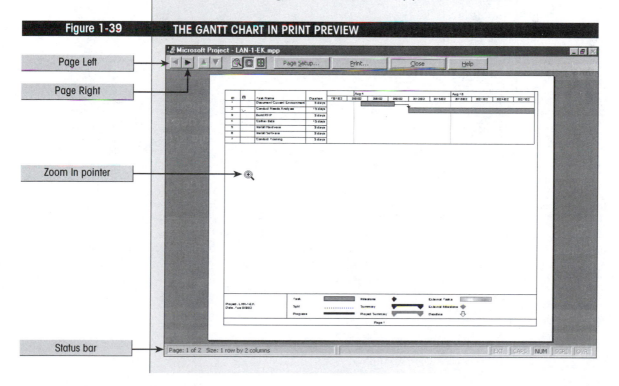

Page Left

Page Right

Zoom In pointer

Status bar

The status bar indicates that it will take two pages to print the Gantt Chart at the current level of magnification. You could use the Page Right button ▶ and Page Left button ◀ to move through the pages of the printout. The Page Up button ▲ and Page Down button ▼ are dimmed because they are unavailable.

2. Move the pointer into the gray area to the right of the image of the Gantt Chart. The pointer changes to the Zoom Out pointer 🔍. Click the Zoom Out pointer 🔍, and the status bar indicates that you are in Multi-Page view. You now can see both pages of the Gantt Chart.

3. Click the **Close** button on the Print Preview toolbar, and then click the **Zoom Out** button 🔍 on the Standard toolbar to decrease the width of the Gantt Chart.

4. Click the **Print Preview** button 🔍 on the Standard toolbar. The printout now fits on one page, as shown in Figure 1-40. Both the status bar "Page 1 of 1" and the dimmed Page buttons indicate that the entire printout fits on one page.

| Figure 1-40 | GANTT CHART FITS ON ONE PAGE |

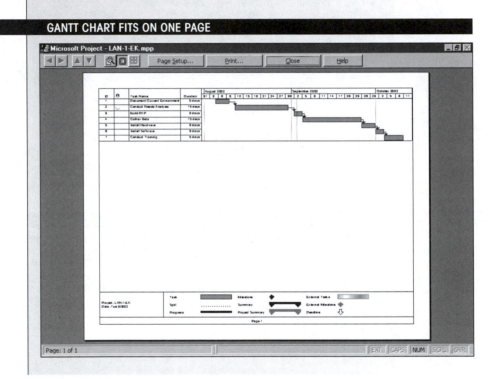

The **legend** appears in the bottom portion of each page to provide information about the bars. The project title and today's date appear to the left of the legend. The default footer appears with the word "Page" and the current page number centered at the bottom of the page.

You can use the **Page Setup** dialog box to change many of the printout's characteristics, including orientation, margins, legend, header, and footer. Header and footer information can be placed in a left-aligned, centered, or right-aligned position.

To set up the page:

1. Click the **Page Setup** button on the Print Preview toolbar. The Page Setup Gantt Chart dialog box opens.

2. Click the **Header** tab, click the **Left** alignment tab, click in the **text box**, and then type **Your Name**, as shown in Figure 1-41. The upper section of the Page Setup dialog box displays a preview of how the information that you specified for the left, center, or right portions of the header will appear on the page.

Figure 1-41   MODIFYING THE HEADER

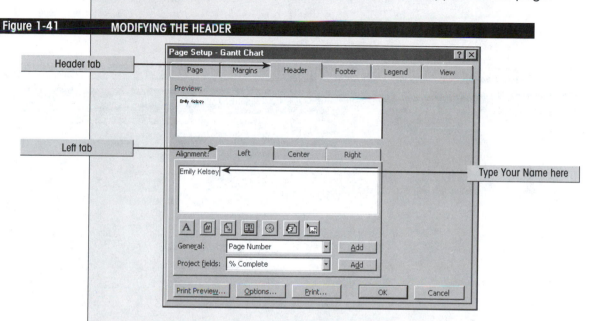

3. Click the **Legend** tab, click the **Left** alignment tab, triple-click to select **Project** and then type **File Name**. Your dialog box should look like Figure 1-42.

Figure 1-42   MODIFYING THE LEGEND

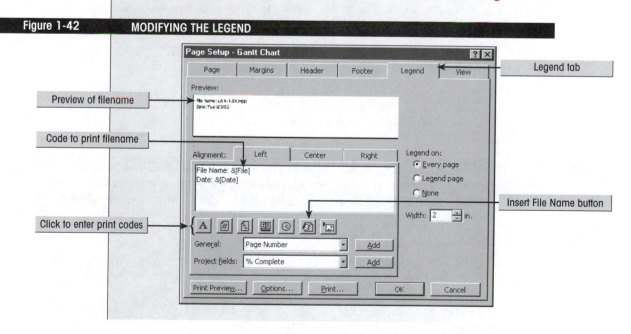

The &(File) code represents the actual filename as shown in the preview section of the Page Setup dialog box. If you change the filename, this code will automatically change the filename on the printout.

4. Click the **OK** button to accept the changes, click the **Print** button on the Print Preview toolbar, then click the **OK** button in the Print dialog box.

Other codes can be entered into the header, footer, and legend by using the other buttons in the Page Setup dialog box, as described in Figure 1-43, or by inserting the codes found in the General and Project fields lists.

Figure 1-43		PRINT CODE BUTTONS IN THE PAGE SETUP DIALOG BOX	
BUTTON NAME	**BUTTON**	**CODE**	**DESCRIPTION**
Format Text Font	A	(no code)	Allows you to format selected text by changing the font, font size, bold, italics, underline, and text color
Insert Page Number	#	& [Page]	Inserts the current page number
Insert Total Page Count		& [Pages]	Inserts the total number of pages for the entire printout
Insert Current Date		& [Date]	Inserts the current date as established by the computer's clock or network server
Insert Current Time		& [Time]	Inserts the current time as established by the computer's clock or network server
Insert File Name		& [File]	Inserts the project's filename
Insert Picture		(no code)	Inserts a picture (for example, clip art, scanned photo, or logo)

Page Setup options vary slightly when printing a Calendar, Network Diagram, or table view. The key aspects of successful printing (zooming to an acceptable magnification level, print previewing your work, and using the Page Setup dialog box to make changes) remain the same regardless of which view you are printing.

Getting **Help**

The Project 2000 Help system provides quick access to information about commands, features, and screen elements. Figure 1-44 describes the options available on the Help menu.

Figure 1-44	THE PROJECT 2000 HELP MENU OPTIONS
MENU OPTION	**DESCRIPTION**
What's This?	Provides **context-sensitive** Help information. When you choose this command, the pointer changes to the Help pointer, which you can then use to click any object or option on the screen, including menu commands, to see a description of the item.
Office Assistant	A context-sensitive, interactive guide to finding information on Microsoft Project 2000 and which sometimes opens automatically to help you with a task. You can also type a direct question to search the Help system for an answer in plain English.
Office on the Web	When you are connected to the Internet, provides up-to-the-minute information, news, and answers to common Project 2000 questions on the Microsoft Web site.
Contents and Index	Enables you to look up information in Project 2000's Help system as you would in an encyclopedia. This option bypasses the Office Assistant and goes directly into the Help manual.

REFERENCE WINDOW **RW**

Getting Help from the Office Assistant

- Click the Microsoft Project Help button on the Standard toolbar (or click Help on the menu bar and then click Show the Office Assistant).
- Type your question in the Office Assistant's text box, and then click the Search button.
- Click a topic from the list of topics displayed.
- Read the information in the Microsoft Project 2000 Help window. For more information, click underlined hyperlinks to navigate through the Help system.
- To display the Index, Answer Wizard, or Contents tab, with which you can also navigate the Help system, click the Show button in the Microsoft Project 2000 Help window. Click the Hide button to hide these tabs.
- To close the Microsoft Project 2000 Help window, click the Close button.
- To hide the Office Assistant, click Help on the menu bar and then click Hide the Office Assistant. You can also right-click the Office Assistant and then click Hide.

By default, the Office Assistant takes the form of an animated paper clip, but your Office Assistant might differ. You can easily change the look of the Office Assistant by right-clicking the Office Assistant, clicking Choose Assistant from the shortcut menu, clicking Next on the Gallery tab to view the Assistant choices, and then clicking the OK button after you have made a choice.

If a light bulb appears above the Office Assistant, click it to see a tip relevant to your recent activity. You'll use the Office Assistant now to learn how to delete a task.

To use the Office Assistant to learn how to delete a task:

1. Click the **Microsoft Project Help** button 🔲 on the Standard toolbar. The Office Assistant opens, offering help on topics related to the task that you most recently performed and asking what you'd like to do.

2. Type **How do I delete a task?** and then click the **Search** button. The Office Assistant window shows topics related to removing and changing tasks.

3. Click **Remove a Task**. The Microsoft Project 2000 Help window opens with specific information on how to delete a task, as shown in Figure 1-45.

   TROUBLE? Depending on how the Help system was used by the last person, it might or might not appear in a maximized window on your screen. It may open either to the left or right side of the Project window. If you do not see the Help window after Step 3, click the Microsoft Project 2000 Help button in the taskbar.

Figure 1-45	STEPS FOR DELETING A TASK

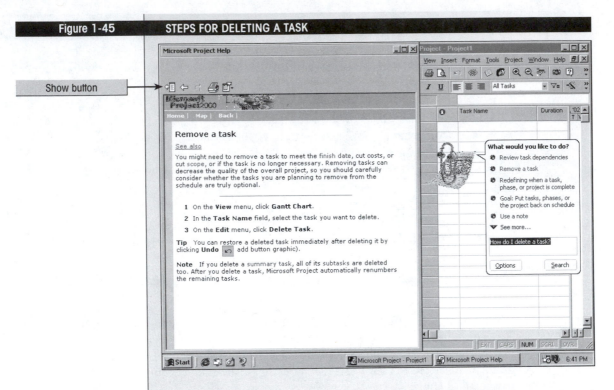

TROUBLE? If the Help window tabs are already on the screen, skip Step 4.

4. Click the **Show** button [icon]. The Show button toggles into the Hide button [icon], and Help window tabs appear, as shown in Figure 1-46.

Figure 1-46	HELP WINDOW TABS

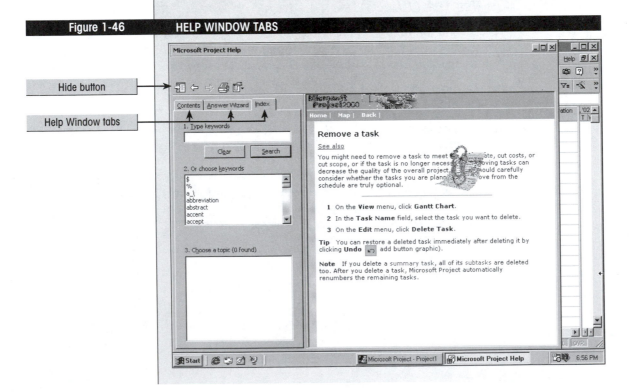

5. Click the **Contents** tab. This tab allows you to search the Help system by general topics.

6. Click the **Expand** button to the left of the **Getting started folder**, click the **Expand** button to the left of the **Build a plan folder**, click the **Expand** button to the left of the **Define a project folder**, and then click **Start a project file**.

   Your screen should look like Figure 1-47. Using the Contents tab is very similar to expanding and collapsing folders in Windows Explorer.

Figure 1-47   **USING THE CONTENTS TAB**

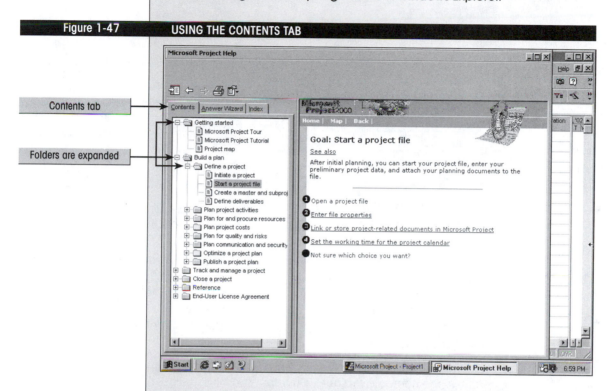

7. Click the **Index** tab.

   The Index tab shows major entries alphabetically in the second list (from which you can scroll and choose a topic), or you can type your search phrase into the Type keywords text box.

8. Type **critical path**, click the **Search** button, and then click **Show the critical path** in the Choose a topic list, as shown in Figure 1-48.

Figure 1-48   **USING THE INDEX TAB**

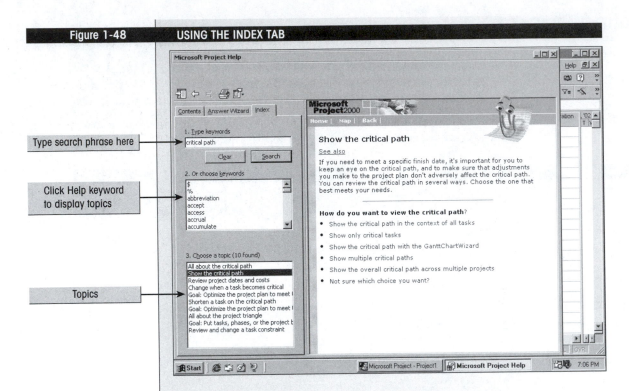

Type search phrase here

Click Help keyword
to display topics

Topics

The Answer Wizard tab allows you to enter an English phrase to search for information in the Help manual just like the Office Assistant. The **Back** button ⇐ and **Forward** button ⇒ next to the Show/Hide button help you to move backward and forward quickly between the Help pages that you have already displayed. The **Options** button 🗐 provides additional printing and navigation options.

8. Click the **Print** button 🖨, click the **OK** button in the Print dialog box, and then close the Microsoft Project 2000 Help window.

Hiding the Office Assistant

You might find that having the Office Assistant open on the screen interferes with your work in Project 2000. You can hide the Office Assistant so that it does not display unless you request help.

To hide the Office Assistant:

1. Right-click the **Office Assistant**. The shortcut menu opens, offering options for working with or modifying the Office Assistant.

2. Click **Hide**. The Office Assistant is now hidden from view. If you need help, click the Office Assistant button on the toolbar, and it will reappear.

Exiting Project 2000

After exploring so many new features and capabilities of this powerful program, you are now ready to **exit**, or quit, Project 2000.

To save the existing project with the same filename and exit Project 2000:

1. Click the **Save** button 🔲 on the Standard toolbar. You should always save your work before exiting the program.

2. Click **Save 'LAN-1-Your Initials.mpp' without a baseline** (if prompted) and then click the **OK** button. You will learn about baselines in a later tutorial.

3. Click the Project 2000 **Close** button ⊠ to exit Project 2000.

Now that you have learned the vocabulary of project management, as well as how to view, navigate, and enter a task in Project 2000, you are ready to build the project for JLB Partners. You will do this in the next tutorial.

Session 1.3 QUICK CHECK

1. What is the default Project 2000 view?

2. What does the Project 2000 title bar display?

3. What is found on Project 2000 toolbars?

4. What categories of task views are provided by Project 2000?

5. What types of graphical views are available within Project 2000?

6. What types of task tables are available within Project 2000?

7. What is the purpose of the form view?

8. How do you open the Task Information dialog box, and what is its purpose?

9. Explain how zooming out changes the timescale on the Gantt Chart.

10. Explain how zooming in changes the bars on the Gantt Chart.

11. How do you open the Timescale dialog box?

12. List several tips for successful printing.

13. What is the animated interface (usually in the form of a paperclip) in the Project Help system called?

REVIEW ASSIGNMENTS

A very important component of the LAN installation at JLB Partners involves training the users. It will be your job to coordinate this effort. In this assignment, you will open a partially completed project file that documents training tasks. You will explore the project, add tasks, and print several views.

1. Start Project 2000, and make sure that your Data Disk is in the appropriate disk drive. Open the **Training-1.mpp** file in the Review folder for Tutorial 1.

2. Use the Save As command to save the project file as **Training-1-Your Initials** on your Data Disk so that you do not change the original project file. Save the file without a baseline.

3. Click Project on the menu bar, and then click Project Information to open the Project Information dialog box. Change the Start Date to today's date.

4. Add a task on row 7 with the Task Name "Schedule classes," and leave the duration at 1 day. Add another new task on row 8 with the Task Name "Conduct training" and a duration of 3 days. (*Note*: By default, the task starts on today's date and does not have any predecessors. The next tutorial will explain how to set task relationships so that a task will not be able to start until a prior task is completed.)

5. Change the duration for the first task, "Identify existing skills," from 3 days to 2. (*Hint*: If the duration unit is days, all you need to enter in the Duration column is 2 to indicate 2 days.)

6. Write down your answer to the following question: "Why do some durations appear with a question mark and others do not?"

7. Preview the Gantt Chart printout, and then open the Page Setup dialog box. Change the left section of the legend to display your name instead of Project in the first line.

8. Print the Gantt Chart. It should be one page.

9. Click the Network Diagram button on the View Bar.

10. Click the Zoom Out button until you can see all of the tasks (there are eight total tasks) on the screen.

Explore ▷ 11. Place the pointer over each task and read each task.

12. Preview the Network Diagram printout on the screen, and then open the Page Setup dialog box and change the left section of the header to display your name.

Explore ▷ 13. Click the Print button on the Print Preview toolbar, set Page(s) From: 1 To: 1 in the Print range section of the Print dialog box to specify that only the first page of the Network Diagram is to be printed, and then print the page.

14. Click the Calendar button on the View Bar, and then preview the Calendar view. Open the Page Setup dialog box. Change the left section of the footer to display your name. Use the Zoom Out pointer to preview all three pages on the screen, and then print the First Page Calendar view.

15. Use the Office Assistant to search for the phrase "Start date."

Explore ▷ 16. Click "Change a project start or finish date." Write down the steps to set a project Start date or Finish date. Write down the answer to the following question: "Why can't you set *both* the project's Start date and Finish date?"

Explore 17. Begin at the Microsoft Project Help Welcome page. Click Tutorial. Complete the Help system's tutorial on "The Basics." (*Hint*: It has three parts: What is project management?, Getting around, and Getting help.) Write down a sentence or two about one new item that you learned about from each part of this tutorial. Close Help.

18. Save **Training-1-Your Initials** without a baseline, close the project file, and then exit Project 2000.

CASE PROBLEMS

Case 1. Building a House You have a part-time job working for a general contractor, BJB Development, Inc., which manages residential construction projects. The manager has asked you to use Project 2000 to enter and update some of the general tasks involved in building a new home.

1. Start Project 2000 and make sure that your Data Disk is in the appropriate disk drive. Open the **House-1.mpp** file in the Cases folder for Tutorial 1.

2. Use the Save As command to save the project file as **House-1-Your Initials** in the same folder so that you do not change the original project file. Save the file without a baseline.

3. Click Project on the menu bar, and then click Project Information to open the Project Information dialog box. Change the Start Date to today's date, and write down the date that is displayed in the Finish Date text box.

4. Enter the following new tasks and corresponding durations to the project (in rows 12, 13, and 14): Paint interior, 3 days; Lay carpet, 3 days; Install wood trim, 10 days.

5. Open the Project Information dialog box, and write down the date displayed in the Finish date text box. Explain why the date changed from that in Step 3.

6. Change the duration for the first two tasks—Secure financing and Purchase lot—to 4 days each. Open the Project Information dialog box, and write down the date displayed in the Finish date text box. Explain why the date did not change from that in Step 5.

7. Preview and then print a Gantt Chart view of this project, using the Page Setup dialog box to enter your name in the left portion of the header.

8. Preview and then print a Calendar view of this project, using the Page Setup dialog box to enter your name in the left portion of the header.

9. Preview the Network Diagram. Enter your name in the left portion of the header using the Page Setup dialog box.

Explore 10. Print the Network Diagram.

Explore 11. On the printout, identify which task is on the critical path. Also on the printout, write down two visual cues that indicate that the task you just identified is on the critical path. (*Hint*: One of the cues involves the task's color, which will not be differentiated on a black and white printout.)

12. Use the Office Assistant to search for the phrase "critical path."

Explore 13. Click the All about the critical path option, and then print that page of the Help manual.

Explore   14. Write down at least two reasons why the critical path is so important to project managers. Use the Help manual or any other project management resources to help you to understand the importance of the critical path.

15. Save **House-1-Your Initials.mpp**, close the project file without saving a baseline, and exit Project 2000.

Case 2. Finding a Job   You are currently pursuing a new job that utilizes technical skills that you have recently acquired. Use Project 2000 to organize your job search efforts.

1. Start Project, and make sure that your Student Data Disk is in the appropriate disk drive. Open the **Job-1.mpp** file in the Cases folder for Tutorial 1.

2. Use the Save As command to save the project file as **Job-1-Your Initials.mpp** in the Cases folder so that you do not change the original project file. Save the file without a baseline.

3. Click Project on the menu bar, and then click Project Information to open the Project Information dialog box. Change the Start Date to today's date.

4. Enter the following new tasks and corresponding durations to the project (in rows 9 and 10): Write cover letter, 1 day; Purchase interview clothes, 2 days.

5. Change the duration of the second task, Edit resume, from 1 day to 3 days.

6. Double-click the timescale to open the Timescale dialog box. Change the Timescale so that the major scale is Thirds of Months with the label January Beginning, January Middle, and the minor scale is Days with the label Su, Mo, Tu. View the Gantt Chart.

7. Preview the Gantt Chart view, open the Page Setup dialog box, click the Legend tab, click the Left alignment tab. Enter your name as the third line of the legend, and then print the Gantt Chart view.

8. Change the timescale back to months on the major scale.

9. Click the Calendar button on the View Bar, and then zoom in so that you see two weeks on the screen and all tasks are visible on the calendar.

Explore   10. Preview the Calendar view, and then use the Page Setup dialog box to add the text "File Name:" and the filename code in the left section of the header. Enter your name as the right side of the header, and then print the Calendar view.

11. Click the Network Diagram button on the View Bar, and then preview the Network Diagram.

Explore   12. Use the Page Setup dialog box to add the text "File Name:" and the filename code as in the left side of the header. Enter your name in the right side of the header, and then print the Network Diagram.

13. Write down the answer to the following question: "By default, where does the legend print on a Network Diagram?"

Explore   14. Click the Office Assistant, type "Create link," and then click the Search button.

15. Click the Create a dependency between tasks in a project option, and then print that page of the Help manual.

16. Save **Job-1-Your Initials**, close the project file without saving a baseline, and exit Project 2000.

Case 3. Planning a Convention   In your new job at Future Technology, Inc. (FTI), you have been asked to help organize the annual convention in which FTI unveils its new product ideas for customers. You'll use Project 2000 to enter and track the many tasks that must be completed for a successful convention to occur. Since the convention *must* occur March 4, 5, and 6 of the year 2002, you'll schedule the project from a Finish Date and let Project 2000 determine the project Start Date.

1. Start Project, and make sure that your Data Disk is in the appropriate disk drive. Open the **Convention-1.mpp** file in the Cases folder for Tutorial 1.

2. Use the Save As command to save the file as **Convention-1-Your Initials** without a baseline to the Cases folder so that you do not change the original project file.

3. Click Project on the menu bar, and then click Project Information. Make sure that the project is scheduled from a Finish Date of 3/4/02. Write down the current Start Date for the project.

4. Enter the following new tasks and corresponding durations to the project (in rows 9 and 10): Organize mass mailing, 5 days; Make site visit, 2 days.

5. Double-click task 1 to open the Task Information dialog box, click the Advanced tab, and then write down the option for the Constraint type. Click OK to close the Task Information dialog box.

6. Change the timescale so that the major scale is Sun 1/30/00, Mon 1/31/00, Tue 2/1/00, and the minor scale is days Sun, Mon, Tue, ….

7. Click the Network Diagram button on the View Bar, and then zoom out to determine which task(s) are on the critical path.

Explore   8. Preview the Network Diagram, and then use the Page Setup dialog box to enter your name as the first line of the left section of the header and the current date code as the second line of the left section of the Header. Print the Network Diagram.

9. On the printout, identify which task(s) are on the critical path. Write a sentence or two that explains why this task (or tasks) establishes the critical path.

10. Click the Calendar button on the View Bar, and then use the Page Setup dialog box to enter your name as the first line of the left section of the Header and the current date code as the second line of the left section of the Header. Print the calendar.

Explore   11. Use the Help system to explain what "Overflow Tasks" on the calendar printout means.

Explore   12. Return to the Calendar view, and then zoom in or drag the top edge of the bar that separates the weeks so that all tasks are visible.

Explore   13. Preview the Calendar view, and then open the Page Setup dialog box and click the View tab. Click the Week height as on screen option button, and then click OK. Print the calendar and then compare the results to the printout of Step 10. What are the differences?

14. Save **Convention-1-Your Initials**, close the project file without saving a baseline, and exit Project 2000.

Case 4. Organizing a Fundraiser You have volunteered to lead your neighborhood elementary school's major fundraising effort to purchase new playground equipment. Since the equipment must be ready for school to start on September 16, 2002, you'll schedule the project from a Finish Date and let Project 2000 establish the project Start Date.

1. Start Project 2000, and make sure your Data Disk is in the appropriate disk drive.

2. Click Project on the menu bar, and then click Project Information. (*Hint*: If Project 2000 is already running, you can start a new project by clicking the New button on the Standard toolbar. The Project Information dialog box automatically opens for each new file started within Project 2000.)

3. Change the Schedule from option in the Project Information dialog box to "Project Finish Date," and then change the Finish Date to September 16, 2002. Click the OK button.

4. Enter the following tasks and corresponding durations:

   Identify school sponsor, 5 days

   Research equipment choices, 10 days

   Prepare for PTO meeting, 2 days

   Set monetary goal, 1 day

   Choose fundraiser project, 5 days

5. Double-click task 1 to open the Task Information dialog box, click the Notes tab, and enter the following into the Notes text box: "Start with Mrs. Biheller." Click the OK button.

6. Save the project with the name **Fund-1-Your Initials** in the Cases folder for Tutorial 1. Save the file without a baseline.

7. Preview the Gantt Chart view, and then use the Page Setup dialog box to add the text "File Name:" and the filename code to the left portion of the header. Enter your name in the right portion of the Header, and then print the Gantt Chart view.

Explore 8. Click the Calendar button in the View Bar, and then resize the rows of the calendar so that all of the tasks are visible for the weeks of September 8 and September 15.

9. Write down your answer to the following question: "What visual cue do you see on the calendar to indicate that more tasks are scheduled on a day than are currently visible?"

10. Preview the Calendar view, and then use the Page Setup dialog box to add the text "File Name:" and the filename code to the left portion of the header. Enter your name in the right portion of the header, and then print the calendar.

Explore 11. Click the Network Diagram button on the View Bar, and then use the Page Setup dialog box to change the legend. Specify that the legend is to print on every page instead of the legend page.

12. Add the text "File Name:" and the filename code to the left portion of the header. Enter your name in the right portion of the Header, and then print the Network Diagram.

13. Save the **Fund-1-Your Initials** file, close the project file without saving a baseline, and then exit Project 2000.

INTERNET ASSIGNMENTS

The purpose of the Internet Assignments is to challenge you to find information on the Internet so that you learn more about project management and how to use Microsoft Project 2000 more effectively. The actual assignments are updated and maintained on the Course Technology Web site. Log on to the Internet, and use your Web browser to go to the Student Online Companion that accompanies this text at **www.course.com/NewPerspectives/Project2000**. Click the link for Tutorial 1.

QUICK | CHECK ANSWERS

Session 1.1

1. Defining, organizing, tracking, and communicating information about a project in order to meet a project goal

2. The project goal is achieved when a series of tasks are completed that produce a desired outcome, at a specified level of quality, and within a given time frame and budget.

3. Efficient is doing tasks faster and with fewer resources. Effective is doing the tasks that produce the desired outcome at the desired level of quality.

4. Many possible answers exist, but they should exhibit an acknowledgment of some sense of quality, time frame, and budget. For example: "Write a college-level textbook on the subject of distance education by the end of the year within the publisher's budget."

5. A task is the specific actions that need to be completed in order to achieve the project goal.

   The duration is how long it takes to complete the task.

   The resources are the people, equipment, and facilities (such as a conference room) that need to be scheduled to complete a particular task.

   The project manager is the central point at which all of the details of the project converge for entry into the project plan.

6. The benefits of project management include:

   - Better understanding of overall project goals
   - Better understanding of project tasks, durations, schedule dates, and costs
   - More organized and streamlined way to manage the many details of a project
   - More accurate and reliable project status information
   - More efficient use of project resources
   - Better communication between management, the project manager, and others
   - Faster response to conflicting project goals
   - Greater satisfaction of project progress
   - Faster project completion
   - Lower project costs

7. The Gantt Chart is a graphical visualization of the project that displays each task as a horizontal bar. The length of the bar measures the task's duration as compared to the timescale at the top of the chart. The primary purpose of the Gantt Chart is to graphically display task durations and task schedules.

8. The Network Diagram displays each task as a box. Dependent tasks are linked together through link lines, thus creating a clear picture of how the tasks will

be sequenced. The primary purpose of the Network Diagram is to display the critical path.

Session 1.2

1. Task name and task duration are usually the first two pieces of information entered about a task in Gantt Chart view.

2. The left side of the Standard toolbar contains buttons that are common to almost all applications, such as Save, Print, Cut, Copy, Paste, and Spell Check. On the right side of Project 2000's Standard toolbar are buttons specific to Project 2000, such as Assign Resources Assignment, Zoom In, and Zoom Out.

3. The Formatting toolbar contains buttons that improve the appearance of the project, such as font, bold, italics, and alignment. On the left side of Project 2000's Formatting toolbar are several buttons to help you organize, outline, and filter tasks.

4. The Entry Table

5. Dragging the split bar to the right displays more columns in the underlying table.

6. By default, the major scale is measured in weeks and displays the date for the Sunday of that week. By default, the minor scale is measured in days and displays the first letter of the day of the week.

7. Closing a project leaves Project 2000 running for you to create a project file or open an existing file. Exiting Project 2000 closes any open files and closes the application, returning you to the Windows desktop.

Session 1.3

1. Gantt Chart view is the default view.

2. The title bar displays the name of the current project as well as the name of the application software being used.

3. The toolbars display some of the most popular commands. These commands, and many others, are also found in the menu system.

4. Project 2000 supports chart, sheet 1 table, and form views.

5. Gantt Chart, Network Diagram, Task PERT, and Calendar views are some of the most popular graphical views within Project 2000.

6. Task tables include the Entry, Cost, Schedule, Summary, Tracking, Variance, and Work tables.

7. The purpose of the Form view is to focus on the details of only one task.

8. Double-click a task in any view to open the Task Information dialog box. Its purpose is to show details of a task. You also can edit task details in the Task Information dialog box.

9. Zooming out makes the timescale show larger units of time.

10. Zooming in expands the size of bars, thereby showing fewer tasks on the screen at any time.

11. In Gantt Chart view, double-click the timescale to open the Timescale dialog box.

12. Tips for successful printing include:

    - Set the magnification to an appropriate level.

    - Always print preview before printing.

    - Use the Page Setup dialog box to make appropriate changes to the margins, header, footer, and other elements of the printout.

13. Clipit

OBJECTIVES

In this tutorial you will:

- Start a new project

- Examine scheduling defaults

- Change a project calendar

- Create a task calendar

- Enter and edit tasks, durations, and task dependencies

- Enter and edit recurring tasks and milestones

- Enter lag and lead times

- View project statistics

- Create and manipulate summary tasks

- Apply a work break-down structure

CREATING A PROJECT SCHEDULE

Scheduling Tasks and Durations for a Local Area Network Installation

CASE

JLB Partners

After attending the Microsoft Project 2000 course at the local college, you should be comfortable with project management terminology and the Project 2000 interface. You can use your new knowledge as the project manager at JLB Partners. Your first major effort was to develop a project goal that satisfied the company's management. The project goal, "*network company computers to easily share resources within a time frame of three months and within a budget of $50,000,*" has been approved by Emily Kelsey, the managing partner. Meeting the project goal will determine the success of the project. Your second major effort was to research several LAN installations and create task lists to serve as reference material for this project. With these checklists in hand, you can start defining the specific tasks, durations, milestones, constraints, and dependencies that are appropriate for the local area network (LAN) installation at JLB Partners. Emily has asked that you start creating the project and manage the LAN installation to coordinate the computer resources of the six users at JLB Partners. You start by entering the details of this project into Project 2000.

SESSION 2.1

In this session, you will start a new project by checking important default options, creating a project calendar, and entering tasks, durations, recurring tasks, and milestones.

Starting a New Project and Examining Scheduling Defaults

When you open Project 2000, a new, blank project file is ready for you to start entering tasks and durations. By default, the new project file is scheduled from a project Start Date and all tasks are scheduled to begin as *soon* as possible in order for the overall project to be finished as quickly as possible. Project 2000 calculates the project's Finish Date based on the tasks, durations, and dependencies between the tasks entered into the project file using **as soon as possible** start dates for each task. You can open the Project Information dialog box to review or change these default settings.

REFERENCE WINDOW   **RW**

Changing Default Project Scheduling Options
- Click Project on the menu bar, and then click Project Information.
- If necessary, change the Schedule from option to project Finish Date (project Start Date is the default) in the Project Information dialog box.
- If necessary, change the Start Date or the Finish Date.
- Click the OK button to apply the changes.

You want to examine default project scheduling options and how they affect the scheduling of individual tasks.

To examine default project scheduling options for projects that are scheduled from a Start Date:

1. Start Project 2000. By default, a new project file opens that is scheduled from today's date as the Start Date.

   TROUBLE? If Project 2000 is already open, click the New button 🗋 on the Standard toolbar, and then click the OK button in the Project Information dialog box to start a new project.

2. Press the **Tab** key to move to the **Task Name** cell, type **Document hardware**, press the **Tab** key, type **3**, and then press the **Enter** key.

3. Click **Project** on the menu bar, and then click **Project Information**.

   The default options in the Project Information dialog box confirm the way that the first task was scheduled, that is, to begin as soon as possible based on the project's Start Date. The Schedule from option is project Start Date, the Start Dates of the project and the first task is today's date, and the project Finish Date is calculated as three working days after today's date.

TROUBLE? Your project will be scheduled as of the Current Date (as determined by your computer's internal clock). Therefore, your project dates will not always match those shown in the figures of this textbook.

Figure 2-1	PROJECT INFORMATION DIALOG BOX

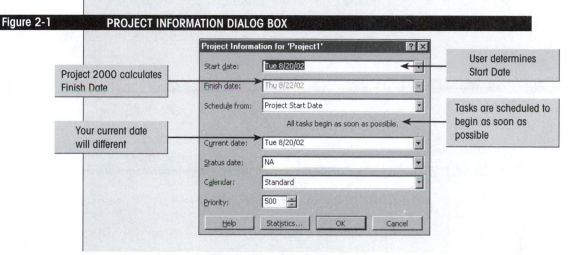

Project 2000 calculates Finish Date

Your current date will different

User determines Start Date

Tasks are scheduled to begin as soon as possible

The Project Information dialog box can be used to affect the way the project is scheduled after one or more tasks have already been entered.

To further examine default project scheduling options:

1. Click the **OK** button in the Project Information dialog box, click the **second Task Name** cell, type **Document software**, press the **Tab** key, type **5**, and then press the **Enter** key.

    The second task has a longer duration than the first, so the project's calculated Finish Date should have changed to accommodate this task.

2. Click **Project** on the menu bar, and then click **Project Information**.

    The Finish Date is now calculated as five working days after the project Start Date. If either task spans a nonworking day (such as a weekend), the Finish Date will be more than five days after the Start Date.

3. Click the **OK** button to close the Project Information dialog box, click the project **Close Window** button ⊠, and then click **No** to close the sample project without saving changes.

    TROUBLE? If you are returned to the desktop and Project 2000 is no longer running, you exited Project 2000 by clicking the Project 2000 Close button rather than closing the file by clicking the project file Close Window button. Restart Project 2000 to continue with the tutorial.

If your project should be scheduled from a Finish Date (such as a convention that is planned for a specific date), you must change the Schedule from option in the Project Information dialog box.

To examine default project scheduling options for projects that are scheduled from a Finish Date:

1. Click the **New** button 🗋 on the Standard toolbar, click the **Schedule from** list arrow in the Project Information dialog box, click **Project Finish Date**, click the **Finish date** list arrow, click the **next month** arrow on the calendar as shown in Figure 2-2, and then click the **OK** button.

Figure 2-2	PROJECT SCHEDULED FROM A FINISH DATE

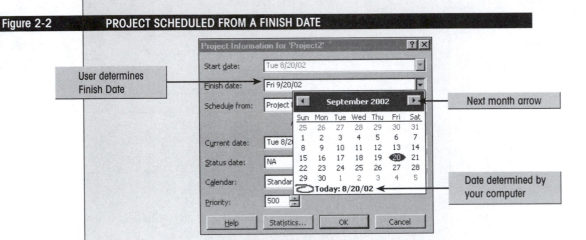

You can also enter a date directly into the project Finish Date text box if you do not want to use the calendar. When a project is scheduled from a Finish Date, all tasks are scheduled to begin as *late* as possible in order for the over-all project to be started as late as possible and yet still meet the required Finish Date. In this case, Project 2000 calculates the project's Start Date based on the tasks, durations, and dependencies between the tasks using **as late as possible** start dates for each task.

2. Press the **Tab** key to move to the first **Task Name** cell, type **Document hardware**, press the **Tab** key, type **3**, and then press the **Enter** key.

3. Click the **Task Name** cell for the second row, type **Document software**, press the **Tab** key, type **5**, and then press the **Enter** key.

Although the specific dates will differ, your screen should look similar to Figure 2-3. In this case, the project Finish Date was entered as 8/20/02 in the Project Information dialog box, and therefore the second task, Document software is scheduled to finish on 8/20/02 and start five working days earlier using as late as possible scheduling.

Figure 2-3	PROJECT SCHEDULED FROM A FINISH DATE

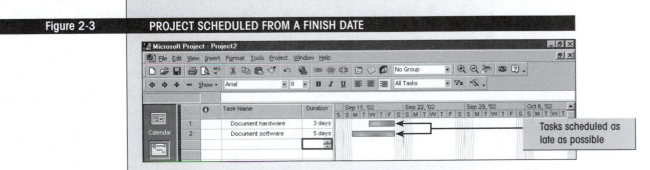

Check the Project Information dialog box to determine the Start Date for the project.

4. Click **Project** on the menu bar, and then click **Project Information**.

When a project is scheduled from a Finish Date, all tasks are scheduled with as late as possible start dates as shown in Figure 2-4.

Figure 2-4   PROJECT INFORMATION DIALOG BOX

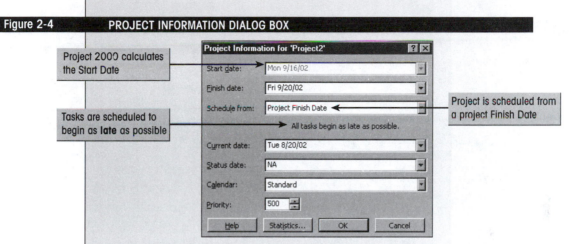

Project 2000 calculates the Start Date

Tasks are scheduled to begin as **late** as possible

Project is scheduled from a project Finish Date

The Project Information dialog box controls the scheduling assumptions for all new tasks that are added to the project.

5. Click the **OK** button. The Project Information dialog box closes.

The Task Information Dialog Box

The Task Information dialog box is a comprehensive collection of all of the information about each task organized into five categories represented by these tabs: General, Predecessors, Resources, Advanced, and Notes. The Task Information dialog box is another type of view by which you can examine and enter data about a task.

You can change the As Soon As Possible or As Late As Possible scheduling constraint for an individual task by using the Task Information dialog box.

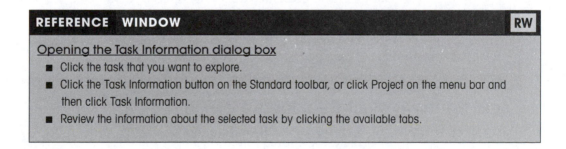

REFERENCE WINDOW   **RW**

Opening the Task Information dialog box
- Click the task that you want to explore.
- Click the Task Information button on the Standard toolbar, or click Project on the menu bar and then click Task Information.
- Review the information about the selected task by clicking the available tabs.

To examine scheduling constraints using the Task Information dialog box:

1. Click **task 1**, click the **Task Information** button 📧 on the Standard toolbar, and then click the **Advanced** tab, as shown in Figure 2-5.

   You can also double-click a task to open its Task Information dialog box.

Figure 2-5	TASK INFORMATION DIALOG BOX

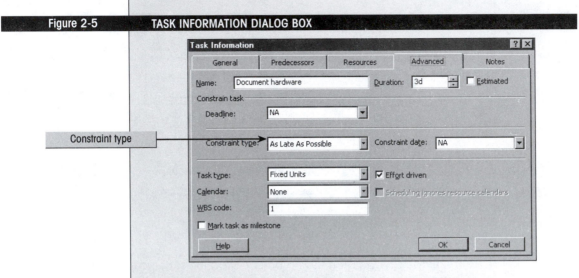

2. Click the **Constraint type** list arrow. You can see that many options are available for Constraint types. You will learn how each of these affects the project schedule later in the tutorials.

3. Click **As Soon As Possible**, and then click the **OK** button. The Document hardware bar moved to the left. The project will still finish on the specified Finish Date, but the first task is now scheduled to start as soon as possible.

From this example, you can see that careful attention to how the project is originally scheduled (from a Start Date or from a Finish Date) is extremely important because this choice determines the initial Constraint type (as soon as possible or as late as possible) for each task. This initial decision has a tremendous impact on the calculated start and finish dates for each task entered into the project. Always take the time to examine the Project Information dialog box before starting a new project.

Now that you've examined the Project Information dialog box, its affect on how tasks are scheduled, and how to access the Project and Task Information dialog boxes to make changes, you are ready to examine the project calendar.

Examining **Project Calendars**

By default, the entire project, each task, and each resource is scheduled according to the Standard calendar. The **Standard calendar** specifies that Monday through Friday are working days with eight hours of work completed each day. Saturday and Sunday are designated as nonworking days. You can modify these calendars to identify holidays or other nonworking days or times in which work should not be scheduled. You can also create unique calendars for tasks and resources that do not follow the working and nonworking times specified by the Standard calendar.

Changing the Project Calendar

The **project calendar** (also called the **Standard calendar**) is the base calendar used by Project 2000 to schedule new tasks within the project. It specifies **working time**, the hours during which work can occur, by default 8:00 AM to 12:00 PM and 1:00 PM to 5:00 PM Monday through Friday. It also specifies **nonworking time**, the hours of a 24-hour day that are not specified as working time, as well as any other global working time issues (such as a scheduled holiday) that affect the entire project.

REFERENCE WINDOW   **RW**

Changing the Project Calendar

- Click Tools on the menu bar, and then click Change Working Time.
- To change working and nonworking days, click the date on the calendar and then select the appropriate nonworking or working option.
- To change working hours, click the working date on the calendar and then change the From and To times that specify the working hours.
- Click the OK button to apply the changes.

JLB Partners closes the office on certain days. So you need to examine the project calendar and mark several days as nonworking days. When you start a new project by clicking the New button, you will always be presented with the Project Information dialog box. When you first start Project 2000, however, it automatically loads Project1, which is scheduled from a Start Date, without presenting the Project Information dialog box.

To change a project calendar:

1. Click the project's **Close Window** button ⊠, click **No** when prompted to save the changes to the project, and then click the **New** button 🗋 on the Standard toolbar to start a new project.

2. Click the **OK** button in the Project Information dialog box to schedule the project from a project Start Date.

3. Click **Tools** on the menu bar, and then click **Change Working Time**.

   The Change Working Time dialog box opens as shown in Figure 2-6. You can modify all project, task, and resource calendars by using this dialog box. Currently, the Standard (Project Calendar) is selected. It serves as the base calendar for the entire project.

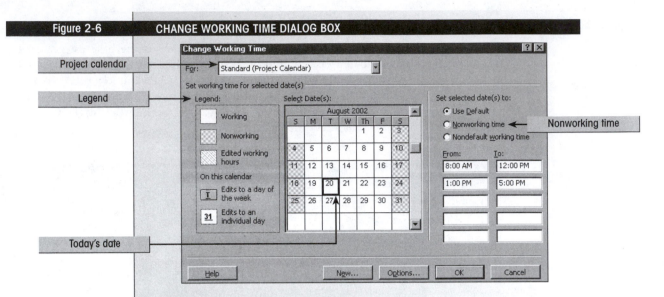

Figure 2-6   **CHANGE WORKING TIME DIALOG BOX**

The Legend provides the key to the shading on the calendar. Working days appear as white, nonworking days as light gray, and edited working hours with gray diagonal lines. If a day of the week such as Monday or Tuesday is edited, the day's abbreviation is underlined. If an individual day is edited, the day's number is underlined.

4. Click the **scroll arrows** on the calendar until you reach the month of **September 2002**.

   Project 2000 does not assume that any special holidays will be observed. If on any day the entire project will rest and all offices will be closed, you need to mark that day as a nonworking day. JLB Partners closes on Labor Day.

5. Click the box for **Monday September 2** on the calendar, and then click the **Nonworking time** option button in the Set selected date(s) to section of the Change Working Time dialog box.

   The number "2" is now underlined on the calendar to indicate that the date was edited. Some holidays span more than one day. You can change more than one day at the same time.

6. Click the **scroll arrows** on the calendar until you reach the month of **November 2002**, click the box for **Thursday November 28**, drag through the box for **Friday November 29**, and then click the **Nonworking time** option button. If you had to select non-contiguous days, you would click the first day and then press and hold the CTRL key while clicking the other days to select them as a group.

   You can also modify the number of hours worked during any day of the week.

7. Click the **F** column (for Friday), double-click **5** in the To time 5:00 PM text box, and then type **4**. The Friday workday now ends at 4:00 PM as shown in Figure 2-7. By modifying that one day of the week, you specify that every Friday for the duration of the project will have only seven hours' work to be scheduled and completed. If you further modified individual Fridays, the individual day changes would override the change made to all Fridays.

Figure 2-7 **CHANGING FRIDAYS FOR THE ENTIRE CALENDAR**

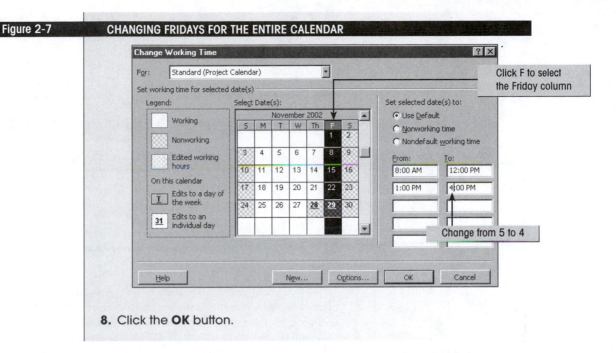

8. Click the **OK** button.

Changes to the project calendar can be made at any time during the development of the project.

Now that you've examined the project calendar and made changes that affect the entire project, you will create an individual task calendar.

Creating Task Calendars

An individual **task calendar** can be created for any task that does not follow the working and nonworking times specified by the project calendar. For example, your company might have a policy that training tasks may occur only from 8:00 AM to 12:00 PM. To accommodate this, you could create a task calendar called Training Calendar and apply it to the training tasks and thereby prevent Project 2000 from scheduling any training activities in the afternoon.

Likewise, an individual **resource calendar** can be created for a resource that does not follow the working and nonworking times specified by the project calendar. For example, contracted electricians might want to work from 7:00 AM to 11:30 AM and 12:30 PM to 4:00 PM. By assigning a resource to a resource calendar, you allow the resource to be worked on the days and times specified by the resource calendar rather than the project calendar. By default, all tasks and resource assignments inherit the project calendar unless you specify something else. That is why it is so important that you first set up all of the holidays and nonworking times in the project calendar. How resource calendars affect task scheduling is discussed in more detail in a later tutorial.

Creating a Task Calendar

- Click Tools on the menu bar, and then click Change Working Time.
- Click the New button within the Change Working Time dialog box, enter a name for the task calendar, determine whether the calendar should be created from scratch (a new base calendar without any holidays or other working time changes) or based on a copy of another calendar, and then click the OK button.
- To change working and nonworking days, click the date on the calendar and then select the appropriate nonworking or working option.
- To change working hours, click the working date on the calendar and then change the From and To times that indicate the working hours.
- Click the OK button to apply the changes.

Emily Kelsey has requested that the installation and training not disrupt the daily activities of JLB Partners. To meet this need, you met with the staff and determined that mornings are generally used for meetings and training could also be scheduled during that time. You create a calendar for the training tasks called Training that allows training tasks to be scheduled only between the hours of 8:00 AM and 12:00 PM.

To create a task calendar:

1. Click **Tools** on the menu bar, and then click **Change Working Time**.

   The Change Working Time dialog box opens.

2. Click **New** in the Change Working Time dialog box, and then type **Training**, as shown in Figure 2-8.

Figure 2-8 CREATING A NEW CALENDAR NAMED TRAINING

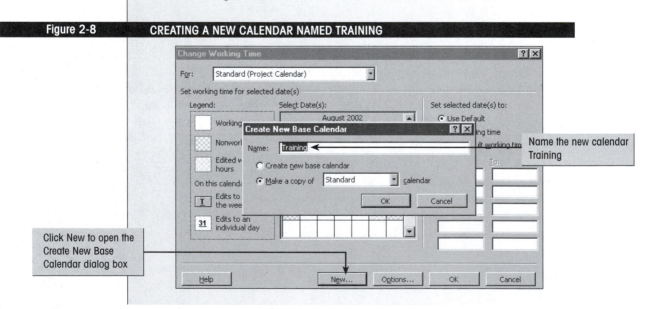

Click New to open the Create New Base Calendar dialog box

Name the new calendar Training

Clicking the Create new base calendar option button creates the Training calendar based on a 40-hour work week (8:00 AM to 12:00 PM and 1:00 PM to 5:00 PM), Monday through Friday, with Saturday and Sunday designated as nonworking days. Clicking the Make a copy of Standard calendar option button applies all of the holidays and working time changes made to the Standard (Project Calendar) calendar to this task calendar as well.

3. Click the **Make a copy of Standard calendar** option button (if it is not already selected), and then click the **OK** button. Click and drag from the **M** of Monday through the **Th** of Thursday on the calendar so that the first four working day columns are highlighted. You will change the working time for Monday through Thursday on the Training calendar.

4. Select **1:00 PM** in the From text box, press the **Delete** key, press the **Tab** key to select **5:00 PM** in the To text box, and then press the **Delete** key. The training now will take place only from 8:00 AM to 12:00 PM, Monday through Friday. Since the working hours for Friday were changed in the Standard (Project Calendar), you must additionally make the change to the working hours for Friday.

5. Click the **F** to select the Friday column, select the **1:00 PM** in the From text box, press the **Delete** key, press the **Tab** key to select **4:00 PM** in the To text box, and then press the **Delete** key. The Training calendar now specifies Nondefault working time for Monday through Friday from 8:00 AM to 12:00 PM.

Your screen should look like Figure 2-9.

| Figure 2-9 | **MODIFYING THE TRAINING CALENDAR** |

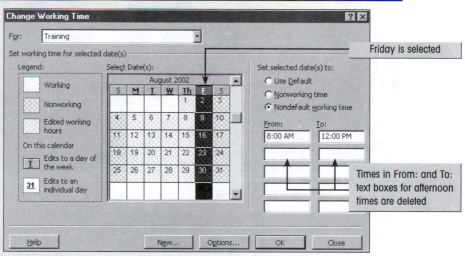

6. Click the **OK** button. The Standard (Project Calendar) and Training calendars are now set up in the project file.

By default, all new tasks follow the Standard (Project Calendar), but you can easily apply a different calendar by using the Task Information dialog box.

It is important that you test the new calendar with a sample task to see the effects of your changes.

To apply a task calendar to a task:

1. Press the **Tab** key to move to the **Task Name** cell for the first row, type **Train Users**, press the **Tab** key, type **2** for the duration, and then press the **Enter** key.

   By default, the new task is completed in two days (16 hours). You need to open the Task Information dialog box to modify the calendar by which the task is scheduled.

   TROUBLE ? If this task is scheduled on a Friday, remember that only seven hours of work are now completed on Fridays because of the time change from 5:00 PM to 4:00 PM on the Standard (Project Calendar). This will push the last hour of work into a third day.

2. Double-click **Train Users** to open the Task Information dialog box for that task, and then click the **Advanced** tab. The calendars that are available for this project appear in the Calendar list on the Advanced tab of the Task Information dialog box.

3. Click the **Calendar** list arrow, and then click **Training**, as shown in Figure 2-10.

Figure 2-10	CHOOSING A TASK CALENDAR

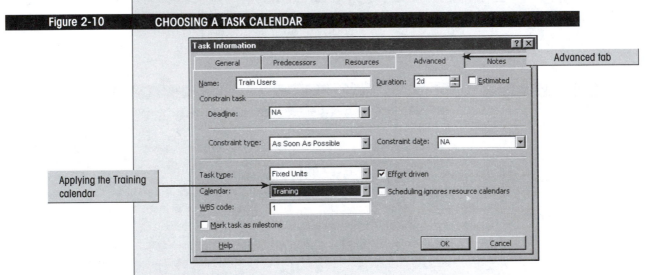

4. Click the **OK** button, and then click **Train Users**. Your screen should look like Figure 2-11. Although the duration did not change (a two-day duration still equals 16 hours of work), the task bar on the Gantt Chart extended to reflect the fact that this task can be completed only according to the working hours on the Training calendar, that is, 8:00 AM to12:00 PM.

Figure 2-11	TRAIN USERS TASK ASSIGNED TO THE TRAINING TASK CALENDAR

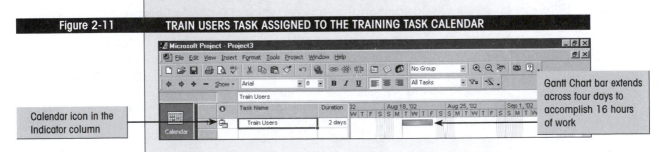

5. Point to the **Calendar indicator** 🖼 in the Train Users task Indicators cell. The ScreenTip "The calendar 'Training' is assigned to the task." appears. Many of the changes that you make within the Task Information dialog box, especially those that affect default settings, have corresponding icons and ScreenTips that appear in the Indicators cell for that task.

6. Click the **Print Preview** button 🔍 on the Standard toolbar, click the **Page Setup** button, add your name in the left section of the header, and then print the Gantt Chart.

7. Close the project file without saving the changes.

Once you have finished the calendars, you are ready to enter tasks and durations for the project. Although you can alter the project calendar and create task calendars at any point during the project's creation, the more work that you put into developing realistic calendars up front the more accurately Project 2000 will schedule task start and finish dates.

Entering Tasks and Durations in the Entry Table

After you have gathered all of the preliminary information during the planning phase of developing your project, entering tasks and durations is probably the single most important effort in developing the project. If tasks are omitted or durations underestimated, the value of the project's scheduling and cost information is compromised and the success of the project might be jeopardized. To gather the task and duration information, ask whether similar projects have been completed within your company and interview the staff members who have been involved so that you can document their experiences. If the project is a first-time endeavor, work with vendors and research the project on the Internet. The more sample task lists, checklists, and real-world experiences that you can implement into your project, the more likely that your project will represent realistic dates and costs.

To enter tasks and durations:

1. Click the **New** button 🗋 on the Standard toolbar, and then click the **OK** button in the Project Information dialog box to open a new project file using today's date as the Start Date.

   Task names and durations are usually entered in the Entry table. The table portion of the project file is very similar to a spreadsheet. Before entering or editing the contents of a cell in the table, you must select it to make it the active cell. The **active cell** is the cell that you are editing; a dark border surrounds it. Pressing the Enter key moves the active cell down one row in the same column. Refer to Figure 2-12 for more information on ways to navigate within a table.

Figure 2-12 **METHODS TO NAVIGATE WITHIN A TABLE**

KEYS TO PRESS	RESULT
↑ ↓ ← →	Move the active cell, up, down, left, or right one cell.
[Tab], [Shift]+[Tab]	Move the active cell right or left one cell.
[Pg Up], [Pg Dn]	Move the active cell one screen up or down.
[Home], [End]	Move the active cell to the first or last column in that row.
[Ctrl]+[Home], [Ctrl]+[End]	Move the active cell to the first column of the first row or the last column of the last row (that contains a task name).
Left click	Moves the active cell to the cell to which you are pointing.

2. Beginning with task 1, enter the following tasks and durations in the Entry table: **Document Current Environment**, 5 days; **Conduct Needs Analysis**, 15 days; **Build RFP**, 2 days; **Gather Bids**, 15 days; **Choose Vendors**, 2 days; **Install Hardware**, 3 days; **Install Software**, 3 days; **Conduct Training**, 5 days. This project started on August 5, 2002, as shown in Figure 2-13. Your project will start on the current day as determined by your computer.

   Because days is the default duration and the durations for these tasks are specified in days, you only have to enter the number portion of the duration.

   TROUBLE? Recall that the Entry table has many columns of information, some of which are currently covered by the Gantt Chart. If the active cell moves under the Gantt Chart, press the Home key to position the active cell in the first column of that row.

Figure 2-13 **INITIAL TASKS AND DURATIONS**

Drag the edge of a column heading to change the column's width

Active cell has a dark border

Split bar

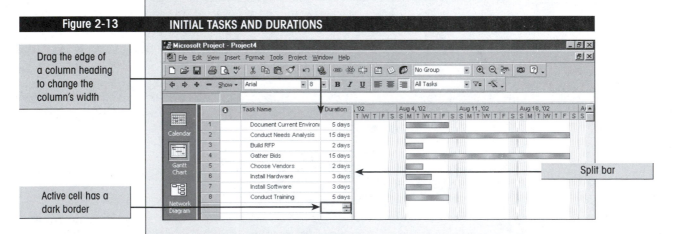

3. Save the project with the filename **LAN-2-Your Initials** in the Tutorial folder of your Data Disk for Tutorial 2. If prompted to save a baseline, save the project without a baseline.

When you are building a new project, your goal is to enter all of the task names and durations correctly and in the order in which they are to be completed. Often, however, you'll need to change an existing task or insert, delete, or move a task.

Editing Tasks and Durations in the Entry Table

Project 2000 makes it very easy to edit an existing project. If you have experience with working on spreadsheets, many of the editing skills that you gained when editing a spreadsheet will apply to a project table. To change an existing entry, you first navigate to the cell. Once there, you have several options: Retype the entry, edit the entry directly in the cell, or edit an entry in the Entry bar.

Basic Editing Techniques

Project 2000 provides many different ways to edit existing entries in a current project. As you work with the program, you will develop your own preferences for the best way to navigate among and edit entries.

To change an existing entry:

1. Click the **2 days** duration cell for the Choose Vendors task (task 5), click the **up arrow** in the spin box to change the entry to **3 days**, and then press the **Enter** key.

   You can use the Entry bar to make specific edits to any part of a cell entry.

2. Click the **Build RFP task** (task 3), click to the right of **RFP** in the Entry bar, press the **Backspace** key three times to delete RFP, type **Request for Proposal**, and then press the **Enter** key.

   Your screen should look like Figure 2-14.

Figure 2-14	EDITING EXISTING TASK ENTRIES

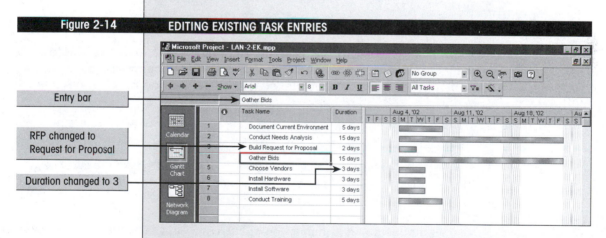

Project 2000 allows **in-cell editing**, that is, an edit made directly within the cell instead of using the Entry bar.

3. Click the **Gather Bids task** (task 4), and then click between **Gather** and **Bids** in the task name. A blinking cursor appears in the cell.

   TROUBLE? If you double-clicked the task instead of single-clicking it twice, you opened its Task Information dialog box. Close the Task Information dialog box and then single-click the task to select it. Single-click it a second time to position the insertion point at the specific location where you wish to edit the entry.

4. Press the **Spacebar**, type **Vendor**, and then press the **Enter** key. The entry is edited.

   In-cell editing can also be used to delete text.

5. Click the **Gather Vendor Bids task** (task 4), click between the "n" and "d" of the word **Vendor**, press the **Backspace** key three times, and then press the **Delete** key four times. You used two methods to erase the word "Vendor" and the extra space between the words "Gather" and "Bids."

6. Press the **Enter** key. The edit is complete.

Inserting and deleting tasks are common editing activities. As you continue to plan the project by conducting research and meeting with management, you might find that new tasks are required.

REFERENCE WINDOW   **RW**

Inserting a Task
- Click any cell in the Entry table in the row where you want to insert the new task.
- Click Insert on the menu bar, and then click New Task. You can also insert a new task by pressing the Insert key.
- Enter the Task Name and Duration information.

To insert a task:

1. Click the **Install Hardware task** (task 6), and then press the **Insert** key.

   A new row in the Entry table appears, ready for you to enter the new task name. The task that formerly occupied row 6 has been moved down to row 7; all subsequent tasks have moved down one row and been renumbered as well.

   If you prefer to use menus to insert a new task from the menu bar, click the Insert menu option and then click New Task.

2. Type **Install Cabling**, press the **Tab** key, type **1**, and then press the **Enter** key. The new task is inserted as task 6 in the project.

Sometimes during project planning, you will determine that a task is no longer required and want to delete it.

REFERENCE WINDOW   **RW**

Deleting a Task
- Click any cell in the Entry table in the row that you want to delete.
- Click Edit on the menu bar, and then click Delete Task. You can also delete a task by pressing the Delete key.

To delete a task and use the undo button:

1. Click any cell for **task 1** (Document Current Environment), and then press the **Delete** key. The task is deleted from the project file. When you delete a task, all tasks below it move up one row and are renumbered.

   You delete the entire row when you press the Delete key in any cell of a project row. This result differs from that of a spreadsheet, in which you delete only the active cell when you press the Delete key.

2. Click the **Undo** button 🔙 on the Standard toolbar to undo the last action which was deleting the task.

   In Project 2000, you can undo only your last action. When you click the Undo button, it changes into a Redo button ↪, as shown in Figure 2-15, so that you can redo the action that was previously undone.

Figure 2-15	INSERTING AND DELETING TASKS

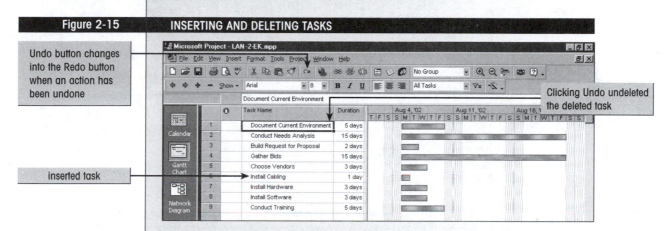

Undo button changes into the Redo button when an action has been undone

inserted task

Clicking Undo undeleted the deleted task

Sometimes you want to clear the contents of an individual cell but not delete the entire task row.

3. Right-click the **Conduct Training task** (task 9), click **Clear Contents** from the shortcut menu, type **Train Users**, and then press the **Enter** key. Using the Clear Contents menu option is often more efficient than pressing either the Backspace key or the Delete key to change a cell's contents.

Copying, pasting, and moving tasks are important task editing skills. Project 2000 offers a variety of tools that you can use to accomplish these common tasks, including menu system options, toolbar buttons, quick keystrokes, and right-click shortcut menus.

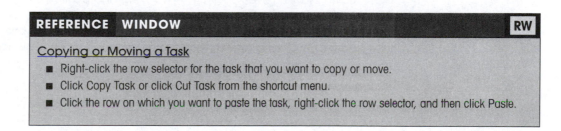

REFERENCE WINDOW	RW

Copying or Moving a Task

- Right-click the row selector for the task that you want to copy or move.
- Click Copy Task or click Cut Task from the shortcut menu.
- Click the row on which you want to paste the task, right-click the row selector, and then click Paste.

To copy and paste a task:

1. Right-click the **row selector** for task 9, and then click **Copy Task** from the short-cut menu. The row is selected and the task copied to the Clipboard.

   TROUBLE? If you right-click a cell instead of the task number 9 to the left of the task row, the shortcut menu will display Copy Cell instead of Copy Task. Copy Cell copies only the contents of a single cell.

2. Right-click the **row selector for task 10** (the blank row selector below 9), and then click **Paste**. The task is copied to the new row, as shown in Figure 2-16.

Figure 2-16	COPYING AND PASTING A TASK

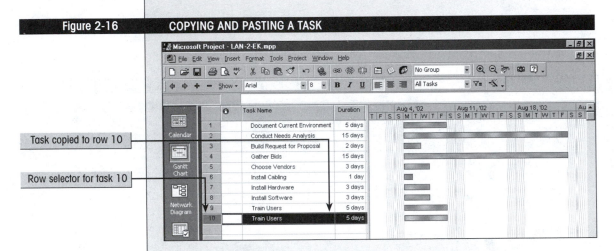

Task copied to row 10

Row selector for task 10

It doesn't matter whether you use the right-click shortcut menu options, the Copy 📋 and Paste 📋 buttons on the Standard toolbar, or the Copy and Paste options from the Edit menu to copy and paste tasks. What does matter is that you first click the *row selector* before initiating the Copy command if you want to copy all of the information for that particular task and not copy only the active cell's contents.

3. Click **Train Users** (task 10), click in the **Entry Bar**, double-click **Users**, type **Management**, and then press the **Enter** key.

4. Click **Choose Vendors** (task 5), click and drag to select **Vendor** (omit the "s"), click the **Copy** button 📋 on the Standard toolbar, click **Gather Bids** in task 4, click between **Gather** and **Bids** in the active cell, press the **Spacebar**, and then click the **Paste** button 📋 on the Standard toolbar. Copying and pasting can be used for task names as well as parts of task names.

   Moving tasks is even easier than copying and pasting them. You could use the Cut ✂ and Paste 📋 buttons on the Standard toolbar, the Cut and Paste options from the Edit menu, or the Cut Task and Paste options from the shortcut menus. Another easy way to move tasks is to drag their row selector.

5. Click the **row selector for task 10** (Train Management), and then drag it up between tasks 8 and 9 as shown in Figure 2-17. The task, Train Management, is now 9, and the task Train Users is renumbered as 10.

Figure 2-17	MOVING A TASK

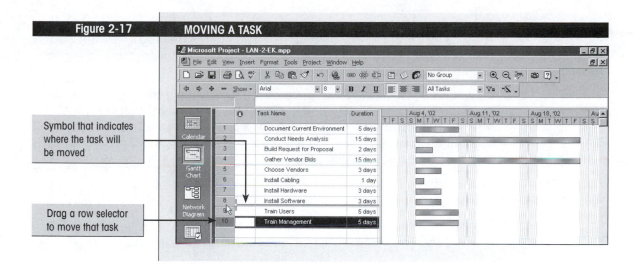

Symbol that indicates where the task will be moved

Drag a row selector to move that task

If several task durations are the same, you can use either the copy and paste features to quickly enter the durations or the **fill handle** to populate cells. If you have used the fill handle in Excel or another spreadsheet product, you will find it a very similar process in Project 2000. The fill handle is a small square that appears in the lower corner of the selected cell. When you drag a fill handle, the contents of the active cell are copied.

To use the fill handle to copy and paste information:

1. Click the **3 days** duration for task 8 (Install Software), point to the small square in the lower right-hand corner of the duration cell so that your mouse pointer changes to ┿, and then drag down two rows so that the outline surrounds the duration cells for tasks 9 and 10. When you release the left mouse button, the three-day duration for task 8 fills in the duration for tasks 9 and 10, as shown in Figure 2-18.

   TROUBLE? You might want to move the split bar slightly to the right so that the fill handle for the duration cells is easier to access.

Figure 2-18	USING THE FILL HANDLE

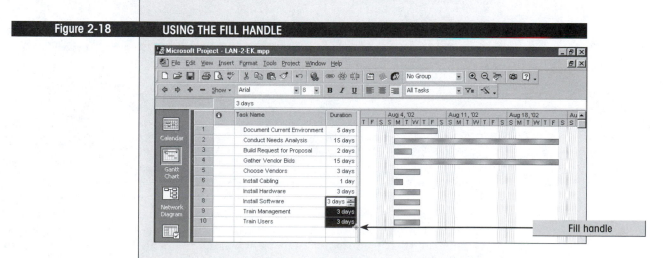

Fill handle

Tasks 8, 9, and 10 now have three-day durations. You can also use the fill handle to fill task names. However, the fill handle cannot be used when affected cells are not contiguous. To copy a task name or duration to a task that is not in the next row, use the Copy and Paste buttons.

2. Click the **5 days duration for task 1** (Document Current Environment), click the **Copy** button 📋 on the Standard toolbar, click the **1 day duration for task 6** (Install Cabling), and then click the **Paste** button 📋 on the Standard toolbar. The duration cell entry for task 1 is copied and pasted to the duration cell for task 6.

3. Click the **Undo** button ↰ on the Standard toolbar.

The Undo button undoes your last action to the current project, whether it was to paste a cell entry, delete a task, or modify some other aspect of the current project. The Undo button will not undo such actions as saving, printing, or closing a project file.

4. Click the **Save** button 💾 on the Standard toolbar, and then save the file without a baseline.

Working with Duration Units of Measure

Entering and editing durations involves understanding the units of measure available for them. The default unit of measure is "day" and therefore does not need to be entered. To use any other unit, you must type it using the abbreviations shown in Figure 2-19.

Figure 2-19	UNITS OF MEASURE ABBREVIATIONS

TYPE THIS ABBREVIATION	TO GET THIS UNIT OF MEASUREMENT
m	minute
h	hour
d (default)	day
w	week
mon	month
em	elapsed minute
eh	elapsed hour
ed	elapsed day
ew	elapsed week
emon	elapsed month

Elapsed refers to clock time rather than working time. Some tasks are completed over an elapsed period of time regardless of whether the time is working or nonworking. An example is the task "Allow paint to dry." The paint will dry in exactly the same amount of time regardless of whether it dries on a workday, a weekend, or a holiday. If it takes one day to dry, the duration should be entered as 1ed.

If you are not sure about a task's duration and want to be reminded to study it later, enter a question mark (?) after the duration entry to indicate that the duration is an estimated duration. Later you will learn how to quickly find and filter tasks based on estimated durations.

To enter and edit durations and print the Gantt Chart:

1. Click the **15 days duration for task 2** (Conduct Needs Analysis), type **3w**, and then press the **Enter** key.

   Fifteen days of work is equal to three weeks of work in a standard five workday week, but you might prefer to show the duration in the week unit of measure.

2. Click the **15 days duration for task 4** (Gather Vendor Bids), type **3w?**, and then press the **Enter** key.

   Your screen should look like Figure 2-20.

Figure 2-20	MODIFYING TASK DURATIONS

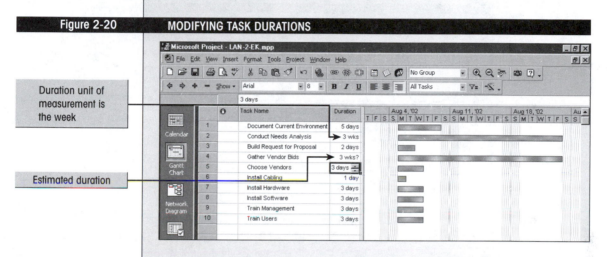

Duration unit of measurement is the week

Estimated duration

TROUBLE? If you do not enter a duration for a task, Project 2000 displays a default duration of 1d?.

3. Save the project without a baseline.

4. Click the **Print Preview** button on the Standard toolbar, and then click the **Page Setup** button. The Page Setup dialog box opens so that you can customize the printout.

5. Click the **Header** tab, click the **Left Alignment** tab, type **Your Name** in the left section of the header, click the **OK** button to close the dialog box, click the **Print** button, and then click the **OK** button to print the Gantt Chart.

While most of your task and duration entry and editing will be done in the Entry table displayed to the left of the Gantt Chart, tasks can be entered and edited in any view.

Editing Tasks and Durations in Other Views

Anything changed in one view is automatically changed in all of the other views. You can use the View Bar to quickly switch between views. As you learned in Tutorial 1, the way the data is displayed differs by view and often satisfies different communication and reporting needs as the project develops.

To edit durations in the Gantt Chart:

1. Point to the **Gantt Chart bar for task 3** (Build Request for Proposal). The pointer changes to the ✛ mouse pointer, and a ScreenTip appears that gives information about the task's name, duration, and start and finish dates.

2. Point to the **right edge of the Gantt Chart bar for task 3** (Build Request for Proposal). The ▶ mouse pointer appears on the right edge of the bar, thereby indicating that you can drag the length of the bar to the right to increase the duration for that task. ScreenTips guide your work as you work in Project 2000.

3. Drag the ▶ pointer to the right until the ScreenTip displays a duration of 4d, as shown in Figure 2-21.

Figure 2-21	CHANGING A TASK DURATION USING THE GANTT CHART

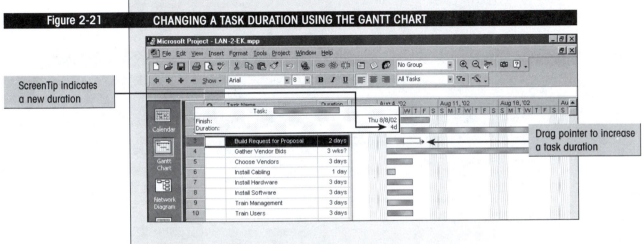

ScreenTip indicates a new duration

Drag pointer to increase a task duration

Notice that when you stop dragging the pointer, the duration also has changed in the Duration column of the Entry table.

The graphical views of the Gantt Chart, Network Diagram, and Calendar views are usually not used for heavy data entry. However, if you are viewing your project in one of these views and need to edit a task, Project 2000 provides a way.

To enter and edit durations in the Network Diagram and Calendar views:

1. Click the **Network Diagram** button 🗗 on the View Bar, scroll to view task 1, click the **5 days** duration for task 1 (Document Current Environment), type **4**, and then press the **Enter** key. The duration for task 1 is changed to four days.

2. Click the **Calendar** button ▦ on the View Bar, and then point to the **top edge** of the second week. The mouse pointer changes to ↕.

3. Drag ↕ down so that all of the tasks that start in the first week are visible, as shown in Figure 2-22.

Figure 2-22   **EXPANDING THE SIZE OF THE WEEKS ON THE CALENDAR**

Calendar button

Drag down to expand the size of the week on the calendar

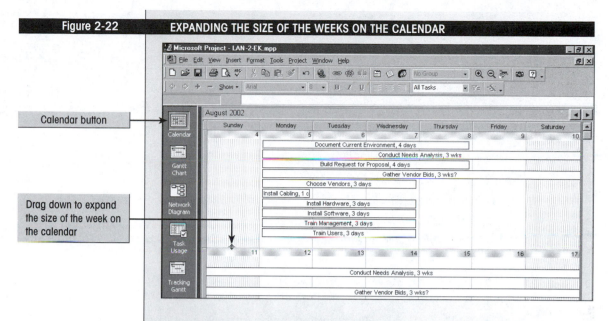

4. Point to the **right edge of Install Hardware, 3 days**, the mouse pointer changes to ⊬, then drag the **Install Hardware task** to the left until the ScreenTip displays a duration of two days. You can increase or decrease the length of the bars in Calendar view to increase or decrease the duration of a task.

   Regardless of the view used, you can edit any task by double-clicking it to open its Task Information dialog box.

5. Double-click the **Train Management task**, and then click each **Tab** in the Task Information dialog box (General, Predecessors, Resources, Advanced, and Notes) to observe the types of task information that can be modified on each tab. The task name appears on each tab.

6. Double-click **Management** in the Name text box, type **Mgmt**, and then click the **OK** button. Regardless of which tab in the Task Information dialog box you use to change the task name, it is changed for the task and in all views.

7. Click the **Gantt Chart** button 🔲 on the View Bar, and observe the changes to tasks 1, 7, and 9 made in other views.

8. Save the project without a baseline.

9. Click the **Print Preview** button 🔎 on the Standard toolbar, click the **Page Setup** button, verify that your name is in the left section of the header, and then print the Gantt Chart.

As you work with Project 2000, you will become more familiar with each view and learn which is the best representation of the data for different purposes.

Entering **Recurring Tasks**

A **recurring task** is a task that repeats at a regular interval. A Monday morning status meeting is a good example of a recurring task that needs to be scheduled for each week of the project. In Project 2000, you can define a recurring task one time. Project 2000 then handles the details of scheduling the task on each Monday for the entire project or for the time period you specify.

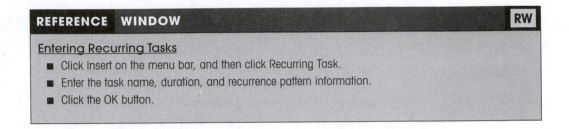

REFERENCE   WINDOW   RW

Entering Recurring Tasks

- Click Insert on the menu bar, and then click Recurring Task.
- Enter the task name, duration, and recurrence pattern information.
- Click the OK button.

To enter a recurring task:

1. Click the empty **Task Name** cell for task 11, click **Insert** on the menu bar, and then click **Recurring Task**.

   The Recurring Task Information dialog box opens, prompting you for the task name, duration, and recurrence pattern information.

2. Type **Status Meeting** in the Task Name text box, press the **Tab** key, type **2h** in the Duration text box, and then click the **Monday** check box.

   The Recurring Task Information dialog box should look like Figure 2-23. You scheduled a two-hour status meeting for every Monday. The Start and End by dates reflect the current Start Date and Finish Date for the project and will change as the project is developed. If you enter specific dates or a number of occurrences for the recurring task, those choices will override the default assumption that the recurring task is to be scheduled for each Monday throughout the life of the project.

| Figure 2-23 | RECURRING TASK INFORMATION DIALOG BOX |

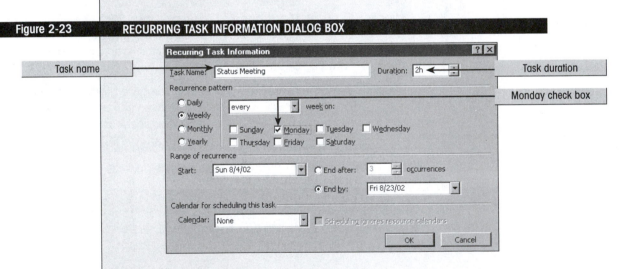

3. Click the **OK** button.

   The Gantt Chart shows the recurring task for each Monday. A recurring task symbol ↻ appears in the Indicators column, and if you point to the symbol, a ScreenTip will appear providing information about the task.

   TROUBLE? If the Duration column displays a series of pound (##) signs, the information is too wide to display within the width of the column. You need to widen the column. Point to the right edge of the line that separates the Duration heading and the Start heading (you might need to drag the split bar to the right to see this line). Then double-click ↔ to widen the column to display the widest entry.

4. Click the Status Meeting task (task 11) **Expand** button ⊞ to see the details of the recurring task, as shown in Figure 2-24.

Figure 2-24 **EXPANDING A RECURRING TASK**

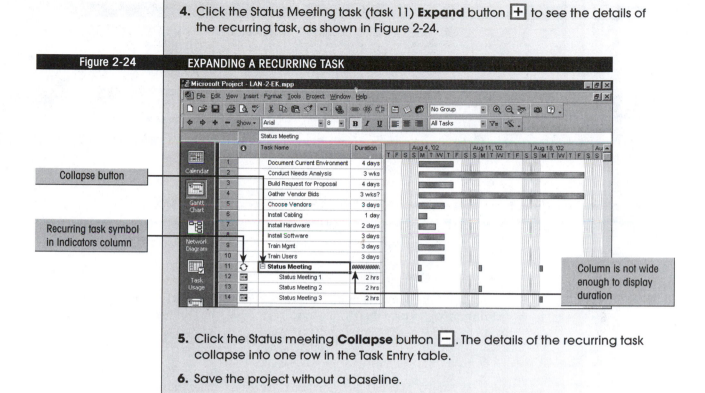

Collapse button

Recurring task symbol in Indicators column

Column is not wide enough to display duration

5. Click the Status meeting **Collapse** button ⊟. The details of the recurring task collapse into one row in the Task Entry table.

6. Save the project without a baseline.

Recurring tasks can be expanded to show all of the individual tasks within them or collapsed to one line, depending on how the user wants to view the Task Entry table and Gantt Chart.

Entering Milestones

A **milestone** is a task that marks a significant point in time or progress checkpoint. It has a zero duration and is therefore a symbolic task that is used mainly to communicate progress or to mark the end of a significant phase of the project. Examples include the signing of a contract or the announcement of a new product. Milestones can also be used to motivate project participants by recognizing accomplishments. Many project managers identify milestones early in a project so as to help build momentum toward the project's completion.

To enter a milestone:

1. Click **Install Cabling** (task 6), and then press the **Insert** key to insert a blank task row for the new task.

2. Type **Sign Contracts**, press the **Tab** key, type **0**, and then press the **Enter** key. Notice that the entry in the Gantt Chart is a black diamond symbol, as shown in Figure 2-25. The date of the milestone appears beside the symbol in the month/day format.

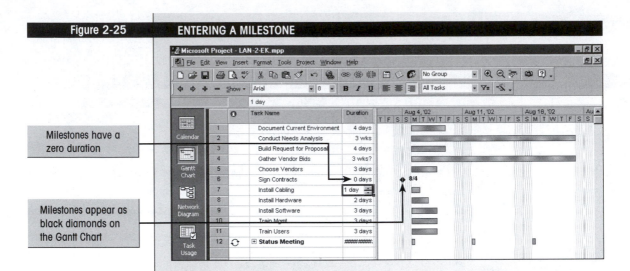

Figure 2-25   ENTERING A MILESTONE

Milestones have a zero duration

Milestones appear as black diamonds on the Gantt Chart

3. Save the project without a baseline.

4. Click the **Print Preview** button [icon] on the Standard toolbar, and then click the **Print** button to print the Gantt Chart.

5. Close the **LAN-2-Your Initials.mpp** project file, saving any changes.

Since milestones have no duration, they are scheduled without regard to working and nonworking time. Therefore, if you enter this milestone task for a weekend, your milestone might be scheduled during the nonworking weekend before the tasks themselves, as shown in Figure 2-25. Obviously, this milestone cannot occur until tasks 1 through 5 are finished. The next session introduces you to *task dependencies* that help determine the sequencing and scheduling for each task in the project, including milestones.

Session 2.1 QUICK CHECK

1. What is the default Schedule from option in the Project Information dialog box?

2. If the Schedule from option is Project Finish Date in the Project Information dialog box, who controls the project Start Date and Finish Date?

3. If the Schedule from option is Project Start Date in the Project Information dialog box, what constraint is used to assign individual start dates to tasks?

4. What calendar do you use to schedule the entire project?

5. If you click in a duration cell and press the Delete key, what will you erase?

6. How do you enter an estimated duration for three months?

7. What is the difference between a duration and an elapsed duration?

8. How do you change the duration of a task in the Calendar view?

9. How do you enter a recurring task?

10. What is the duration of a milestone?

Now that you have finished entering tasks (including recurring tasks and milestones) and their associated durations, you are ready to establish task dependencies.

SESSION 2.2

In this session, you will enter *task dependencies*, the rules that determine which tasks must precede (come before) or succeed (follow) another. Together with the task durations, dependencies provide the key information used to calculate individual task start and finish dates, as well as the overall Finish or Start Date for the project.

Understanding Task Dependencies

Four **task dependencies** define the relationships between tasks in a project. They are summarized in Figure 2-26. By far the most common is the Finish-to-Start (FS) dependency, which indicates that the first task must be finished before the second task can start. Once you establish task dependencies, Project 2000 will provide a realistic Finish Date for the overall project and appropriate start and finish dates for the individual tasks of installing a LAN.

Figure 2-26	TASK DEPENDENCIES

DEPENDENCY TYPE	ABBREVIATION	EXPLANATION	HOW IT LOOKS ON A GANTT CHART	EXAMPLE
Finish-to-Start	FS	Task 1 must finish before task 2 can start.		A computer must be installed (task 1) before application software can be installed (task 2).
Start-to-Start	SS	Task 1 must start before task 2 can start.		As soon as you start installing hardware (task 1), you can start documenting serial numbers (task 2).
Finish-to-Finish	FF	Task 1 must finish before task 2 can finish.		A computer backup (task 1) must be finished before the shutdown of the system is completed (task 2).
Start-to-Finish	SF	Task 1 must start before task 2 can finish.		In the event of a power interruption, the UPS must start (task 1) before the operator can finish shutting down the system in an orderly fashion (task 2).

By linking tasks in finish-to-start relationships, you establish the required sequence of tasks. Project 2000 uses these relationships to set start and finish dates for each task. When no dependencies are defined, all tasks start on the project Start Date in as soon as possible scheduling and all tasks finish on the project Finish Date in as late as possible scheduling. The first task described in the dependency is called the **predecessor task**. The second task described in the dependency type is called the **successor task**.

Creating Task Dependencies

Project 2000 makes it easy to create, and remove, FS relationships between tasks by providing the **Link Tasks** 🔗 and **Unlink Tasks** 🔗 buttons on the Standard toolbar.

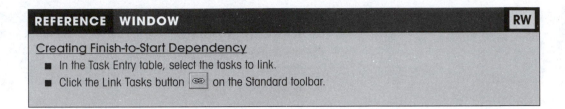

REFERENCE WINDOW   RW

Creating Finish-to-Start Dependency
- In the Task Entry table, select the tasks to link.
- Click the Link Tasks button 🔗 on the Standard toolbar.

The installation of the LAN at JLB Partners requires linked tasks. You determine that finish-to-start (FS) dependencies between the tasks of the LAN project are the most appropriate. Emily did some work on your original project file and wants you to continue working on that file.

To create an FS dependency between tasks using the Task Entry table:

1. Open the project file **LAN-2-2.mpp** from the Tutorial folder for Tutorial 2 on your Data Disk.

2. Click **File** on the menu bar, click **Save As**, type **LAN-2-2-Your Initials** in the File name text box, and then click **Save**. Save the file without a baseline. Emily scheduled the project from a Start Date of 8/12/02.

3. Click **Document Current Environment** (task 1) in the Task Entry table, and then drag ✚ down to select **Conduct Needs Analysis** (task 2) in the Task Entry table.

   You want to link these two tasks, so you select both. Notice that the mouse pointer changes to ✚ when you select cells in a Table view in Project 2000. When you select multiple cells in a project table, the first cell in the selection is surrounded by a black border and all subsequent selected cells appear in reverse image, with a black background and white text. This resembles how multiple-cell selections appear in a spreadsheet program.

4. Click the **Link Tasks** button 🔗 on the Standard toolbar.

   The Gantt Chart adds a finish-to-start link line between the tasks, as shown in Figure 2-27.

Figure 2-27   **ESTABLISHING A FINISH-TO-START RELATIONSHIP USING THE TASK ENTRY TABLE**

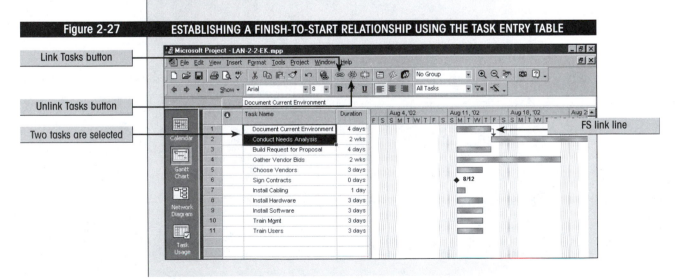

You know that you can enter a task in graphical views. Task dependencies also can be established in the graphical views.

To create a finish-to-start dependency between tasks using the Gantt Chart view:

1. Point to the middle of **task 2** (Conduct Needs Analysis) in the Gantt Chart. The pointer changes to ⊕.

   TROUBLE? Be sure that you point to the *middle* of the bar to create an FS relationship between two tasks in Gantt Chart view. When you press the left mouse button while the pointer is on the middle of the Gantt Chart bar and then begin to drag, the pointer will change to 🔗, the linking pointer.

2. Drag the 🔗 pointer to the middle of the bar for **task 3** (Build Request for Proposal), as shown in Figure 2-28.

Figure 2-28	CREATING A FINISH-TO-START RELATIONSHIP USING THE GANTT CHART VIEW

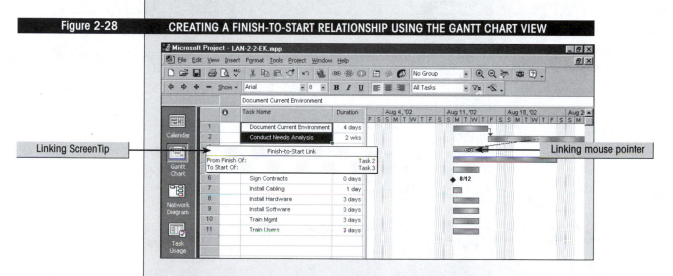

Linking ScreenTip

Linking mouse pointer

The mouse pointer changes to 🔗 when you are creating a link between tasks in any of the graphical views (Gantt Chart, Network Diagram, and Calendar).

Task 3 immediately moves to a new position after task 2 in the Gantt Chart because of the new dependency. As you would expect, creating task dependencies affects the start and finish dates of the linked tasks. Changing and linking tasks also affects the critical path. The **critical path** consists of the tasks that must be completed with the given schedule dates in order for the overall project to be completed in the shortest amount of time. Project 2000 defines the critical path as consisting of those tasks that have zero slack. **Slack** is the amount of time by which an activity may be delayed from its scheduled start date without the delay's setting back the entire project.

Graphical views in Project 2000 take a graphical (pictures and icons) approach to representing information about the project. In the Network Diagram view, the **critical tasks**—tasks that are on the critical path—are displayed within a red border. A task that is not on the critical path is a **non-critical task**, that is, it doesn't necessarily have to start on its currently scheduled start date in order for the overall project to be completed on time.

To create an FS dependency between tasks using the Network Diagram view:

1. Click the **Network Diagram** button 🖼 on the View Bar.

   Tasks 1, 2, and 3 and their FS dependencies represent the shortest amount of time required to complete the project; they are the current critical path. Before further relationships are established, Gather Vendor Bids and Choose Vendors are displayed as noncritical tasks. The milestone, Sign Contracts, is also currently a noncritical task. Tasks 4 and 5 should be linked together in an FS relationship.

2. Point to the middle of **task 4** (Gather Vendor Bids) so that the mouse pointer changes to ✚, and then drag 🔗 to the middle of **task 5** (Choose Vendors), as shown in Figure 2-29.

| Figure 2-29 | CREATING A FINISH-TO-START RELATIONSHIP USING THE NETWORK DIAGRAM VIEW |

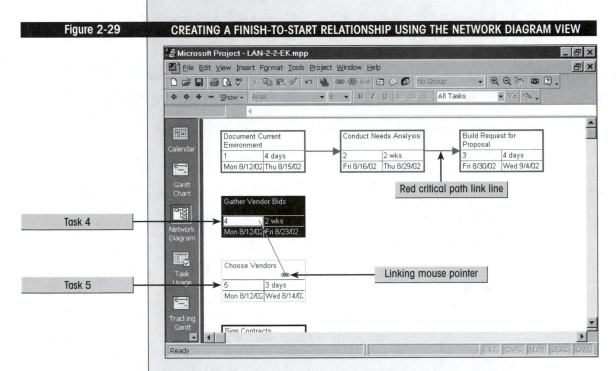

The Network Diagram changes to display tasks 4 and 5 on the same row with a linking line between them. Since these tasks are not on the critical path, they are still displayed with a black border.

3. Click the **Zoom Out** button 🔍 on the Standard toolbar. You should be able to see task 1 through task 3 on the top row.

4. Point to the middle of **task 3** (Build Request for Proposal) so that the mouse pointer changes to ✚, drag 🔗 to the middle of **task 4** (Gather Vendor Bids), and then click the **Zoom Out** button 🔍 on the Standard toolbar so that your screen looks like Figure 2-30.

Figure 2-30	THE NEW CRITICAL PATH IN THE NETWORK DIAGRAM

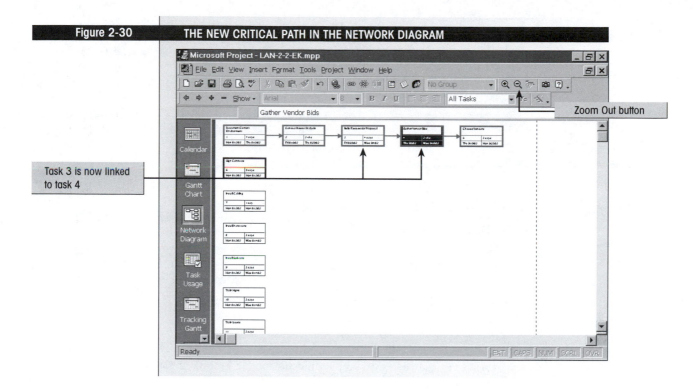

Now that task 3 is related to task 4 with an FS relationship, both tasks 4 and 5 appear in red boxes because they are now also on the critical path. The Network Diagram is used mainly to view and analyze the critical path. More information on how to change and manage this important view is provided in Tutorial 3.

To create an FS dependency between tasks using the Calendar:

1. Click the **Calendar** button on the View Bar, and press and hold the **Alt** key as you press the **Home** key. The first day of the first task in the project is visible on your screen.

2. Point to the middle of the **Install Hardware task bar**, and then drag the pointer to the middle of the **Install Software task bar**.

   The Install Software task bar immediately moves after the Install Hardware task bar, as shown in Figure 2-31. The Link pointer is available and works the same as it does in the Gantt Chart and Network Diagram views. Link lines are not shown in the Calendar view, but you might want to view and print the Calendar view because it most clearly indicates the tasks that are occurring, in a weekly and monthly format.

Figure 2-31   **CREATING A FINISH-TO-START RELATIONSHIP USING THE CALENDAR VIEW**

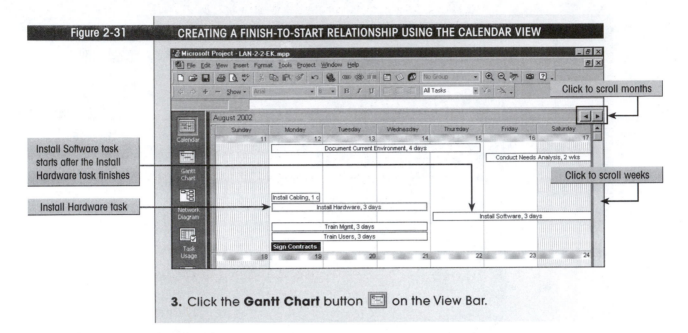

Install Software task starts after the Install Hardware task finishes

Install Hardware task

3. Click the **Gantt Chart** button on the View Bar.

You can enter and edit task relationships in any view. As project planning continues, you might discover that certain tasks should no longer be linked together. In such cases, you must delete the task relationships.

REFERENCE WINDOW   **RW**

Deleting Task Dependencies

- Select the task or tasks in the Task Entry table.
- Click the Unlink Tasks button on the Standard toolbar. You can also double-click the link line to open the Task Dependency dialog box and then click Delete.

To delete a task dependency:

1. Click **Document Current Environment**, and then click the **Go To Selected Task** button on the Standard toolbar. You have repositioned the Gantt chart to the first task in the project.

2. Click and drag through **task names 1 and 2** (Document Current Environment and Conduct Needs Analysis), and then click the **Unlink Tasks** button on the Standard toolbar.

   The Gantt Chart deletes the finish-to-start link line between the tasks. Task 2 is now scheduled to start on the project Start Date of 8/12/02 because it no longer has a predecessor task.

3. Click the **Save** button on the Standard toolbar and save your changes to the project without a baseline.

Using Form View to Create Task Dependencies

Sometimes a task is a predecessor to more than one other task and therefore the process of dragging link lines in a graphical view becomes laborious. Using a Form view of the project can make entering many details for a single task easier.

To enter task dependencies using a Form view:

1. Click **Window** on the menu bar, and then click **Split**.

   The Task Entry table and Gantt Chart view appear in the top pane of the screen and a Form view appears in the bottom pane. By default, the Form view displays resources on the left side and predecessors on the right side of the form. However, to analyze each task's relationship, you want it to display predecessors and successors.

2. Right-click the **form**, and then click **Predecessors & Successors**.

   The form changes to display the predecessors on the left side of the form and successors on the right side.

3. Click **task 9** (Install Software) in the Task Entry table.

   Corresponding form information always displays for the selected task in the Task Entry table. You want to specify task 10 (Train Mgmt) and task 11 (Train Users) as successors to task 9.

   TROUBLE? The columns in the form are actually cells even though the rows are not clearly differentiated. A selected cell will appear with a border.

4. Click the **first Successor ID** cell in the form, type **10**, press the **Enter** key, and then type **11**, as shown in Figure 2-32. You can enter as many predecessor and successor task IDs in the form as needed.

Figure 2-32   CREATING FINISH-TO-START RELATIONSHIP USING THE FORM VIEW

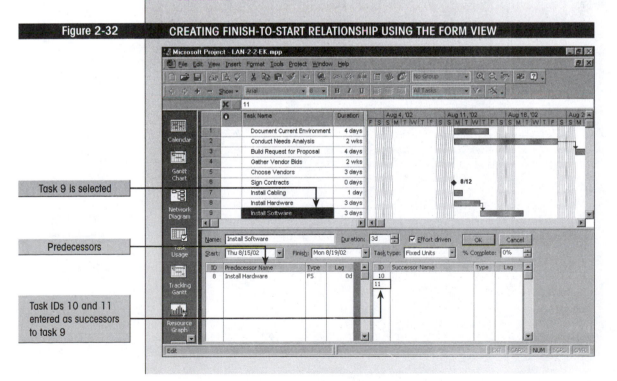

Task 9 is selected

Predecessors

Task IDs 10 and 11 entered as successors to task 9

To have Project 2000 process the information, you confirm your entries by clicking the OK button.

5. Click the **OK** button in the form. Project 2000 adds the task names for tasks 10 and 11 to the Successor Name column in the form and adds the appropriate link lines to the Gantt Chart.

The OK and Cancel buttons in the form that appear when you are editing information change to the Previous and Next buttons to move through the tasks of the project.

6. Click the **Next** button in the form. Train Mgmt (task 10) is selected in the Entry table, and Install Software (task 9) appears in the Predecessor Name column.

7. Click the **Next** button in the form. Train Users (task 11) is selected in the Entry table, and Install Software (task 9) appears in the Predecessor Name column. Notice the link line that appears in the Gantt Chart.

8. Point to the **horizontal split bar** so that your mouse pointer changes to ⯭, as shown in Figure 2-33, and then double-click the **split bar** to remove the split.

Figure 2-33	REMOVING THE SPLIT

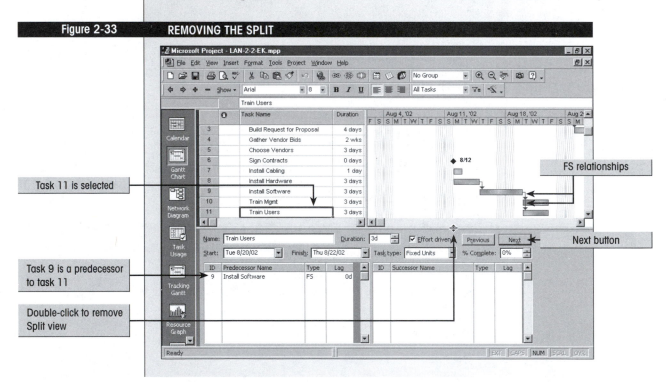

After carefully assessing the tasks required for the LAN installation, you determine the rest of the required task relationships and next must enter them into the project file. You are developing preferences for your working style and know that you can quickly create links between consecutive tasks in the Task Entry table, the most common way to create task dependencies.

To create task dependencies using the Task Entry table:

1. Click **Choose Vendors** (task 5), drag ⊹ to select the task names Choose Vendors (task 5) through Install Hardware (task 8), and then click the **Link Tasks** button ⊜ on the Standard toolbar. The bars on the Gantt Chart are no longer visible in the window because linking these tasks in an FS relationship moved the dates further down the calendar.

2. Save the **LAN-2-2-Your Initials.mpp** project without a baseline.

3. Click the **Print Preview** button ▣ on the Standard toolbar, click the **Page Setup** button, add your name in the left section of the header, and then print the Gantt Chart.

You have learned how to create finish-to-start task dependencies in the Task Entry table and in the Gantt Chart, the Network Diagram, the Calendar, and Form views. You can also double-click a task in the Task Entry table or in any view and add relationships using the Predecessors tab of the Task Information dialog box.

Yet another way to add relationships between tasks is to drag the split bar to the right in Gantt Chart view so that more columns of the Task Entry table are available. You can specify task IDs to relate two tasks in the Predecessors column of the Task Entry table.

Editing **Task Dependencies**

Task dependencies start as FS dependencies because that type of dependency is by far the most common relationship between tasks. To change the dependency type, you must open the Task Dependency dialog box. There, you can change the relationship type from FS (finish-to-start) to SS (start-to-start), FF (finish-to-finish), or SF (start-to-finish). You usually edit task relationships in the Gantt Chart or Network Diagram view because it is easy to double-click the link line in these views to open the Task Dependency dialog box.

REFERENCE WINDOW | **RW**

Editing Task Dependencies
- Double-click the link in either the Gantt Chart or Network Diagram view.
- Make the changes in the Task Dependency dialog box.
- Click the OK button.

To edit a task dependency:

1. Click the Gantt Chart **horizontal scroll bar** until you can view the link between **Install Cabling** (task 7) and **Install Hardware** (task 8). You can use ScreenTips to verify that you are viewing the correct link.

2. Point to the **link line** from Install Cabling to Install Hardware. A ScreenTip appears to confirm that you have located the correct link line.

   TROUBLE? If the ScreenTip doesn't confirm the correct link, point to another line until you are sure that you have identified the correct link.

3. Double-click the **link line** from Install Cabling to Install Hardware in the Gantt Chart. The Task Dependency dialog box opens, describing the dependency type.

4. Click the **Type** list arrow, and then click **Start-to-Start (SS)**, as shown in Figure 2-34. Because the hardware installation can start as soon as the cabling installation starts, the SS dependency more clearly indicates the relationship between these two tasks.

Figure 2-34	TASK DEPENDENCY DIALOG BOX

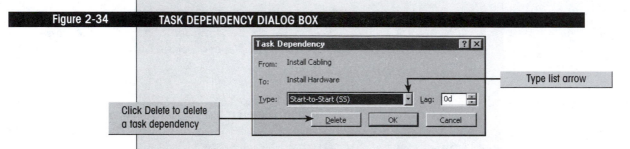

5. Click the **OK** button.

The Gantt Chart link line changes to point from the left edge (the start) of the Install Cabling bar to the left edge (the start) of the Install Hardware bar to indicate that an SS relationship exists between the two tasks.

You can also edit the relationships between tasks in the Task Information dialog box by using the Predecessors column of the Task Entry table. Alternatively, you can use a Form view that displays predecessor and successor information. To remove a task dependency, double-click the link line and then click the Delete button in the Task Dependency dialog box.

Entering **Lag and Lead Times**

When a project is scheduled from a Start Date, lag and lead times refer to an amount of time that the second task of a relationship is moved backward (lead) or forward (lag) in time. **Lead time** moves the second task *backward* in time so that the two tasks overlap. For example, suppose that two tasks have an FS relationship such as Installing Hardware and Installing Software, and yet the second task (Installing Software) can be started *before* the finish date of the first. You can create an FS relationship between the two tasks with a lead time of 50% so that the successor task (Installing Software) starts when the predecessor task (Installing Hardware) is 50% completed.

Lag time is the opposite of lead time. It moves the second task *forward* in time so that the tasks are further separated. Consider the tasks Sign Contracts and Install Cabling, which have an FS relationship. While in theory the second task (Install Cabling) could be started immediately upon completion of the first (Signs Contract) task, you might want to allow for some lag time (a gap of time between the finish of the first task and the start of the second) to give your project team a well-deserved rest between the contract negotiation and project installation phases of the project. Figure 2-35 illustrates lag and lead times for a project that is scheduled from a Start Date.

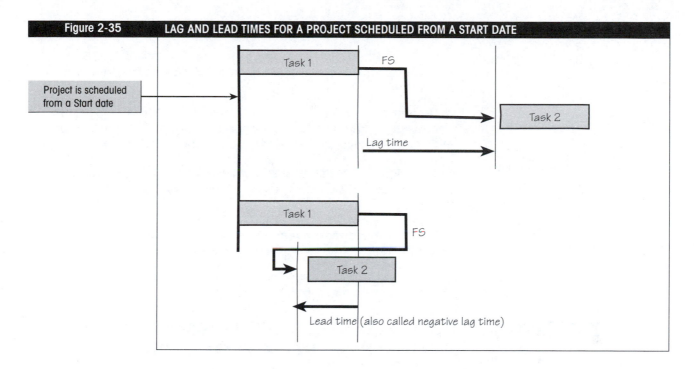

Figure 2-35   LAG AND LEAD TIMES FOR A PROJECT SCHEDULED FROM A START DATE

Project 2000 combines the concepts of lag and lead times into one term, **lag time**. When a project is scheduled from a Start Date, **positive lag time** moves the second task forward in time. (Positive lag time is the traditional definition of lag time in general project management discussions.) **Negative lag time** moves the second task backward in time so that the tasks overlap. (Negative lag time is called lead time in general project management discussions.) The rest of this text, therefore, always refers to lag time in Project 2000 terminology (as either positive or negative). In Figure 2-35, the first example shows how positive lag time affects the second task. The second example shows how negative lag time affects the second task.

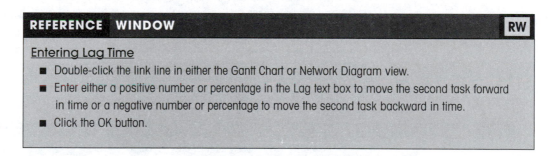

REFERENCE   WINDOW   **RW**

Entering Lag Time
- Double-click the link line in either the Gantt Chart or Network Diagram view.
- Enter either a positive number or percentage in the Lag text box to move the second task forward in time or a negative number or percentage to move the second task backward in time.
- Click the OK button.

Lag durations use the same duration units (d for days, h for hours, and so forth) used for task durations. You also can enter a positive or negative percentage that will calculate the lag as a percentage of the duration of the first task. In a finish-to-start relationship, +25% lag time pushes the second task forward in time. The second task will not start until after the first task is completed plus an additional 25% of the duration of the first task. A –25% lag time pulls the second task backward in time. In this case, the second task will start when the first task is 75% completed.

To enter lag time for tasks that are assigned relationships:

1. Scroll in the Gantt Chart to view the **link line between tasks 2 and 3** (Conduct Needs Analysis and Build Request for Proposal), and then double-click the **link line**.

   The Task Dependency dialog box opens for tasks 2 and 3 (Conduct Needs Analysis and Build Request for Proposal). You can change lag time by using the spin box arrows or typing a value directly into the Lag spin box.

   TROUBLE? If the Task Dependency dialog box displays other tasks, click Cancel, use the ScreenTips on the link lines to locate the correct line, and then double-click the correct line.

2. Click the **Lag** down arrow in the spin box twice to set the lag at **-2d**, and then click the **OK** button.

   Your screen should look like Figure 2-36. Negative lag has moved the start date of the second task backward in time.

Figure 2-36	ENTERING NEGATIVE LAG TIME ON AN FS LINK

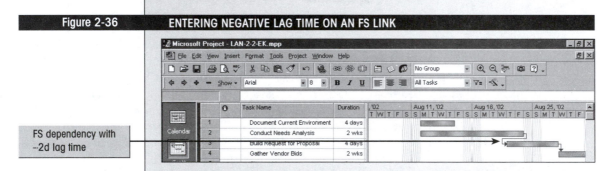

FS dependency with −2d lag time

3. Scroll in the Gantt Chart to view the **link line between tasks 6 and 7** (Sign Contracts and Install Cabling), and then double-click the **link line**. The Task Dependency dialog box opens for From: Sign Contracts To: Install Cabling.

4. Click the **Lag** up arrow in the spin box five times to set the lag at **5d**, and then click the **OK** button.

5. Scroll so that your screen looks like Figure 2-37. Positive lag has moved the start date of the second task forward in time.

Figure 2-37	ENTERING POSITIVE LAG TIME ON AN FS LINK

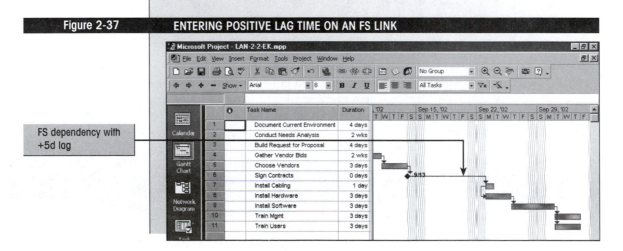

FS dependency with +5d lag

6. Double-click the **link line between tasks 7 and 8** (Install Cabling and Install Hardware).

7. Double-click **0d** in the Lag text box, type **50%**, and then click the **OK** button.

   Task 8 is moved slightly forward in time, when task 7 is 50% completed. Lag can be applied to any type of dependency. In this case, it is applied to a SS dependency. Regardless of the dependency type, lag always moves the start date of the second task when projects are scheduled from a Start Date.

8. Double-click the **link line between tasks 8 and 9** (Install Hardware and Install Software).

9. Double-click **0d** in the Lag text box, type **–50%**, and then click the **OK** button.

   Task 9 is moved backward in time when task 8 is 50 percent completed. Your screen should look like Figure 2-38.

Figure 2-38	ENTERING LAG PERCENTAGES

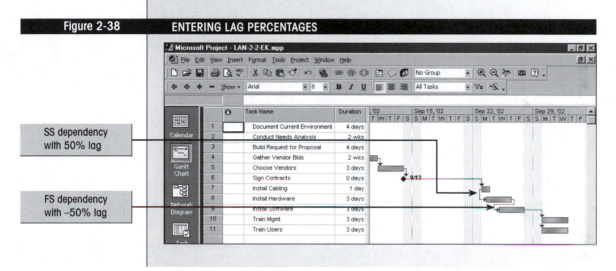

Once the tasks, durations, and relationships are entered, you should check the Project Information dialog box to determine the project's calculated Finish Date, if the project is scheduled from a Start Date, or calculated Start Date, if the project is scheduled from a Finish Date.

To check for lag time effects on Start or Finish Dates:

1. Click **Project** on the menu bar, and then click **Project Information**.

   The Finish Date of 10/2/02 was calculated based on the Start Date of 8/12/02. The original project file had a calculated Finish Date of 8/23/02 prior to your entering task dependencies and lag times. As you can see, entering task dependencies greatly affects project scheduling.

2. Click the **Cancel** button, and then save the **LAN-2-2-Your Initials.mpp** project file without a baseline.

3. Click the **Print Preview** button on the Standard toolbar, click the **Page Setup** button, verify that your name is in the left section of the header, and then print the Gantt Chart.

4. Close the **LAN-2-2-Your Initials** project.

When a project is scheduled from a Start Date, applying negative lag time to task dependencies that are on the critical path is a common way to shorten the critical path because it allows tasks to overlap. When you apply negative lag time, the second task is allowed to start before the first task is completely finished.

When a project is scheduled from a Finish Date, all tasks have as late as possible schedules and lag time affects the *first* task rather than the second. Figure 2-39 shows how positive and negative lag times affect the first task of a project scheduled from a Finish Date.

Figure 2-39	LAG TIME FOR A PROJECT SCHEDULED FROM A FINISH DATE

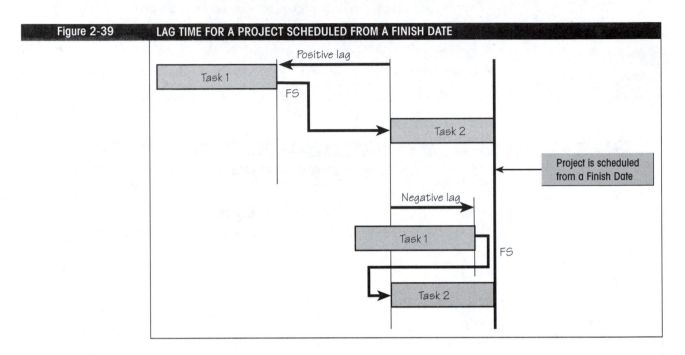

Confusing negative and positive lag times is easy, especially when examining them for both a project that is scheduled from a Start Date and one scheduled from a Finish Date. Remember, positive lag time always *increases* the amount of time between tasks and negative lag time always causes the tasks to *overlap*. This rule holds true regardless of whether the project is scheduled from the Start Date or the Finish Date.

Session 2.2 QUICK | CHECK

1. What are the four types of task dependencies?

2. Which is the most common type of task dependency?

3. Give an example of the finish-to-start dependency between two tasks.

4. What is a critical path?

5. How do the tasks on a critical path appear in the Network Diagram?

6. How do noncritical tasks appear in the Network Diagram?

7. When a project is scheduled from a Start Date, how does positive lag time affect two tasks in a finish-to-start relationship?

8. When a project is scheduled from a Start Date, how can you use lag time to shorten the critical path?

9. When a project is scheduled from a Finish Date, how does positive lag time affect two tasks in a finish-to-start relationship?

Now that you have worked with Emily to establish the task dependencies and lag times, the project starts to provide realistic start and finish dates for each task and predict the overall Finish Date for the project.

SESSION 2.3

In this session, you will further organize your project by using summary tasks, indented tasks, work breakdown structures, and grouped tasks.

Outlining with Summary Tasks

A **summary task** is a grouping of tasks that logically belong together. It also is called a **phase**. When developing a new, large project, some project managers prefer to start with summary tasks and then break them down into individual tasks using the **rule of 20s**. The rule of 20s heuristic (rule of thumb) directs you to list no more than 20 summary tasks and then break them down into individual tasks until you have defined the entire project. Planning a project by starting with the summary tasks is called the **top-down method**. Other project managers prefer to list all of the individual tasks, and then collect them into logical phases—the **bottom-up method**. A phase is defined as a group of related tasks that completes a major step in a project. Summary tasks organize phases. Outdenting and indenting create summary tasks in Project 2000.

Outdenting and Indenting Tasks

Once you have identified your summary tasks and are ready to create them in the project, the actual technique for creating the summary task is simple. The Outdent button and the Indent button are the first two buttons on the Formatting toolbar. **Outdenting** moves a task to the left (a higher level in the outline), and **indenting** moves a task to the right (a lower level in the outline).

To create a summary task:

1. Open the **LAN-2-3.mpp** project file from the Tutorial folder on your Data Disk for Tutorial 2, click **File** on the menu bar, and then click **Save As**, saving the file as **LAN-2-3-Your Initials** to the Tutorial folder on your Data Disk. Do not save a baseline.

2. Click **Train Mgmt** (task 10), press the **Insert** key, type **Training** as the name of the summary task, and then press the **Enter** key.

The summary task is named Training and consists of the individual tasks Train Mgmt and Train Users. You need not specify a duration for a summary task because it is calculated based on the durations and relationships of the individual tasks within that summary task.

3. Press and hold the **Shift** key, click **Train Users** (task 11) to select both tasks 10 and 11, and then click the **Indent** button ⮕ on the Formatting toolbar. Your screen should look like Figure 2-40.

| Figure 2-40 | CREATING THE TRAINING SUMMARY TASK |

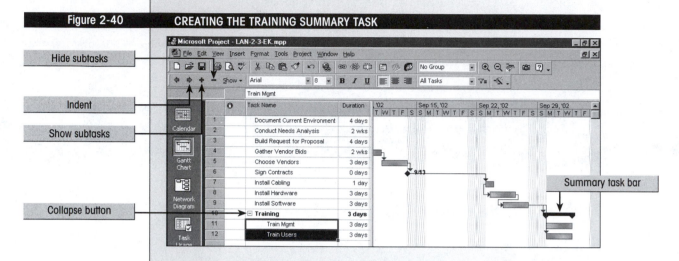

Training is now a summary task with a calculated duration of three days. Summary tasks are listed in bold text in the Task Entry table and display a Collapse/Expand button to the left of the task so that you can easily show or hide the individual tasks within that summary task. In the Gantt Chart, a summary task bar displays as a solid black line with arrow-like markers that indicate where the summary task starts and stops. The duration cell of a summary task cannot be directly edited; it is calculated from the durations and relationships of the individual summary tasks within that phase.

4. Click the **Link Tasks** button 🔗 on the Standard toolbar to link tasks 11 and 12 in an FS relationship. Note the change in the duration of the summary task from three to six days.

5. Click **Install Cabling** (task 7), press the **Insert** key, type **Installation**, and then press the **Enter** key. Installation is the name of the summary task consisting of the next three individual tasks.

6. Drag ✛ to select **Install Cabling** (task 8) through **Install Software** (task 10), and then click the **Indent** button ⮕ on the Formatting toolbar.

Your screen should look like Figure 2-41. The Installation summary task's duration was calculated at five days.

Figure 2-41	CREATING THE INSTALLATION SUMMARY TASK

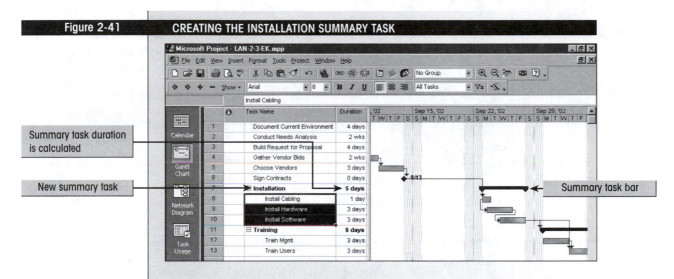

Summary task duration is calculated

New summary task

Summary task bar

7. Click **Document Current Environment** (task 1), press the **Insert** key, type **Analysis**, and then press the **Enter** key. You have inserted a new task that will become a summary task. The task, Document Current Environment, is selected.

8. Drag ✛ to select **Document Current Analysis** (task 2) and **Conduct Needs Analysis** (task 3), and then click the **Indent** button ⇨ on the Formatting toolbar.

   The two individual tasks were added to the summary task Analysis, which has a calculated duration of ten days. You need to enter one more phase, named Design.

9. Click **Build Request for Proposal** (task 4), press the **Insert** key, type **Design**, and then press the **Enter** key.

   Because you are inserting a task at an indented level, the new task 4 (Design) is also inserted at this indented level. Design is the phase name for the final summary task, so you must outdent that task.

10. Click **Design** (task 4), and then click the **Outdent** button ⇦ on the Formatting toolbar.

    Task 4 has been promoted to a higher level and is no longer an individual task within the Analysis phase.

11. Click **Build Request for Proposal** (task 5), drag ✛ to select the tasks **Build Request for Proposal** (task 5) through **Sign Contracts** (task 8), and then click the **Indent** button ⇨ on the Formatting toolbar. Design is now a phase that has four tasks and a calculated duration of 17 days.

12. Press and hold the **Alt** key, press the **Home** key to move to the beginning of the Gantt Chart, and then click the **Zoom Out** button 🔍 on the Standard toolbar twice. You now can see the entire project. Your screen should look like Figure 2-42.

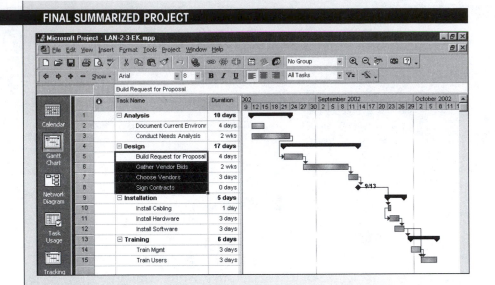

Figure 2-42 FINAL SUMMARIZED PROJECT

TROUBLE? If the timescale on your screen doesn't match the figure, zoom as needed.

13. Save the **LAN-2-3-Your Initials.mpp** project file without a baseline.

You can create a summary task bar for the entire project (it appears at the top of the Gantt Chart) by clicking Tools on the menu bar, Options, the View tab, and then the Project summary task check box. Summary tasks not only improve the clarity of the project and calculate the total duration for that phase, but they also help identify areas that are not yet fully developed. In this project, for instance, the addition of summary tasks clearly identifies the fact that no tasks for testing the final LAN installation have been scheduled. Further, summary tasks can be nested to create multiple levels of summary tasks if needed to define your project.

Expanding and Collapsing Tasks

Once your project has been organized into summary tasks, you can easily expand (show) and collapse (hide) the individual tasks within each phase. As your project at JLB Partners develops, you will find that you need to view different phases in various levels of detail. You use three buttons on the Formatting toolbar as well as the Expand and Collapse buttons within the Task Entry table to display and hide individual tasks.

To expand and collapse tasks:

1. Click the **Analysis** (summary task in row 1) **Collapse** button, and then click the **Design** (summary task in row 4) **Collapse** button.

Your screen should look like Figure 2-43. When you click the Collapse button of a summary task, the tasks within it are hidden and the Collapse button changes to the Expand button. Clicking the Expand button displays the individual tasks again. To expand and collapse more than one summary task at a time, use the buttons on the Formatting toolbar.

TROUBLE? If you do not see a Collapse button to the left of the summary tasks, click Project on the menu bar, point to Outline, and then click Show Outline Symbols.

Figure 2-43	COLLAPSING SUMMARY TASKS

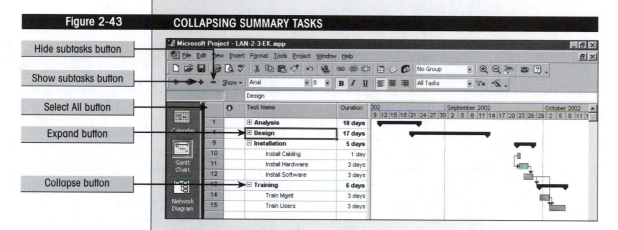

2. Click the **Select All** button, and then click the **Hide Subtasks** button [−] on the Formatting toolbar.

    The Select All button selects the entire Task Entry table. Each summary task is collapsed at the same time.

    When working on a project, you might often want to get an overview of the entire project by looking only at the summary tasks. There is a quick way to get that information.

3. Click the **Show Subtasks** button [+] on the Formatting toolbar.

    All summary tasks are expanded at the same time. When multiple levels of summary tasks exist, every detail task is displayed.

4. Click the **Show** button [Show ▾] on the Formatting toolbar, and then click **Outline Level 1**.

    Only the summary tasks are displayed.

5. Click the **Show** button [Show ▾] on the Formatting toolbar, and then click **Outline Level 2**.

    This project has only two levels of tasks, so clicking Outline Level 2 displays all the tasks for each summary task. Had you created multiple levels of summary tasks, you could choose exactly which level of detail you wanted to display using the Show button.

6. Click **Analysis (task 1)** to deselect the table.

    As you continue to work on developing your project, you will find that viewing various levels of detail provides different information. Another way to expand, hide, indent, and outdent tasks is to use the menu bar. Click Project on the menu bar, point to Outline, point to Show, and then click the Outline Level that best meets your needs at the time.

Using Work Breakdown Structures

A **work breakdown structure (WBS)** is a way to use an alphanumeric code to represent each task's position within the hierarchical structure of the project. A WBS code helps identify and group project tasks for communication, documentation, or accounting purposes.

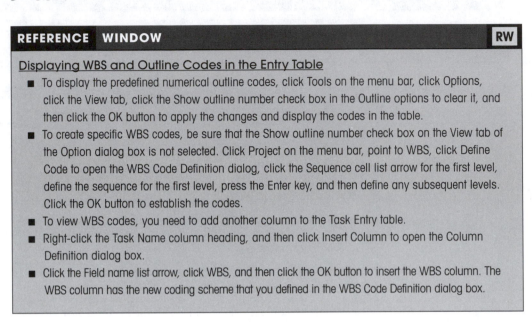

REFERENCE WINDOW | **RW**

Displaying WBS and Outline Codes in the Entry Table

- To display the predefined numerical outline codes, click Tools on the menu bar, click Options, click the View tab, click the Show outline number check box in the Outline options to clear it, and then click the OK button to apply the changes and display the codes in the table.
- To create specific WBS codes, be sure that the Show outline number check box on the View tab of the Option dialog box is not selected. Click Project on the menu bar, point to WBS, click Define Code to open the WBS Code Definition dialog, click the Sequence cell list arrow for the first level, define the sequence for the first level, press the Enter key, and then define any subsequent levels. Click the OK button to establish the codes.
- To view WBS codes, you need to add another column to the Task Entry table.
- Right-click the Task Name column heading, and then click Insert Column to open the Column Definition dialog box.
- Click the Field name list arrow, click WBS, and then click the OK button to insert the WBS column. The WBS column has the new coding scheme that you defined in the WBS Code Definition dialog box.

Project 2000 lets you create and modify a WBS with outline numbers. The default WBS code is the task's outline number, but you can create your own custom WBS code.

To add outline numbers to the project:

1. Click **Tools** on the menu bar, click **Options**, click the **View** tab, click the **Show outline number** check box in the Outline options for LAN-2-3-Your Initials.mpp section, and then click **OK**.

   Your screen should look like Figure 2-44. Each summary task is numbered sequentially, and subtasks are sequentially numbered within each summary task.

Figure 2-44	OUTLINE NUMBERS ADDED TO TASKS

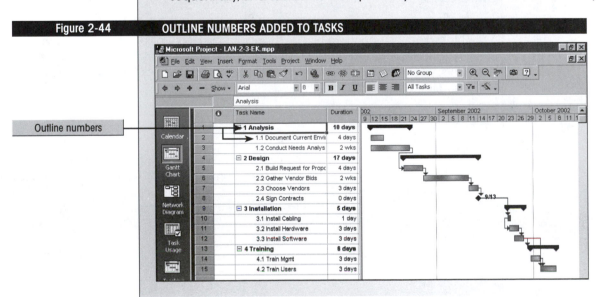

Outline numbers

2. Click **Tools** on the menu bar, click **Options**, click the **Show outline number** check box in the Outline options for **LAN-2-3-Your Initials.mpp** on the View tab to clear it, and then click the **OK** button.

This numbering system works well when you want to numerically code each task and do not care how the WBS should be structured. To develop your own coding system, however, you first must define the WBS codes.

To create WBS codes:

1. Click **Project** on the menu bar, point to **WBS**, and then click **Define Code**.

   The WBS Code Definition dialog box opens in which you can determine how each level of tasks should be coded.

2. Click the **Sequence** cell list arrow for the first level, and then click **Uppercase Letters (ordered)**. This option creates a sequence for the first level that follows a pattern A, B, C, and so forth.

3. Press the **Enter** key, click the **Sequence** cell list arrow for the second level, click **Numbers (ordered)**, and then press the **Enter** key to move to the Sequence cell for the third level.

   Your screen should look like Figure 2-45. The Code preview text box shows you a sample of how the WBS code will appear for each task. If you had more than two levels, you would continue defining each level's code within the WBS Code Definition dialog box.

Figure 2-45	WBS CODE DEFINITION DIALOG BOX

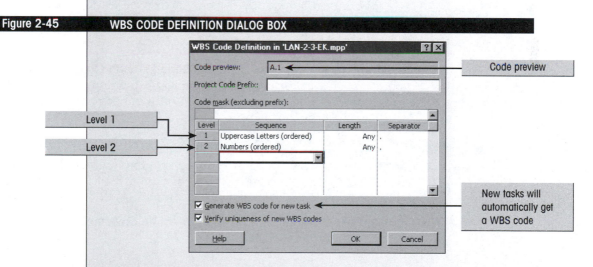

4. Click the **OK** button. Even though you established the codes, the Entry table hasn't changed. To view WBS codes, you need to add another column to the Task Entry table.

5. Right-click the **Task Name column heading**, and then click **Insert Column**. The Column Definition dialog box opens.

6. Click the **Field name** list arrow, scroll the alphabetical list of Field names, click **WBS**, and then click the **OK** button.

Your screen should look like Figure 2-46. The WBS column is inserted between the Indicator column and the Task Name column. This WBS column has the new coding scheme that you defined in the WBS Code Definition dialog box.

Figure 2-46	ENTRY TABLE WITH NEW WBS COLUMN

New WBS column

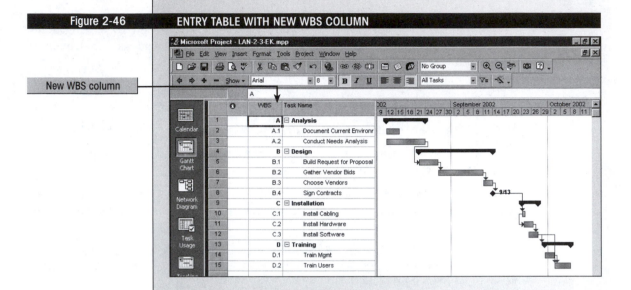

The WBS field uses the coding system defined in the WBS Code Definition dialog box to make a default entry for each field. Since the WBS field is user-created, however, you can override the default entry and enter something else, provided that it follows the hierarchical coding rules that you previously established (in this case, for example, the first part of the code must be a capital letter).

7. Click the **WBS code** cell for the Sign Contracts task (task 8), type **B.99**, and then press the **Enter** key.

Sometimes WBS codes are used to correlate tasks and their associated costs to a cost accounting structure that was previously created, so you must be able to edit them manually. Other times, WBS codes are edited to enable the user to find, filter, and report on them.

8. Save the **LAN-2-3-Your Initials.mpp** project file without a baseline.

9. Click the **Print Preview** button 🔍 on the Standard toolbar, click the **Page Setup** button, add your name in the left section of the header, and then print the Gantt Chart.

10. Close the **LAN-2-3-Your Initials.mpp** project file, save the file without a baseline, and then exit Project 2000.

A project does not need to be outlined in order for you to use the WBS column, but the outline helps visually clarify the phases of the project. The ability to expand and collapse different phases enables you to quickly display or print only the information needed. Creating summary tasks, displaying different levels of detail, and adding a WBS clarify and enhance the project but do not change any of the scheduled start and finish dates.

Session 2.3 QUICK CHECK

1. What is a summary task, and how do you create one in Project 2000?

2. Identify two methods for entering tasks into a new project.

3. How does a summary task help you manage your project?

4. The outlining buttons are found on which toolbar?

5. What is the purpose of the WBS codes?

6. How can you manually change a WBS code?

REVIEW ASSIGNMENTS

Part of the LAN installation involves training its users. In this assignment, you will open a partially completed project file that documents training tasks. You have to make some changes to the project calendar. You will explore the project, add tasks, create summary tasks, change the durations, create relationships between tasks, organize the tasks using the Outline features, and print the Gantt Chart view to show the relationships.

1. Start Project and make sure that your Data Disk is in the appropriate disk drive. Open the **Training-2.mpp** project file in the Review folder for Tutorial 2.

2. Use the Save As command to save the project as **Training-2-Your Initials** to the Review folder on your Data Disk without a baseline.

3. Click Project on the menu bar, and then click Project Information to open the Project Information dialog box. This project was scheduled from a Start Date, 8/5/02. On a separate piece of paper, record the project Finish Date, and then close the Project Information dialog box.

4. Change the duration for task 3 (Develop Training Document) from 15 days to three weeks.

5. Use the fill handle to copy the duration of two days from task 5 (Hire Trainers) to task 6 (Secure Lab Space).

6. The company picnic is Friday, August 9, 2002. Open the Change Working Time dialog box and change that day to a nonworking day on the Standard (Project Calendar).

7. Create a new calendar by making a copy of the Standard (Project Calendar) and naming it Hiring. Select Monday through Friday, and then delete the afternoon hours so that the working time for the Hiring calendar is only four hours a day, from 8:00 AM to 12:00 PM.

8. Double-click Hire Trainers (task 5) to open the Task Information dialog box for that task, and apply the Hiring calendar on the Advanced tab.

9. Use the Insert menu to enter the task name Write Progress Report as a recurring task in row 7. The duration should be two hours, and the task should be scheduled for every Monday throughout the project's duration.

10. Use the Calendar view to link task 1 (Identify Existing Skills) and task 2 (Identify Needed Skills) in an FS relationship.

11. Use the Network Diagram view to link task 2 (Identify Needed Skills) and task 3 (Develop training document) in an FS relationship.

12. Use the Gantt Chart view to edit the relationship between task 2 (Identify Needed Skills) and task 3 (Develop training documentation) with a –50% lag time.

13. Use the Gantt Chart view to link tasks 3, 4, 5, and 6 with an FS relationship.

14. Edit the relationship between task 5 (Hire trainers) and task 6 (Secure lab space) so that it is an SS relationship with a lag time of one day.

15. Insert a new task 1 with the task name Documentation. Indent tasks 2, 3, and 4 beneath task 1 to make Documentation a summary task.

16. Insert a new task 5 with the task name Trainers. Outdent task 5, and then indent tasks 6 and 7 to make Trainers a summary task.

17. Insert a new task 8 with the task name Lab. Outdent task 8, and then indent task 9 to make Lab a summary task.

18. Insert a new task 10 with the task name Sign Lab Contract. Make the duration zero so that the task is a milestone, and then link tasks 9 and 10 with an FS relationship.

19. Zoom out so that all of the task bars are visible on the Gantt Chart, and then print the Gantt Chart view with your name in the left part of the header.

20. Click Project on the menu bar, and then click Project Information to open the Project Information dialog box. Record the project's new Finish Date on your paper.

21. Save **Training-2-Your Initials.mpp** without saving a baseline, close the project file, and then exit Project 2000.

CASE PROBLEMS

Case 1. Building a House You have a part-time job working for BJB Development, a general contracting company that manages residential construction projects. The manager has asked you to use Project 2000 to enter and update some of the general tasks involved in building a new home. You have created and entered some of the tasks and now must further develop the project by creating summary tasks, creating task dependencies, and working with the Outline features.

1. Start Project 2000 and make sure that your Data Disk is in the appropriate disk drive. Open the **House-2** file in the Cases folder for Tutorial 2 on your Data Disk.

2. Use the Save As command to save the project as **House-2-Your Initials** without a baseline to your Data Disk.

3. Click Project on the menu bar, and then click Project Information to open the Project Information dialog box. This project was scheduled from a Start Date, 8/5/02. Record the project Finish Date.

4. Insert a new task 1 with the task name Planning.

5. Indent task 2 (Secure financing) and task 3 (Purchase lot) to make task 1 a summary task.

6. Insert a new task 4 with the task name Exterior.

7. Outdent task 4, and then indent tasks 5 through 10 to create the Exterior summary task.

8. Insert a new task 11 with the task name Interior.

9. Outdent task 11, and then indent tasks 12 through 14 to create Interior as a summary task.

10. Select tasks 1 through 14, and create an FS relationship between them by clicking the Link Tasks button.

11. Edit the task relationship between tasks 2 and 3 to reflect a –2 day lag time.

Explore ▶ 12. View the Network Diagram, noticing the tasks on the critical path. Click summary task 4 (Exterior), press and hold the Ctrl key as you click summary task 11 (Interior), and then click the Unlink Tasks button on the Standard toolbar. View the Network Diagram again, and write down an explanation for the changes to the critical path.

13. Click task 10 (Brick exterior), press and hold the Ctrl key as you click task 12 (Install plumbing), and then click the Link Tasks button on the Standard toolbar. You can link summary tasks or individual tasks in FS relationships.

Explore ▶ 14. Click the first blank Task Name cell in the Task sheet at the end of the project, click Insert on the menu bar, and then click Recurring Task to open the Recurring Task Information dialog box. Insert a recurring task for a weekly two-hour meeting on every Tuesday and name the task Meet with Building Inspector.

15. Add a milestone after the task of purchasing the lot and name it Review and Sign All Contracts.

16. Click Project on the menu bar, and then click Project Information to open the Project Information dialog box. Record the project's new Finish Date.

17. Zoom out so that all of the task bars are visible on the Gantt Chart, and then print the one-page Gantt Chart view with your name in the left part of the header.

18. Save **House-2-Your Initials.mpp**, close the project file without saving a baseline, and exit Project 2000.

Case 2. Finding a Job   You are seeking a new job that utilizes technical skills that you have recently acquired. Use Project 2000 to organize your job search efforts. You have created and entered some of the tasks and now must further develop the project by creating summary tasks, creating task dependencies, adding appropriate lag times, and working with the Outline features to better see what needs to be done.

1. Start Project 2000 and make sure that your Data Disk is in the appropriate disk drive. Open the **Job-2** file in the Cases folder for Tutorial 2 on your Data Disk.

2. Use the Save As command to save the project as **Job-2-Your Initials** on your Data Disk without saving the baseline.

3. Click Project on the menu bar, and then click Project Information to open the Project Information dialog box. This project was scheduled from a Start Date, 8/5/02. On a piece of paper, record the project Finish Date.

4. Insert a new task 1 with the task name Resume.

5. Indent tasks 2 and 3 so that Resume becomes a summary task.

6. Insert a new task 4 with the task name Research.

7. Outdent Research and then indent tasks 5, 6, and 7 to make Research a summary task.

8. Insert a new task 8 with the task name Phone Calls.

9. Outdent Phone Calls, and then indent tasks 9, 10, and 11 to make Phone Calls a summary task.

10. Insert a new task 10 with the task name Existing Contacts.

Explore   11. Indent tasks 11 and 12 so that Existing Contacts becomes a second-level summary task.

12. Insert a new task 13 (a new row) with the task name New Contacts.

13. Outdent New Contacts.

Explore   14. Copy and paste tasks 11 and 12 to rows 14 and 15.

15. Indent tasks 14 and 15 so that New Contacts becomes a second-level summary task at the same level as task 10 (Existing Contacts).

16. Select tasks 1 through 15, and click the Link Tasks button on the Standard toolbar to link all 15 tasks in an FS relationship.

17. Double-click the link line between task 4 (Research) and task 8 (Phone Calls) in the Gantt Chart and add a –50% lag time.

18. Open the Project Information dialog box, and record the project's new Finish Date.

19. Print preview the Gantt Chart, make sure that it will print on one page and that your name is in the left part of the header, and then print the Gantt Chart view.

20. Save **Job-2-Your Initials.mpp**, close the project file without saving a baseline, and then exit Project 2000.

Case 3. Planning a Convention In your new job at Future Technology, Inc., you have been asked to help organize the annual convention at which the company will unveil its new product ideas for customers. You'll use Project 2000 to enter and track the many tasks that must be completed for a successful convention. Since the convention *must* occur December 4, 5, and 6 of the year 2002, you scheduled the project from a Finish Date and let Project 2000 determine the project Start Date. Now you must continue to work on the project by creating summary tasks, establishing dependencies between tasks, and adding lag times. You will keep a watchful eye on the critical path as you work on this file.

1. Start Project 2000 and make sure that your Data Disk is in the appropriate disk drive. Open the **Convention-2** file in the Cases folder for Tutorial 2 on your Data Disk.

2. Use the Save As command to save the file as **Convention-2-Your Initials** without a baseline.

3. Open the Project Information dialog box. You have scheduled the project from a Finish Date of 12/4/02. Click the OK button, and then reopen the Project Information dialog box and record the project Start Date on a piece of paper.

4. Click the Network Diagram view. Record which task(s) are on the critical path and explain why they are on the path. *(Hint:* Remember that whether a task is on the critical path depends on its duration and dependencies.)

5. Use the Network Diagram view to link tasks 1 and 2 with an FS relationship. Now which tasks are on the critical path? Record this information on your paper.

6. Use the Network Diagram view to link tasks 2 and 3 with an FS relationship. Now which tasks are on the critical path? Record this information on your paper.

7. Use the Network Diagram view to link tasks 3 to 4, 4 to 5, 5 to 6, and 7 to 8 in FS relationships. *(Hint:* Zoom out in Network Diagram view in order to expand the number of task boxes that you can see on the screen.)

Explore　8. In the Task sheet of the Gantt Chart view, drag task 3 (Determine number of attendees) between tasks 1 and 2 so that it becomes task 2 (task 3 becomes Determine convention goals).

9. Add three summary tasks:

Task 1, Research, which contains tasks 2, 3, and 4

Task 5, Financial Planning, which contains tasks 6 and 7

Task 8, Activity Planning, which contains tasks 9, 10, and 11

Explore　10. Edit the relationship between task 6 (Set budget) and task 7 (Set agenda) so that the tasks overlap by two days.

11. Create an SS relationship between task 9 (Book entertainment) and task 10 (Determine menu).

12. Edit the relationship between task 10 (Determine menu) and task 11 (Develop promotional brochure) so that it is an SS relationship with a one-day lag.

13. Open the Project Information dialog box, and record the project's new Start Date.

14. Preview the Gantt Chart so that all of the task bars are visible on one page of the chart, and then print the Gantt Chart with your name in the left part of the header.

15. Save **Convention-2-Your Initials.mpp** to the Cases folder for Tutorial 2 without saving a baseline, close the project file, and then exit Project 2000.

Case 4. *Organizing a Fund-Raiser* You have volunteered to lead your neighborhood elementary school's major fund-raising effort to purchase new playground equipment. The equipment must be ready by the start of school on September 16, 2002, so you'll schedule the project from a Finish Date and let Project 2000 establish the project Start Date. You must establish the task relationships and create summary tasks.

1. Start a new project.

2. Make sure that your Data Disk is in the appropriate disk drive.

3. Change the Schedule from option in the Project Information dialog box to Project Finish Date, and then change the Finish Date to September 16, 2002.

4. Add the following in rows 1, 2, and 3 as the first three tasks: Planning, Fund-Raising, and Building.

5. Add new tasks and outline them so that Planning, Fund-Raising, and Building are summary tasks containing at least two subtasks each.

6. Create an FS relationship between the three summary tasks.

7. Save the project with the name **Fund-2-Your Initials** to the Cases folder for Tutorial 2 on your Data Disk.

8. Open the Project Information dialog box, and record the project Start Date.

Explore 9. Establish a WBS structure for the project, and define your own WBS code for two levels.

10. Insert a WBS column after the Indicators column in the Entry table.

Explore 11. Preview the Network Diagram view of the project with your name in the left side of the header. Change the Legend to include the name of the school in the center.

Explore 12. Use the Fit to option in the Print dialog box so that the Network Diagram is forced to fit on two pages wide by one page high.

13. Print the Gantt Chart with your name on the left side of the header.

14. Print the Calendar view of the project with your name in the left side of the header. How does a summary task appear in the Calendar view? *(Hint:* Does a summary task appear in the Calendar view?)

15. Save **Fund-2-Your Initials.mpp** without a baseline, close the file, and then exit Project 2000.

INTERNET ASSIGNMENTS

The purpose of the Internet Assignments is to challenge you to find information on the Internet so that you learn more about project management and can more effectively use Project 2000. The actual assignments are updated and maintained on the Course Technology Web site. Log on to the Internet, and use your Web browser to go to the Student Online Companion that accompanies this text at **www.course.com/NewPerspectives/Project2000**. Click the link for Tutorial 2.

QUICK | CHECK ANSWERS

Session 2.1

1. Project Start Date

2. The user enters the Finish Date and Project 2000 calculates the Start Date.

3. With the as soon as possible constraint

4. The Standard calendar

5. The entire task

6. 3mon?

7. Elapsed durations are not affected by working and nonworking times.

8. Drag the right edge of the task bar left or right.

9. Choose Insert from the menu bar, and then click Recurring Task.

10. Zero, 0

Session 2.2

1. Finish-to-Start, FS

   Start-to-Start, SS

   Finish-to-Finish, FF

   Start-to-Finish, SF

2. The finish-to-start is by far the most common. It states that task 1 must finish before task 2 starts.

3. A computer must be installed (task 1) before application software can be installed (task 2).

4. The critical path consists of the tasks that must be completed within the given schedule dates in order for the overall project to be completed in the shortest amount of time.

5. A critical task appears within a red-bordered shape in the Network Diagram view.

6. Noncritical tasks appear within a rounded rectangle in Network Diagram view. The border is blue, and the interior is light blue.

7. When scheduling is done from a project Start Date, positive lag always pushes the second task forward in time.

8. When a project is scheduled from a Start Date, applying negative lag time to task dependencies that are on the critical path is a common way to shorten the critical path because it brings the second task *backward* in time, thereby causing the tasks to overlap.

9. When a project is scheduled from a Finish Date, all tasks have as late as possible schedules and lag time affects the *first* task rather than the second. Positive lag time always *increases* the amount of time between tasks and therefore pushes the first task backward in time.

Session 2.3

1. A summary task is a group of tasks that belong together in a logical group; it is also called a phase. Summary tasks in Project 2000 are created by outdenting and indenting tasks using the first two buttons on the Formatting toolbar.

2. You can plan a project by starting with the summary tasks (the top-down method) and then dividing them into individual tasks. Or you can list all of the individual tasks and then collect them into logical phases (the bottom-up method).

3. Summary tasks improve the clarity of the project and calculate the total duration for a phase, as well as help identify areas that are not yet fully developed.

4. Formatting

5. A work breakdown structure (WBS) is a way to code each task. The code helps identify and group project tasks for communication, documentation, or accounting purposes.

6. Click the WBS code in the Entry table, and type a new code that follows the convention that you set.

OBJECTIVES

In this tutorial you will:

- Examine the critical path
- Filter tasks
- Format a Gantt Chart
- Enter and edit tasks and dependencies in a Network Diagram
- Expand, collapse, move, and filter tasks in a Network Diagram
- Format a Network Diagram
- Crash the critical path by using task durations, relationships, and lag time
- Analyze task constraints
- Use task reports

COMMUNICATING PROJECT INFORMATION

Improving the LAN Project Plan

CASE

JLB Partners

Emily Kelsey reviewed the Project 2000 file that you have been developing. She examined the tasks, durations, and dependencies that you determined are necessary to install a local area network (LAN) for the CPA firm, JLB Partners. The Finish Date that Project 2000 calculated is two weeks later than she had anticipated, so Emily has asked you to use the features within Project 2000 such as filters and custom formats to emphasize, analyze, and condense the critical path.

SESSION 3.1

In this session, you will work with the project's critical path using filters, custom formatting, and the Network Diagram.

Understanding the Critical Path

Recall from Tutorial 2 that the **critical path** consists of the tasks and durations that determine the shortest period to complete the project. Any task on the critical path is called a **critical task.** The critical path will often change as activities are completed ahead of or behind schedule. A simple example is the garden improvement project shown in Figure 3-1.

| Figure 3-1 | GANTT CHART FOR THE GARDEN IMPROVEMENT PROJECT |

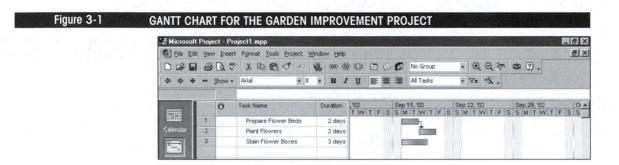

Tasks 1 and 2 currently represent the critical path. Another way to define the critical path is that it consists of those tasks having a float of zero. **Float**, also called **total slack**, is the amount of time that a task can be delayed from its planned start date without delaying the project Finish Date. Total slack differs from free slack. **Free slack** is the amount of time that a task can be delayed without delaying any successor tasks; it is examined further in a later tutorial.

The project, as currently planned, will be completed in four days. This is represented by the durations and finish-to-start (FS) relationship between tasks 1 and 2. Task 3 has a float of one day, so it is not a critical task and is not currently on the critical path. Figure 3-2 shows the current Network Diagram for this project.

| Figure 3-2 | NETWORK DIAGRAM FOR THE GARDEN IMPROVEMENT PROJECT |

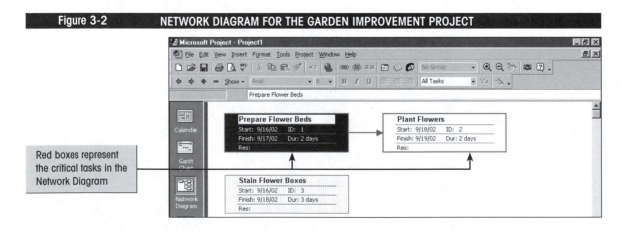

Red boxes represent the critical tasks in the Network Diagram

How would the critical path change, however, if task 1 was completed as scheduled but task 3 had not yet been started? Because two days had elapsed and the float of task 3 was only one day, task 3 would become a critical task and its duration would then represent the shortest period of time required to complete the entire project, the critical path. Figure 3-3 shows the Network Diagram for such a scenario.

Figure 3-3   **NEW NETWORK DIAGRAM**

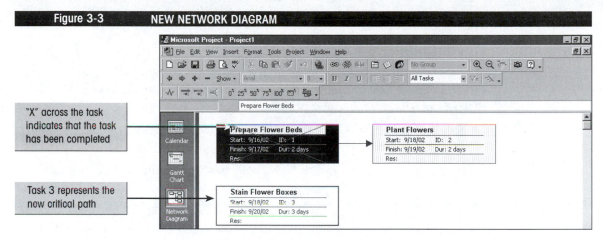

"X" across the task indicates that the task has been completed

Task 3 represents the new critical path

Even in this small example it is easy to see how the critical path can quickly change as the project is progressing. It is very important for a project manager to have excellent skills in finding, analyzing, and communicating information about the critical path throughout the life of the project. Filters, formats, and special presentations of the Network Diagram help the manager accomplish this.

Filtering **Tasks for Information**

Filtering tasks within Project 2000 is very similar to filtering within an Excel spreadsheet or an Access database. A **filter** temporarily hides some of the tasks so that only those that you are interested in are displayed. Thus filters help you to focus your attention on specific aspects of the project based on different criteria. Project 2000 offers many built-in filters, available as a list on the Formatting toolbar. One of the most popular filters is Critical, because it filters out all tasks not currently on the critical path.

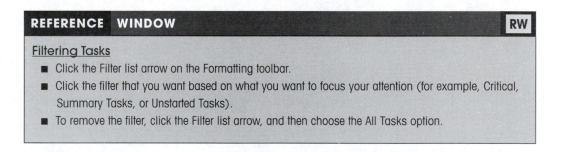

REFERENCE WINDOW   **RW**

Filtering Tasks
- Click the Filter list arrow on the Formatting toolbar.
- Click the filter that you want based on what you want to focus your attention (for example, Critical, Summary Tasks, or Unstarted Tasks).
- To remove the filter, click the Filter list arrow, and then choose the All Tasks option.

As project manager at JLB Partners, you have been working diligently to enter all of the tasks and durations in the LAN project file. Now that you have completed that important step, you can begin to work with the file and use more-advanced features of Project 2000. You want to take a look at all the critical tasks in the file. You use the filtering capabilities of Project 2000 to quickly display those tasks on the critical path.

To filter tasks in the Entry table and the Gantt Chart view:

1. Start Project 2000 and open the **LAN-3.mpp** file from the Tutorial folder on your Data Disk for Tutorial 3.

   The LAN project with all of the tasks opens.

2. Click **File** on the menu bar, click **Save As**, click the **Save in** list arrow to locate the Tutorial folder on your Data Disk, then save the file with the name **LAN-3-Your Initials** without a baseline.

   The file contains 23 tasks in six phases. The filter, which displays on the Formatting toolbar, is currently set for All Tasks.

3. Click the **Filter** list arrow on the Formatting toolbar, and then click **Critical**.

   Only the critical tasks, those tasks on the critical path, are now displayed, as shown in Figure 3-4. Not all tasks are on this project's critical path; tasks 2, 13, 14, 15, 16, 18, and 20 are hidden. Nothing has changed in the project file, only the way that you view the data has changed.

Figure 3-4	FILTERING FOR CRITICAL TASKS IN THE GANTT CHART

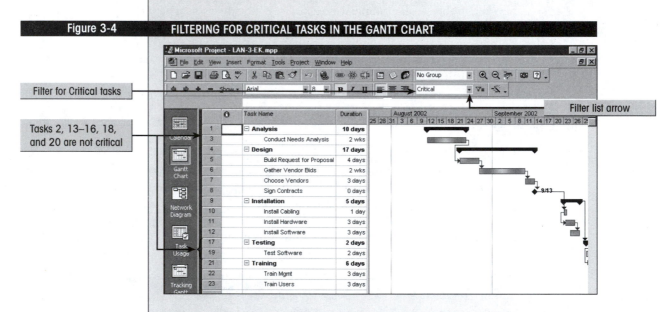

Filter for Critical tasks

Tasks 2, 13–16, 18, and 20 are not critical

Filter list arrow

Filters can be applied in any view, but each view is filtered independently of the others.

4. Click the **Network Diagram** button on the View Bar.

   The Filter list in the Formatting toolbar displays All Tasks, thereby indicating that all tasks are currently visible in this view.

5. Click the **Filter** list arrow on the Formatting toolbar. The available filters are listed in alphabetical order. Scroll down the list, and then click **Summary Tasks**.

   The Network Diagram displays only the six summary tasks within the project, as shown in Figure 3-5.

   TROUBLE? If you can't see all of the summary tasks in the window, click the Zoom Out button.

Figure 3-5	FILTERING FOR SUMMARY TASKS IN THE NETWORK DIAGRAM

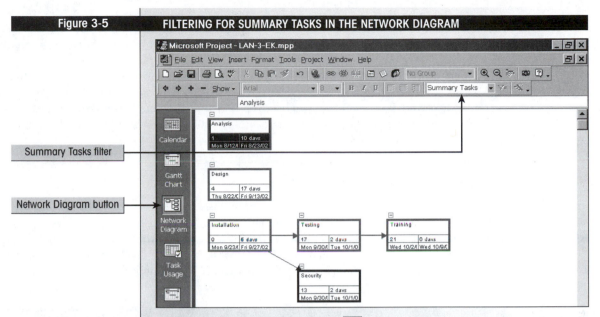

Summary Tasks filter

Network Diagram button

6. Click the **Gantt Chart** button on the View Bar, click the **Filter** list arrow, scroll down the list, and then click **Summary Tasks**.

The Gantt Chart now displays summary rather than critical tasks. The Filter list offers many more filters, some of which filter for resource allocations and progress tracking information. Those filters are used after the actual project is underway.

Other filters such as Milestones, Task Range, and Date Range can be used at any time. Filters such as Date Range require that you enter parameters to specify the exact details of the filter. For the Date Range, for example, you must enter parameters to specify criteria for start or finish after and start or finish before dates. As you plan for this LAN installation, you want to see everything that is going on during the first two weeks of September.

To filter for a date range:

1. Click the **Filter** list arrow, and then click **Date Range**. The Date Range dialog box opens. You want to find all tasks that are scheduled between 9/1/2002 and 9/15/2002.

2. Type **9/1/2002**, click the **OK** button, type **9/15/2002**, and then click the **OK** button.

Your screen should look like Figure 3-6, with only three tasks displayed because of the date range filter.

Figure 3-6	FILTERING FOR A DATE RANGE

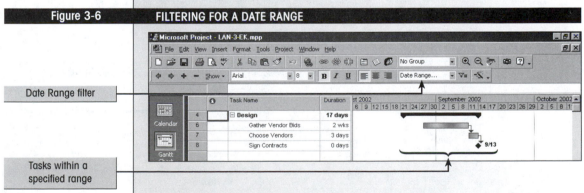

Date Range filter

Tasks within a specified range

3. Click the **Filter** list arrow, and then click **All Tasks** so that all tasks in the project are displayed again.

Filters temporarily hide those tasks that do not meet the filter criteria. They never delete tasks, and each view's filters are independently applied and removed. Each view of the project can have a different filter applied at the same time. It is also important to note that filters are only "correct" as of the moment they are applied. They do not dynamically update the current view of the project as the project is modified. In other words, if you make a change to a filtered project, you must reapply the filter to make sure that the tasks that meet the filter's criteria are currently displayed. For example, if you have the "Critical" filter applied and make a change to a task (such as shortening its duration) that causes it to be noncritical, it will still be displayed until you reapply the Critical filter.

Using the AutoFilter

You can use another type of filter, the **AutoFilter**, to display only those tasks that meet specified criteria. You determine the criteria by selecting from the existing information in each column. The AutoFilter creates lists that you choose from by clicking list arrows in the column headings of a Sheet view. AutoFilters are available in all Sheet views in Project 2000. If you are familiar with using AutoFilters in Excel, you will notice that this feature works similarly in Project 2000.

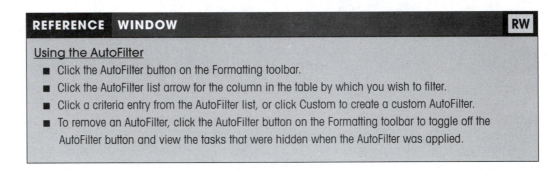

REFERENCE WINDOW   **RW**

Using the AutoFilter
- Click the AutoFilter button on the Formatting toolbar.
- Click the AutoFilter list arrow for the column in the table by which you wish to filter.
- Click a criteria entry from the AutoFilter list, or click Custom to create a custom AutoFilter.
- To remove an AutoFilter, click the AutoFilter button on the Formatting toolbar to toggle off the AutoFilter button and view the tasks that were hidden when the AutoFilter was applied.

To use an AutoFilter:

1. Click the **AutoFilter** button ⏷= on the Formatting toolbar.

   AutoFilter arrows appear at the top of each column of the Entry table.

2. Drag the **split bar** to the right of the Finish column so that five columns of information are displayed in the Entry table, as shown in Figure 3-7.

Figure 3-7   ENTRY TABLE WITH AUTOFILTERS

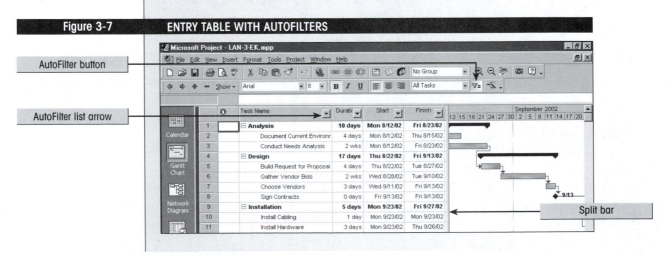

AutoFilter button

AutoFilter list arrow

Split bar

3. Click the **Start AutoFilter** list arrow to display the list of available criteria for the Start column, and then click **Mon 8/12/02**.

Only those tasks that start on Monday, 8/12/02, are displayed. Notice that the column heading, Start, is now blue—this indicates the filtered column in the table. The Filter list and AutoFilters can be used together.

4. Click the **Filter** list arrow on the Formatting toolbar, and then click **Critical.**

Only one task starts on 8/12/02 and is on the critical path. Summary tasks that include critical tasks also are included in the filter. AutoFilters and filters applied through the Filter list must be removed individually.

5. Click the **AutoFilter** button ⍌= on the Formatting toolbar to clear all AutoFilters, click the **Filter** list arrow, and then click **All Tasks** so that all tasks are visible.

Custom filters are useful to filter the columns by two values or to compare criteria. Comparison operators such as Greater Than >, Less Than <, Less Than or Equal To <=, and Greater Than or Equal To >= can be combined with the logical operators AND and OR to create conditions to display very specific information that you might need in the project. The Custom AutoFilter dialog box makes creating these criteria very simple. You can apply custom filters using the AutoFilter buttons.

To use Custom AutoFilters:

1. Click the **AutoFilter** button ⍌= to display the AutoFilter list arrows, click the **Duration AutoFilter** list arrow, and then click **(Custom)**.

The Custom AutoFilter dialog box opens as shown in Figure 3-8.

Figure 3-8	AUTOFILTER DIALOG BOX

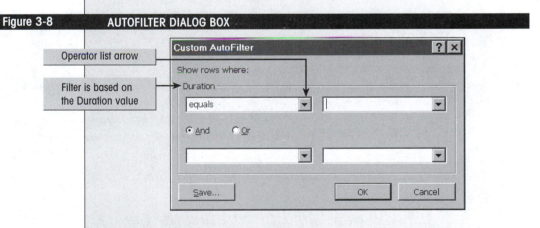

2. Click the **Duration Operator** list arrow, click **is greater than**, press the **Tab** key, type **5** to specify that you want to display the tasks with a duration greater than five days, and then click the **OK** button.

Five rows are displayed that meet the custom criteria. Each task has a duration of more than five days. In addition to a custom filter, the Duration AutoFilter list provides many handy options from the list itself, including > 1 day, > 1 week, and Estimated Duration (a duration that displays a question mark).

3. Click the **Print Preview** button 🔍 on the Standard toolbar, click the **Page Setup** button, click the **Header** tab, click the **Left** tab, type **Your Name**, click the **Right** tab, type **Tasks greater than 5 days**, click the **Print** button, and then

> click the **OK** button. The Gantt Chart view of the filtered project provides you
> with an excellent communication tool to share with your staff.
>
> 4. Click the **AutoFilter** button ▽= to view all tasks.
>
> 5. Click the **Save** button 🔲 and then click the **OK** button to save your work
>   without a baseline.

You can print any filtered view of a project. Entering information into the header and
footer sections to clearly identify the information on the printout is very helpful when presenting a filtered list of tasks.

Formatting a Project

Sometimes you want to highlight information in a project by changing the appearance of
the default views. For example, you might change the color of certain types of task bars
within the Gantt Chart or change the text font size within a table. Project 2000 provides
many ways to format the colors, shapes, and text within each project view to help you clearly
communicate your message.

Formatting a Gantt Chart

Project 2000 applies default formatting choices such as blue for task bars and black for summary bars. You can change the default options individually or by using the Gantt Chart
Wizard. Enhancing the appearance of certain task bars of a Gantt Chart customizes the project and helps you communicate the information to management.

REFERENCE WINDOW   **RW**

Formatting a Gantt Chart
- Click Format on the menu bar, and then click Bar Styles.
- Click the type of task that you want to modify, and then choose the formatting changes using the
  options in the lower section of the dialog box.
- When you are finished making formatting choices, click the OK button.
- To format a Gantt Chart using the Gantt Chart Wizard, click the GanttChartWizard button on the
  Formatting toolbar and follow the steps to work through the wizard.

To format the Gantt Chart using the Gantt Chart Wizard:

1. Click the **GanttChartWizard** button 🔳 on the Formatting toolbar. A welcome
   message is presented in the opening wizard dialog box.

2. Click the **Next** button.

   The second step of the Gantt Chart Wizard asks you to choose from one of four
   standard Gantt Chart formatting options (Standard, Critical Path, Baseline, or
   Other) or to create a custom Gantt Chart. You can click any of these option
   buttons or choose an option from the Other list to see a quick preview of the
   Gantt Chart formatting changes in this dialog box. Choosing Custom Gantt
   Chart will give you the most formatting choices.

3. Click the **Custom Gantt Chart** option button, and then click the **Next** button.

4. Read the Step 3 dialog box, click the **Yes, please** option button if it is not already selected to format critical and noncritical bars in a different way, and then click the **Next** button.

5. Click the **Next** button to accept the default options for formatting the critical tasks in red with a default pattern and no end shapes, and then click the **Next** button to accept the defaults to format noncritical tasks in blue.

   In the Step 6 dialog box, you determine the styles for how summary tasks should be formatted. You want to change the pattern for summary tasks.

6. Click the **Bar style** list arrow, and then click the second to the last option. Your Step 6 dialog box should look like Figure 3-9.

Figure 3-9	THE GANTT CHART WIZARD

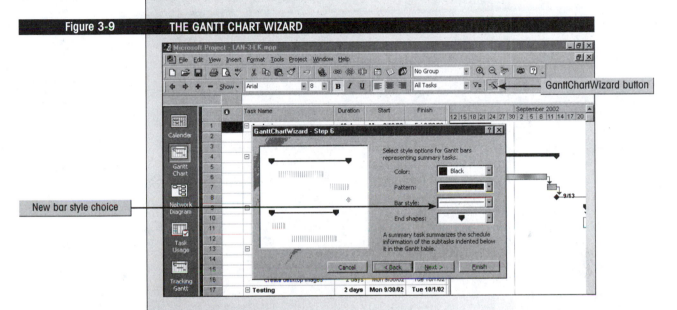

7. Click the **Next** button to progress to the Step 7 dialog box, where you select the style for milestones, click the **Shape** list arrow, scroll down the list, click the last shape (it's a **star**) in the list to change the milestone shape to a star, and then click the **Next** button.

   The Gantt Chart Wizard continues to ask you questions regarding the formatting of each part of the Gantt Chart. The preview panel displays the choices that you have made. Once you start the project and enter the actual task start and finish dates, you might also want to display baseline bars. (Recall that a baseline is an iteration of the project from which you want to track actual progress.) **Slack bars** help show how many days a noncritical task can be delayed and not affect the project Finish Date.

8. Click the **Total Slack** option button, and then click the **Next** button.

   Step 9 asks whether you want to show resource or date information on the Gantt Chart. The preview window can be used to display the effects of any of the selections.

9. Click the **Resources** option button, and then click the **Dates** option button and notice that either option clutters the Gantt Chart. Click the **None, thanks** option button, and then click the **Next** button.

Step 13 asks if you want to show link lines between dependent tasks. This is a very useful visual aid in the Gantt Chart.

10. Click the **Yes, please** option button if it is not already selcted, and then click the **Next** button.

11. Click the **Format It** button in the congratulatory GanttChartWizard Step 14 dialog box, click the **Exit Wizard** button, and then drag the **split bar** to the left so that your formatted Gantt Chart looks like Figure 3-10.

Figure 3-10	FORMATTED GANTT CHART

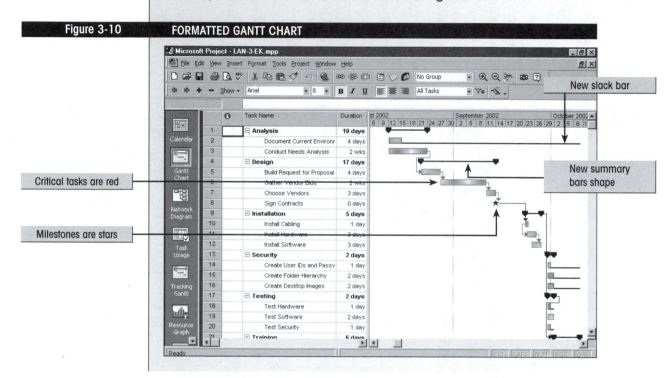

The Gantt Chart Wizard is a very powerful and easy tool that you can use as many times as you want to format the Gantt Chart. You have even more formatting choices by using the Bar Styles dialog box.

To format the Gantt Chart bars using the Bar Styles dialog box:

1. Click **Format** on the menu bar, and then click **Bar Styles**.

The Bar Styles dialog box opens as shown in Figure 3-11, displaying the current formatting choices for each type of task that appears in the Gantt Chart. This dialog box provides more formatting choices than the Gantt Chart Wizard. You can view task categories by clicking any Show For ... Tasks cell and then clicking the list arrow. The most common task categories include normal, critical, noncritical, milestone, and summary. Other task categories define tasks that are partially or completely finished and are useful when the actual project is underway.

Figure 3-11	BAR STYLES DIALOG BOX

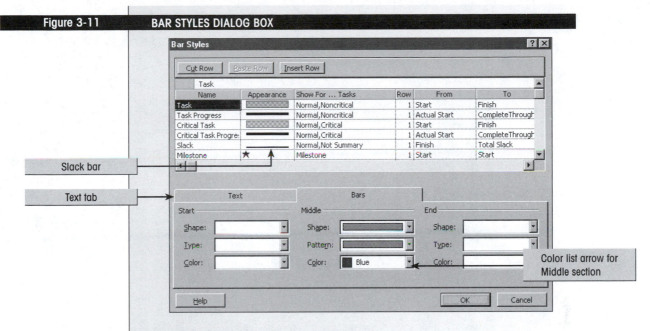

Slack bar

Text tab

Color list arrow for Middle section

2. Click the **Slack bar** Appearance cell, click the **Color** list arrow for the Middle section on the Bars tab, and then click **Blue**.

   Formatting slack bars in blue instead of black will help differentiate them from the black summary bars.

3. Click the **Milestone star** Appearance cell, click the **Text** tab, click the **Right** cell, click the **Right** list arrow, scroll through the alphabetical list, and then click **Name**.

   This formatting change will display the task's name to the right of the milestone marker.

4. Click the **OK** button.

   The Gantt Chart should look like Figure 3-12. Both formatting changes improve the readability and communication value of the Gantt Chart for your purposes.

Figure 3-12   **FINAL FORMATTED GANTT CHART**

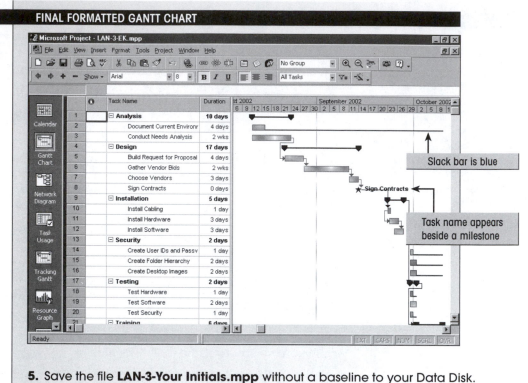

5. Save the file **LAN-3-Your Initials.mpp** without a baseline to your Data Disk.

6. Click the **Print Preview** button 🔍 on the Standard toolbar, click the **Page Setup** button, verify that your name is in the left section of the header, delete the text in the right section of the header, and then print the Gantt Chart.

The Bar Styles dialog box also allows you to change the way that bars appear within different date parameters or summary tasks. Project 2000 has many formatting options for the Gantt Chart. The key to formatting the Gantt Chart is that the final product should clearly and quickly communicate the information that is important to the project manager and management. As the project progresses, you can always reformat the Gantt Chart to highlight any new important messages.

Formatting a Table

Formatting a table is similar to formatting cells within Excel or tables within Word. You can click any cell within the table and choose a new font, font size, font effect, or color from the Formatting toolbar or Formatting menu options. Rather than making a change to a single task entry, however, you'll often want to apply formatting changes consistently to all of the tasks of one type. For example, you might want to change the text color of critical tasks to red or emphasize milestone tasks with a different font face. By visually organizing the tasks, you help communicate what needs to be done in the project. To make changes to all of the tasks of one type, you use the Text Styles dialog box.

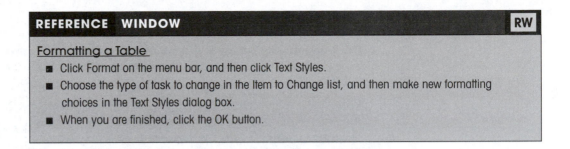

Formatting a Table

- Click Format on the menu bar, and then click Text Styles.
- Choose the type of task to change in the Item to Change list, and then make new formatting choices in the Text Styles dialog box.
- When you are finished, click the OK button.

To format the table using the Text Styles dialog box:

1. Click **Format** on the menu bar, and then click **Text Styles**. The Text Styles dialog box opens. It looks similar to text style dialog boxes that you might have encountered in your word processor or spreadsheet programs, offering options to change the font, as well as its style, size, and color.

2. Click the **Item to Change** list arrow, and then click **Critical Tasks**. Whatever formatting changes you make will apply to the critical tasks in the project file.

3. Click the **Color** list arrow, and then click **Red**. The sample in the dialog box shows you that all critical tasks will display in Arial 8 pt red font. You can add attributes for additional emphasis.

4. Click **Bold** in the Font style list, as shown in Figure 3-13, and then click the **OK** button.

| Figure 3-13 | TEXT STYLES DIALOG BOX |

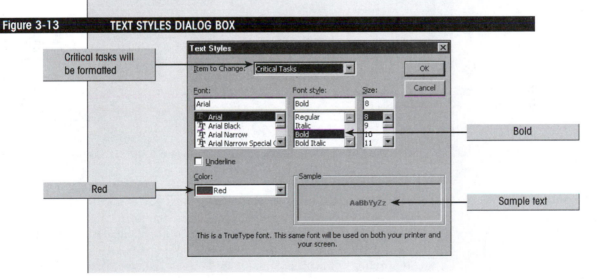

The project now displays all critical tasks in red, bold text. Since both the Gantt Chart and table formatting changes were made to a *category* of tasks (as opposed to an individual bar or row), any task that changes categories (for example, if a noncritical task becomes a critical task) will automatically be formatted to match its new category.

Task 2 (Document Current Environment) should be linked to task 3 (Conduct Needs Analysis) in a finish-to-start (FS) relationship. You can see how this new relationship changes the formatting for task 2.

To see how formatting changes are dynamic:

1. Click **Document Current Environment** (task 2), drag ✛ to select tasks 2 and 3, click the **Link Tasks** button 🔗 on the Standard toolbar, and then click **Analysis** (task 1).

   Your screen should look like Figure 3-14. Notice that for task 2, both the text in the Entry table and the bar in the Gantt Chart automatically change formatting characteristics. After tasks 2 and 3 were linked, task 2 became critical and thus now displays the special formatting for critical task text and bars.

| Figure 3-14 | THE NEW CRITICAL PATH INCLUDES TASK 2 |

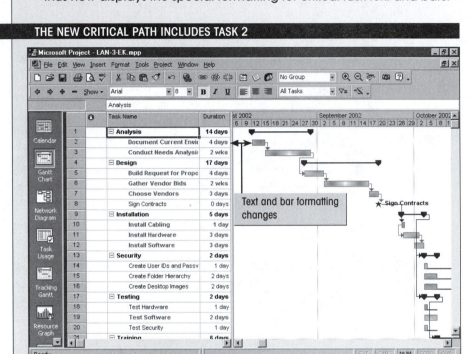

2. Save the **LAN-3-Your Initials.mpp** project file without a baseline to your Data Disk.

Formatting tasks by category through the Text Styles and Bar Styles dialog boxes is a powerful tool because the task will always display the formatting specified for its category. The task automatically changes formatting when it changes from one category to another (for example, from noncritical to critical) to highlight a change in the project and communicate important information. Sometimes, however, you might want to make individual task formatting changes.

Formatting Individual Items in the Entry Table and Gantt Chart

Many options on the Formatting toolbar and Format menu are used for individual task formatting changes that override the choices determined by the task category. For example, you might want to format the tasks that you have assigned to an outside contractor with an italic font face. Or, you might want to temporarily change the color of a Gantt Chart bar to highlight it for a meeting.

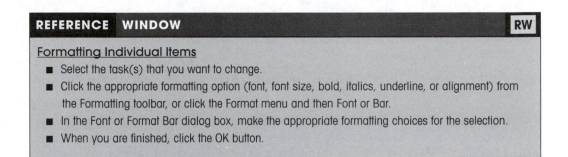

REFERENCE   WINDOW   **RW**

Formatting Individual Items

- Select the task(s) that you want to change.
- Click the appropriate formatting option (font, font size, bold, italics, underline, or alignment) from the Formatting toolbar, or click the Format menu and then Font or Bar.
- In the Font or Format Bar dialog box, make the appropriate formatting choices for the selection.
- When you are finished, click the OK button.

You have hired an outside contractor to install the cabling and hardware and want to format both the Entry table and Gantt Chart bars for these tasks in bright green.

To format individual items in the Entry table and Gantt Chart:

1. Click **Install Cabling**, drag ✛ to select **Install Cabling** (task 10) and **Install Hardware** (task 11), click **Format** on the menu bar, and then click **Font**.

   The Font dialog box opens, in which you can make text formatting changes for the selected tasks.

2. Click the **Color** list arrow, click **Green**, and then click the **OK** button.

3. With the two tasks still selected, click **Format** on the menu bar, and then click **Bar**.

   The Format Bar dialog box opens, in which you can change the formatting characteristics for the selected tasks. To format an individual bar, you also can double-click the bar in Gantt Chart view to open the Format Bar dialog box for that individual task.

4. Click the **Color** list arrow in the Middle Bar section, click **Green**, click the **OK** button, and then click **Analysis** (task 1).

   Your screen should look like Figure 3-15. Even though tasks 10 and 11 are still critical, they were formatted individually to display in a green font.

Figure 3-15   **INDIVIDUAL FORMATTING CHANGES**

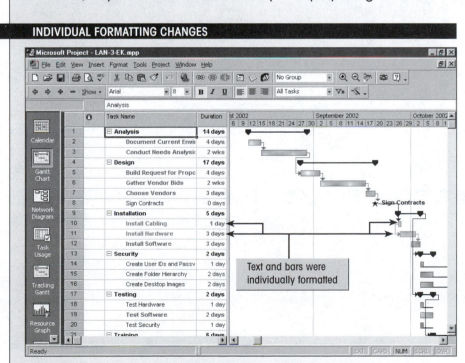

You can make many other minor formatting changes in the Gantt Chart view, such as changing the timescale, gridlines, and link lines.

To format the timescale, gridlines, or link lines:

1. Click **Format** on the menu bar, click the **double down arrows** if necessary, and then click **Timescale**.

   The Timescale dialog box opens in which you can change the way that the major (upper) and minor (lower) scales are measured, labeled, and aligned (beyond the default changes to the timescales when you zoom in and out). You have already learned how to change the timescales and labels. The Nonworking Time tab allows you to format nonworking time bars in the Gantt Chart.

2. Click the **Nonworking Time** tab, click the **In front of task bars** option button, click the **OK** button, and then press and hold the **Alt** and **Home** keys to reposition the Gantt Chart to the beginning of the project.

   You can also click any task in the Entry table and then click the Go To Selected Task button 📯 on the Standard toolbar to quickly readjust the Gantt Chart to display that particular task.

3. Click the **Zoom Out** button 🔍 and the **Zoom In** button 🔍 on the Standard toolbar and reposition the Scroll bars until your screen looks like Figure 3-16.

Figure 3-16	FORMATTING THE TIMESCALE

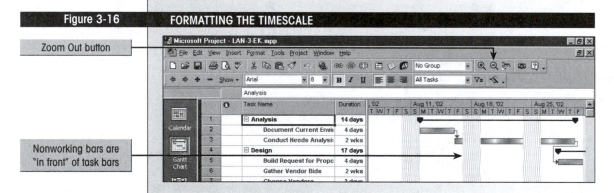

4. Click **Format** on the menu bar, and then click **Gridlines**.

   The Gridlines dialog box opens. Gridlines can provide a visual guide to help you interpret the bars. The Gantt Chart has several different gridlines that can be formatted many different ways.

5. Click **Project Start** in the Line to change list box, click the **Color** list arrow, click **Automatic**, click the **Type** list arrow, click the last dashed line as shown in Figure 3-17, and then click the **OK** button.

Figure 3-17	GRIDLINES DIALOG BOX

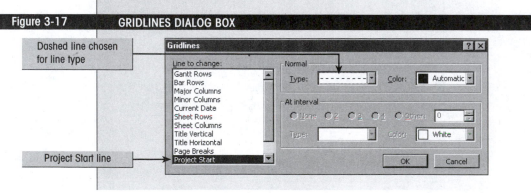

A dashed line appears, marking the project Start Date, August 12, 2002.

6. Click **Format** on the menu bar, and then click **Layout**.

The Layout dialog box provides several formatting options for the link lines and bars.

7. Click the **Always roll up Gantt bars** check box, click the **Hide Rollup bars when summary expanded** check box, and then click the **OK** button.

These layout changes will change the way that the Gantt Chart summary bars are formatted when the summary task is collapsed.

8. Click the **Zoom Out** button 🔍 on the Standard toolbar, click the **Collapse** button ⊟ to the left of task 1 (Analysis), and then click the **Collapse** button ⊟ to the left of task 4 (Design).

Your screen should look like Figure 3-18. The updated Gantt Chart displays many formatting changes.

| Figure 3-18 | FORMATTED GANTT CHART |

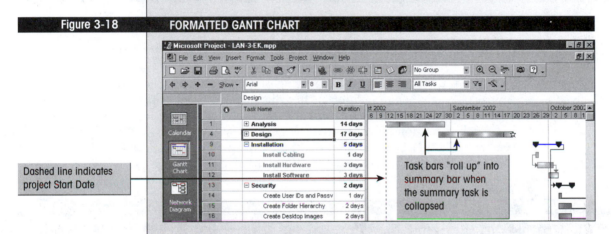

Dashed line indicates project Start Date

Task bars "roll up" into summary bar when the summary task is collapsed

9. Save the **LAN-3-Your Initials.mpp** project file without a baseline to your Data Disk, print the Gantt Chart with your name in the left section of the header, and then close the **LAN-3-Your Initials.mpp** file.

As you have seen, formatting options are available to help you communicate project information to management as you work with Project 2000. You should use these options wisely. Formatting is intended to clearly illustrate the information, as well as to present a pleasing picture of what is going on. You don't want to create a confusing array of lines, colors, and designs. As you work with Project 2000, you will develop personal preferences for the types of formatting that best suit your communication needs.

Session 3.1 QUICK CHECK

1. Why is the critical path important to project managers?

2. Explain how a noncritical task could become a critical task as a project progresses. Use float as part of your answer.

3. What is the purpose of filtering? Name two common filters.

4. Besides using the Gantt Chart Wizard, how else can you format all of the bars of one task type within the Gantt Chart?

5. What steps would you follow to format the text in the Entry table for milestone tasks with a different font face and size?

6. Why must you first select a task or tasks before using the Font or Bar options (but not the Text Styles or Bar Styles options) on the Format menu?

7. Identify four types of gridlines that can be changed using the Gridlines dialog box.

8. Identify three items that can be modified using the Layout dialog box.

SESSION 3.2

In this session, you'll work more with the Network Diagram, the project view that best shows the critical path of the entire project as well as the relationships between tasks. You'll use the Network Diagram to enter and edit tasks and relationships, to expand, collapse, move, and filter tasks, and to format task boxes.

Working with the Network Diagram

The Gantt Chart view and accompanying Entry table are most commonly used to enter the initial task names and durations. After this initial data entry process, however, emphasis often shifts to the Network Diagram because it most clearly identifies the dependencies (also called relationships) between the tasks, as well as the critical path. While both the Gantt Chart and Network Diagram can be used to enter and edit tasks, durations, and dependencies, each has its strengths, as summarized in Figure 3-19.

Figure 3-19	COMPARISON OF THE GANTT CHART AND NETWORK DIAGRAM		
PROJECT 2000 VIEW	**OTHER COMMON NAMES**	**STRENGTHS**	**ACTIONS COMMONLY COMPLETED IN THIS VIEW**
Gantt Chart	■ Bar Chart	■ Displays a sequential listing of task names (in the Entry table). ■ Graphically displays durations as bar lengths. ■ Displays a timeline at the top of the chart that helps communicate approximate task start and finish dates.	■ Entering tasks and durations ■ Editing tasks and durations ■ Moving tasks ■ Linking tasks ■ Updating task completion progress ■ Creating task dependencies ■ Editing task dependencies
Network Diagram	■ PERT Chart ■ Critical Path Diagram	■ Displays relationships between tasks. ■ Displays the critical path.	■ Creating task dependencies ■ Editing task dependencies

Entering and Editing Tasks

While the Gantt Chart is usually the primary view in which to enter and edit tasks, you need to be able to complete basic actions such as entering and editing tasks in any view that you use.

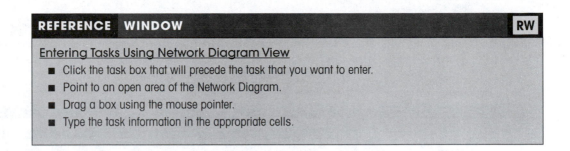

REFERENCE WINDOW **RW**

Entering Tasks Using Network Diagram View

- Click the task box that will precede the task that you want to enter.
- Point to an open area of the Network Diagram.
- Drag a box using the mouse pointer.
- Type the task information in the appropriate cells.

To create a task in the Network Diagram:

1. Open the **LAN-3-2.mpp** file in the Tutorial folder in the folder for Tutorial 3 on your Data Disk, and then save the file as **LAN-3-2-Your Initials** to the Tutorial folder on your Data Disk without a baseline.

2. Click the **Network Diagram** button 🖳 on the View Bar.

Your screen should look like Figure 3-20. Each task is represented by a geometrical shape that is further divided into cells of information that contain the task name, duration, ID, scheduled task start date, scheduled task finish date, and percentage completed. Task boxes are shape- and color-coded. Red boxes indicate a critical task. Summary tasks are displayed in the first column with a Collapse button just above the left edge of the task box.

Figure 3-20 **THE NETWORK DIAGRAM**

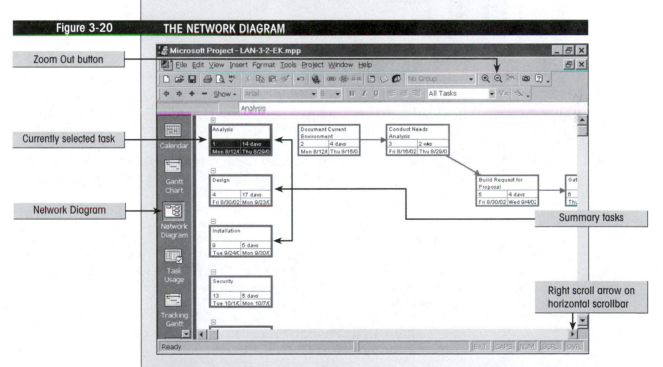

3. Click the **right scroll arrow** on the horizontal scroll bar until the link between task 3 (Conduct Needs Analysis) and task 5 (Build Request for Proposal) is visible in the window.

You need to add a new task, Set Budget, between these two tasks.

4. Click **task 3** (Conduct Needs Analysis) to make it the current task, place the pointer in the **white space** below task 3, press and hold the left mouse button and drag ➕ to draw a rectangle the same size as the box for task 3 as shown in Figure 3-21. You have created a new task.

| Figure 3-21 | CREATING A NEW TASK IN THE NETWORK DIAGRAM |

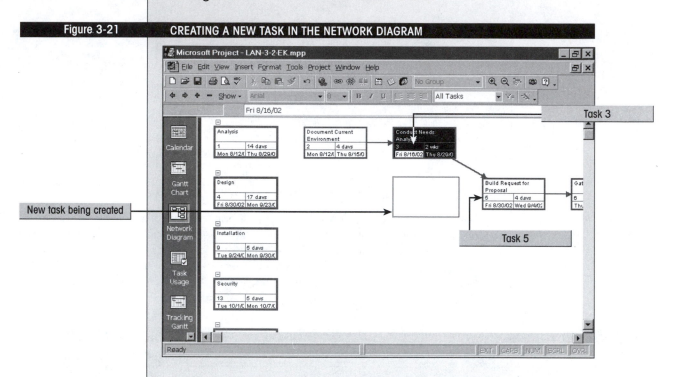

As soon as you release the mouse button, the new task appears below task 2 with an ID of 4. The previous task 5 has been renumbered to become task 6. The project tasks are organized as if you had inserted the task using the Entry table. The new task appears below task 2 instead of task 3 because no relationships are yet set for this task. It currently is scheduled to start at the same time as task 2. The Network Diagram attempts to put task boxes in chronological order according to when they are scheduled. The task shape takes the default format for a noncritical task.

TROUBLE? If you are unsure if the task you entered is correct, you can return to the Gantt Chart view to analyze the project from that familiar standpoint and then return to Network Diagram view. The insertion point is in the Task Name cell of the new task rectangle, ready for you to name the new task. Notice how the Entry Bar above the Network Diagram displays the information as you enter the task information.

5. Type **Set Budget**, press the **Tab** key twice, type **2** as the duration, and then press the **Enter** key.

You have identified the new task and entered a duration, as shown in Figure 3-22.

Figure 3-22   ENTERING A TASK NAME AND DURATION IN THE NETWORK DIAGRAM

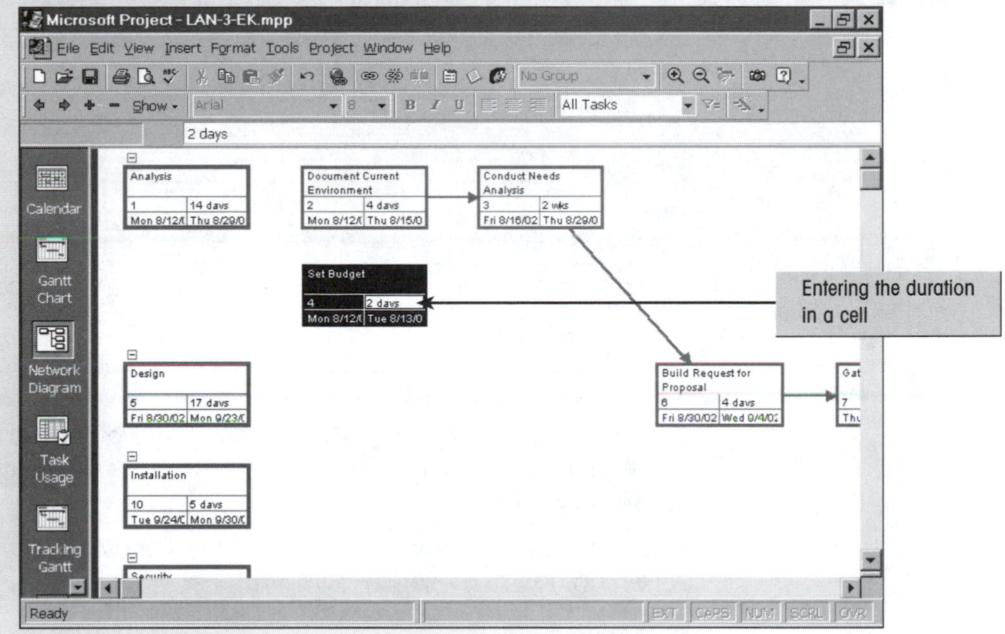

You can click any cell within a task box in the Network Diagram view to enter or edit task information. You can work either directly in the task box or in the Entry Bar. If you double-click a task box, you will open its Task Information dialog box to gain access to all of the fields of information about that task, not just those that are displayed in the task box.

Examining Relationships and the Critical Path

The primary purpose of the Network Diagram is to clearly illustrate the sequential progression of tasks and the critical path. Therefore, project managers often use this view to enter and edit task relationships.

To enter a relationship in the Network Diagram:

1. Click in the middle of **task 3** (Conduct Needs Analysis), drag the ⬚⬚ pointer to the middle of the new **task 4** (Set Budget), and then click **task 3**.

   A link line showing a Finish-to-Start (FS) dependency between tasks 3 and 4 is created, as shown in Figure 3-23. Also task 4 is moved to a new position to indicate that it will start at about the same time as task 6. The color and shape of the task 4 box indicates that it is still not on the critical path.

Figure 3-23   **CREATING A TASK RELATIONSHIP IN THE NETWORK DIAGRAM**

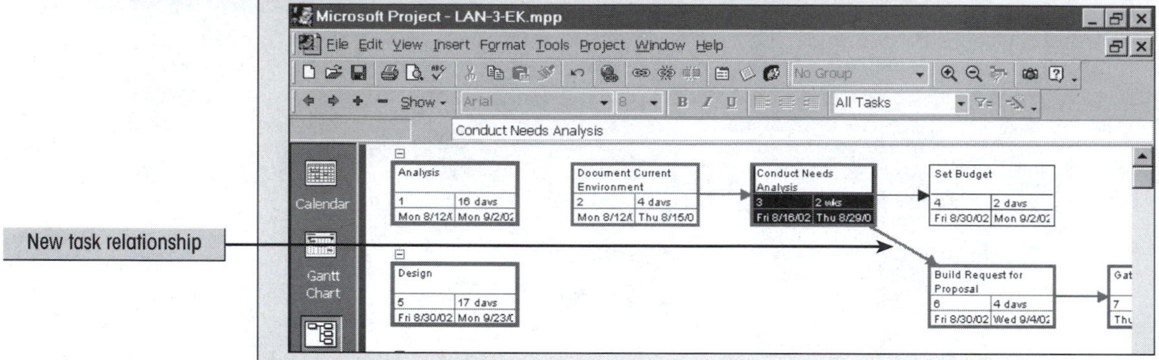

New task relationship

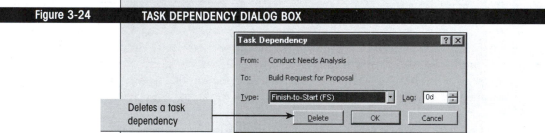

After further analyzing the Network Diagram, you realize that task 6 (Build Request for Proposal) depends on the new task 4 (Set Budget) rather than task 3 (Conduct Needs Analysis).

2. Double-click the **link line** between tasks 3 and 6 to open the Task Dependency dialog box, as shown in Figure 3-24.

Figure 3-24   **TASK DEPENDENCY DIALOG BOX**

Deletes a task dependency

The Task Dependency dialog box displays the task names of the relationship that you are examining. It also allows you to change the relationship type (from FS to SS, FF, or SF), enter lag time, or delete the relationship.

3. Click the **Delete** button.

Deleting this relationship changes the critical path. Now neither task 3 nor 4 is a critical task. This will soon change.

4. Click in the middle of **task 4** (Set Budget), and then drag the ⟨⟩ pointer to the middle of **task 6** (Build Request for Proposal). You have created a Finish-to-Start (FS) dependency between the two tasks.

5. Click the **Zoom Out** button 🔍 on the Standard toolbar as many times as necessary so that you see the linked tasks, and then point to the currently selected task, as shown in Figure 3-25.

Figure 3-25	ZOOMING OUT IN THE NETWORK DIAGRAM

Zoom Out button

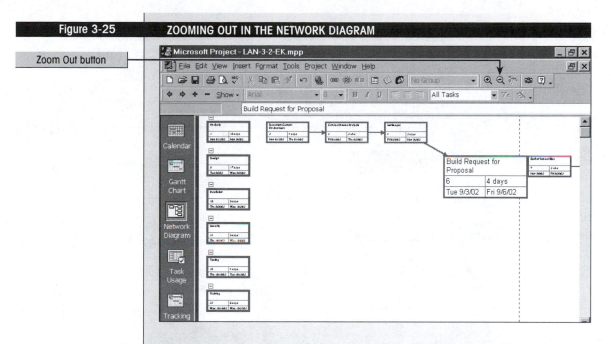

Pointing expanded that task on the screen so that you could read the information.

6. Point to each task box in the Network Diagram to see the details for each.

7. Save the file **LAN-3-2-Your Initials.mpp** without a baseline to your Data Disk.

Because zooming out lets you see more task boxes and thereby obtain a larger perspective on the entire project with less detail about each task, you can read the details of a particular task box by pointing to that task to expand it on the screen.

Expanding and Collapsing Tasks in the Network Diagram

In Network Design view, you can expand and collapse summary tasks by clicking the Expand button ⊞ and Collapse button ⊟, just as you can in the Entry table.

To expand and collapse tasks in the Network Diagram:

1. Click the **Zoom In** button ⊕ twice, scroll to the beginning of the Network Diagram to view the summary tasks in a column on the left side of the window, and then click the **Collapse** button ⊟ for task 1 (Analysis).

Your screen should look like Figure 3-26. Tasks 2, 3, and 4 are now hidden, and the Collapse button for summary task 1 has become an Expand button. The task boxes appear to the right of summary task 5 (Design). All of the other summary tasks are still expanded.

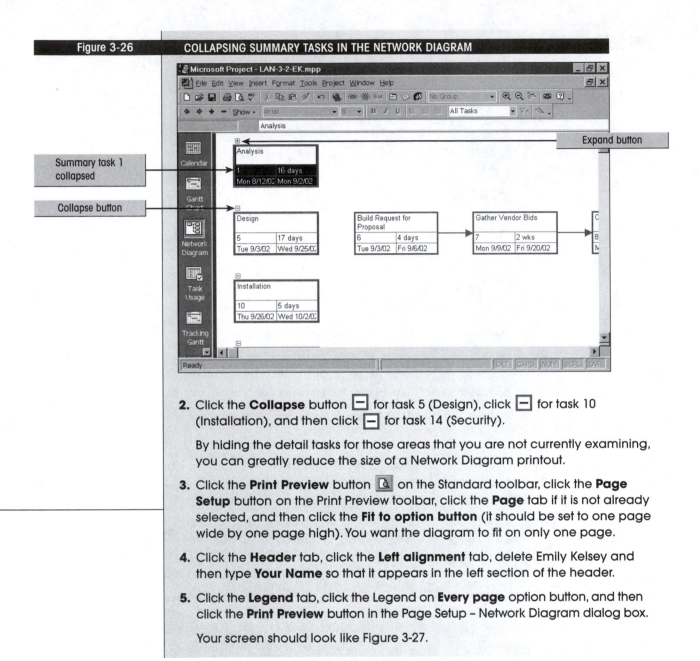

Figure 3-26   COLLAPSING SUMMARY TASKS IN THE NETWORK DIAGRAM

2. Click the **Collapse** button ⊟ for task 5 (Design), click ⊟ for task 10 (Installation), and then click ⊟ for task 14 (Security).

By hiding the detail tasks for those areas that you are not currently examining, you can greatly reduce the size of a Network Diagram printout.

3. Click the **Print Preview** button 🔍 on the Standard toolbar, click the **Page Setup** button on the Print Preview toolbar, click the **Page** tab if it is not already selected, and then click the **Fit to option button** (it should be set to one page wide by one page high). You want the diagram to fit on only one page.

4. Click the **Header** tab, click the **Left alignment** tab, delete Emily Kelsey and then type **Your Name** so that it appears in the left section of the header.

5. Click the **Legend** tab, click the Legend on **Every page** option button, and then click the **Print Preview** button in the Page Setup – Network Diagram dialog box.

Your screen should look like Figure 3-27.

Figure 3-27	PREVIEWING THE NETWORK DIAGRAM

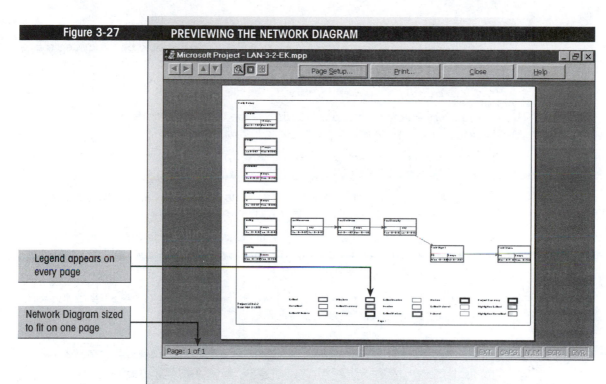

Legend appears on every page

Network Diagram sized to fit on one page

6. Click the **Print** button on the Print Preview toolbar, and then click the **OK** button. The single-page Network Diagram is sent to the printer.

Always try to reduce printouts to a single page, although you don't want to sacrifice legibility for the convenience of a single-page printout.

Moving Tasks

Network Diagram printouts can be quite wide, so you might want to move tasks in order to better arrange them for printouts. You have to consider the purpose of these printouts. If you plan to show them to your colleagues or to management, they must be organized so as to best communicate the information.

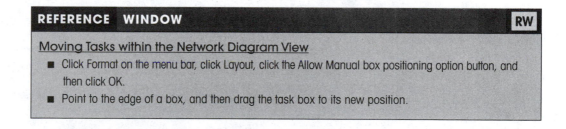

REFERENCE WINDOW   **RW**

Moving Tasks within the Network Diagram View
■ Click Format on the menu bar, click Layout, click the Allow Manual box positioning option button, and then click OK.
■ Point to the edge of a box, and then drag the task box to its new position.

To move tasks in the Network Diagram:

1. Click the **Expand** button ⊞ for **task 1** (Analysis), click the **Expand** button ⊞ for **task 5** (Design), be sure that all other subtasks are collapsed, and then click the **Zoom Out** button 🔍 on the Standard toolbar to view all of the subtasks in the diagram.

TROUBLE? If you are unsure that you have correctly expanded or collapsed the tasks, note that the first two tasks in the column, 1 and 5, should be expanded (have a minus sign) and the rest of the tasks should be collapsed (have a plus sign).

2. Click **Format** on the menu bar, and then click **Layout**.

    The Layout dialog box opens to display the different options available. You want to be able to move the boxes in the window.

3. Click the **Allow manual box positioning** option button, and then click the **OK** button.

    Since tasks 6, 7, 8, and 9 are part of summary task 5, you want to manually position those four tasks on the same row as summary task 5.

4. Place the pointer on the tasks to identify **task 6**, click **task 6**, point to the edge of **task 6**, and then drag it using the move pointer ✛ to the right of summary task 5 (Design), as shown in Figure 3-28.

    TROUBLE? Don't drag the linking pointer. Be sure to point to the edge of the task box and drag with the move pointer.

| Figure 3-28 | MOVING A TASK IN THE NETWORK DIAGRAM |

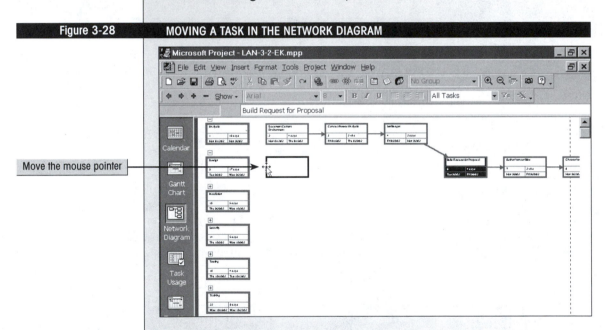

Move the mouse pointer

TROUBLE? If you point to the *middle* of the task rather than the edge, you will expand the task box. Move your mouse away from the task box and try again.

5. Drag tasks 7, 8 and 9 using ✛ so that they line up on the second row to the right of task 5, and then click the **Print Preview** button ▣.

    Your screen should look like Figure 3-29. Scaling is still set to one page wide by one page high, but because the task boxes are organized on two rows, the printout is easier to read.

Figure 3-29	PREVIEWING A NEW TASK BOX ARRANGEMENT

6. Click the **Print** button on the Print Preview toolbar, and then click the **OK** button.

7. Save the project file without a baseline.

Filtering in the Network Diagram

Filtering in the Network Diagram is almost exactly the same as filtering in Gantt Chart view, except that you cannot use the AutoFilter option (which is applied to the columns of the Entry table portion of the Gantt Chart). Filtering is useful for zeroing in on particular aspects of the project based on specified criteria. You want to be able to show Emily the critical tasks of the project at JLB Partners within a specific date range.

To filter tasks in the Network Diagram:

1. Click **Format** on the menu bar, click **Layout**, click the **Automatically position all boxes** option button, and then click the **OK** button to remove manual positioning. Notice that the layout you set up is no longer visible and the Network Diagram places the tasks automatically on one line.

2. Click the **Show** button `Show ▾` on the Formatting toolbar, and then click **All Subtasks** to show all tasks.

3. Click the **Filter** list arrow on the Formatting toolbar, and then click **Date Range**.

4. Type **9/1/2002**, press the **Enter** key, type **9/15/2002**, and then press the **Enter** key. You can see immediately how the filter removed many of the tasks from view.

5. Click the **Zoom In** button to expand the size of the task boxes, and then move the pointer from task to task to read the start and finish dates for each task. Each should start or finish between 9/1/2002 and 9/15/2002.

6. Click the **Filter** list arrow, and then click **All Tasks**.

Filtering only hides tasks from view; it doesn't remove them. Filtering offers a logical view of the project. A logical view is a way of looking at the project, not actually changing the data.

Formatting a Network Diagram

Formatting a Network Diagram is very similar to formatting a Gantt Chart. You can make changes to all of the tasks of one type (for example, Critical, Noncritical, Milestone), or you can format an individual task box. You format all of the tasks of one type using the Box Styles dialog box. Individual task box formatting changes can also be done using the Format Box dialog box. Individual formatting changes override any changes made to the task category. Clicking their corresponding commands on the Format menu opens both the Box Styles and Format Box dialog boxes.

To format tasks within the Network Diagram:

1. Click **Format** on the menu bar, and then click **Box Styles**. The Box Styles dialog box opens. It includes a preview pane to help you as you design the view.

   You use the Box Styles dialog box to format tasks of one type. You want to differentiate the critical summary task boxes from their individual tasks.

2. Click **Critical Summary** if it is not already selected, click the **Shape** list arrow in the Border section, and then click the **second rectangle** in the list, as shown in Figure 3-30.

Figure 3-30	BOX STYLES DIALOG BOX

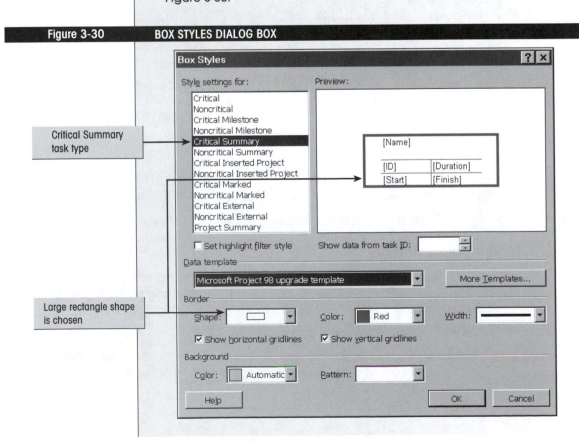

In addition to changing the box shape, you can modify the border color, the border width, the background color, and the background pattern. If your company requires that a standard set of formatting choices be applied to each Network Diagram, you can save the choices as a template and apply the template to other projects.

3. Click the **OK** button.

Each critical summary task is modified with the new task shape.

In addition to formatting all of the tasks of one type, you will often want to format an individual task box to bring attention to it alone. For example, if you are currently working within the first phase of the project, you might want to format the first critical summary task to be different from the rest.

You use the Format Box dialog box to format individual tasks. Because you are formatting an individual task, you must select it before opening the Format Box dialog box.

4. Click the **Zoom In** button 🔍, click **Summary Task 1** (Analysis), click **Format** on the menu bar, and then click **Box**.

The Format Box dialog box opens with the currently selected task displayed in the Preview window.

5. Click the **Color** list arrow in the Background section, click **Yellow**, click the **Pattern** list arrow, and then click the **solid** pattern, as shown in Figure 3-31.

Figure 3-31	FORMAT BOX DIALOG BOX

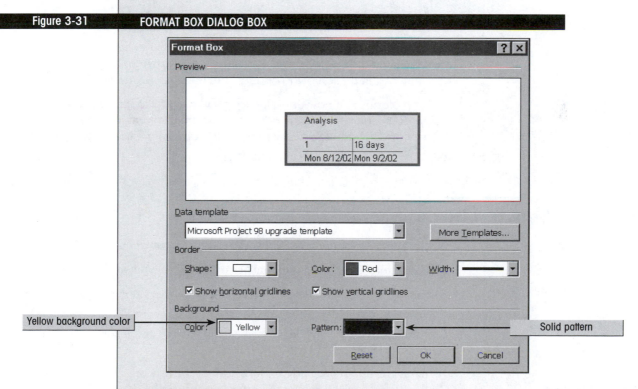

If the project is to be viewed on the computer screen or from a color printout, color can be effectively used to emphasize and clarify information. If you will be distributing the Network Diagram through a printed black and white report, however, you probably want to use different shapes as a means of highlighting certain tasks, since solid colors often print as solid black boxes on a black and white printer or fax machine.

6. Click the **OK** button, and then click **Task 2** (Design) so that you can observe the background color change made to Summary Task 1.

   Your screen should look like Figure 3-32.

| Figure 3-32 | THE FINAL FORMATTED NETWORK DIAGRAM |

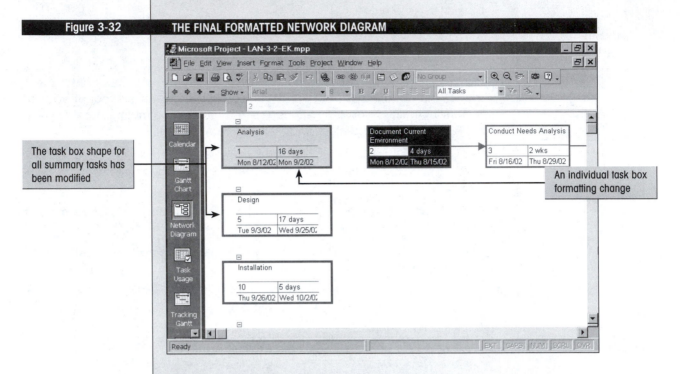

The task box shape for all summary tasks has been modified

An individual task box formatting change

7. Save the project file without a baseline, print the Network Diagram with your name in the left section of the header, and then close **LAN-3-2-Your Initials.mpp**.

   You can clearly see how using the formatting and filtering capabilities of Project 2000 can help you in your efforts to communicate the project information to Emily and the contractors working on the LAN installation at JLB Partners.

Session 3.2 QUICK CHECK

1. What information does the Network Diagram most clearly show?

2. What actions are most commonly performed in the Network Diagram view?

3. If you add a task in the Network Diagram view, how do you know what its task ID will be? (Where in the sequential order of tasks will it be added?)

4. What actions must you take to manually rearrange task boxes in the Network Diagram view?

5. What is the difference between formatting the Network Diagram using the Box Styles dialog box and using the Format Box dialog box?

SESSION 3.3

ity. Now that you've learned how to find, format, and display the critical path, in this session you will use several methods to *crash the path*, that is, shorten the amount of time that it takes to complete a project. You can crash the path by changing task information—by working directly with task durations, task dependencies, or task schedule dates—or by applying additional resources to tasks on the critical path. Creating and applying resources is tackled after the project tasks and dependencies are defined.

Crashing the Critical Path By Using Task Information

Directly modifying the task information for a critical task is the easiest way to crash the path. For example, if a critical task has an initial duration of three days and is modified to be completed in two days, the critical path will automatically be reduced by one day. Important to this discussion, however, is the assumption that any direct change to task information must be a true reflection of reality. To crash the path only for the sake of shortening the project on paper serves no meaningful purpose—it only confuses and stresses out the project participants. Strive to find ways to crash the path by using techniques that can be readily accomplished once the project is started. Refer to Figure 3-33 for different techniques to crash the critical path by directly modifying task information.

Figure 3-33	WAYS TO CRASH THE CRITICAL PATH BY MODIFYING TASK INFORMATION

1. Shorten task durations for critical tasks.

2. Delete finish-to-start (FS) dependencies between two critical tasks.

3. Change finish-to-start (FS) dependencies between two critical tasks to start-to-start (SS) or finish-to-finish (FF) dependencies.

4. Add negative lag time to a finish-to-start (FS) relationship between two critical tasks, thereby allowing the tasks to overlap.

5. Modify the calendar on which the task is based to expand the available working time.

6. Eliminate date constraints, especially those that require that a task start on a particular date.

Changing Task Durations

Probably the quickest way to shorten the critical path is by directly shortening the durations of critical tasks. However, this method, while it works well on paper, in reality must be examined to determine whether the tasks can be accomplished in the shorter time frame.

To crash the path by changing task durations:

1. Open **LAN-3-3.mpp** from the Tutorial folder of your Data Disk for Tutorial 3, click **File** on the menu bar, and then click **Save As** to save the file as **LAN-3-3-Your Initials** without a baseline.

   The file opens to display the Gantt Chart view with only one summary task, Installation, expanded. Four tasks (11, 12, 13, and 14) make up the Installation summary task.

2. Click **Project** on the menu bar, and then click **Project Information**.

Observe the current project Finish Date of 11/8/02. Emily has indicated that the LAN must be installed no later than November 1 to provide a comfortable transition into the new year. You need to crash the path to bring the current Finish Date forward by one week.

3. Click the **OK** button, click the **Filter** list arrow on the Formatting toolbar, and then click **Critical.**

All four tasks within the Installation summary task are still displayed, thereby indicating that they are all critical tasks. You have discussed tasks 13 (Install Hardware) and 14 (Install Software) with your installation subcontractor and have renegotiated the duration to be no more than four days for each task.

4. Click the **Duration** cell for task 13 (Install Hardware), and then click the **down arrow** in the spin box to change the duration to four days.

5. Click the **Duration** cell for task 14 (Install Software), click the **down arrow** in the spin box to change the duration to four days, and then press the **Enter** key.

The duration for both the current task and the Installation summary task change to reflect the shorter duration. Next, check the new scheduled Finish Date for the project.

6. Click **Project** on the menu bar, and then click **Project Information**.

Your screen should look similar to Figure 3-34. Because two days were cut from the durations of critical tasks, the project Finish Date was also cut by two days, to 11/6/02.

Figure 3-34	CRASHING THE PATH BY CHANGING THE DURATION OF TASKS ON THE CRITICAL PATH

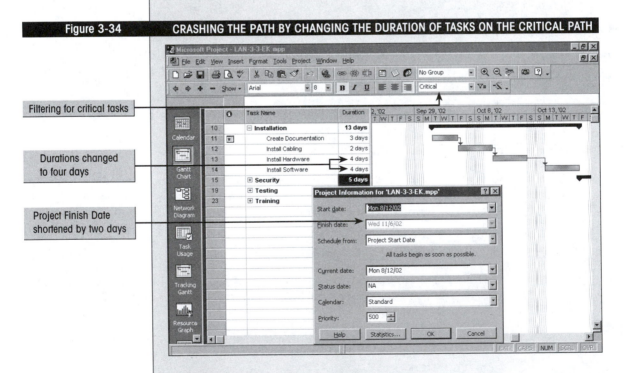

Filtering for critical tasks

Durations changed to four days

Project Finish Date shortened by two days

TROUBLE? The Current date entry (the date as determined by your computer's internal clock or by your LAN) in the Project Information dialog box will be different on your screen than it is in these figures. This date isn't significant unless you are entering tasks (whose start dates, by default, are the Current date) or recording actual progress on an existing project. Later you will learn how to track progress on an existing project and how to work with the Current date in that context.

7. Click the **OK** button, and then save the project without a baseline to your Data Disk.

You have taken two days off of the project's original Finish Date, but you still need to find ways to cut another five days from the schedule in order to please the management at JLB Partners. There are other ways to shorten the critical path that you can explore.

Changing Task Dependencies

Another common way to crash the critical path is to examine and modify task dependencies. Linking tasks in finish-to-start (FS) dependencies is easy using several techniques. Sometimes a finish-to-start (FS) dependency is created when it is not necessary, or when a dependency that requires less total time such as a start-to-start (SS) or finish-to-finish (FF) relationship would be appropriate.

To crash the path by changing task dependencies:

1. Click the **Expand** button ⊞ to the left of summary task 15 (Security).

In reviewing the project with your information systems consultant, you learn that task 16 (Create User IDs and Passwords) does not have to be finished before task 17 (Create Folder Hierarchy) begins. In fact, no relationship exists between the two tasks; they are independent of each other. You only have to consider the fact that they both must be completed during the security phase.

2. Drag ✛ to select **task 16** (Create User IDs and Passwords) and **task 17** (Create Folder Hierarchy), and then click the **Unlink Tasks** button 🔗 on the Standard toolbar.

The dependency between the two tasks is deleted. This results in task 17's being scheduled on the first day of the project because it no longer depends on any predecessor tasks. This in turn extends the duration of the Security phase to 50 days because task 17 is scheduled so much earlier than the other tasks. Task 17 still depends on the software installation task; task 14, so you need to add this dependency to the project.

3. Click **task 14** (Install Software), press and hold the **Ctrl** key as you click **task 17** (Create Folder Hierarchy), and then click the **Link Tasks** button 🔗 on the Standard toolbar.

By making task 17 depend on task 14 instead of task 16, the Security phase is now at four days—and you have shaved one more day off of the critical path.

4. Click **Project** on the menu bar, then click **Project Information**.

The Project Information dialog box indicates that the calculated Finish Date is now 11/5/02. You are well on your way toward the target Finish Date of November 1.

5. Click the **OK** button, and then click **summary task 10** (Installation).

Your screen should look like Figure 3-35.

| Figure 3-35 | CRASHING THE PATH BY DELETING FINISH-TO-START (FS) RELATIONSHIPS |

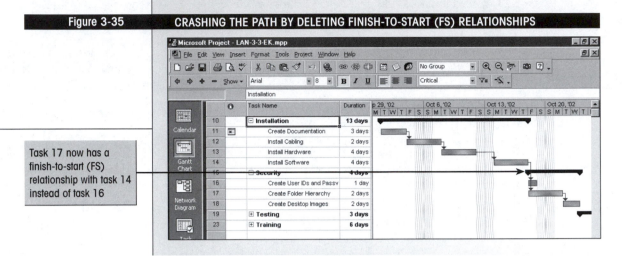

Task 17 now has a finish-to-start (FS) relationship with task 14 instead of task 16

Another technique to crash the path, in addition to deleting unnecessary finish-to-start (FS) relationships, is to add negative lag time to an existing finish-to-start (FS) relationship between two critical tasks. Negative lag time always allows the tasks to overlap, regardless of whether the project is scheduled from a given Start or Finish Date. When a project is scheduled from a given Start Date, negative lag time pulls the second task in the dependency backward in time. This in turn pulls the calculated Finish Date backward. When a project is scheduled from a given Finish Date, negative lag time pushes the first task in the dependency forward in time. This then pushes the calculated Start Date closer to the specified Finish Date.

After further discussions with the Information Systems consultant, you have learned that task 14 (Install Software) can start one day earlier than the finish date of task 13 (Install Hardware). The Installation phase currently has a duration of 13 days. You use negative lag to reflect this.

To crash the path by adding negative lag time:

1. Double-click the **link line** between task 13 (Install Hardware) and task 14 (Install Software) to open the Task Dependency dialog box.

2. Click the **down arrow** in the Lag spin box to change the lag to –1d, and then click the **OK** button.

The Gantt Chart updates to reflect the change in the start of task 14. Because both tasks 13 and 14 were on the critical path, this action also removed one day from the total duration of the project. Installation is now at 12 days.

Yet another way to use dependencies to crash the path is to change the dependency type from finish-to-start (FS) to finish-to-finish (FF) or start-to-start (SS), in which the task durations automatically overlap. You have learned that task 12 (Install Cabling) and task 13 (Install Hardware) can be given a start-to-start (SS) relationship. The hardware technician plans to start one day after the cabling technician starts. Installation is currently at 12 days.

To crash the path by changing the type of dependency:

1. Double-click the **link line** between task 12 (Install Cabling) and task 13 (Install Hardware), click the **Type** list arrow, click **Start-to-Start (SS)**, and then click the **OK** button.

   Without lag time, the tasks start on the same day. You have gained two more days on the project Finish Date, but the new date is not realistic. Enter positive lag time for this relationship to indicate that task 13 starts one day after task 12 starts.

2. Double-click the **link line** between task 12 (Install Cabling) and task 13 (Install Hardware), click the **up arrow** in the Lag spin box to change the lag to 1d, and then click the **OK** button.

   Installation is back up to 11 days, but the changes to the relationships and lag time should have shortened the project's overall duration. Check the Project Information dialog box to determine the effect on the calculated Finish Date.

3. Click **Project** on the menu bar, and then click **Project Information**.

   Your screen should look like Figure 3-36. The Project Information dialog box indicates that the calculated Finish Date is now 11/1/02. You have met your target date.

Figure 3-36	CRASHING THE PATH BY USING LAG TIME AND A START-TO-START (SS) RELATIONSHIP

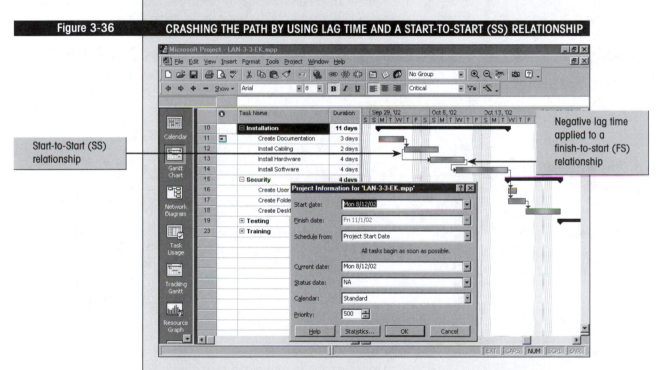

Start-to-Start (SS) relationship

Negative lag time applied to a finish-to-start (FS) relationship

Your efforts have cut several days from the total duration of the project. However, you should always consider all options to bring a project in sooner, to plan for any potential delays. Always check for all ways to crash the path even if you have met the desired Finish Date.

4. Click the **OK** button to close the Project Information dialog box.

5. Save the project file without a baseline.

Changing Calendar and Task Constraints

Because work is performed only during working hours, nonworking hours such as weekends and scheduled holidays extend the project's duration. If you know of a task whose working time does not follow that of the Standard calendar, you should create a special calendar with the appropriate working and nonworking times and assign it to that task.

You notice that task 14 (Install Software) spans a weekend (two nonworking days). Your software vendor is willing to work on Saturday and Sunday afternoons (1:00 PM to 5:00 PM) at no extra expense, so you have created a new calendar called Software Installation Team to apply to that task.

To crash the path by changing the calendar:

1. Click **task 14** (Install Software) in the Entry table, and then click the **Task Information** button 🗒 on the Standard toolbar.

   The Task Information dialog box opens.

2. Click the **Advanced** tab, click the **Calendar** list arrow, and then click **Software Installation Team**, as shown in Figure 3-37. By assigning this calendar to the task, you enable the software installation to occur over the weekend and the project schedule to reflect the work that occurs on those days.

Figure 3-37	ASSIGNING A CALENDAR

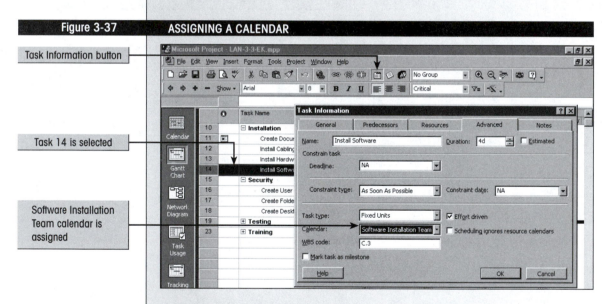

3. Click the **OK** button.

   The Gantt Chart readjusts the length of the bar for task 14 because four hours of work are being completed on Saturday and four hours on Sunday. A calendar indicator icon appears in the Indicators column to alert you to the fact that a special calendar applies to this task.

4. Point to the **calendar indicator** icon for more information about that icon. The ScreenTip confirms that the Software Installation Team calendar is assigned to the task.

Yet another way to crash the path is to analyze and eliminate unnecessary date constraints that have been applied to the tasks within your project. A **constraint** is a restriction that you put on a task's start or finish date. Constraints can extend the overall time to complete a project because they minimize or eliminate some of Project 2000's ability to freely move the scheduled start and finish dates of individual tasks. See Figure 3-38 for a listing of the types of constraints. The table also details the new constraint that Project 2000 automatically applies when you manually enter a task start or finish date in the Entry table.

Figure 3-38	CONSTRAINT TYPES
CONSTRAINT	**DESCRIPTION**
As Soon As Possible	Schedules a task as soon as possible. This is the default constraint for tasks that are entered into a project with an assigned Start Date.
As Late As Possible	Schedules a task as late as possible. This is the default constraint for tasks that are entered into a project with an assigned Finish Date.
Finish No Earlier Than	Schedules the finish date of the task on or after the date that you specify. If the project is scheduled from a Start Date and you enter a finish date into the Entry table for a task, then Project 2000 will automatically apply this constraint type to that task.
Finish No Later Than	Schedules the finish date of the task on or before the date that you specify. If the project is scheduled from a Finish Date and you enter a finish date into the Entry table for a task, then Project 2000 will automatically apply this constraint type to that task.
Start No Earlier Than	Schedules the start date of the task on or after the date that you specify. If the project is scheduled from a Start Date and you enter a start date into the Entry table for a task, then Project 2000 will automatically apply this constraint type to that task.
Start No Later Than	Schedules the start date of the task on or before the date that you specify. If the project is scheduled from a Finish Date and you enter a start date into the Entry table for a task, then Project 2000 will automatically apply this constraint type to that task.
Must Start On	Schedules the start date of a task on the date that you specify.
Must Finish On	Schedules the finish date of a task on the date that you specify.

Some constraints cannot be avoided or changed. For example, if your project contains a task in the middle of the project called Attend Multimedia Conference and that task is scheduled for September 6 through 9, no task that depends on this conference can be started until after September 9, regardless of how fast the first half of the project is completed. Therefore, be very careful about entering date constraints because they will definitely remove some flexibility in recalculating individual task start and finish dates. Fortunately, Project 2000 places an icon in the Indicator column for any constraint other than As Soon As Possible and As Late As Possible to alert you to this situation.

To crash the path by changing constraints:

1. Double-click **task 11** (Create Documentation) to open its Task Information dialog box, and then click the **Advanced** tab (if necessary), as shown in Figure 3-39.

   The Must Start On constraint was previously added with a constraint date of 10/1/02. That was the first day that a new hire who was to create the LAN documentation was to start work at JLB Partners. You have learned, however, that this person can start much earlier than previously assumed and that the constraint can be removed.

| Figure 3-39 | TASK INFORMATION DIALOG BOX SHOWING THE MUST START ON CONSTRAINT |

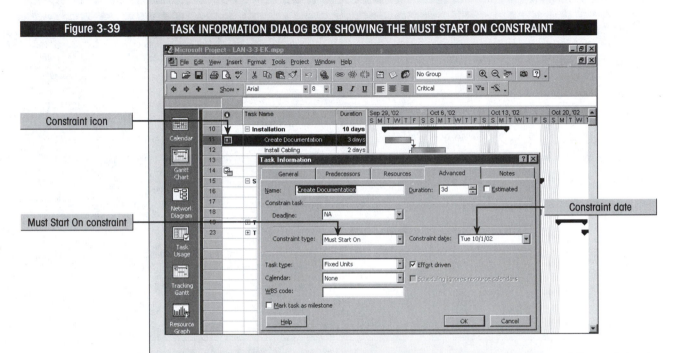

2. Click the **Constraint type** list arrow, click **As Soon As Possible**, and then click the **OK** button. Because of these additional changes to the project's calendar and constraints, you'll want to keep a watchful eye on the project Finish Date.

3. Click **Project** on the menu bar, and then click **Project Information**.

   Your updated project is now predicting a 10/29/02 Finish Date, a few days before the November 1 goal set by management.

4. Click the **OK** button, and then save the project without a baseline.

5. Click the **Filter** list arrow on the Formatting toolbar, click **All Tasks**, click the **Show** button Show ▾ on the Formatting toolbar, and then click **All Subtasks**. You can see all of the subtasks in the project. This quick review confirms that you have done a fine job. The management at JLB Partners will be very pleased with the project plan for the LAN installation.

6. Preview and print the Gantt Chart view with your name in the left section of the header.

   TROUBLE? If the Gantt Chart printout is more than two pages, zoom to an appropriate magnification so that the printout is two pages.

Using **Task Reports**

In addition to standard Gantt Chart and Network Diagram printouts, Project 2000 provides a variety of predeveloped reports. A **report** is a detailed or summarized collection of information about a particular aspect of the project, such as task, resource, cost, date, or progress data. Figure 3-40 lists Project 2000's predefined Overview and Current Activity reports that are useful in the project planning stages. Each of these can be edited to meet your individual needs, thereby making the reporting possibilities almost endless.

Figure 3-40	REPORTS THAT ASSIST PROJECT PLANNING EFFORTS	
CATEGORY	**NAME**	**DESCRIPTION**
Overview	Project Summary	A summary of the project dates, durations, work, costs, and the status of tasks and resources
	Top-Level Tasks	A report on summary tasks
	Critical Tasks	Entry table information about critical tasks (task ID, name, duration, start date, finish date, predecessors, and resources)
	Milestones	Entry table information about milestones
	Working Days	A summary of the working hours for the Standard calendar
Current Activities	Unstarted Tasks	Entry table information about tasks not yet started
	Tasks Starting Soon	Information about tasks between start and finish dates that you specify

To preview an Overview report:

1. Click **View** on the menu bar, and then click **Reports**.

The Reports dialog box appears, as shown in Figure 3-41, displaying the six categories of reports: Overview, Current Activities, Costs, Assignments, Workload, and Custom.

Figure 3-41	REPORTS DIALOG BOX

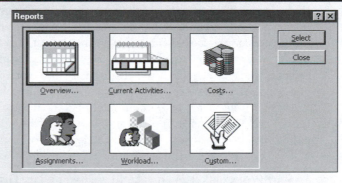

2. Double-click the **Overview** icon.

Five predefined Overview reports are available, as shown in the Overview Reports dialog box. You can select a report as is or customize any to best meet your individual needs.

3. Click the **Top-Level Tasks** icon, and then click the **Select** button.

The Top Level Tasks report appears in a print preview window, listing several columns of information about each summary task. The report is as of today's date.

4. Click the **Page Setup** button, add your name in the left section of the header, and then print the report.

5. Click the **Close** button in the Reports dialog box.

6. Save the project file without a baseline, close **LAN-3-3-Your Initials.mpp**, and then exit Project 2000.

Session 3.3 QUICK CHECK

1. What does "crash the path" mean?

2. Identify five ways to crash the path.

3. What is a constraint?

4. How do constraints relate to the critical path?

5. What are the default constraint types for projects scheduled from both a Start Date and a Finish Date?

6. What are Project reports?

7. List the six report categories.

REVIEW ASSIGNMENTS

Part of the LAN installation will involve training the users. In this assignment, you will open a partially completed project file that documents the training tasks that will be required once the LAN installation is complete at JLB Partners. You will work on formatting the Gantt Chart, work with filters to get a better understanding of the tasks in the project, take a close look at the critical path, and work with the Network Diagram to enter new tasks. You will work with the formatting features and the Gantt Chart Wizard to create a Gantt Chart that better communicates the information about the tasks. You will also format the Network Diagram. You then will use the various techniques for crashing the path to bring in the project sooner. Once you have completed your work on the file, you will use the Reports feature to print a report to share with your colleagues.

1. Start Project 2000 and make sure that your Data Disk is in the appropriate disk drive. Open the **Training-3**.mpp file in the Review folder for Tutorial 3.

2. Use the Save As command to save the project as **Training-3-Your Initials** without a baseline to the Review folder for Tutorial 3 on your Data Disk.

3. Click Project on the menu bar, and then click Project Information. On a piece of paper, record the project's scheduled Finish Date, and then close the Project Information dialog box.

4. Double click Hire trainers, click the Advanced tab in the Task Information dialog box, click the calendar list arrow and apply the Hiring calendar.

5. Filter for critical tasks in the Gantt Chart. On your paper, write down how many tasks (not including summary tasks) are critical.

6. Filter for all tasks, and then click the AutoFilter button and the Custom AutoFilter to filter for those tasks greater than or equal to three days. Print the Gantt Chart view for those filtered tasks, ensuring that your name is in the left section of the header, and then remove the filter.

7. Use the Gantt Chart Wizard to format the Gantt Chart for critical path information. Choose custom task information to display with the Gantt bars, and specify that the duration is to appear on the left side of the bars. Specify that the name is to appear on the left side of the summary and milestone Gantt bars. Show the link lines.

8. Open the Format Bar dialog box for task 6 (Develop contract), and then specify that a diamond shape start and end the bar. This is your way of visually signaling that the company attorney needs to be involved in this task.

9. Click Format on the menu bar, click Text Styles, and then format all critical tasks with an italic font style.

10. Select task 10 (Sign lab contract), click Format on the menu bar, click Font, and change this individual task name to a bold, red font style because you want to draw special attention to it.

11. Double-click the timescale to open the Timescale dialog box, and change the minor scale label to a 1/31/00, 2/1/00 style. Save your work without a baseline.

12. Print the final formatted Gantt Chart view (zoom to a magnification that enables the chart to print on one page only, ensuring that your name is in the left section of the header.

13. Click the Network Diagram button on the View Bar, zoom out until you can see a portion of several pages on the screen, and then click task 4 (Develop Training Documentation). (*Hint*: If you point to a task in the Network Diagram, a ScreenTip appears with more information about that task.)

14. Drag a small box below the selected task 4 to insert a new task 5. The task box will automatically appear below task 2 because it does not depend on any other tasks and can therefore start at the same time that the project starts. Double-click the new task 5 task box to open its Task Information dialog box. Enter Distribute training manual as the task name, and specify a duration of two hours.

15. Drag a link line between task 4 and the new task 5 to link them in a finish-to-start (FS) relationship.

Explore ▷ 16. You want to create a one-page printout of the summary tasks as well as the individual tasks within summary task 1. Move whichever tasks you determine necessary (even the new task) to the first page. Click Format on the menu bar, click Layout, click the Allow manual box positioning option button, and then close the Layout dialog box.

17. Move tasks 4 and 5 down and to the left so that all of the task boxes and linking lines are clearly displayed.

18. Click Format on the menu bar, click Box Styles, and then specify that all of the Critical Summary and Noncritical Summary tasks be given a trapezoidal shape, which is the last shape on the Shape list. Close the Box Styles dialog box.

19. Click the task 2 (Identify existing skills), click Format on the menu bar, and then click Box to format this task box individually. Change the background to yellow, and make the border width as thick as possible.

20. Save the project file without a baseline, click File on the menu bar, and then click Print. Use the Pages option to specify that only page 1 be printed, and print this page of the Network Diagram.

21. Return to Gantt Chart view, double-click the link line between task 2 (Identify existing skills) and task 3 (Identify needed skills), and change the relationship type to Start-to-Start.

22. Change the duration for task 4 (Develop Training Documentation) to four days.

23. Double-click task 8 (Hire trainers), and click the Advanced tab in the Task Information dialog box. Change the calendar to None. (*Note:* The Hiring calendar specified only 20 hours of working time each week.)

24. Double-click the link line between task 3 (Identify needed skills) and task 4 (Develop training documentation), and specify a –50% lag time.

25. Click Project on the menu bar, and then click Project Information. On your paper, record the project's new scheduled Finish Date, and then click the OK button in the Project Information dialog box.

26. Save the file without a baseline. Print the entire Gantt Chart on one page, ensuring that your name is in the left section of the header.

27. Click View on the menu bar, and then click Reports. Double-click the Overview icon, and then double-click the Critical Tasks icon. Print the two-page Critical Tasks report, ensuring that your name is in the left section of the header.

28. Save **Training-3-Your Initials.mpp** without a baseline, close the project file, and then exit Project 2000.

CASE PROBLEMS

Case 1. Building a House You have a part-time job working for BJB Development, Inc., a general contracting company that manages residential construction projects. The manager has been working on the Project 2000 file and has asked you to review it to see if you can format the Gantt Chart and Network Diagram to better communicate the information. You try to help out and to bring the project in earlier than currently scheduled, using the skills that you have learned by working with Project 2000 to format and update some of the task information for the tasks involved in building a new home.

1. Start Project 2000 and make sure that your Data Disk is in the appropriate disk drive. Open the **House-3.mpp** file in the Cases folder for Tutorial 3 on your Data Disk.

2. Use the Save As command to save the project without a baseline as **House-3-Your Initials** to the Cases folder on your Data Disk.

3. Click Project on the menu bar, and then click Project Information. On a piece of paper, record the project's scheduled Finish Date, and then close the Project Information dialog box.

4. Delete the finish-to-start (FS) dependency between task 9 (Roof house) and task 10 (Install insulation). Add a finish-to-start (FS) dependency between task 8 (Frame house) and task 10 (Install insulation).

5. Use the Gantt Chart Wizard to display critical path information. Choose to display dates and link lines with the Gantt bars.

6. Double-click the Gantt bar for task 2 (Secure financing), and then change the middle bar color to green.

Explore ▷ 7. Double-click the Gantt bar for task 8 (Frame house), and then change the Start shape and End shape to the diamond within a circle shape.

8. Double-click the Gantt Chart timescale, and then change the minor scale Count to 7.

9. Save the file without a baseline. Preview and then print the Gantt Chart (it should be one page), ensuring that your name is in the left section of the header.

10. Click the Network Diagram button on the View Bar, zoom out so that you can see a portion of four pages on the screen, and then collapse all summary tasks except task 7 (Exterior).

11. Click Format on the menu bar, click Layout, and then click the Allow manual box positioning option button.

12. Move task 10 (Install insulation) and task 11 (Brick exterior) to the left so that they are directly below task 8 (Frame house) and task 9 (Roof house), respectively.

13. Click Format on the menu bar, and then click Box Styles. Change the Background color of the Noncritical tasks to White.

14. Preview the Network Diagram, and then add your name to the left section of the header. Change the legend so that it prints on every page. Print the Network Diagram.

15. Click the Gantt Chart button on the View Bar, and then show all subtasks.

16. Change the duration for task 8 (Frame house) to 14 days.

17. Add −1d lag to the dependency between task 14 (Install electrical) and task 15 (Install dry wall).

18. Click Project on the menu bar, and then click Project Information. On your paper, record the project's new scheduled Finish Date, and then close the Project Information dialog box.

19. Save **House-3-Your Initials.mpp** without a baseline, close the project file, and then exit Project 2000.

Case 2. Finding a Job You are currently pursuing a new job that utilizes technical skills that you have recently acquired. You continue to work on the Project 2000 file that you are using to organize your job search efforts.

1. Start Project 2000 and make sure that your Data Disk is in the appropriate disk drive. Open the **Job-3.mpp** file in the Cases folder for Tutorial.03 on your Data Disk.

2. Use the Save As command to save the project without a baseline as **Job-3-Your Initials** to the Cases folder for Tutorial 3 on your Data Disk without a baseline.

Explore ▸ 3. Filter the Gantt Chart for critical tasks. On a piece of paper, explain why only one task is on the critical path. Include a definition of the critical path in your explanation, and explain how task 9 relates to that definition.

4. Delete task 9 (Meet with Uncle Ralph), and then refilter for critical tasks.

Explore ▸ 5. On your paper, explain why tasks 1, 2, and 8 are on the critical path now, but they were not the first time that you filtered for critical tasks. (*Hint*: Consider that task 9 was date-constrained and how that created slack for some of the other tasks. With task 9 gone, what happens to the total slack for tasks 1, 2, and 8?)

6. Filter for all tasks, and then save your file without a baseline.

7. Use the Gantt Chart Wizard to display critical path information and custom task information.

8. Specify that the task name is to display on the right side of the Gantt bars, that the Start Date display on the left side of the summary Gantt bar, and that the Finish Date display on the right side of the summary Gantt bars. Do not display any extra information with the milestone symbols. Show link lines.

9. Click Format on the menu bar, and then click Bar Styles to open the Bar Styles dialog box. Change the pattern for both of the first two bars (Task and Critical Task) to the first Pattern choice (clear) in the list.

10. Drag the split bar between the Entry table and the Gantt Chart to the left so that no columns from the Entry table are visible.

11. Click Tools on the menu bar, click Options, click the View tab, click the Project Summary task check box, and then close the dialog box.

12. Save the file, preview the Gantt Chart, add your name to the left side of the header, and then print the Gantt Chart (it should be one page).

Explore ▸ 13. Based on the printout, you see that clear bars don't work that well. Change the bars to an opaque color that you feel works better.

14. In Network Diagram view, filter for critical tasks, click task 1 (Create resume), and then drag a box directly below task 1 to add a new task 2. Double-click task 2, and then enter the name Design a business card and specify a duration of four hours.

15. Drag a link from task 2 (Design a business card) to task 1 (Create resume) so that they are linked in a finish-to-start (FS) relationship.

16. Return to Gantt Chart view, and then drag the split bar to the right so that the Start and Finish columns of the Entry table are visible again.

Explore ▸ 17. In the Entry table, drag task 2 (Design a business card) above task 1 (Create resume) to switch their positions. (*Hint*: Drag the task number to the left of the Entry table to move task positions in the table.) On a piece of paper, explain what happened to the dependency between tasks 1 and 2 when they were moved in the Entry table.

18. Select tasks 1 and 2, and link them in an (FS) relationship.

Explore ▸ 19. Click the Start date for task 1 (Design a business card), click the list arrow, and then click August 7, 2002 on the calendar. On your paper, explain what happened in the Indicators column.

Explore 20. Click the Start date list arrow for task 2 (Create resume), and then click August 9, 2002 on the calendar. On your paper, write down the three options that you are given by the Planning Wizard. Choose the second option, to move the task and keep the link. On your paper, explain why task 1 is no longer on the critical path because of this action.

21. Preview the project in Gantt Chart view. Print the Gantt Chart view with your name in the left section of the header.

22. Save **Job-3-Your Initials.mpp** without a baseline, close the project file, and then exit Project 2000.

Case 3. Planning a Convention In your new job at Future Technology, Inc., you have been asked to help organize the annual convention in which the company will unveil its new product ideas for customers. You have been using Project 2000 to enter and track the many tasks that must be completed for a successful convention. Since the convention *must* occur December 4, 5, and 6 of the year 2002, you scheduled the project from a Finish Date and let Project 2000 determine the project Start Date. Now you need to format the Gantt Chart and Network Diagram to share with your colleagues and work to try to crash the path.

1. Start Project 2000 and make sure that your Data Disk is in the appropriate disk drive. Open the **Convention-3.mpp** file in the Cases folder for Tutorial 3 on your Data Disk.

2. Use the Save As command to save the project file without a baseline as **Convention-3-Your Initials** to the Cases folder for Tutorial 3.

3. Use the Gantt Chart Wizard to display critical path and custom task information. Display the duration on the left side of normal and summary task bars. Display the task name to the left of milestone tasks, and display link lines.

Explore 4. Enter a new task 9 with the name Mail invitations and a duration of three days. Enter a new task 10 with the name Enroll attendees and a duration of three months.

5. Select tasks 8, 9, and 10, and then click the Link Tasks button on the Standard toolbar to create finish-to-start (FS) relationships among them.

6. Click the first task, and then click the Go To Selected Task button on the Standard toolbar to reposition the Gantt Chart to the beginning of the project, if it is not visible.

7. Click Project on the menu bar, and then click Project Information. On a piece of paper, record the project's scheduled Start Date, and then close the Project Information dialog box.

8. Open the Task Dependency dialog box between task 1 (Survey customers) and task 2 (Determine convention goals), and enter a –50% lag.

9. Open the Task Dependency dialog box between task 4 (Set budget) and task 5 (Set agenda) and enter a –50% lag. On your paper, explain which task moves in the schedule when negative lag is applied to a finish-to-start (FS) dependency in a project that is scheduled from a Finish Date.

Explore 10. Open the Format Bar dialog box for task 10 (Enroll attendees), and change the shape of the Middle bar to the third bar from the top of the Shape list (a thin bar).

Explore 11. In Network Diagram view, click Format on the menu bar, click Layout, and then choose the Straight Link style option button. Click the Arrangement list arrow, and then click Top Down by Week. Close the Layout dialog box. Now the task boxes are arranged with each week's tasks in a new column.

12. Save your work without a baseline, and preview the Network Diagram, adding your name to the left section of the header. Print the Network Diagram.

13. Return to Gantt Chart view, and then add a new task 11 with the name Start convention and a duration of 0.

14. Double-click the timescale, and change the minor scale units to weeks.

15. Preview the Gantt Chart, adding your name in the left section of the header.

16. Print the Gantt chart.

17. Click Project on the menu bar, click Project Information, and record the new Finish Date on your paper.

18. Save **Convention-3-Your Initials.mpp** without a baseline, close the project file, and then exit Project 2000.

Case 4. Organizing a Fund-Raiser You have volunteered to lead your neighborhood elementary school's major fund-raising effort to purchase new playground equipment. The equipment must be ready by the time that school starts on September 16, 2002, so you scheduled the project from a Finish Date and let Project 2000 establish the project Start Date. You cannot start this project until August 1, so you have to find ways to crash the path. Also, working with the school district, you want to present attractive reports and printouts to explain the project plan.

1. Start Project 2000 and make sure that your Data Disk is in the appropriate disk drive. Open the **Fund-3.mpp** file in the Cases folder for Tutorial 3 on your Data Disk.

2. Use the Save As command to save the project file as **Fund-3-Your Initials** without a baseline in the Cases folder for Tutorial 3.

3. Click Project on the menu bar, and then click Project Information. On a piece of paper, record the project's scheduled Start Date, and then click the OK button.

4. Use the Gantt Chart Wizard to format critical path information on the Gantt Chart. Do not display any task information on the bars but do show the link lines.

5. You've already spent some time identifying a school sponsor (task 2) as well as researching equipment choices (task 3), so you can shave some time off of both of those tasks. Lower the duration for both by two days each.

6. Change the dependency between task 2 (Identify school sponsor) and task 3 (Research equipment choices) to Start-to-Start.

Explore ▷ 7. Click Tools on the menu bar, and then click Change Working Time. Create a calendar called Volunteer based on the Standard calendar. The volunteers that will build the playground are willing to work on the weekend, so you change both Saturday and Sunday to nondefault working time.

Explore ▷ 8. Specify the Volunteer calendar for task 11 (Build playground).

9. Open the Project Information dialog box, and record the scheduled Start Date. You still need to cut a week out of this schedule because you cannot start the project until August 1.

10. You decide to schedule the installation (task 10) in conjunction with the contractor negotiations (task 9). Change the dependency between tasks 9 and 10 to Finish-to-Finish.

11. Apply the Volunteer calendar to task 9 (Choose contractor).

12. Click Project on the menu bar, and then click Project Information. You should have reached your project Start Date goal.

13 Double-click the timescale, and change the Minor scale Count to 2.

14. Preview the Gantt Chart, add your name to the left section of the Header, and then print the chart.

15. Create and print a report that shows critical tasks. Add your name to the left section of the header, and print the report.

16. Save and close **Fund-3-Your Initials.mpp** without a baseline, and then exit Project 2000.

INTERNET ASSIGNMENTS

The purpose of the Internet Assignments is to challenge you to find information on the Internet so that you can learn more about project management and more effectively use Project 2000. The actual assignments are updated and maintained on the Course Technology Web site. Log on to the Internet, and use your Web browser to go to the Student Online Companion that accompanies this text at **www.course.com/ NewPerspectives/Project2000**. Click the link for Tutorial 3.

QUICK | CHECK ANSWERS

Session 3.1

1. Because the critical path represents the shortest amount of time required to complete a project, project managers are constantly analyzing it to make sure that those tasks are completed on time.

2. Tasks that compose the critical path often change as a project is being completed. For example, if a noncritical task has a float of one day but has not been started two days after its scheduled start date, it will become a critical task.

3. Filtering is used to display only those tasks that meet certain criteria in order to better clarify and communicate information about the project. Filtering for critical, summary, milestone tasks, or tasks within a certain date range are all common.

4. You can use the Bar Styles dialog box to format all of the bars of one task type.

5. Click the Format menu, and then click Text Styles. The Text Styles dialog box allows you to change the text formatting for all milestone tasks at the same time.

6. Both the Font and Bar options on the Format menu format individual tasks, not categories of tasks. Therefore, you must select which tasks you want to format before using those menu options. The Text Styles and Bar Styles options apply to categories of tasks, so you do not need to first select the task or tasks that you want to change.

7. Gantt Rows, Bar Rows, Major Columns, Minor Columns, Current Date, Sheet Rows, Sheet Columns, Tile Vertical, Tile Horizontal, Page Breaks, Project Start, Project Finish, Status Date

8. Link arrows, bar date format, bar height, whether or not Gantt bars are rolled up into summary bars, bar rounding, bar splits, and whether or not drawings are shown

Session 3.2

1. The Network Diagram most clearly communicates information about dependencies between tasks as well as the critical path.

2. The Network Diagram is commonly used to create and edit task dependencies.

3. Tasks added in Network Diagram view are inserted after the currently selected task. For example, if task 3 is selected, the new task will become task 4 and every other task after task 4 will increment by one.

4. First, click the Format menu, click the Layout option, click the Allow Manual box positioning option button, and then click OK. Then, point to the edge of a box and drag the task box to its new position.

5. The Box Styles dialog box provides a way to format all of the tasks of one type (for example, critical or milestone) in the same way. The Format Box dialog box provides a way to format a single task box.

Session 3.3

1. "Crash the path" means to shorten the amount of time that it takes to complete a project. It requires analyzing those tasks that are on the critical path and determining ways to complete those tasks faster.

2. Ways to crash the path:
   - Shorten task durations for critical tasks.
   - Delete finish-to-start dependencies between two critical tasks.
   - Change finish-to-start dependencies between two critical tasks to start-to-start or finish-to-finish.
   - Add negative lag time to a finish-to-start relationship between two critical tasks, thus allowing the tasks to overlap.
   - Modify the calendar on which the task is based to expand the available working time.
   - Eliminate date constraints, especially those that require a task to start on a particular date.

3. A constraint is a restriction that you put on a task's start or finish date.

4. Constraints can extend the overall time to complete a project because they minimize or eliminate some of Project 2000's ability to freely move the scheduled start and finish dates of individual tasks.

5. Default constraint types:
   - As Soon As Possible: Schedules a task as soon as possible. This is the default constraint for tasks that are entered into a project that has a given Start Date.
   - As Late As Possible: Schedules a task as late as possible. This is the default constraint for tasks that are entered into a project that has a given Finish Date.

6. Reports are detailed or summarized information about a particular aspect of the project, such as task, resource, cost, date, or progress information.

7. There are six report categories: Overview, Current Activities, Costs, Assignments, Workload, and Custom.

ASSIGNING RESOURCES AND COSTS

Scheduling Resources and Determining Costs for the LAN Installation

CASE

JLB Partners

You have created a Project 2000 file that contains the tasks, durations, and dependencies necessary to install the local area network (LAN) for the CPA firm, JLB Partners. To complete the project, you need to hire contractors, purchase equipment, and commit resources and costs to accomplish the tasks. Emily Kelsey, the managing partner, has asked you to expand the information that you report to her to include resource management information and project cost data. You'll accomplish this by entering, scheduling, and analyzing resource and cost information in the project file.

SESSION 4.1

In this session, you will work with resource and cost views to enter, edit, and group resources within a project file.

Entering Resource and Cost Data

A significant component to planning and managing your project is accurately controlling and tracking cost and resource data. A **cost** is an expenditure made to accomplish a task. It includes both variable and fixed costs. **Variable costs** are determined by the number of resource units assigned to a task as well as the hourly or per use cost for that resource. Variable costs can be associated with labor costs or material consumable resources. **Fixed costs** are expenses such as insurance, a legal fee, or a travel expense that are associated with a task but do not vary according to the length of the task or the number of resources assigned to the task. After establishing costs, you can prepare to track and manage them so that your project stays within the budget. The **budget** is the amount of money based on estimated costs that you have allocated for the project. A **resource** is the person(s) equipment, or materials used to complete a task in a project. You can enter resource and cost data about a project in many different project views, but for the initial data entry effort, the **Resource Sheet** view shown in Figure 4-1 is commonly used. Like all sheet views, the Resource Sheet view presents information in an easy-to-use row and column format. In this case, each row represents a different resource and each column represents a field of information about the resource.

Figure 4-1   RESOURCE SHEET VIEW

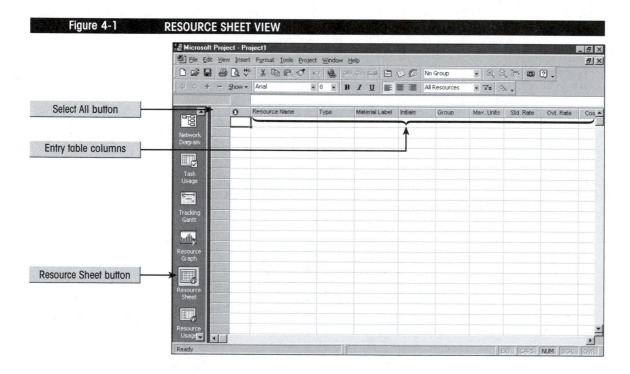

The table that is currently applied determines the columns displayed within the sheet. By default, the Entry table is applied to the Resource Sheet. The Entry table's columns are the fields of information used to enter new resources. See Figure 4-2 for a description of the fields presented by the Entry table.

Figure 4-2	FIELDS PRESENTED BY THE ENTRY TABLE APPLIED TO THE RESOURCE SHEET
FIELD	**DESCRIPTION**
Indicator	A calculated field that automatically displays small icons to represent various conditions about the resource. For example, a **note icon** indicates that an associated note is stored about the resource. An **exclamation point icon** means that the resource needs to be **leveled**, a process that reconciles resource overallocations. An **overallocation** occurs when a resource has been assigned more work than it can complete on a given day. (By default, a working day consists of eight hours of work, as defined by the Standard calendar.)
Resource Name	Stores the resource name entered by the user.
Type	Specifies whether the resource is a **Work (hourly) resource** or **Material (consumable) resource**, and is used to filter and find Work and Material resources. Resources such as people, rooms, and equipment that have associated hourly costs are Work types. Resources such as building materials or supplies are Material types. Work and Material are the only two choices for the Type field.
Material Label	Stores a material label value that can be displayed and printed on various views and reports.
Initials	Stores an initials entry that can be used to identify resources instead of the longer entry in the Resource Name field.
Group	Stores an entry by which the user can define groups of resources. For example, you might want to group all management, subcontractor, department, or union resources together with the same entry in the Group field for later filtering, finding, and reporting purposes.
Max. Units	Determines the maximum number of units or portion of a unit of the resource that is available for the project. By default, the Max. Units field is 100%. If a resource is available on, for example, a half-time basis, the entry will be 50%. If the resource entry represents two people (for example, two electricians) or two items (two trucks), the entry will be 200%.
Std. Rate	The standard hourly rate for a single resource of that type. By default, the Std. Rate and Ovt. Rate entries are costs per hour. You can override this assumption by entering the value and a new unit of measure as follows: /m (per minute), /d (per day), /w (per week), /mon (per month), or /y (per year).
Ovt. Rate	The overtime hourly rate for a single resource of that type.
Cost/Use	The one-time cost per use for a single resource of that type. This cost may be used with or instead of hourly charges. For example, some resources might charge a flat fee for a service regardless of the number of hours of service that are rendered. An initial consultation with an attorney or physician might fit into this category. Other resources, such as a rental car, might charge a minimum fee plus a daily or hourly rate.
Accrue At	Determines when the costs associated with that resource will be applied to any task to which it has been assigned. Three choices are available for this field: Start, Prorated, and End. Prorated is the default entry.
Base Calendar	Determines which base calendar that the resource calendar uses to determine working and nonworking time. By default, Project 2000 provides three base calendars (Standard, Night Shift, and 24 Hours). Standard is the default choice for the Base Calendar field.
Code	Contains any code, number, or abbreviation that you want to enter to help identify that resource. Often used to identify the resource's cost center.

Other tables (Cost, Hyperlink, Summary, Usage, and Work) can be applied by right-clicking the sheet's Select All button, and then choosing the appropriate table from the shortcut menu.

You can display the Resource Sheet view by scrolling down the View Bar and clicking the Resource Sheet button or by clicking View on the menu bar and then clicking Resource Sheet.

<u>Entering and Editing Resources</u>

■ Click the Resource Sheet button on the View Bar, or click View on the menu bar and then click Resource Sheet, to display the Resource Sheet view.

■ Right-click the Select All button, and then click Entry to apply the Entry table columns.

■ Enter each resource in its own row in the Resource Sheet. Enter individual fields of data for each resource directly within their corresponding cells at the intersection of each row and column on a sheet by clicking the cell and then typing in the Entry Bar, or by clicking a choice from the cell's drop-down list.

You have the list of resources that you will be using. Use the Resource Sheet view to enter and edit several resources that later will be assigned to individual tasks within the LAN project.

To enter resources in the Resource Sheet view:

1. Start Project 2000 and open the **LAN-4.mpp** file stored in the Tutorial folder of your Data Disk for Tutorial 4. The project file opens in Gantt Chart view and includes all 19 linked tasks in six phases.

2. Click **File** on the menu bar, click **Save As**, click the **Save in** list arrow to find the Tutorial folder for Tutorial 4 or your Data Disk, and then save the file without a baseline with the name **LAN-4-Your Initials**.

3. Click the **View Bar** down arrow button, and then click the **Resource Sheet** button 🖼 on the View Bar.

4. Point to the **Select All** button. The ScreenTip tells you that the Entry table is applied, that this is the Resource Sheet view, and that you right-click to select and change tables.

5. Enter the five resources shown in Figure 4-3. (*Note*: The columns of the Resource Sheet have been narrowed so that all of the columns are visible except for the last column, Code. The Code column does not contain an entry for any of the five resources.) Be sure to enter your name and initials in the second resource row.

   TROUBLE? Since the default unit of measure is hours in the cost fields, be sure to enter 150/d (to enter $150 per day instead of per hour) in the Std. Rate fields for the Laptop and PC Viewer resources. You might also need to resize some of the columns to view all of the data.

Figure 4-3   FIVE RESOURCES ENTERED INTO THE RESOURCE SHEET

Enter your name and initials in the second row

Cost per day

		Resource Name	Type	Material Label	Initials	Group	Max. Units	Std. Rate	Ovt. Rate	Cost/Use	Accrue At	Base Cal
	1	Emily Kelsey	Work		EK	Mgmt	100%	$100.00/hr	$100.00/hr	$0.00	Prorated	Standard
	2	Your Name	Work		YN	PM	100%	$50.00/hr	$50.00/hr	$0.00	Prorated	Standard
	3	Laptop	Work		Lap	Equip	200%	$150.00/day	$0.00/hr	$100.00	Prorated	Standard
	4	PC Viewer	Work		PCV	Equip	100%	$150.00/day	$0.00/hr	$100.00	Prorated	Standard
	5	General Labor	Work		G	Labor	500%	$20.00/hr	$30.00/hr	$0.00	Prorated	Standard

Greater than 100%   Cost per use

You edit entries in the Resource Sheet view by clicking the cell that you want to edit and then making the change directly from the keyboard or choosing the option from the drop-down list. The entry in the **Cost/Use** field is the charge made for the resource regardless of how many hours it is used (rooms and equipment commonly have a cost per use fee). The entry in the **Max. Units** field is the total number of items of that resource that are available, specified as a percentage. You need to edit the General Labor resource.

To edit resources in the Resource Sheet view:

1. Click **Labor** in the Group column for the General Labor resource in row 5, type **Temp**, and then press the **Enter** key. This creates a group named Temp that will be used to track and report on all temporary resources (people) that are hired for this project.

2. Click **Prorated** in the Accrue At column for the Laptop resource in row 3, click the **Prorated** list arrow, and then click **Start**.

   The rental costs associated with this resource must be paid up front, so this change more accurately reflects the costs that have been committed for that task.

3. Click **Prorated** in the Accrue At column for the PC Viewer resource in row 4, click the **Prorated** list arrow, and then click **Start**.

   You also must pay for the PC Viewer at the time of rental.

4. Enter the Receptionist resource in row 6, as shown in Figure 4-4. The Code column to the far right of the Entry table does not contain an entry.

Figure 4-4	EDITING RESOURCES IN THE RESOURCE SHEET

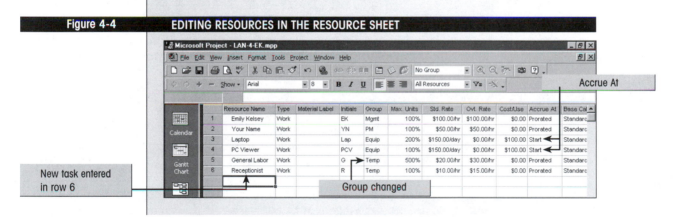

The Resource Sheet has six resources entered, and the necessary corrections have been made.

Using the Resource Information Dialog box

The **Resource Information** dialog box is a comprehensive collection of all of the data stored for a single resource. It is analogous to the Task Information dialog box for a task and is opened either by double-clicking a resource or by clicking a resource and then clicking the Resource Information button on the Standard toolbar.

To open the Resource Information dialog box:

1. Double-click **Receptionist** (resource 6). The Resource Information dialog box opens, as shown in Figure 4-5. It contains four tabs (General, Working Time, Costs, and Notes) to organize the fields of information about that resource.

| Figure 4-5 | RESOURCE INFORMATION DIALOG BOX |

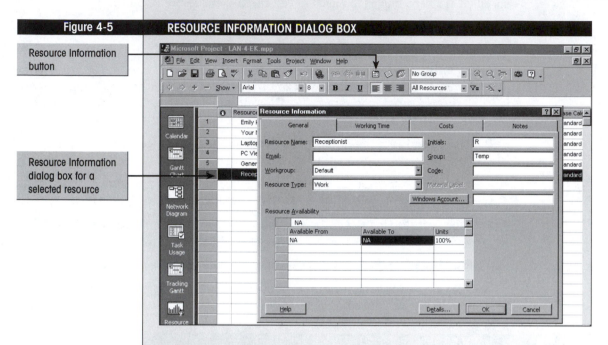

Resource Information button

Resource Information dialog box for a selected resource

2. Click the **Working Time** tab, click the **Costs** tab, click the **Notes** tab, and then click the **General** tab. Each tab provides specific information about the selected resource.

3. Click the **Cancel** button.

Some fields of resource information, such as e-mail, resource availability dates, cost rate tables, and notes, are available only within the Resource Information dialog box. A **resource availability date** documents when a resource unit grows or shrinks. For example, you might want to make an individual available to a project only 50% of the time during a particular portion of the project. Or, you might be purchasing additional units of an existing resource midway through the project. If you were purchasing an additional truck, for example, you could expand the number of units of truck resources to correlate with the delivery date for the new truck.

Cost Rate Tables

A **cost rate table** is a grid of different hourly and per use costs that can be stored for a single resource. For example, you might want to apply three rate tables to the same programmer. The programmer might charge $150/hour for C++ programming, $120/hour for HTML programming, and $100/hour for meeting time. By storing these different rates in the project, you can apply the same resource to many different tasks but the costs associated with that resource will be calculated according to the chosen rate.

You edit resource information to make changes to the e-mail, notes, resource availability date, and cost rate table fields using the Resource Information dialog box.

To use the Resource Information dialog box:

1. Double-click **Emily Kelsey** (resource 1). The Resource Information dialog box opens. You want to record Emily's resource information.

2. Click the **General** tab (if not already selected), click the **Email** text box, and then type **ekelsey@jlb.com** as Emily's e-mail address. Her e-mail address is recorded along with her other information.

   You also want to be sure to track all vacation time.

3. Click the **Working Time** tab, click the **calendar** scroll bar to display September 2002, drag from **September 9** through **11**, and then click the **Nonworking time** option button to mark three days of vacation for Emily. You also want to be able to reach Emily when she's out of the office, so you store her cell phone number along with the other resource information.

4. Click the **Notes** tab, type **Emily's cellular phone is 555-4422**, and then click the **OK** button.

5. Click **General Labor** (resource 5), click the **Resource Information** button 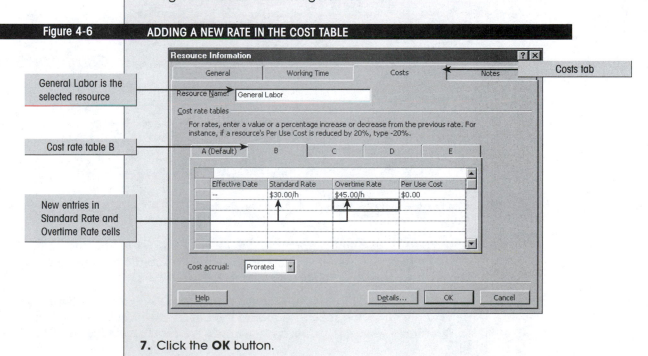 on the Standard toolbar, and then click the **Costs** tab.

   General Labor is a resource that will be contracted from HelpMeRita, a temporary agency, for a variety of tasks during the installation of the LAN, such as moving furniture and installing software. The agency has two different cost rates that will apply depending on the nature of the work. The default standard rate of $20 per hour and $30 per overtime hour apply to labor-intensive tasks. You need to enter a higher rate for more technically challenging work such as installing software and testing passwords. The Cost rate tables are organized by tabs on the Cost tab.

6. Click the **B** tab, click the first **Standard Rate** cell, type **30**, click the **Overtime Rate** cell, type **45**, and then press the **Enter** key. Your Resource Information dialog box should look like Figure 4-6.

Figure 4-6	ADDING A NEW RATE IN THE COST TABLE

Resource Information

General Labor is the selected resource

| General | Working Time | Costs | Notes | → Costs tab |

Resource Name: General Labor

Cost rate tables

For rates, enter a value or a percentage increase or decrease from the previous rate. For instance, if a resource's Per Use Cost is reduced by 20%, type -20%.

Cost rate table B

| A (Default) | B | C | D | E |

Effective Date	Standard Rate	Overtime Rate	Per Use Cost
--	$30.00/h	$45.00/h	$0.00

New entries in Standard Rate and Overtime Rate cells

Cost accrual: Prorated

| Help | | Details... | OK | Cancel |

7. Click the **OK** button.

Resource Availability

Another change that you might want to make using the Resource Information dialog box concerns a change to a resource's availability or cost midway through the project.

To change a resource's capability:

1. Double-click **Your Name** (resource 2), and then click the **General** tab. JLB Partners is involved in a local charity that inspects and repairs furnaces for the elderly. It has given you permission to spend 50% of your time with this charitable organization during the month of December as a corporate donation of time.

2. Click the first **Available From** cell in the Resource Availability section, click the **list arrow**, click the **Calendar** arrow to display December 2002, and then click **1** on the December 2002 calendar.

   You can also use the Entry Bar to make changes within many Project 2000 dialog boxes.

3. Click the first **Available To** cell, click in the **Entry Bar** above the NA entry, press the **Backspace** key twice to delete NA, and then type **1/1/2003**, as shown in Figure 4-7.

Figure 4-7	CHANGING RESOURCE AVAILABILITY

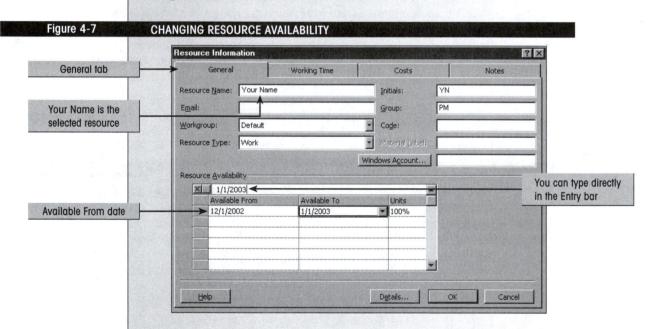

4. Click the first **Units** cell that currently displays 100%, type **50%**, and then press the **Enter** key.

   You have also learned that on January 1, 2003, you will be assigned a new internal rate for all internal projects. You want to record that information in this project in case the project extends into 2003.

5. Click the **Costs** tab, click the **Effective Date** cell in the second row, type **1/1/2003**, click the second **Standard Rate** cell, type **60**, click the second **Overtime Rate** cell, type **60**, and then press the **Enter** key, as shown in Figure 4-8.

Figure 4-8   **ENTERING THE NEW RATE**

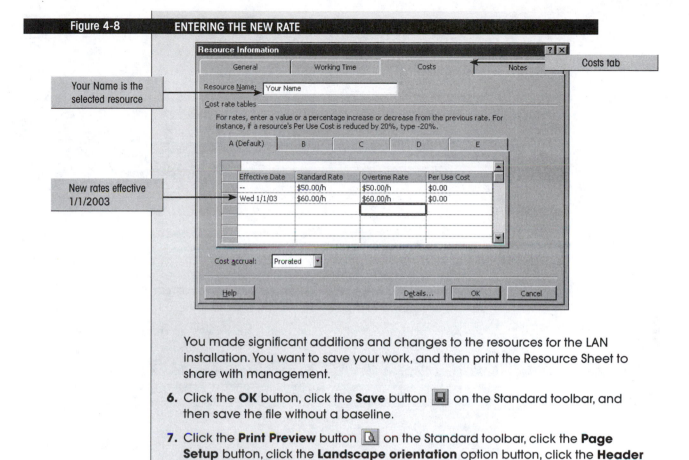

You made significant additions and changes to the resources for the LAN installation. You want to save your work, and then print the Resource Sheet to share with management.

6. Click the **OK** button, click the **Save** button 🖫 on the Standard toolbar, and then save the file without a baseline.

7. Click the **Print Preview** button 🔍 on the Standard toolbar, click the **Page Setup** button, click the **Landscape orientation** option button, click the **Header** tab, delete the code in the Center section, type **Your Name** in the left section, and then print the **Resource Sheet.**

Entering resource information into a project is a considerable effort. As you have seen, you can track many fields of information about each resource. Fortunately the most commonly used fields are presented in the Entry table of the Task Sheet. The others, such as e-mail, availability schedules, cost rate tables, and notes, are found by opening the Resource Information dialog box. After the resource data has been entered, you can start assigning resources to specific tasks. Project 2000 automatically calculates task costs by multiplying task durations by the cost information supplied for each resource.

Assigning **Resources to Tasks**

Project 2000 is designed to give you great flexibility in the way that you enter data. Many methods are available to assign resources to specific tasks. The fastest method uses the Assign Resources button 👤 on the Standard toolbar. You can also use a split screen view that shows both task and resource information at the same time. When assigning resources in a split screen arrangement, you usually position the Gantt Chart at the top of the screen and a resource form at the bottom. Seasoned project managers often prefer this approach because it provides more information about the actual hours of work being assigned to each task. You'll use both techniques to assign resources to tasks.

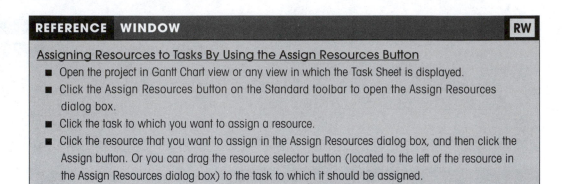

REFERENCE WINDOW   **RW**

<u>Assigning Resources to Tasks By Using the Assign Resources Button</u>

- Open the project in Gantt Chart view or any view in which the Task Sheet is displayed.
- Click the Assign Resources button on the Standard toolbar to open the Assign Resources dialog box.
- Click the task to which you want to assign a resource.
- Click the resource that you want to assign in the Assign Resources dialog box, and then click the Assign button. Or you can drag the resource selector button (located to the left of the resource in the Assign Resources dialog box) to the task to which it should be assigned.

To make resource assignments using the Assign Resources dialog box:

1. Click the **Gantt Chart** button ⊞ on the View Bar, and then click the **Assign Resources** button 🔘 on the Standard toolbar.

   The Assign Resources dialog box opens, as shown in Figure 4-9.

Figure 4-9	ASSIGN RESOURCES DIALOG BOX

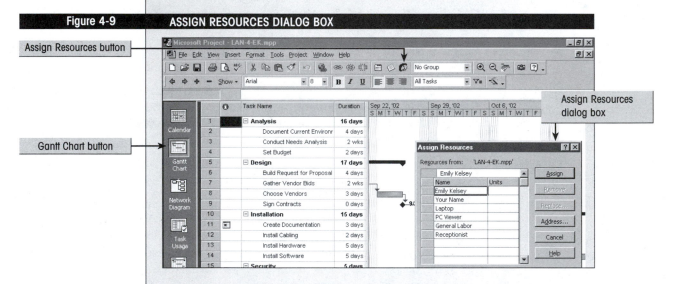

You can use the Assign Resources dialog box to assign resources to a task or to enter new resources (although the Resource Sheet is the preferred way of entering new resources because it provides so many more columns in which to enter information about a new resource). Double-clicking a resource in the Assign Resource dialog box opens the Resource Information dialog box, in which you edit existing resources.

2. Click **Document Current Environment** (task 2), click **Your Name** in the Assign Resources dialog box, click the **Assign** button in the Assign Resources dialog box, and then click the **Go To Selected Task** button 🐎 on the Standard toolbar. The Gantt Chart is positioned on task 2, as shown in Figure 4-10.

| Figure 4-10 | ASSIGNING YOUR NAME TO TASK 2 |

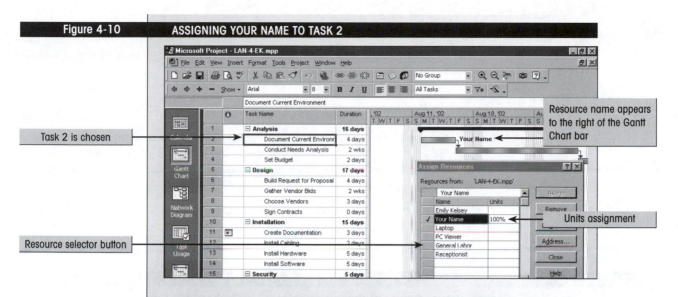

A check mark appears in the resource selector button for Your Name because you have been assigned to the chosen task. The resource is assigned at a 100% units level unless you specify something different. The Gantt Chart displays resource names to the right of the task bar (by default), but you can change this formatting choice by using the Gantt Chart Wizard or by choosing the Bar Styles option from the Format menu.

Now make a resource assignment by dragging the resource selector button to a task.

3. Point to **Your Name's resource selector** button in the Assign Resource dialog box so that the mouse pointer changes to ▟, and then drag ▟ to **Conduct Needs Analysis** (task 3) in the Task Entry table.

Your Name has also been assigned to task 3 at a 100% units level. You can assign more than one resource to a task at the same time.

4. Click **Set Budget** (task 4), click **Emily Kelsey** in the Assign Resources dialog box, press and hold the **Ctrl** key, click **Your Name**, click the **Assign** button, and then click the **Go To Selected Task** button ⧉ on the Standard toolbar to position the Gantt Chart on task 4.

Both you and Emily have been assigned to task 4, and both of your names appear to the right of the task bar in the Gantt Chart.

The maximum unit of a person is obviously 100%, but some resources consist of more than one unit that can be applied to a task. You have five general labor units available for assignment to various tasks in this project.

5. Click **Install Software** (task 14), click the **Units** cell for General Labor in the Assign Resources dialog box, type **200%**, click the **Assign** button, and then click the **Close** button to close the Assign Resources dialog box.

Two general labor workers have been assigned to the duration of the Install Software task.

Assigning a New Rate Table

Recall that there are two labor rates for general labor. You want to change the rate table for this assignment to the higher cost rate.

To change a rate table for a task using the Task Usage view:

1. Click the **Task Usage** button ⊞ on the View Bar. The **Task Usage** view shows tasks with assigned resources indented within each task on the left and the number of hours of each resource that is assigned to each task in a day-by-day format on the right.

2. Click **General Labor** (the resource assigned to task 14), and then click the **Go To Selected Task** button ☞ to position the usage details on task 14, as shown in Figure 4-11.

Figure 4-11	TASK USAGE VIEW

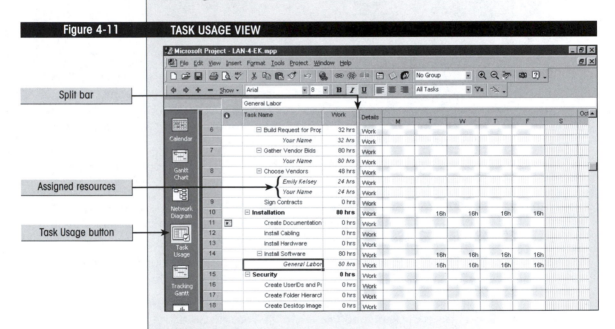

TROUBLE? If your screen does not match the figures, you might need to drag the split bar left or right.

3. Double-click **General Labor** to open the Assignment Information dialog box, and then click the **General** tab (if it is not already selected).

   The Assignment Information dialog box contains all of the information regarding the resource assignment, including the cost rate table used for this assignment. Notice, too, that the cost is currently calculated at $1,600 (80 hours at $20/hour).

4. Click the **Cost rate table** list arrow, and then click **B.** Your dialog box should look like Figure 4-12.

Figure 4-12	ASSIGNMENT INFORMATION DIALOG BOX

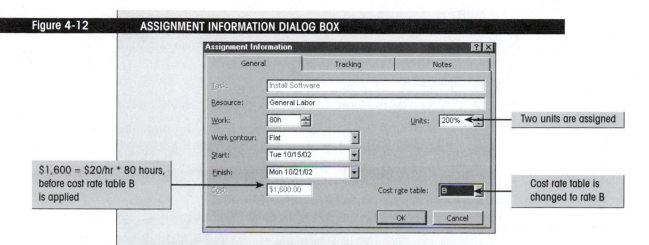

5. Click the **OK** button to apply the change, and then double-click **General Labor** to reopen the Assignment Information dialog box. Cost rate table B is assigned, and the resource cost is calculated at $2,400 (80 hours at $30/hour).

6. Click the **OK** button to close the Assignment Information dialog box.

7. Click the **Gantt Chart** button [icon] on the View Bar, and then click the **Save** button [icon] on the Standard toolbar and save the **LAN-4-Your Initials.mpp** file without a baseline. You will continue to work in Gantt Chart view.

In addition to using the Assign Resources dialog box to make resource assignments (and Task Usage view to modify them), you might want to split the screen so that it presents a resource form in the bottom half. This additional information can be useful when you are analyzing the number of hours of work assigned to a task.

Using the Resource Work Form

Total work for a task is initially calculated as the task duration (converted to hours) multiplied by the number of resources assigned to that task. Total work is initially calculated based on the initial resource assignment and then recalculated when the task duration changes. For example, if one resource is assigned to a task with a duration of one day, the total work would be eight hours. If two people are initially assigned to a task with a duration of one day, the total work would be 16 hours.

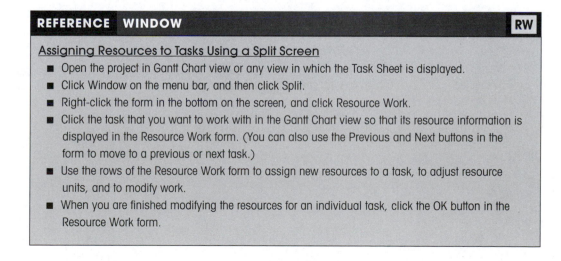

REFERENCE WINDOW   **RW**

Assigning Resources to Tasks Using a Split Screen
- Open the project in Gantt Chart view or any view in which the Task Sheet is displayed.
- Click Window on the menu bar, and then click Split.
- Right-click the form in the bottom on the screen, and click Resource Work.
- Click the task that you want to work with in the Gantt Chart view so that its resource information is displayed in the Resource Work form. (You can also use the Previous and Next buttons in the form to move to a previous or next task.)
- Use the rows of the Resource Work form to assign new resources to a task, to adjust resource units, and to modify work.
- When you are finished modifying the resources for an individual task, click the OK button in the Resource Work form.

To use the Resource Work form to make resource assignments:

1. Click **Conduct Needs Analysis** (task 3), click **Window** on the menu bar, and then click **Split**. The Gantt Chart is in the top of the screen, and a form appears in the bottom.

2. Right-click the **form**, and then click **Resources & Predecessors**.

   The form now displays resource name, units, and work information for the selected task in the left section and predecessor information in the right.

3. Right-click the **form**, and then click **Resource Work**. The Resource Work form opens, as shown in Figure 4-13.

Figure 4-13	RESOURCE WORK FORM DISPLAYED IN A SPLIT VIEW

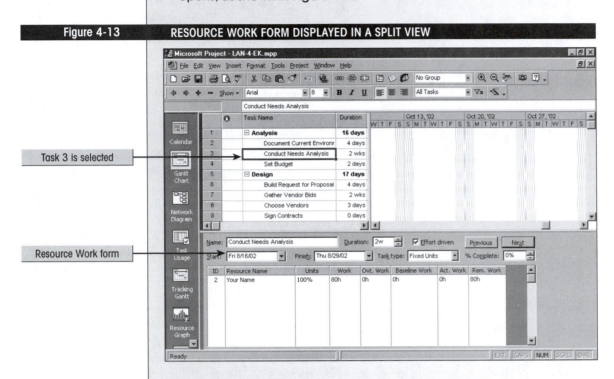

Any form view that displays resource information will provide the three columns of resource information that you are most concerned about when making resource assignments (Resource Name, Units, and Work). The Resource Work form is also very valuable when you are assigning overtime work or tracking how work has advanced on a project in progress.

4. Click **Build Request for Proposal** (task 6) in the Task Sheet, click the first **Resource Name** cell in the Resource Work form, click the **list arrow**, and then click **Your Name**.

   When you are using a form view, the resource assignment isn't finished until you click the OK button in the form.

5. Click the **OK** button in the form.

The work field is calculated at 32 hours, which equals one person working eight hours per day on a four-day task. Once you clicked the OK button, the form's OK and Cancel buttons became Previous and Next buttons.

6. Click the **Next** button in the form to move to task 7 (Gather Vendor Bids), click the first **Resource Name** cell in the Resource Work form, click the **list arrow**, click **Your Name**, and then click the **OK** button.

Since this task has a duration of two weeks, the total work was initially calculated at 80 hours.

7. Click the **Next** button in the form to move to task 8 (Choose Vendors).

Because both you and Emily Kelsey want to be involved in this task, you'll assign both resources in the Resource Work form.

8. Click the first **Resource Name** cell in the Resource Work form, click the **list arrow**, click **Your Name**, press the **Enter** key, click the second **Resource Name** list arrow, click **Emily Kelsey**, and then click the **OK** button.

The initial total work for this task is calculated to be 48 hours as shown in Figure 4-14 (2 resources × 8 hours of working time per day per resource × 3 day task duration = 48 total hours). The Rem. Work column of the Resource Work form shows the remaining work to be completed. This column shows the total of the Work and Ovt. Work (Overtime Work) assignments before the project starts. When you start tracking progress and enter values in the Act. Work (Actual Work) column of the Resource Work form, you'll see the Rem. Work column automatically be recalculated.

| Figure 4-14 | USING THE FORM TO ASSIGN TWO RESOURCES TO A TASK |

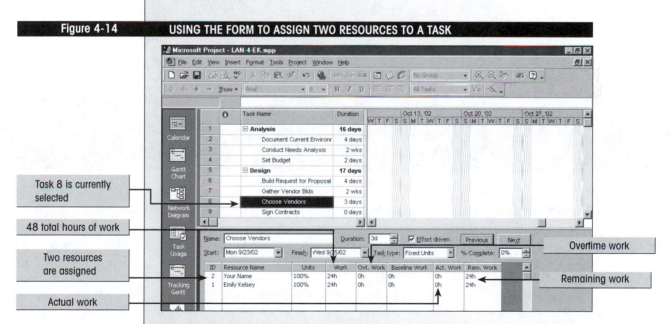

Task 8 is currently selected

48 total hours of work

Two resources are assigned

Actual work

Overtime work

Remaining work

9. Click anywhere on the **Gantt Chart**, click the **Zoom Out** button on the Standard toolbar, and then click the **Print Preview** button on the Standard toolbar to view the Gantt Chart.

You cannot print form views, so the form doesn't appear in the preview screen. Because of the zoom magnification, the Gantt Chart should appear as a single-page report.

10. Click the **Page Setup** button, enter Your Name in the left section of the header, and then print the Gantt Chart.

11. Save the **LAN-4-Your Initials.mpp** file without a baseline, and then close the project file.

A review of the Gantt Chart printout reveals how the project planning process is progressing. The tasks and durations are clearly defined, and now you have begun to assign the resources that will work on the project. The printout is a good way to communicate who is going to be doing what task, when, and for how long. In the next session, you'll continue making resource assignments and learn more about the relationship between duration, work, and resource units.

Session 4.1 QUICK | CHECK

1. Which view and table is most commonly used to enter resources?

2. List two ways to assign resources to tasks by using the Resource Assignment dialog box.

3. How do you open a split screen to show the Gantt Chart in the top portion of the screen and a form in the bottom?

4. How do you change the information that is displayed in a form?

5. What is the benefit of assigning resources by using the Resource Work form versus the Resource Assignment dialog box?

6. How is initial total work calculated?

SESSION 4.2

In this session, you'll explore the important relationship between task duration, work, and resource units. You will create fixed work and fixed duration tasks. You will see the benefits of sorting and filtering resource information. You also will format the project to highlight important resource information.

Understanding the Relationship between Duration, Work, and Units

Your understanding of the relationship between the task duration, the total work for the task, and the number of resource units assigned to a task is very important in order to manage task schedules and costs. By default, work is calculated in hours and follows this formula: **Work = Duration * Units** (W=D*U). Some project managers rewrite this equation as Duration = Work/Units to solve for the Duration, rather than Work. Some interesting exceptions and caveats to this formula exist, especially when multiple resources are assigned to a task. First, consider the task that does not yet have a resource assignment. Currently, the work is calculated as zero hours and costs $0 (even though the latter is obviously not true, unless perhaps the task is a milestone with a zero duration). Because task costs are calculated by multiplying the work for an assigned resource by its hourly rate (plus any cost per use for the task), without a resource assignment, the cost associated with a task will be $0. (*Note*: Project 2000 does enable you to enter a fixed task cost without associating the cost to any particular resource. This capability is explored later in this tutorial.)

Second, consider the task that has *already* been given an initial resource assignment. For example, you might have a task such as Conduct Needs Analysis with one resource assigned. When you add a second resource (when you double the units), what happens to the Work = Duration * Units formula? There are two possibilities. Either the Work value will also double or the Duration value will halve in order to balance the equation. In the case of Project 2000, when you add additional resource units *after* the initial resource assignment, the program assumes that the work will remain constant—this forces the duration to change. This assumption is called **effort-driven scheduling**. Work (effort) remains constant and determines (drives) the way that the W=D*U formula will be calculated. This assumption differs from that of some prior versions of Microsoft Project in which the duration remained constant and the work changed when additional resources were added to a task.

Third, consider the task in which two resources are applied but should not work the same number of hours on the task. For example, if a task has a duration of one day (eight hours), you might need to assign one person to work on the task for eight hours and another for four hours. How does the Work = Duration * Units formula change when each resource is not working the same number of hours? In this case, the duration is driven by the resource with the most amount of work. In other words, the W=D*U formula still holds true for the first resource (8 hours = 1 day * 1 unit). The resource with only four hours of work does not affect the calculation of the task's duration.

To change the name of a resource:

1. Open the **LAN-4-2.mpp** file stored in the Tutorial folder of your Data Disk for Tutorial 4.

   The project opens in split view, with the Gantt Chart and Task Sheet in the top and the Resource Work form in the bottom.

2. Click **File** on the menu bar, click **Save As**, and then save the file without a baseline with the name **LAN-4-2-Your Initials** to the Tutorial folder for Tutorial 4 on your Data Disk.

3. Click the **Assign Resources** button 🖻 on the Standard toolbar, click **Your Name** in the Assign Resources dialog box, type your name, press the **Enter** key, and then click the **Close** button in the Assign Resources dialog box.

   Notice how all of the tasks were automatically updated.

Watch what happens to a task's duration when a second resource is assigned *after* the initial resource assignment. The work hours will remain constant but will be distributed between the existing and new resources.

To explore the default relationship between duration, work, and units:

1. Click **Conduct Needs Analysis** (task 3). Notice that it has a duration of two weeks and you are the only assigned resource.

2. Click the second **Resource Name** cell in the Resource Work form, click the **list arrow**, click **Emily Kelsey**, and then click the **OK** button in the Resource Work form.

As shown in Figure 4-15, the 80 hours of work was redistributed evenly between the two resources and the duration changed from two weeks to one week. Project 2000 doesn't really understand, of course, the true capabilities of the two resources that were just assigned or whether the workload can actually be distributed evenly between them. The assumption that Project 2000 makes when adding new Labor resources is that the resources have equivalent capabilities to perform this task. Because of this assumption, you'll find it particularly helpful to have the form view open so that you can watch the work and duration values change as additional resources are added to a task. Effort-driven scheduling means that adding additional resources redistributes the work and changes the duration.

Figure 4-15   **TASK 3 WITH A SECOND RESOURCE ASSIGNMENT**

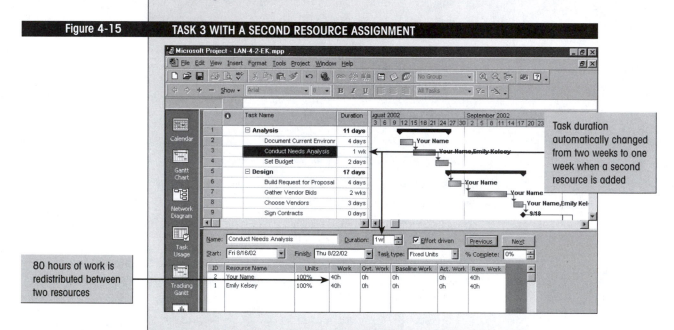

Task duration automatically changed from two weeks to one week when a second resource is added

80 hours of work is redistributed between two resources

In this case, Project 2000's assumption that the work was to remain a constant 80 hours and be redistributed between the two resources was incorrect. You can easily override this change by reentering the correct duration; this will recalculate the work for both resources. The task should have a two-week duration, and each resource should work 80 hours on the task. You make the changes in the Resource Work form.

3. Click the Conduct Needs Analysis **Duration up arrow** in the spin box in the Resource Work form to change it to 2w, and then click the **OK** button in the form.

When you change the duration of an existing task, the work hours automatically adjust for each resource to extend throughout the duration of the task.

If your *initial* task assignment includes two resources, however, Project 2000 assumes that *both* resources are required to complete the task in the initial duration. It is therefore very important that the initial resource assignment be synchronized with the initial task duration in order for Project 2000 to be used most productively. Now make an *initial* assignment of two resources to a task, and note that the initial duration doesn't change simply because you are assigning more than one resource to the task.

4. Click **Set Budget** (task 4) in the Task Entry table, click the first **Resource Name** cell in the Resource Work form, click the **list arrow**, click **Your Name**, click the second **Resource Name** cell, click the **list arrow**, click **Emily Kelsey**, and then click **OK** in the Resource Work form.

Your screen should look like Figure 4-16. Because both resources were initially assigned together, both are assigned to the initial duration.

Figure 4-16   **THE INITIAL RESOURCE ASSIGNMENT WITH TWO RESOURCES**

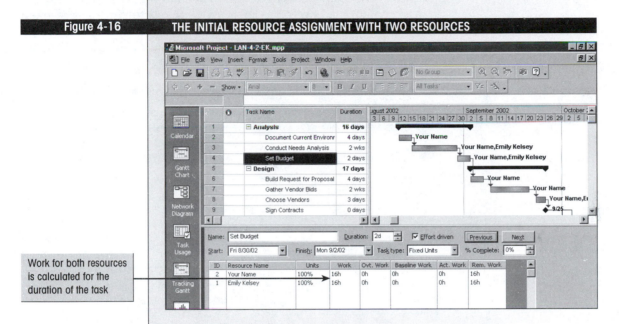

Work for both resources is calculated for the duration of the task

If more than one resource is assigned to a task, but both tasks should not be given the same amount of work, you can manually adjust the number of work hours in the Resource Work form.

5. Click the **Work** cell for Emily Kelsey in the Resource Work form, type **8h**, and then click the **OK** button in the Resource Work form.

In this case, changing the work for Emily to eight hours did not shorten the task duration because the overall task duration is still driven by you, the resource with the most work hours.

Next you want to explore the relationship between work, duration, and units when only one resource is involved. In this case, the Work = Duration * Units formula can be used without any special considerations for multiple resources.

To explore the relationship between duration, work, and units when only one resource is involved:

1. Click the **Next** button in the Resource Work form eight times to select task 12 (Install Cabling).

2. Click the first **Resource Name** cell, click the **list arrow**, click **General Labor**, click the **Units** cell, type **200%**, and then click the **OK** button.

This initial assignment creates 32 hours of work for this task, since two general laborers have been assigned to a task with duration of two days (16 hours). Observe how the duration changes when you change the units after the initial assignment.

3. Click the **Units** cell, type **400%**, and then click the **OK** button.

When the units of one resource were doubled after the initial assignment, the duration was automatically halved to keep the Work = Duration * Units formula balanced, as shown in Figure 4-17.

Figure 4-17	CHANGING THE UNITS FOR AN EXISTING RESOURCE ASSIGNMENT

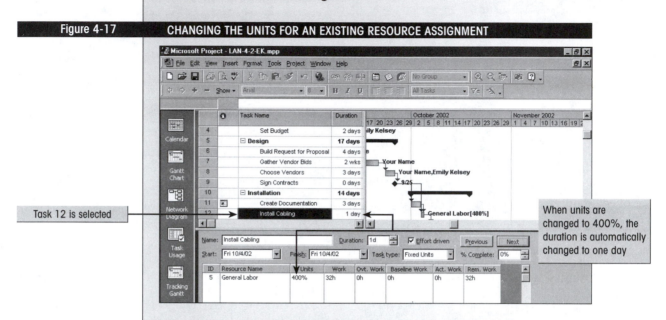

4. Click the **Save** button 💾 on the Standard toolbar, and then save the **LAN-4-2-Your Initials.mpp** file without a baseline.

The initial default relationship between work, duration, and units is summarized in Figure 4-18.

Figure 4-18	THE INITIAL DEFAULT RELATIONSHIP BETWEEN WORK, DURATION, AND UNITS

	WORK	DURATION	UNITS OF RESOURCE
Before resources are assigned	= 0	= the initial duration entry	NA
At the time of the initial resource assignment	= Duration * Units for *each* resource assigned	= the initial duration entry	= the initial units entry

Figure 4-19 explains how the W=D*U formula works after the initial resource assignment is made and an additional resource is added to a task.

Figure 4-19	THE DEFAULT RELATIONSHIP BETWEEN WORK = DURATION * UNITS WHEN CHANGES ARE MADE TO A TASK AFTER A RESOURCE ASSIGNMENT

IF YOU MODIFY/ADD:	THIS ITEM CHANGES TO BALANCE THE WORK = DURATION * UNITS FORMULA:
New resource	Duration
Units on existing resource	Duration
Work	Duration
Duration	Work

Effort-Driven Scheduling

How the relationship between work, duration, and units is balanced is a function of both *effort-driven scheduling* and the *task type*. As you have seen, new tasks are, by default, **effort driven**, that is, when a new resource is added to a task with an existing resource assignment, total work (effort) remains constant and the duration is adjusted (shortened) to accommodate the redistribution of work across multiple resources. When in the previous exercise you added an additional resource (Emily) to a task (Set Budget) that had an existing resource assignment (you), work was redistributed to shorten the duration. As you might suspect, when effort-driven scheduling is turned *off* and a new resource is added to a task with an existing resource assignment, the work (effort) no longer drives the assignment. When effort-driven scheduling is turned off and a new resource is assigned to a task, the *duration* of the task remains constant and the work (effort) is increased. This is called a **fixed-duration task**. You will learn more about fixed-duration tasks shortly.

Task Types

Task type is a task field that refers to what will remain constant when additional resources are added to a task. It may be either Fixed Units, Fixed Duration, or Fixed Work; by default, it is Fixed Units. Figure 4-20 shows how the same task (with an initial duration of four days and one resource assignment) responds to the assignment of an additional resource when different task types are used and effort-driven task scheduling is both on and off.

Figure 4-20	WHAT HAPPENS WHEN AN ADDITIONAL RESOURCE IS ADDED

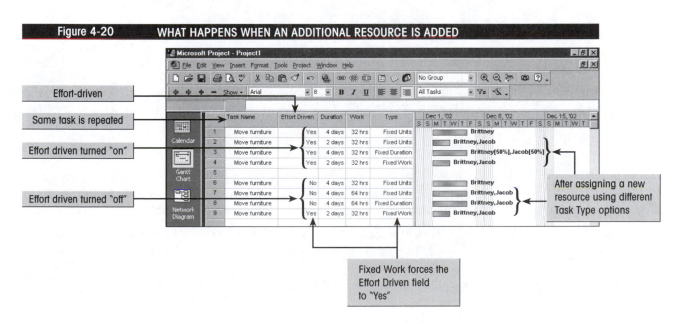

Figure 4-21 explains each task assignment. The default settings for a new task are the Effort-Driven / Fixed Units task. This is the most common combination of scheduling option and task type.

Figure 4-21	EFFORT-DRIVEN SCHEDULING AND TASK TYPE RELATIONSHIPS	
TASK ID	**RESOURCE ASSIGNMENT ACTIVITY**	**DESCRIPTION**
1	Brittney is the initial resource assignment.	Initial work is calculated for an effort-driven task.
2	Jacob is added as a new resource assignment.	Work remains constant due to effort-driven scheduling but is redistributed between Jacob and Brittney. The duration is decreased to balance the W=D*U formula.
3	Jacob is added as a new resource assignment.	Work remains constant due to effort-driven scheduling. The duration remains constant due to a fixed-duration task type. Units are reduced to 50% to balance the W=D*U formula.
4	Jacob is added as a new resource assignment.	Work remains constant but is redistributed between Jacob and Brittney. The duration is decreased. In effort-driven scheduling, Fixed Units and Fixed Work task types react the same way.
6	Brittney is the initial resource assignment.	Initial work is calculated for a task that is not effort driven. The initial work calculation is the same for a task that is effort driven.
7	Jacob is added as a new resource assignment.	The task is not effort driven, so the duration rather than work remains constant. Adding Jacob to the task doubles the amount of work to balance the W=D*U formula. This is a **fixed-duration** task.
8	Jacob is added as a new resource assignment.	The task is not effort driven, so the duration rather than work remains constant. Adding Jacob to the task doubles the amount of work. If a task is not effort driven, Fixed Units and Fixed Duration task types react the same way.
9	Jacob is added as a new resource assignment.	If the task is given a Fixed Work task type, it must be effort driven and the Effort Driven field is automatically set to Yes. This task reacts the same way that tasks 2 and 4 react when a new resource was added. Work was held constant due to effort-driven scheduling, and the duration was decreased.

Creating a Fixed-Duration Task

Some tasks, such as meetings and seminars, should have fixed durations. **Fixed-duration** means that a task's work, rather than the duration, changes when a new resource is assigned. To change a task from effort driven to fixed-duration, clear the Effort driven check box on the Advanced tab of the Task Information dialog box or in the Resource form.

To create a fixed-duration task:

1. Scroll down the Task Entry table, click **Test Software** (task 20, which has a duration of two days), and then click the **Go To Selected Task** button 🖉 on the Standard toolbar to position the Gantt Chart on that task.

   You decide that no matter how many people are asked to test the software, you want the testing process to last a full two days. This decision means that you must change this task to fixed-duration. Notice that on the Resource Work form, the Effort driven check box is checked.

2. Click the **Effort driven** check box in the Resource Work form to uncheck the box.

Now add resources to the task to see how it responds to the assignment of new resources.

3. Click the first **Resource Name** cell in the Resource Work form, click the **list arrow**, click **Your Name**, and then click the **OK** button in the Resource Work form.

   Your Name is the initial resource assignment. Because the initial duration was two days, the initial work calculation is 16 hours.

4. Click the second **Resource Name** cell, type **Gabriel Mitchell**, and then click the **OK** button on the Resource Work form.

   The result is shown in Figure 4-22. Effort-driven scheduling is turned off, so work was *not* held constant. Rather, the duration was held constant (two days). Adding Gabriel Mitchell doubled the work because he was also assigned 16 hours of work.

Figure 4-22	ADDING A NEW RESOURCE FOR A FIXED-DURATION TASK

Effort driven check box is cleared

Duration remains constant

Adding a new resource doubles the work

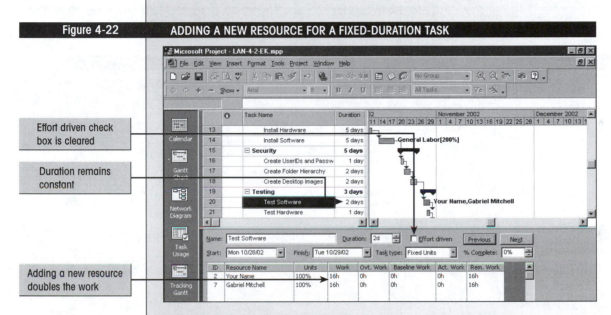

5. Click the third **Resource Name** cell, type **Maureen Hill**, and then click the **OK** button in the Resource Work form.

   Once again, the duration was held constant and the work was increased because the effort-driven scheduling field is currently set to No.

Creating new resources by directly entering them in this form, however, does not provide a field to enter their hourly costs. You can use the Resource Sheet to assign the costs.

To assign costs to a resource:

1. Click the **down scroll arrow** on the View Bar, and then click the **Resource Sheet** button on the View Bar.

The Resource Sheet opens below the Gantt Chart, replacing the Resource Work form. Displaying the Gantt Chart in the top pane and the Resource Sheet in the bottom pane in split view is handy because you view only those resources in the Resource Sheet that are assigned to the currently selected task. From this view, you can enter Gabriel and Maureen's hourly costs.

TROUBLE? If the Resource Sheet appears in the top of the screen instead of in the bottom, the top pane was active. Click the Gantt Chart button to display the Gantt Chart in the top pane again. Then click the form in the bottom of the screen to make it active before clicking the Resource Sheet button.

2. Click the **Std. Rate** cell for Gabriel, type **40**, press the **Tab** key, type **40**, and then press the **Enter** key. Gabriel's rate of $40.00 per hour is entered for both the Standard and the Overtime Rate fields.

3. Click the **Std. Rate** cell for Maureen, type **40**, press the **Tab** key, type **40** for the Ovt. Rate field, and then press the **Enter** key, as shown in Figure 4-23.

Figure 4-23	VIEWING THE GANTT CHART AND RESOURCE SHEET

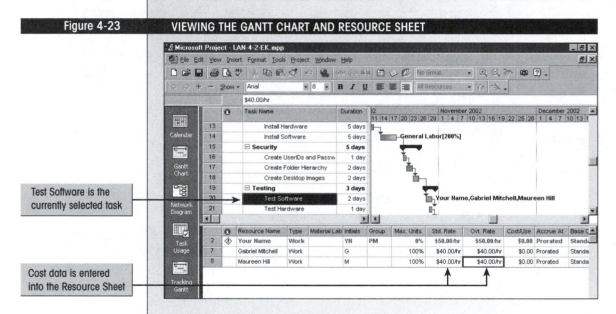

Test Software is the currently selected task

Cost data is entered into the Resource Sheet

4. Click the **Entry table**, press and hold the **Ctrl** key, press the **Home** key to navigate to the first task, and then press the ↓ to move through the tasks in your project.

As you move from task to task, the Resource Sheet will change to display only those resources that are assigned to that task.

5. Click the **Save** button 🖫 on the Standard toolbar, save the project without a baseline, click **Window**, click **Remove Split**, and then close the **LAN-4-2-Your Initials**.mpp file.

Using the Resource Usage View to Examine Resource Information

The **Resource Usage** view shows each resource that has assigned tasks. The left pane is organized similarly to the Task Entry table but contains resource information. The right pane of the view displays the number of hours of each resource that are assigned to each task, in a day-by-day format. You have made the rest of the resource assignments and saved the file as **LAN-4-2B.mpp**.

To filter a project for resource information:

1. Open the **LAN-4-2B.mpp** file stored in the Tutorial folder of your Data Disk for Tutorial 4.

2. Click **File** on the menu bar, click **Save As**, and then save the file with the name **LAN-4-2B-Your Initials** without a baseline in the Tutorial folder of your Data Disk for Tutorial 4.

3. Click the **down scroll arrow** twice on the View Bar, and then click the **Resource Usage** button 🗓 on the View Bar. The Resource Usage view displays in the Project window.

   Resources appear in the Resource Name column, similarly to how summary tasks display. The tasks are indented below each resource. The Indicators column displays the relevant icons for any special conditions for each resource, and a Work column displays the number of hours for each task and the total hours assigned for each resource. The right pane of the view displays the number of hours of each resource that are assigned to each task in a day-by-day format. Resources in red are overallocated.

4. Click the **Collapse** button ⊟ to the left of Emily Kelsey (row 1) in the Resource Name column, and then click the **Collapse button** ⊟ to the left of Your Name (Row 2). Both resources are collapsed. You can expand and collapse individual resources within the Resource Usage view just as you can expand and collapse summary tasks within a Task Sheet view.

5. Click the **Testing** task for the Laptop resource, and then click the **Go To Selected Task** button 🖼 on the Standard toolbar, as shown in Figure 4-24.

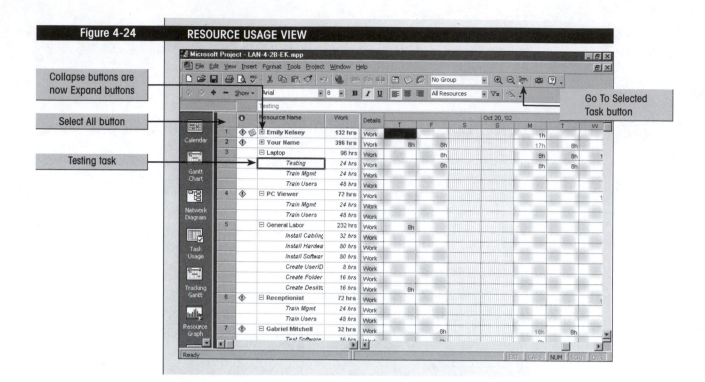

Figure 4-24   RESOURCE USAGE VIEW

Collapse buttons are now Expand buttons

Select All button

Testing task

Go To Selected Task button

Sorting Tasks for Resource Information

The sorting capabilities of Project 2000 highlight specific resource information. You use **sorting** to reorder the resources in an ascending or descending sort order based on the values in the resource fields.

To sort a project for resource information:

1. Click the **Select All** button to select the entire Resource Usage sheet, and then click the **Hide Subtasks** button ⊟ on the Formatting toolbar to collapse all tasks within each resource.

2. Click **Project** on the menu bar, point to **Sort**, click **by Cost**, and then click **Your Name** (the first resource listed in the sheet).

    The resources are now listed from highest cost (Your Name) to least cost (Contract Trainer).

3. Click **Project** on the menu bar, point to **Sort**, and then click **by Name**.

    Now the resources are listed in alphabetical order, as shown in Figure 4-25.

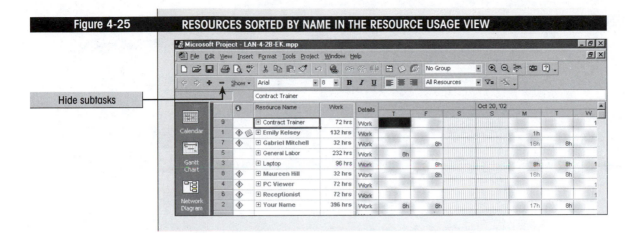

Figure 4-25   RESOURCES SORTED BY NAME IN THE RESOURCE USAGE VIEW

You sort Task Sheets similarly to how you sort Resource Sheets, except that the sort fields differ. You can sort Task Sheets by Start Date, Finish Date, Priority, Cost, and ID. You can sort Resource Sheets by Cost, Name, and ID. You can also open the Sort dialog box by clicking Project on the menu bar, pointing to Sort, and then clicking Sort by. The Sort dialog box lets you specify more than one sort field, as well as whether the fields are to be sorted in ascending or descending order.

Filtering Tasks for Resource Information

You can use the Resource Usage view to **filter** resources to show a subset of resources that meet certain criteria. For example, soon you will need to focus on the overallocated resources (those that have more than eight hours of work assigned for a given day or days). You can filter Resource Sheets using the AutoFilter button ▾= or Filter list, similarly to the way that you filter Task Sheets.

> *To filter a project for resource information:*
>
> **1.** Click the **Filter** list arrow, and then click **Overallocated Resources**.
>
> Only those resources that are overallocated are now showing on the Resource Sheet. The numbers in red in the day-by-day grid on the right represent overallocations.
>
> **2.** Click the **Expand** button ⊞ to the left of Gabriel Mitchell.
>
> You can now see which two tasks create the overallocation for Gabriel on Monday, October 21, 2002, as shown in Figure 4-26. He is scheduled on that day to spend eight hours testing software and eight hours testing hardware.

Figure 4-26   **FILTERING AND EXAMINING A SPECIFIC OVERALLOCATION**

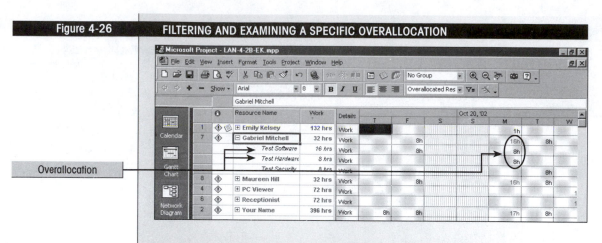

3. Click the **Print Preview** button [icon] on the Standard toolbar to preview the Resource Sheet. You often will want to print this information to communicate resource information with your planning and management staff.

4. Click the **Page Setup** button, enter Your Name in the left section of the header, and then **print** the first page of the filtered Resource Sheet.

5. Click the **Collapse** button [−] to the left of Gabriel Mitchell in the Resource Name column.

6. Click the **Filter** list arrow, and then click **All Resources** to view all resources.

7. Click the **Save** button [icon] on the Standard toolbar, save the project without a baseline, and then close the **LAN-4-2B-Your Initials.mpp** file.

You can see how filtering and sorting in the Resource view helps you to determine how your resources are allocated and helps you highlight significant information about your project.

Session 4.2 QUICK | CHECK

1. What is the general formula to calculate work for a task?

2. How is work calculated for a task that does not yet have a resource assignment?

3. How is the duration of a task scheduled when two resources are assigned and they are given different work entries? (For example, the first task is assigned eight hours of work and the second four hours of work.)

4. With effort-driven scheduling, what is held constant and what is increased in the $W=D*U$ formula when an additional resource is added?

5. With fixed-duration scheduling, what is held constant and what is increased in the $W=D*U$ formula when an additional resource is added?

6. What is the default task type?

7. What is a resource overallocation?

8. Differentiate filtering from sorting.

9. Differentiate the Resource Usage view from the Task Usage view.

SESSION 4.3

In this session, you'll finish the resource and cost portions of building a project by leveling overallocated resources, reviewing project costs, entering fixed costs, and analyzing summary statistics. Of course, you don't want to lose sight of the project goal: to *network six computers to easily share resources within a timeframe of three months and within a budget of $50,000*. So you'll also analyze and crash the critical path by manipulating resources. Finally, you'll review cost and resource reports.

Leveling Overallocations

A resource is overallocated if it is assigned more work in a given time period than it has working hours. Usually this means that a resource has been assigned more than eight hours of work in a day. **Leveling** means to correct overallocations so that no resource is assigned more work than is available in the given time period.

Note that overallocations can occur not only when resources are scheduled to do more than eight hours of work in a day, but also if they are scheduled to do more than 60 minutes of work in a given hour of the day. If you suspect this latter problem, because an overallocation exists for a resource that is assigned fewer than eight hours of work in a day, change the timescale to hours instead of days in the Task Usage or Resource Usage view in order to find the overallocation.

Many ways are available to level resources. Project 2000 will assist you in that process as well. Figure 4-27 identifies some of the ways to level an overallocation.

Figure 4-27	LEVELING OVERALLOCATIONS		
METHOD	**DESCRIPTION**	**PROS**	**CONS**
Delay a task	When you ask Project 2000 to level overallocated resources, it will delay tasks and reschedule their start and finish dates to a period of time in which the assigned resource is free.	• Project 2000 can automatically delay and reschedule tasks. • This method is very fast and easy to implement.	• The length of the project is increased.
Split a task	When you ask Project 2000 to level overallocated resources, it might **split** a task so as to reschedule remaining work in a period of time in which the assigned resource is free.	• Project 2000 can automatically split and reschedule the remainders of tasks. • This method is very fast and easy to implement.	• The length of the project is increased. • The nature of the task might not accommodate splitting.
Assign a different resource	Replace the overallocated resource with a free resource.	• This method does not increase the project's length.	• Sometimes it is difficult or impossible to find an equivalent and also free resource to assign.
Assign overtime	Assign hours of work to the overallocated resource outside of the regular working day.	• This method does not increase the project's length.	• It usually increases the project cost because of overtime labor rates. • Overtime might not be an effective way to accomplish some tasks or use some resources.
Assign additional resources	If more resources are assigned to an effort-driven task, the work will be redistributed among all of the resources, thereby decreasing the number of hours required for the overallocated resource.	• This method does not increase the project's length.	• It is sometimes difficult or impossible to find an equivalent and also free additional resource to assign to the task.
Shorten the task duration or the hours of work assigned to a task	Shorten the duration or work of the task with an overallocated resource so that fewer hours of work are required.	• If you shorten a task duration, you might also shorten the project's length. • Directly decreasing the duration or work hours for an overallocated resource is an effective way to level it.	• This method is appropriate only for those tasks whose durations or work hours were initially overestimated.

Manually Leveling Overallocations

When leveling resources, you probably want to examine the overallocated resources yourself first and use leveling techniques that do not extend the project's length (reassign work, assign overtime, add additional resources, and shorten task duration) before using the Project 2000 leveling tool. Project 2000 provides a powerful leveling tool that delays and splits tasks to reassign work to free periods. While this is a fast and effective way to deal with overallocations, it also extends the duration of the overall project—this might not be acceptable.

REFERENCE WINDOW   **RW**

Examining and Adjusting Overallocations Using the Resource Management toolbar
- Click the Filter list arrow on the Formatting toolbar, and then click Overallocated Resources to view only overallocations.
- Click View on the menu bar, point to Toolbars, and then click Resource Management to display the Resource Management toolbar, which has many useful buttons.
- Click the Resource Allocation view button on the Resource Management toolbar to find and examine overallocations.
- Enter any changes to work assignments that you deem necessary and appropriate at this time.

To manually level overallocations by reducing work:

1. Open the **LAN-4-3.mpp** project file in the Tutorial folder of the Data Disk for Tutorial 4.

   The project should open to the Resource Usage view.

2. Click **File** on the menu bar, click **Save As**, and then save the file with the name **LAN-4-3-Your Initials** without a baseline. You can see that several resources display in red, thereby indicating that they are overallocated.

3. Click the **Filter** list arrow on the Formatting toolbar, and then click **Overallocated Resources** to focus on just those resources that need leveling. Notice that all of the resources have the yellow exclamation point indicator ⬦.

4. Point to the ⬦ icon for Your Name, read the ScreenTip, click **View** on the menu bar, point to **Toolbars**, and then click **Resource Management**.

   The first button on the Resource Management toolbar, the **Resource Allocation view** button 🖼, is very helpful in finding and examining overallocations.

5. Click the **Resource Allocation View** button 🖼 on the Resource Management toolbar, click the **Filter** list arrow and then click **Overallocated Resources**.

6. Click **Project** on the menu bar, point to **Sort**, click **by Name**, scroll up as necessary to view Gabriel Mitchell as the first row in the Entry table in the top left pane, and then click the **Expand** button ➕ to expand Gabriel Mitchell's tasks, as shown in Figure 4-28.

The **Resource Allocation View** in Figure 4-28 shows resources and hours in the top pane and the tasks that they are assigned to, via Gantt chart bars, in the bottom pane. With this view, you can see both work information by task within a resource (top), as well as task relationships to one another in the Gantt Chart (bottom).

| Figure 4-28 | RESOURCE ALLOCATION VIEW |

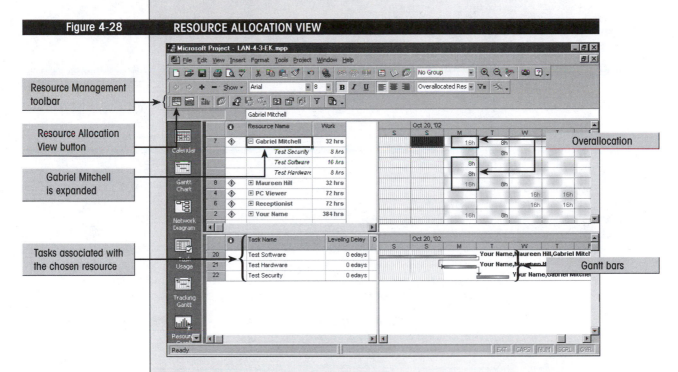

You decide that Gabriel needs to spend only four hours of work on both the Test Software and Test Hardware tasks on Monday, October 21.

7. Click **8h** in the Monday, October 21, cell for the Test Software task, type **4h**, press the **Enter** key, type **4h** for the Monday, October 21, cell for the Test Hardware task, and then press the **Enter** key.

You immediately notice a few changes to the Resource Allocation View. Icons are entered for the two tasks in the Indicators column, thereby showing that the assignment has been edited. Refer to Figure 4-29. You can see that Gabriel Mitchell is no longer overallocated—his information is displayed in black and the ⟨!⟩ icon is no longer in the Indicators column.

TROUBLE? If you cannot see the hourly entries for the chosen task on the left, click the task that you want to display and then click the Go To Selected Task button 🖼 to show that task's information on the right.

Figure 4-29	CHANGING WORK ENTRIES IN THE RESOURCE ALLOCATION VIEW

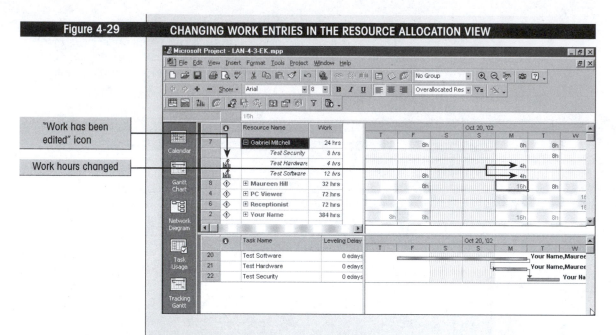

"Work has been edited" icon

Work hours changed

This direct approach to lowering the number of hours of work assigned to a resource on a given day is an efficient way to level an overallocation. It is appropriate, however, only if the initial allocation was incorrect (too high) to begin with or if work has been redistributed to other resources.

8. Click the **Save** button 🖫 on the Standard toolbar, and then save the **LAN-4-3-Your Initials.mpp** file without a baseline.

Manually leveling overallocations by lowering work assignments in the Resource Allocation view is often not appropriate if the number of work hours cannot be reduced. Another way to manually level an overallocation without lowering work hours or increasing the project's duration is to assign the work to a different resource or to assign overtime. You can make both types of assignments in the task entry form that is displayed in the bottom of the screen by splitting a Gantt Chart view or by clicking the Task Entry View button 🖫 on the Resource Management toolbar.

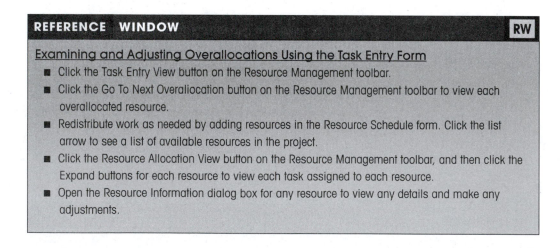

REFERENCE WINDOW   RW

Examining and Adjusting Overallocations Using the Task Entry Form
- Click the Task Entry View button on the Resource Management toolbar.
- Click the Go To Next Overallocation button on the Resource Management toolbar to view each overallocated resource.
- Redistribute work as needed by adding resources in the Resource Schedule form. Click the list arrow to see a list of available resources in the project.
- Click the Resource Allocation View button on the Resource Management toolbar, and then click the Expand buttons for each resource to view each task assigned to each resource.
- Open the Resource Information dialog box for any resource to view any details and make any adjustments.

To manually level resources by redistributing work:

1. Click the **Task Entry View** button 📇 on the Resource Management toolbar.

   You are already familiar with the Task Entry view because you used it to make initial resource assignments. This view shows the Gantt Chart with an accompanying task sheet in the top pane and a form in the bottom. This is the view that you will often use to redistribute work to level an overallocation as well. By default, the Resource Schedule form is displayed in the bottom of the Task Entry view, but you could right-click the form to display the Resource Work or any other form at any time.

2. Click the **Go To Next Overallocation** button 📊 on the Resource Management toolbar.

   Task 20 (Test Software) is selected, and Your Name, Maureen Hill, and Gabriel Mitchell appear as the only assigned resources in the form. You decide to use temporary workers from the General Labor resource to finish some of the Test Software tasks so that Your Name and Maureen Hill are no longer scheduled for eight hours of work for both the Test Software and Test Hardware task on Monday, October 21.

3. Click below Gabriel Mitchell in the fourth **Resource Name** cell in the Resource Schedule form, click the **list arrow**, click **General Labor**, click the **Work** cell for General Labor, type **16**, click the **Work** cell for Your Name, type **8**, click the **Work** cell for Maureen Hill, type **8**, and then click the **OK** button in the Resource Schedule form.

   Your screen should look like Figure 4-30. You took eight hours from Maureen and eight hours from Your Name and assigned it to the General Labor resource. Redistributing the work to a new resource is a common way to handle an overallocation.

| Figure 4-30 | REDISTRIBUTING WORK TO NEW RESOURCES TO ELIMINATE AN OVERALLOCATION |

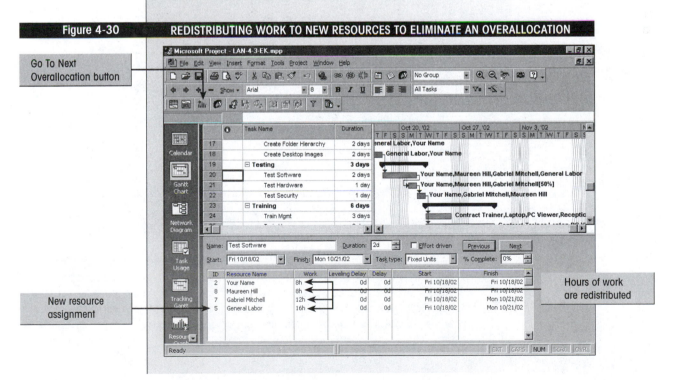

You can always examine the Resource Information or Task Information dialog box to answer questions about why a task appears to be or not to be overallocated.

To make changes to resources through the Resource Information dialog box:

1. Click **Test Software**, click the **Go To Next Overallocation** button 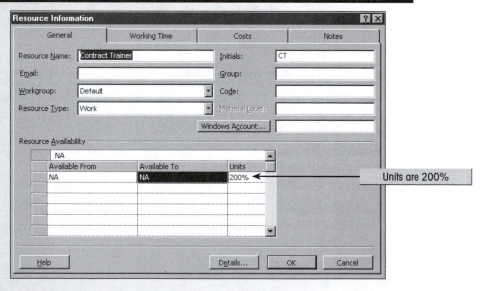 on the Resource Management toolbar, examine the resources for task 24, click the **Next** button in the form to examine the resources for task 25, and then click the **Previous** button in the form to return to task 24.

   Task 24 (Train Mgmt) is selected. It appears that all four resources assigned to task 24 are also assigned to task 25 (Train Users). Since the tasks are scheduled on overlapping days, an overallocation occurs.

2. Click the **Resource Allocation View** button on the Resource Management toolbar, press the **Ctrl** key, press the **Home** key to move to the first resource in the sheet (Contract Trainer), and then click the **Expand** button to the left of Contract Trainer in the Resource Name column.

   You can't figure out why this resource isn't showing up in red as overallocated, since it is scheduled for eight hours of work for two tasks (Train Mgmt and Train Users) on the same day.

3. Double-click **Contract Trainer** to open its Resource Information dialog box, and then click the **General** tab, as shown in Figure 4-31.

Figure 4-31   **RESOURCE INFORMATION DIALOG BOX FOR THE CONTRACT TRAINER RESOURCE**

The General tab of the Resource Information dialog box for Contract Trainer explains why it is not overallocated. There are 200% units of this resource available, so 16 hours of working time are available on a single day. Any time that a resource, task, relationship, or assignment is not responding as expected, double-click it to open its corresponding information dialog box to examine its characteristics.

You were not able to hire two contract trainers as planned, however, so you need to change the units available to 100%.

4. Click the **200%** Units cell, type **100**, and then click the **OK** button in the Resource Information dialog box. Now the Contract Trainer is overallocated. It displays in red, since only eight hours of work are available each working day. The original plan to have two laptops has also changed.

5. Press the ↓ key as many times as needed to select the **Laptop** resource, double-click **Laptop** to open its Resource Information dialog box, click the **200%** Units cell, type **100** in the Units cell, and then click the **OK** button. The Laptop is now overallocated and appears in red.

6. Click the **Go To Next Overallocation** button [icon] on the Resource Management toolbar to select Contract Trainer.

7. Click the **Go To Next Overallocation** button [icon] as needed to review the Laptop, PC Viewer, and Receptionist overallocations. A dialog box opens, indicating that there are no more overallocations after 10/23/2002 at 8:00 AM.

8. Click the **OK** button to close the dialog box.

9. Click the **Save** button [icon] on the Standard toolbar, and save the file **LAN-4-3-Your Initials.mpp** without a baseline.

After examining the project, you have a good idea of where the overallocations are located. You corrected some of them and will let Project 2000's leveling tool help you with the rest.

Using the Leveling Tool

Project 2000 provides a powerful leveling tool that levels resources for you based on some assumptions. First, it does not adjust task durations, work entries, or resource assignments. Second, the leveling tool levels overallocations by delaying and splitting tasks so that the work can be completed by the assigned resource during the available working time. Therefore, the tool generally extends the project's length as it moves tasks into time periods when a resource is available.

REFERENCE WINDOW   **RW**

Leveling Overallocations By Using the Leveling Tool
- Click Tools on the menu bar, and then click Resource Leveling.
- Adjust the options within the Resource Leveling dialog box for items such as the leveling date range.
- Click the Level Now button.

You have reviewed all of the overallocations and made adjustments to durations, resource assignments, and work entries where possible to alleviate the overallocations. Now you want to use Project 2000 to level the remaining overallocations.

To use Manual resource leveling through the Resource Leveling dialog box:

1. Click **Tools** on the menu bar, and then click **Resource Leveling** to open the Resource Leveling dialog box, as shown in Figure 4-32.

Figure 4-32	RESOURCE LEVELING DIALOG BOX

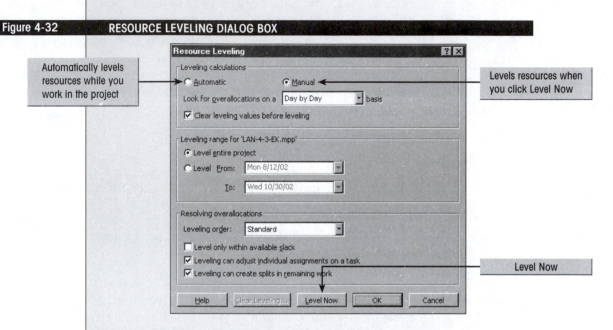

The options in the Resource Leveling dialog box can be used to modify the way that leveling is processed. The most important option is Leveling Calculations, which offers two alternatives: Automatic or Manual. Automatic automatically levels your project *as you enter and adjust the schedule.* Manual levels the project only after you click the Level Now button in the Resource Leveling dialog box.

2. Click the **Level Now** button in the Resource Leveling dialog box, and then click the **OK** button in the Level Now dialog box to level the Entire Pool of resources.

    Green leveling bars appear in the lower pane. You can apply a view that more clearly shows leveling information for the entire project.

3. Click **Window** on the menu bar, click **Remove Split**, click **View** on the menu bar, click **More Views** in the Views dialog box, click **Leveling Gantt**, and then click the **Apply** button.

4. Click **task 23** (Training), click the **Go To Selected Task** button ![icon], then scroll and drag the **split bar** as necessary to position the Gantt Chart so that you can clearly see the Gantt bars for tasks 23, 24, and 25, as shown in Figure 4-33.

| Figure 4-33 | LEVELING THE GANTT CHART |

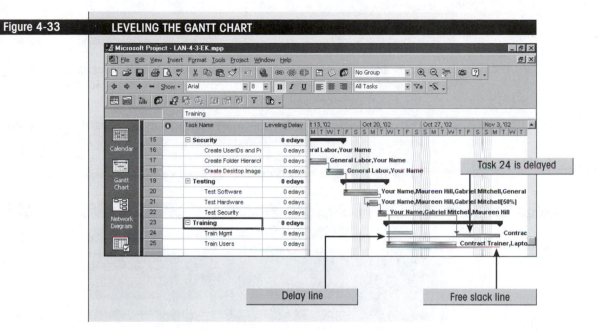

The Task Entry table now has a new column, Leveling Delay.

Leveling Gantt Chart

This column tells you the delay in completing each task created by the resource leveling tool. In the **Leveling Gantt Chart**, green bars represent the schedule for the preleveled task and blue bars represent the new schedule for the leveled task. These highlight the effects of leveling on the schedule. The brown bar preceding task 24 represents a leveling delay, imposed by Project 2000 to level overallocated resources. The dark green bar following task 25 represents **free slack**. Recall from Tutorial 3 that free slack is the amount of time that the task could be delayed without the delay's affecting the subsequent task. Because you have already leveled all of the tasks prior to task 24, those green (preleveled) and blue (leveled) bars appear the same. If a task had been split, you would see blue dashed lines between the blue task bars. In the Leveling Delay column, **edays** represents elapsed days.

In this case, Project 2000 pushed task 24 behind task 25 in an effort to level the tasks. However, you want task 24 to be completed *before* task 25 so you will revisit the Resource Leveling dialog box and fine-tune the leveling options.

To use the Resource Leveling dialog box to level resources by specifying priorities:

1. Click **Tools** on the menu bar, and then click **Resource Leveling** to open the Resource Leveling dialog box. First, you want to clear the effects of your manual leveling so that you can approach leveling in a new way.

2. Click the **Clear Leveling** button in the Resource Leveling dialog box, and then click the **OK** button to clear the leveling for the entire project. Notice that the Leveling Delay column now displays zeros for all of the tasks and the green leveling bars are the same lengths as the blue bars.

TROUBLE? You cannot clear leveling in every view of the project. Display the Gantt Chart or Leveling Gantt Chart view before attempting to clear leveling.

3. Click **Tools** on the menu bar, click **Resource Leveling**, click the **Leveling Order** list arrow in the Resolving overallocations section, click **ID Only**, and then click the **Level Now** button.

The result is shown in Figure 4-34. When resolving an overallocation, now Project 2000 uses the task ID to determine the priority on which task should be delayed. In this example, this allows task 20 to be completed according to the original plan and delays task 21.

Figure 4-34	LEVELING BY TASK ID

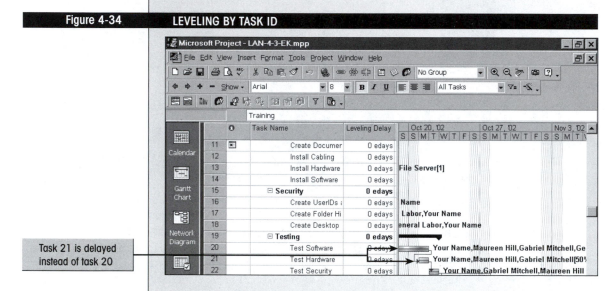

Task 21 is delayed instead of task 20

4. Click the **Save** button 🖫 on the Standard toolbar, and save the file without a baseline.

You want to share the results of your work on resource allocation with the staff to see if they agree with the plan, so you print the Leveling Gantt Chart.

5. Click the **Print Preview** button 🔍 on the Standard toolbar to preview the Leveling Gantt Chart. The chart will print on three pages.

6. Click the **Page Setup** button, enter Your Name in the left section of the header, and then print the Leveling Gantt Chart.

The default leveling priority, Standard, looks at a combination of factors including dependencies, slack, dates, and priorities when leveling tasks. To make sure that a task is given the highest **leveling priority**, open its Task Information dialog box and enter a priority value greater than 500 (the default value). A value of 1,000 means that the task will *never* be delayed or split when this task is leveled against other overallocations.

Reviewing Project Costs

When you assign a resource to a task, Project 2000 automatically calculates costs for the task by multiplying the resource's hourly rate by the task's duration. Some costs, however, are not associated with per hour (work) resource assignments, but rather are material or fixed costs. A **material cost**, for a project such as the JLB Partners LAN installation, is a cost associated with a consumable item or items, such as cabling, supplies, or computers. A **fixed cost** is a cost inherent to the task itself and is not driven by the number of resource assignments made, such as a room charge, a convention entry fee, or a fixed travel expense.

The **resource Type field** has two allowable values: Work and Material. Work (the default) causes the resource cost to be driven by the duration of the task multiplied by the hourly cost of the resource (cost/use charges if applicable). Material causes the resource cost to be driven by the number of units of the resource that have been assigned to the task multiplied by the unit cost of the resource (entered in the Std. Rate field).

Both work and material costs are entered in the Resource Sheet. They are assigned to tasks in the same way. Their cost for a task varies based on the number of units assigned to the task. In Project 2000 terminology, work and material costs are therefore considered variable costs. Fixed costs are entered in the Fixed Cost field of a Task Sheet. The Fixed Cost field is a single value for each task and does not vary based on the task's duration or resource assignments.

Material Costs

You enter *material costs* into the Resource Sheet with the entry Material in the Type field. You apply Material resources to tasks similarly to how you assigned work resources.

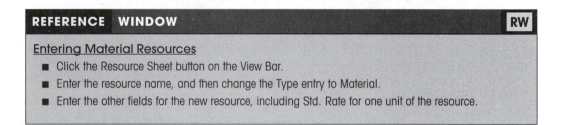

REFERENCE WINDOW **RW**

Entering Material Resources
- Click the Resource Sheet button on the View Bar.
- Enter the resource name, and then change the Type entry to Material.
- Enter the other fields for the new resource, including Std. Rate for one unit of the resource.

You have decided to enter the material costs of cabling drops, computers, printers, and the file server to the Resource Sheet and then apply them to the appropriate tasks in the LAN installation project so that the total cost of these tasks also includes the costs of the equipment and materials.

To enter material resources:

1. Click the **down scroll arrow** in the View Bar as necessary, and then click the **Resource Sheet** button on the View Bar. The Resource Sheet lists the resources that you have entered and have been working with for the LAN installation. Nine resources are currently listed.

2. Refer to Figure 4-35 and enter the four material resources in rows 10–13 and their associated costs. Be sure to change the Type from Work to Material. Then type the initials for each resource shown, and enter the Std. Rate (you don't have to type the $ sign). The Std. Rate is the cost for one unit of that resource.

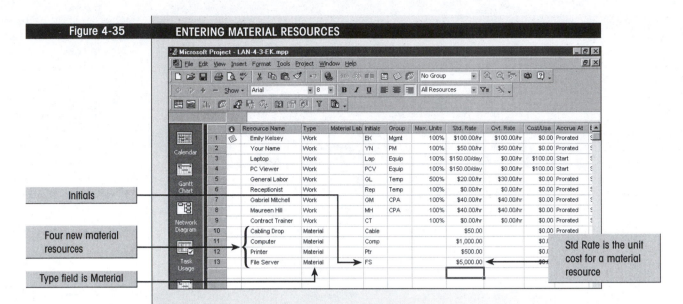

Figure 4-35   ENTERING MATERIAL RESOURCES

Initials

Four new material resources

Type field is Material

Std Rate is the unit cost for a material resource

3. Click the **Save** button 🖫 on the Standard toolbar, and then save the **LAN-4-3-Your Initials.mpp** file without a baseline.

After you have entered the *material resources costs* into the Resource Sheet, you can assign them to a task by using the Resource Assignment dialog box or by using a split screen with a resource form in one pane, as you did when assigning work resources to a task.

To assign material resources to a task:

1. Click the **Gantt Chart** button 📊 on the View Bar, click **Window** on the menu bar, click **Split**, right-click the **form** in the bottom pane, and then click **Resource Work**.

   The Resource Work form is often used to enter and assign resources, regardless of whether they are work or material resources.

2. Scroll down the **Task Entry** table, and then click **task 12** (Install Cabling).

3. Click the second **Resource Name** cell in the form, click the **list arrow**, click **Cabling Drop**, click the **Units** cell for that resource, type **6**, and then click the **OK** button in the form.

   Six units of cabling drop at $50/drop were assigned to this task. You can review and change the cost information for the cabling drop by double-clicking the resource and opening its Resource Information dialog box.

4. Click the **Next** button in the form to move to task 13 (Install Hardware). Currently, the only assigned resource is General Labor.

5. Use the Resource Work form to assign six computers, three printers, and one file server. Refer to Figure 4-36.

Figure 4-36 | **ASSIGNING MATERIAL RESOURCES TO A TASK**

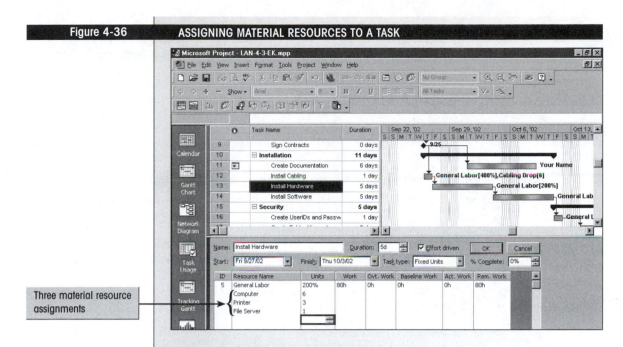

Three material resource assignments

TROUBLE? You will have to scroll through the resources in the Resource Name list to find some of the material resources added at the end of the Resource Sheet.

6. Click the **OK** button on the form. The resources are entered and Project 2000 completes the calculations.

Fixed Costs

You enter fixed costs into the Fixed Cost field for a task. The easiest way to find the Fixed Cost field is to view a Task Sheet with the Cost table applied. The Fixed Cost field is the second column in the sheet.

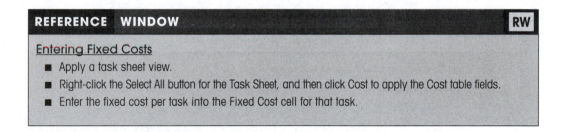

Entering Fixed Costs
- Apply a task sheet view.
- Right-click the Select All button for the Task Sheet, and then click Cost to apply the Cost table fields.
- Enter the fixed cost per task into the Fixed Cost cell for that task.

To enter a fixed cost:

1. Click **Window** on the menu bar, and then click **Remove Split**.

2. Right-click the **Select All** button for the Entry table, and then click **Cost**.

3. Scroll down the Task Sheet, and then click the **Fixed Cost** cell for task 24 (Train Mgmt), as shown in Figure 4-37.

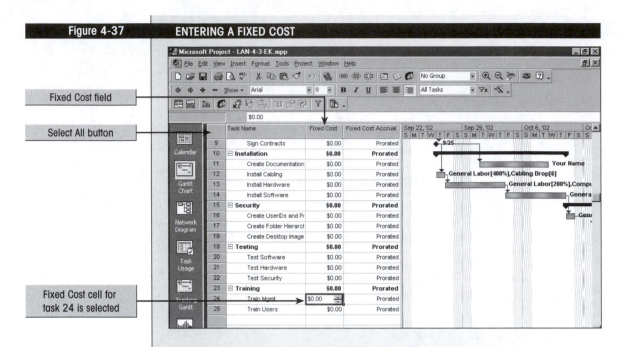

Figure 4-37   **ENTERING A FIXED COST**

Fixed Cost field

Select All button

Fixed Cost cell for task 24 is selected

Both task 24 (Train Mgmt) and task 25 (Train Users) have a $500 fixed cost for renting the room in which the training will take place.

4. Type **500**, press the **Enter** key, type **500**, and then press the **Enter** key. You have entered the fixed costs of $500.00 for each of these tasks.

5. Click the **Save** button 🖫 on the Standard toolbar, and then save the file without a baseline.

Project **Summary Information**

After you have added all of the work and material resources to your project, you likely will be interested in obtaining project summary information, especially as it relates to costs. Two ways to show summary information for a project include adding a project summary bar and reviewing the project's properties.

Project Summary Task Bar and Options Dialog Box

You can add a **project summary task bar** to the project that summarizes the timeline of your project. This bar is always added as task 0 in the first row of the Task Sheet, and its corresponding Gantt bar always appears at the top of the Gantt Chart.

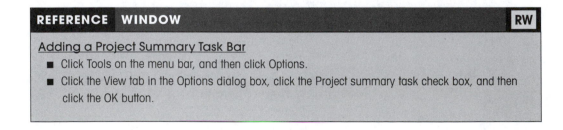

REFERENCE WINDOW   **RW**

Adding a Project Summary Task Bar
- Click Tools on the menu bar, and then click Options.
- Click the View tab in the Options dialog box, click the Project summary task check box, and then click the OK button.

You want to add a project summary bar to your LAN installation project.

To add a project summary bar:

1. Click **Tools** on the menu bar, and then click **Options**. The Options dialog box opens for the project file.

2. Click the **View** tab of the Options dialog box (if it is not already selected), and then click the **Project summary task** check box in the Outline options section, as shown in Figure 4-38.

Figure 4-38   **OPTIONS DIALOG BOX**

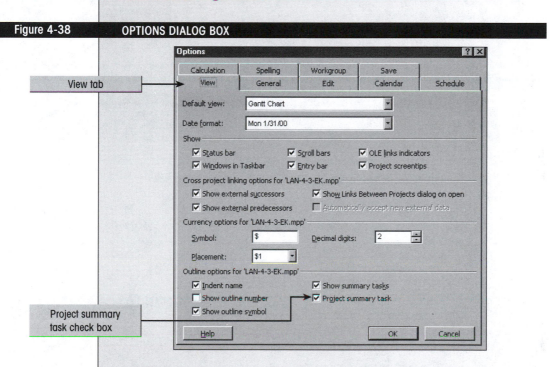

---

3. Click the **OK** button, and then navigate to the first row of your project. Project 2000 uses the filename as the default name for the project summary task. You prefer something more descriptive.

4. Click **LAN-4-3** (task 0), type **LAN Installation** in the Entry Bar, press the **Enter** key, and then point to the **LAN Installation summary task bar** in the Gantt Chart.

   The ScreenTip identifies the project Start and Finish Dates, as well as the project's duration.

The **Options** dialog box not only provides a way to display a project summary task bar, but also contains a number of important default setting choices, summarized in Figure 4-39.

Figure 4-39	CHOICES IN THE OPTIONS DIALOG BOX
TAB	**TYPES OF CHOICES**
View	Default view, default date format, whether various screen elements such as the status bar and ScreenTips will automatically appear, default currency options, and default outline options
General	Startup options such as whether Help is automatically loaded, PlanningWizard options, and default units of measure for standard and overtime rates
Edit	Sheet editing options, unit of measure abbreviations, and hyperlink options
Calendar	Default calendar assumptions such as the first day of the week, and the number of working hours in a day
Schedule	Defaults for duration and work units, effort-driven status, and estimated duration settings
Save	Default file type and location settings and Auto Save features
Calculation	Calculation defaults such as whether to calculate multiple critical paths, how to handle slack when calculating critical tasks, and how to update resource and project status
Spelling	Spelling defaults such as which fields to spell check and how to use the dictionary
Workgroup	Workgroup and Web Server settings for sending and sharing project information across a network

Project Properties

A project **property** is a characteristic of the entire project. After you have entered the initial tasks, durations, relationships, resource assignments, and fixed costs, you'll likely find that reviewing the project properties is very valuable because they present summary cost and date statistics for the entire project.

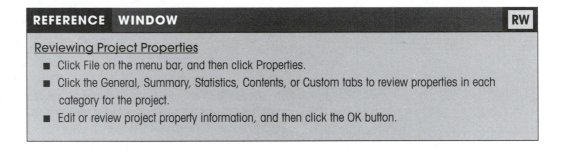

REFERENCE WINDOW   **RW**

Reviewing Project Properties
- Click File on the menu bar, and then click Properties.
- Click the General, Summary, Statistics, Contents, or Custom tabs to review properties in each category for the project.
- Edit or review project property information, and then click the OK button.

You want to review the project properties for the LAN Installation project.

To review or edit project properties:

1. Click **File** on the menu bar, click **Properties,** and then click the **Summary** tab if it is not already selected.

   The project's Properties dialog box opens, as shown in Figure 4-40.

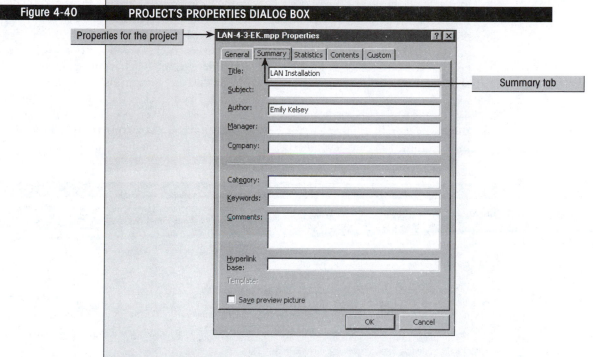

Properties for the project

Summary tab

Your Properties dialog box might have more or less information automatically entered in the fields of the Summary tab depending on how Project 2000 was initially installed on your computer. The **Title** field corresponds with the task name in task 0, the project summary task. Changing the task name for the project summary task either on the Task Entry Sheet itself or within this dialog box automatically changes it in the other location. The other fields on the Summary tab can be specified in the header and footer of printouts.

2. Click the **General** tab to observe information about the project file: its location, size, and date.

3. Click the **Statistics** tab to observe additional date information, as well as the number of revisions and total file editing time.

4. Click the **Contents** tab to observe valuable information about the project's Start Date, Finish Date, Duration, Total Work, Total Cost, and percentage completion statistics.

5. Click the **Custom** tab to view information about additional custom fields that can be added to the project.

6. Click the **Cancel** button to cancel any changes that you might have made in the Properties dialog box.

7. Click the **Save** button 🔲, save the file without a baseline, and then close **LAN-4-3-Your Initials.mpp** file.

Understanding the Relationship between the Critical Path and Slack

Now that you have entered all of your project's tasks, durations, relationships, resources, and fixed cost assignments, it's important to take a closer look at the critical path. The critical path was defined earlier in the book as the tasks that must be completed with the given schedule dates in order for the overall project to be completed in the shortest amount of time. While this is true in a general sense, it is important to understand the precise way that Project 2000 determines whether a task is critical. With this information, you'll understand why Project 2000's portrayal of the critical path might in certain situations differ slightly from your expectation.

To Project 2000, a critical task is a task with zero slack, as well as possessing several other conditions as described in Figure 4-41. In this definition, "slack" represents total slack. **Total slack** is the amount of time that a task can be delayed without delaying the project's Finish Date. Do not confuse total slack with free slack. **Free slack** is the amount of time that a task can be delayed without delaying any successor tasks. When project managers discuss slack, they are generally referring to total slack. Total and free slack are extremely valuable pieces of information. You can view both by applying the Schedule table to any Task Sheet view.

Figure 4-41	CONDITIONS UNDER WHICH A TASK BECOMES CRITICAL

1. The task has 0 slack.

2. The task has a Must Start On or Must Finish On date constraint.

3. The task has an As Late As Possible constraint in a project scheduled from a Start Date.

4. The task has an As Soon As Possible constraint in a project scheduled from a Finish Date.

5. The task has a scheduled finish date that is the same or beyond its deadline date. A deadline date doesn't constrain a task, but it does provide a visual indicator if a scheduled finish date slips beyond the deadline date.

Using Project 2000's definition of a critical task, you might run into situations in which a task *appears* that it should be critical but it isn't calculated as such within the project. An example is when a calendar with additional weekend working hours is applied to a task in the middle of a critical path. If that task finishes on a Friday but the next task cannot start until Monday because it uses the working hours of the Standard calendar, slack will occur for the task that was assigned the new calendar because work on that task could be delayed into the weekend without affecting the project Finish Date. In other words, the task with additional potential working hours will be calculated as noncritical because it has positive slack, even though it is the single predecessor to a critical task.

The training vendor that you using for the LAN installation has seen some of your project files and has asked you to help create a project file for the installation of its new PC Lab.

To explore critical tasks and total and free slack:

1. Open the **PCLab-4.mpp** project file from your Tutorial folder for Tutorial 4.

2. Click **File** on the menu bar, click **Save As**, and then save the project with the name **PCLab-4-Your Initials** without a baseline in your Tutorial folder for Tutorial 4. You see that you and an assistant are the only resources assigned to this project at this time.

3. Click the **Gantt Chart** button on the View Bar, click **Install hardware** (task 1), and then click the **Go To Selected Task** button on the Standard toolbar. The project window displays the Gantt Chart. Task 1 (Install hardware) is selected in the Entry table and is visible in the Gantt Chart.

   You used the Gantt Chart Wizard to format the critical path in red to show that the critical path consists of tasks 1 through 5.

Notice that the first task, Install Hardware, starts on a Friday and finishes on a Monday because it has a two-day duration. Currently, all tasks use the default working days defined by the Standard calendar.

4. Double-click **Install hardware**, click the **Advanced** tab, click the **Calendar** list arrow, click **24 Hours**, and then click the **OK** button.

Notice what happens when a task finishes before the working hours of the next task's start. The blue Gantt bar indicates that task 1 is no longer critical, as shown in Figure 4-42, even though it has a finish-to-start relationship with the previous task. This is because the 24 Hours calendar, when applied to task 1, introduces slack for this task. In other words, task 1 finishes before the working hours for task 2 allow it to start. (Task 1 finishes on the weekend, and task 2 cannot start until 8:00 AM on Monday morning.)

Figure 4-42 **CHANGING THE CRITICAL PATH**

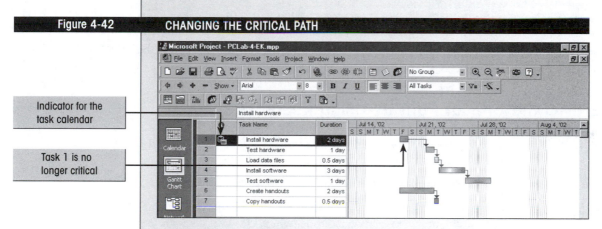

You use the Schedule table applied to the Task Sheet to examine scheduling dates and slack values.

5. Right-click the **Select All** button for the Entry table, click **Schedule**, and then drag the **split bar** to the right so that the Total Slack column is visible, as shown in Figure 4-43.

Figure 4-43 **THE SCHEDULE TABLE APPLIED TO THE TASK SHEET**

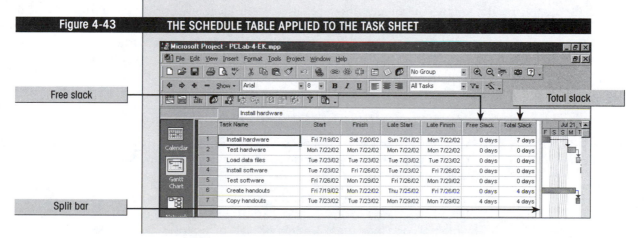

The Schedule table displays information to help you to manage schedule dates and slack. The **Start** and **Finish** date fields are the currently scheduled start and finish dates as calculated by Project 2000. The **Late Start** and **Late Finish** date fields are calculated as the latest start date and latest finish date that the task could start or finish without affecting the project's Finish Date. The **Free Slack** field is the number of days that the task could be delayed without affecting its successor task. When the **Total Slack** field is calculated as zero, the task is critical and the Start/Late Start and Finish/Late Finish dates are the same. For tasks on the critical path, Free Slack equals Total Slack.

Since task 2 cannot start until Monday, but task 1 is finished with working hours to spare (remember that task 1's working hours are driven by a 24 Hours calendar), slack is introduced for task 1. Any positive value in the Total Slack field will make a task noncritical. The Total Slack value for task 1 is calculated as seven days. (The seven-day calculation was derived by finding the total number of hours that the task could slide [56 hours] and dividing that total by 8, the number of hours in a regular workday.)

Task 6 (Create Handouts) has free slack of 0, meaning that no slack exists between it and its successor task, Copy handouts. Yet task 6 has four days of Total Slack, that is, it could be delayed up to four days without the delay's affecting the project Finish Date.

In summary, whenever you are working with a project that appears to calculate the critical path incorrectly, apply the Schedule table to the Task Sheet and check total slack to see if it is positive. Also examine the task constraint and deadline dates. Project 2000 uses each of these values to determine whether a task is critical.

Crashing the Critical Path By Using Resources

You have already looked at many ways to crash the critical path by using task information with such techniques as

- shortening the durations of tasks on the critical path,
- removing unnecessary task date constraints, and
- entering negative lag time, which allows tasks with finish-to-start relationships to overlap.

You also can crash the critical path by manipulating resources. For example, if you assign additional resources to a critical effort-driven task, the additional assignment will shorten the task's duration. Another way to crash the path by manipulating resource data is to assign overtime (which expands the number of working hours in a day and thus results in the task's being completed faster).

Both of these techniques, however, usually introduce additional costs and risks to the project. Overtime rates are obviously more expensive than standard rates. Additional resource assignments must be carefully examined to make sure that they can accomplish the task as efficiently as the original assignment and do not introduce extra complexity or productivity issues by splitting the work among several resources.

To crash the path by adding resources:

1. Right-click the **Select All** button, click **Entry** to apply the Entry fields, and then drag the **split bar** to the left so that the Duration field is the last column displayed in the sheet.

2. Drag the ✚ to select **tasks 1 through 7**, click the **Assign Resources** button 🖽 on the Formatting toolbar, replace **Your Name** with your actual name in the first Name cell, and then press the **Enter** key. All of the tasks are still selected in the table, and you can assign yourself to these tasks with a single click.

3. Click **Your Name**, click the **Assign** button, and then click the **Close** button in the Assign Resources dialog box. You are assigned at 100% to all seven tasks. Because Your Name follows the Standard calendar, the work for task 1 that is assigned to Your Name can be accomplished only in eight hours per day on Monday through Friday. Task 1's total slack is now 0, and the task has become critical.

Using the Project Summary Bar

You want to be able to see how the changes to resources affect the project Finish Date. A project summary bar will help you see this.

To add a project summary bar to help analyze the project Finish Date:

1. Click **Tools** on the menu bar, click **Options**, click the **View** tab, click the **Project summary task** check box, and then click the **OK** button.

   You can display the Finish Date with the project summary task bar.

2. Double-click the **Project summary task bar** to open the Format Bar dialog box, click the **Bar Text** tab, click the **Right** cell, click the **list arrow**, press the **F** key to quickly scroll the list, click **Finish**, then click the **Enter** button ☑ on the Entry Bar.

   Your dialog box should look like Figure 4-44.

Figure 4-44	FORMATTING THE PROJECT SUMMARY TASK BAR

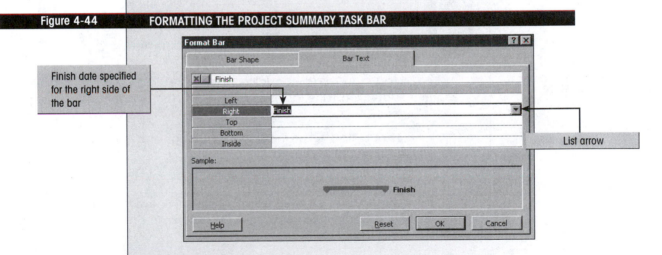

Finish date specified for the right side of the bar

List arrow

3. Click the **OK** button to close the Format Bar dialog box.

   The project summary task bar is formatted so that the project Finish Date appears to the right of the bar. The current schedule date is July 30. You want to crash the critical path so that the project can be wrapped up by 7/26 and will change resource assignments to do so. You will be working with additional resource assignments, so you decide to use a split view so that more fields of resource information are visible.

4. Click **Window** on the menu bar, and then click **Split**.

   The Resources & Predecessors form appears below the Gantt Chart.

5. Click **Install hardware** (task 1), click the **second Resource Name** cell in the form, click the **list arrow**, click **Your Assistant**, and then click the **OK** button in the form.

The project summary task bar indicates that one day was shaved off the project, as shown in Figure 4-45. The addition of one more resource to the task reduced its duration to one day.

Figure 4-45 | ADDING RESOURCES TO CRASH THE CRITICAL PATH

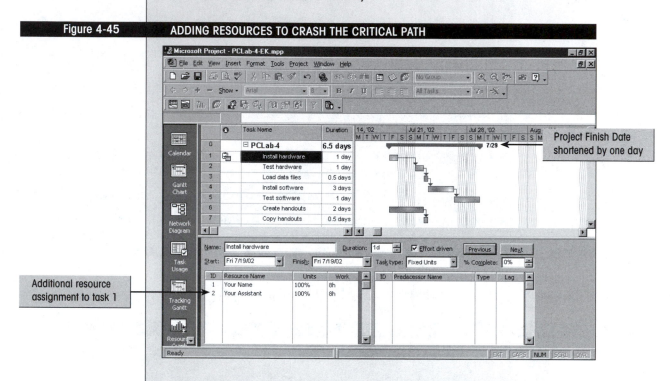

Project Finish Date shortened by one day

Additional resource assignment to task 1

As you already know, adding additional resources to an effort-driven task shortens its duration. If the task is critical, adding the additional resource will crash the path.

6. Click the **Save** button 🖫 on the Standard toolbar, and then save the file without a baseline.

Adding **overtime hours**, work hours outside of those specified by the calendar, to resources assigned to critical tasks is another way to crash the critical path. To assign overtime hours, use the Resource Work form.

To crash the path by adding overtime hours:

1. Right-click the **form**, and then click **Resource Work**. Install software is currently scheduled for three days. You feel that this time can be shortened.

   You are willing to work two 12-hour days to get this task finished faster. The total work for this task is 24 hours, so if you assign eight hours of overtime (four hours per day), you will finish this task in two days.

2. Click **Install software** (task 4), click the **Ovt. Work** cell for Your Name, type **8**, and then click the **OK** button, as shown in Figure 4-46.

Figure 4-46   **ASSIGNING OVERTIME**

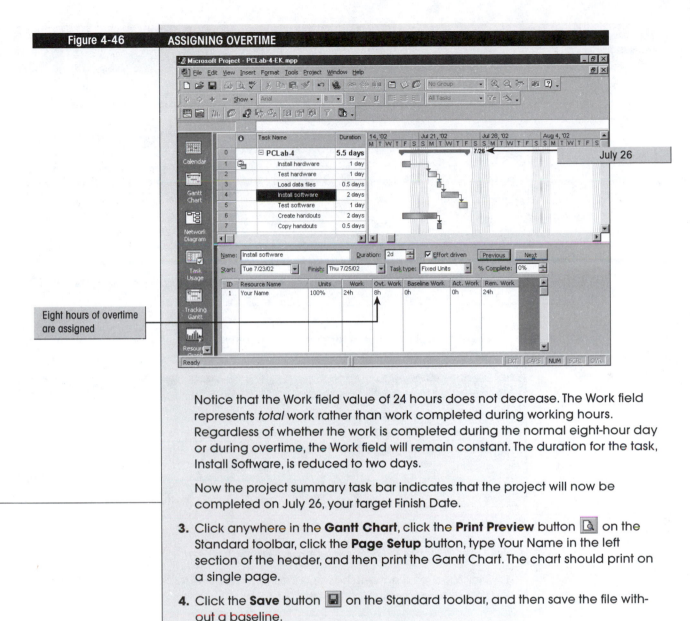

Eight hours of overtime are assigned

Notice that the Work field value of 24 hours does not decrease. The Work field represents *total* work rather than work completed during working hours. Regardless of whether the work is completed during the normal eight-hour day or during overtime, the Work field will remain constant. The duration for the task, Install Software, is reduced to two days.

Now the project summary task bar indicates that the project will now be completed on July 26, your target Finish Date.

3. Click anywhere in the **Gantt Chart**, click the **Print Preview** button 🔍 on the Standard toolbar, click the **Page Setup** button, type Your Name in the left section of the header, and then print the Gantt Chart. The chart should print on a single page.

4. Click the **Save** button 💾 on the Standard toolbar, and then save the file without a baseline.

Using Cost and Assignment Reports

Project 2000 includes several predeveloped cost and resource assignment reports. Some of these are summarized in Figure 4-47.

Figure 4-47	PREDETERMINED COST AND ASSIGNMENT REPORTS	
CATEGORY	**REPORT NAME**	**REPORT DESCRIPTION**
Costs	Cash Flow	Provides a weekly summary of task costs.
Assignments	Who Does What	Lists each resource and its associated tasks. For each task, provides the work hours and scheduled start and finish dates.
	Who Does What When	Lists each resource and its associated tasks. For each task, summarizes the number of hours assigned to the task for each day.
	To-Do List	Lists the tasks assigned for a single resource in a weekly organization. Shows task details such as duration, scheduled start and finish dates, and predecessors.
	Overallocated Resources	Lists the resources that are overallocated, as well as details regarding the tasks, dates, and work to which the resource is assigned.
Workload	Task Usage	Arranges tasks and assigned resources in the first column. The column headings are the weeks of the project. The number of hours of work assigned for each resource and task is shown within the intersection of each column and row.
	Resource Usage	Very similar to the Task Usage report, except that tasks are organized within resources instead of resources organized within tasks.

You want to explore some of the cost and assignment reports for the PCLab-4 project.

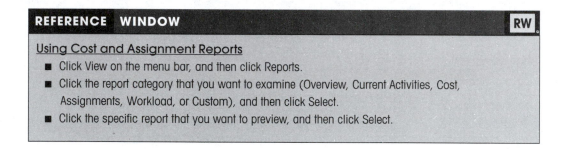

To use Project 2000's cost and assignment reports:

1. Click **View** on the menu bar, and then click **Reports** to open the Reports dialog box, as shown in Figure 4-48.

Figure 4-48	REPORTS DIALOG BOX

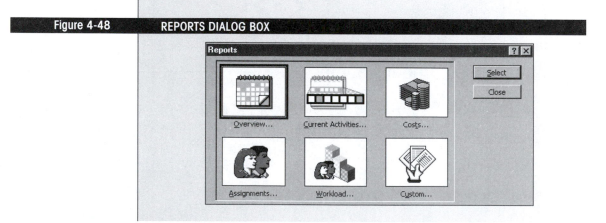

2. Double-click **Assignments** in the Reports dialog box, and then double-click **Who Does What When** in the Assignment Reports dialog box. The report is generated and opens in a preview window on your screen.

3. Click the **Page Setup** button, enter your name in the left section of the header, and then print the report.

   You notice that Your Name is assigned more than eight hours of work on several days and decide to examine this further.

4. Double-click **Assignments** in the Reports dialog box, and then double-click **Overallocated Resources** in the Assignment Reports dialog box.

5. Click the **Page Setup** button, enter your name in the left section of the header, and then print the report.

   You see that you have to reassign the work to help with the overallocations. The two workload reports help you to examine resources within tasks and tasks within resources.

6. Double-click **Workload**, and then double-click **Task Usage**. You can use the Zoom pointer to analyze this in the Preview window. You can review the task assignments for the project.

7. Click the **Close** button on the Print Preview toolbar, double-click **Workload** in the Reports dialog box, double-click **Resource Usage**, click the **Zoom** button 🔍 on the Print Preview toolbar. This report shows you how your time is spent on each task.

   The Task Usage and Resource Usage reports correspond to the Task Usage and Resource Usage views that you used when assigning and analyzing resource assignments.

8. Click the **Close** button on the Print Preview toolbar, and then click the **Close** button in the Reports dialog box.

9. Click the **Save** button 💾 on the Standard toolbar, save the file without a baseline, and then close the **PCLab-4-Your Initials.mpp** project file.

10. Exit Project 2000.

Session 4.3 QUICK CHECK

1. What is the relationship between overallocations and leveling?

2. What are two techniques that you can use to level overallocations? What are two techniques that Project 2000 uses to level overallocations?

3. Because Project 2000 provides a leveling tool, why would you individually examine overallocations yourself? In other words, why not use Project 2000's leveling tool as the first response to overallocations?

4. Which view would you use to see Gantt bars for preleveled and leveled tasks?

5. Differentiate between material and fixed costs.

6. How do you add a project summary task bar to a project? How do you view project properties?

7. What is the difference between total and free slack, and which is used to determine if a task is critical?

8. What conditions make a task critical according to Project 2000?

9. What techniques could you use to alter resources to crash the critical path?

10. Which category of reports would you select to access Task Usage and Resource Usage reports?

REVIEW ASSIGNMENTS

Part of the LAN installation will involve training the users. In this assignment, you will open a partially completed project file that documents training tasks. You will enter resources in the Resource Sheet, assign them to tasks, handle overallocations, crash the critical path by using resource information, and print various resource and cost reports.

1. Start Project 2000 and make sure that your Data Disk is in the appropriate disk drive. Open the **Training-4.mpp** file in the Review folder for Tutorial 4.

2. Use the Save As command to save the project as **Training-4-Your Initials** on your Data Disk without a baseline.

3. Click the Resource Sheet view button on the View Bar, and then enter the following resources in the Resource Sheet view.

RESOURCE NAME	TYPE	MATERIAL LABEL	INITIALS	GROUP	MAX. UNITS	STD. RATE	OVT. RATE	COST/USE	ACCRUE AT	BASE CALENDAR	CODE
Mark Douglas	Work		MD		100%	$100.00/h	$120.00/h	$0.00	Prorated	Standard	
Joy Peterson	Work		JP		100%	$75.00/h	$100.00/h	$0.00	Prorated	Standard	
Manuals	Material		Man			$30.00		$0.00	Prorated		

4. Return to the Gantt Chart, click the Assign Resources button on the Standard toolbar, and use the Assign Resources dialog box to make an initial assignment, Mark Douglas, to tasks 2, 3, 4, 6, 7. Make an initial assignment of both Mark Douglas and Joy Peterson, to tasks 9 and 10.

5. Close the Assign Resources dialog box, and then click the Resource Usage button on the View Bar.

6. Apply a filter to show only overallocated resources. Expand the tasks for the resource, and then print the Resource Usage view with your name in the left section of the header.

7. Click the first task within the resource, and then click the Go To Selected Task button on the Standard toolbar to make sure that you are starting at the first task. Display the Resource Management toolbar, and then click the Go To Next Overallocation button to determine on which day(s) the overallocation occurs. On your printout, use a highlighter to identify which days contain overallocations and the tasks within each overallocation. (*Hint*: You are using the Standard calendar, so overallocations will occur when work exceeds 8 hours per day.)

8. Click the Task Usage button on the View Bar, click Window on the menu bar, and then click Split. Apply the Resource Work form to the bottom pane, and then use your navigation skills and the Go To Next Overallocation button to find the first overallocation. (*Hint:* Identify Needed Skills is the first overallocation.)

9. Resolve the overallocation by assigning a new employee, Daniel Lions, to the task instead of Mark Douglas. Be careful not to change the duration of three days or to change the work.

10. Click the Task Entry View button on the Resource Management toolbar, and then go to the next overallocation, Hire Trainers. Click Project on the menu bar, and then click Project Information. On a piece of paper, record the project's scheduled Finish Date (it should be 9/16/02) and then click the OK button to close the Project Information dialog box.

11. Use the Project 2000 leveling tool to resolve the remaining overallocations. Click Tools on the menu bar, click Resource Leveling, click the Level Now button, and then click the OK button. Click Project on the menu bar, and then click Project Information. On a piece of paper, record the project's scheduled Finish Date (it should be 9/17), and then click OK to close the Project Information dialog box.

12. Click View on the menu bar, click More Views, and then double-click Leveling Gantt.

13. Preview the Leveling Gantt Chart, and then print it with your name added to the left section of the header. On the printout, identify which task(s) were rescheduled when you used the leveling tool. On the printout, identify the original project Finish Date and the project Finish Date after the project was leveled.

14. Click the Gantt Chart button on the View Bar, click Identify existing skills (task 2), and then assign Daniel Lions to the task in addition to Mark Douglas. Daniel will only be observing Mark during this task, so make sure that after the assignment is made, the duration is still three days and the work for both resources is 24 hours.

15. Navigate to task 11 (Conduct Training), and assign ten units of the Manuals resource to it. Even though the task is effort-driven and an additional resource was added, the duration (five days) did not change. On a piece of paper, explain why.

16. Assign Daniel Lions to task 7. On a piece of paper, explain what happened to the duration and why, then undo the assignment.

17. Clear the effort-driven check box for task 7, and then assign Daniel Lions to the task again. This time, the duration stays at two days. On a piece of paper, explain why.

18. Click Window on the menu bar, and then click Remove Split. Click the Resource Sheet button on the View Bar, and then enter 20 in the Std. Rate and 30 in the Ovt. Rate cells for Daniel Lions. Resize all of the columns of the Resource Sheet so that all information is still visible and yet prints on one page in landscape orientation. Preview and then print the Resource Sheet with your name in the left section of the header.

19. Click the Gantt Chart button, and then apply the Cost table to the Task Sheet. Enter $1,000 in the Fixed Cost cell to pay for the lab space in the Conduct Training task.

20. Click Tools on the menu bar, click Options, and then click the View tab. Click the Project summary task check box to add a project summary task bar to the Gantt Chart. Click the Task Name cell for task 0, and type "Training for JLB."

21. Double-click the project summary task bar to open the Format Bar dialog box, and then add the Cost field to the right of the bar.

22. Reapply the Entry table to the Task Sheet, and move the split bar so that you can clearly see the Duration column (if not already visible). Zoom and scroll in the Gantt Chart so that you can see all bars, including the cost associated with the project summary bar. Record the total cost for the project on a piece of paper.

23. Apply a split screen with the Resource Work form in the bottom pane. Mark Douglas has decided to work one hour of overtime for ten days on task 4 (Develop training documentation) to help the project finish sooner. Enter 10 in the Ovt. Work cell for Mark Douglas for task 4. Be sure to click the OK button in the form. What happened to the total cost for the project? Record your answer on your paper.

24. Preview the Gantt Chart (it should fit on one piece of paper), and then print it with your name in the left section of the header.

25. Click View on the menu bar, click Reports, and then print both the Resource Usage and Task Usage reports from the Workload category with your name in the left section of the header. On your paper, briefly explain how the two reports differ.

26. Save the file **Training-4-Your Initials.mpp** without a baseline, close the project file, and then exit Project 2000.

CASE PROBLEMS

Case 1. *Building a House* You have a part-time job working for BJB Development, a general contractor that manages residential construction projects. The manager has asked you to use Project 2000 to track resource information and make sure that unplanned overallocations do not occur. You'll also track fixed costs and print helpful resource and cost reports.

1. Start Project 2000 and make sure that your Data Disk is in the appropriate disk drive. Open the **House-4.mpp** file in the Cases folder for Tutorial 4 on your Data Disk.

2. Use the Save As command to save the project as **House-4-Your Initials** on your Data Disk for Tutorial 4 without a baseline.

3. Enter the following resources in the Resource Sheet view.

RESOURCE NAME	TYPE	MATERIAL LABEL	INITIALS	GROUP	MAX. UNITS	STD. RATE	OVT. RATE	COST/USE	ACCRUE AT	BASE CALENDAR	CODE
Your Name	Work		YN		100%	$0.00/h	$0.00/h	$0.00	Prorated	Standard	
General Contractor	Work		GC		100%	$0.00/h	$0.00/h	$0.00	Prorated	Standard	
General Laborer	Work		GL		500%	$30.00/h	$45.00/h	$0.00	Prorated	Standard	

4. Make an initial assignment of Your Name to tasks 2 and 3. Make an initial assignment of General Laborer (100% units) to tasks 5, 6, 8, 9, 10, 11, 13, 14, and 15. Close the Assign Resources dialog box.

5. Click Tools on the menu bar, and then click Options. Click the View tab, click the Project summary task check box, and then click the OK button. Click task 0 and type Your Name's House in the Entry Bar to identify this project with your name.

6. Double-click the summary task bar, and then add the "Finish" (date) text to the right side of the bar. On a piece of paper, record the initial Finish Date for the project (it should be October 25).

7. Click Window on the menu bar, and then click Split. Display the Resource Work form in the bottom pane, navigate to task 5 (Dig foundation), and change the units of the General Laborer resource to 300% so that the duration changes to one day.

8. Navigate to task 6 (Pour cement), and change the units of the General Laborer resource to 300% so that the duration changes to one day.

Explore 9. Add a one-day lag to the link between task 6 (Pour cement) and task 8 (Frame house) to give the cement time to dry.

10. Navigate to task 8 (Frame house), and change the units of the General Laborer resource to 500% so that the duration changes to three days.

11. Navigate to task 11 (Brick exterior), and change the units of the General Laborer resource to 500% so that the duration changes to two days.

12. View the project summary bar, and record the new scheduled Finish Date for the project (it should be 10/4).

13. Click the Resource Allocation View button on the Resource Management Toolbar, click the Resource Sheet in the upper half of the window, use the Go To Selected Task button to navigate to the first day for the first resource, and then click the Go To Next Overallocation button to find any overallocations. Record the resource, dates, and number of the overallocated days.

Explore 14. On a piece of paper, explain why this number of hours causes an overallocation for this resource. (*Hint*: Multiply eight hours of working time per day times the number of units of this resource to figure out the maximum number of hours that can be assigned for this resource before an overallocation occurs.) Remove the split window.

15. Click Tools on the menu bar, click Resource Leveling, click the Level Now button, and then level the entire pool.

16. Click View on the menu bar, click More Views, and then double-click Leveling Gantt. Print the Leveling Gantt Chart with your name in the left section of the header. On the printout, identify which tasks were rescheduled by the leveling tool.

17. Apply the Cost table to the Resource sheet, and then enter the following fixed costs: Task 1 (Planning): $50,000; Task 4 (Foundation): $20,000; Task 7 (Exterior): $5,000; Task 12 (Interior): $25,000.

Explore 18. Save the file without a baseline, click View on the menu bar, click Reports, and then double-click Costs. Print the Cash Flow report with your name in the left section of the header.

19. Save the **House-4-Your Initials.mpp** project file without a baseline, close the file, and then exit Project 2000.

Case 2. Finding a Job You are currently pursuing a new job that utilizes technical skills that you have recently acquired. After reviewing your task list, the job training counselor, Derek Martinez, has volunteered to help you with some of the work. Many tasks overlap, so use Project 2000 and its leveling tools to gain a true picture of the time that it will take to find a job. You decide to accept Mr. Martinez's offer to help wherever possible so as to cut the number of days that it will take you to find a job.

1. Start Project 2000 and make sure that your Data Disk is in the appropriate disk drive. Open the **Job-4.mpp** file in the Cases folder for Tutorial 4 on your Data Disk.

2. Use the Save As command to save the project as **Job-4-Your Initials** to the Cases folder for Tutorial 4 on your Data Disk without a baseline.

3. Click the Assign Resources button on the Standard toolbar, and then enter Your Name as the only resource.

4. Assign Your Name to tasks 1 through 9.

5. Click File on the menu bar, click Properties, click the Contents tab, record the currently scheduled project Finish Date on a separate piece of paper, and label the date "Project Finish Date before leveling."

6. Click the Resource Allocation View button on the Resource Management toolbar to determine if there are any overallocations.

7. Click the task Create resume in the upper pane, and then click the Go To Selected Task button to position the calendar on the first task. For each overallocation, record the day and number of hours of assigned work for Your Name in that day.

8. Click Tools on the menu bar, click Resource Leveling, click Level Now, and then level the entire pool.

9. Click File on the menu bar, click Properties, and then click the Contents tab if it is not already selected. On the paper that you have been keeping, record the currently scheduled project Finish Date. Label the date "Project Finish Date after leveling." The new date is unacceptable, however, so you decide to hire an assistant, a friend of yours, to help with some of the job finding tasks.

10. Click the Task Entry View button on the Resource Management Toolbar.

11. Click task 2 (Edit resume), and then enter your friend's name in the second Resource Name cell in the form in the bottom pane. (*Hint*: Apply the Resource Work form, if it isn't already applied.)

12. Click task 4 (Develop contact database), click the second Resource Name cell in the form, click the list arrow, and then assign your friend to that task.

13. Click task 4 (Develop contact database), and enter four hours of overtime for your friend. Clear the leveling for the entire project and then relevel the entire project.

14. Click File on the menu bar, click Properties, then view the Contents tab, and write down the currently scheduled project Finish Date. Label the date "Project Finish Date after getting help." How many days did the additional resource help you shave from your project?

15. Click View on the menu bar, click Reports, double-click Assignments, and then print the Who Does What When report with your name in the left section of the header. Also print the To-Do List report in the Assignments category for your friend.

16. Click Window on the menu bar, and then click Remove Split. Click View on the menu bar, click More Views, and then double-click Leveling Gantt.

17. Preview and then print the Leveling Gantt Chart with your name in the left section of the header. Note that task 4 (Develop contact database) is scheduled to be completed in 2.5 days instead of the original 3 days. On your printout, give the reasons why this task was compressed.

Explore ▷ 18. On your Leveling Gantt Chart printout, identify which task has the longest total slack.

Explore ▷ 19. On your Leveling Gantt Chart printout, identify which task was delayed the longest from the original schedule.

20. Save the file **Job-4-Your Initials.mpp** without a baseline, close the project file, and then exit Project 2000.

Case 3. Planning a Convention In your new job at Future Technology, Inc., you have been asked to help organize the annual convention at which the company will unveil its new product ideas for customers. You'll use Project 2000 to enter and track the resources (you and two consultants) that will be assigned to each task. Since the convention *must* occur December 4, 5, and 6 of the year 2002, you scheduled the project from a Finish Date and let Project 2000 determine the project Start Date.

1. Start Project 2000 and make sure that your Data Disk is in the appropriate disk drive. Open the **Convention-4.mpp** file in the Cases folder for Tutorial 4 on your Data Disk.

2. Use the Save As command to save the file as **Convention-4-Your Initials** to the Cases folder on your Data Disk for Tutorial 4 without a baseline.

3. Enter the following resources in the Resource Sheet view.

RESOURCE NAME	TYPE	MATERIAL LABEL	INITIALS	GROUP	MAX. UNITS	STD. RATE	OVT. RATE	COST/USE	ACCRUE AT	BASE CALENDAR	CODE
Your Name	Work		YN		100%	$30.00/h	$45.00/h	$0.00	Prorated	Standard	
Joe Biel	Work		JB	Consultant	100%	$75.00/h	$100.00/h	$0.00	Prorated	Standard	
Ruth Biel	Work		RB	Consultant	100%	$75.00/h	$100.00/h	$0.00	Prorated	Standard	

4. Return to Gantt Chart View, click the Assign Resources button on the Standard toolbar, and then make an initial assignment of Your Name to tasks 2 through 6.

5. Make an initial assignment of Your Name and Joe Biel to task 1 (Survey customers).

6. Make an initial assignment of Your Name and Ruth Biel to tasks 6, 7, and 8. Change the duration for task 6 back to four days, since the initial assignment of only Your Name was incorrect.

7. Click Tools on the menu bar, and then click Options. Check the Project summary task check box on the View tab, and then click OK. Change the name of the summary task 0 to FTI Convention.

8. Double-click the summary task bar, and then add the "Cost" text to the right side of the bar.

Explore   9. Expand the columns to display all of the data for task 0.

10. Apply the Cost table to the Resource Sheet, and then enter the following Fixed Costs for the following tasks: Survey customers: $5,000; Book entertainment: $25,000; Determine menu: $20,000; Develop promotional brochure: $1,000. On a piece of paper, record the initial cost for the project.

11. Because you are using Joe and Ruth Biel as consultants, you will not need to spend as many hours on the tasks that they are helping you with. Click Window on the menu bar, click Split, and then apply the Resource Work form to the bottom pane.

Explore   12. Click task 1 (Survey customers), and then change the work for Your Name to ten hours. Notice that the duration for the task didn't change from five days when work was lowered. On a piece of paper, explain why.

13. Change the work for Your Name to four hours for tasks 6, 7, and 8. Remove the Split window. What affect does this have on the cost of the project? Record your answer on your paper.

14. Click the Resource Allocation View button on the Resource Management toolbar, and then click the Go To Next Overallocation button several times to determine which resources are overallocated and when.

15. Filter for overallocated resources, expand the resources that are overallocated so that you can see the tasks within each resource, and then preview and print the Resource Allocation view with your name in the left section of the header. On the printout, use a highlighter to highlight which days and tasks are affected by the overallocations.

16. Click the Task Entry View button on the Resource Management toolbar, and then click task 7 (Determine menu). Joe is going to take care of this task, so switch the Ruth Biel resource to Joe Biel. Click the Resource Allocation View button. Describe how this action affected the resource overallocations.

17. Click Tools on the menu bar, click Resource Leveling, click Level Now, and then level the entire pool.

18. Click View on the menu bar, click More Views, and then apply the Leveling Gantt Chart view. Preview and then print the Leveling Gantt Chart with your name in the left section of the header.

Explore   19. On your Leveling Gantt Chart printout, identify which task has the longest total slack and which task was delayed the longest from the original schedule.

20. Save the file **Convention-4-Your Initials.mpp**, without saving a baseline, close the project file, and then exit Project 2000.

Case 4. Organizing a Fund-Raiser You have volunteered to lead your neighborhood elementary school's major fund-raising effort to purchase new playground equipment. The equipment must be ready by the start of school on September 16, 2002, so you scheduled the project from a Finish Date and let Project 2000 establish the project Start Date. Now you enter the resources and assignments to finish planning the project and then print some key reports to share with the school administrators.

1. Start Project 2000 and make sure that your Data Disk is in the appropriate disk drive. Open the **Fund-4.mpp** file in the Cases folder for Tutorial 4 on your Data Disk.

2. Use the Save As command to save the file as **Fund-4-Your Initials** in the Cases folder for Tutorial 4 on your Data Disk without a baseline.

3. Click the Assign Resources button, and then enter the following six resources into the Assign Resources dialog box: Your Name, Principal, PTO President, Contractor, Sunset Room, School Sponsor.

4. Using the Assign Resources dialog box, make the following initial assignments:

   - Task 2 (Identify school sponsor): Your Name and Principal
   - Task 3 (Research equipment choices) and Task 5 (Send informational flyers): Your Name and School Sponsor
   - Task 6 (Hold informational meeting) and Task 7 (Set fund-raiser goals): Your Name, PTO President, Sunset Room, and School Sponsor
   - Task 9 (Choose contractor): Your Name and School Sponsor
   - Task 10 (Schedule installation) and Task 11 (Build playground): Your Name, Contractor, and School Sponsor

5. Close the Assign Resources dialog box. Open the Resource Sheet view, and then change the Type field from Work to Material for the Sunset Room. Click OK when prompted that the change will affect resource assignments. Enter $50 for the Std. Rate for the Sunset Room resource.

Explore ▷ 6. Open the Gantt Chart, and try to determine how the change from Work to a Material for the Sunset Room resource affected the project. (*Hint*: The Sunset Room is assigned only to tasks 6 and 7, and the original duration of task 6 was one day.) On a piece of paper, explain what happened to the duration of task 6 when the Sunset Room's Type entry was changed from Work to Material.

7. Change the duration for task 6 (Hold informational meeting) to one day.[1]

8. Open the Resource Sheet view. Resize the columns of the Resource Sheet view so that it fits on one page in landscape orientation. Print the Resource Sheet view with your name in the left section of the header.

Explore ▷ 9. Click View on the menu bar, and then click Reports. Double-click the Assignments category, click the Who Does What When report, and then click the Edit button. Delete "Who Does What When" in the Name text box, enter "Fund-Raiser Master To Do List," click the OK button, and then close the dialog box.

---

[1] Sort the tasks in descending order based on the Duration field and print the Grantt Chart View.

10. Double-click the Custom category in the Reports dialog box, click Fund-Raiser Master To Do List, and then click the Preview button. Print this report with your name in the left section of the header. Close the Reports dialog box.

11. Return to the Gantt Chart, click Tools on the menu bar, and then click Options. On the View tab, click the check box for Project summary task, and then click the OK button.

12. Change the task name for task 0 to Playground Project.

13. In the Gantt Chart, add the Start field to the left section of project summary bar text.

14. Preview and then print the Gantt Chart with your name in the left section of the header.

15. Save the file without a baseline, close **Fund-4-Your Initials.mpp**, and then exit Project 2000.

INTERNET ASSIGNMENTS

The purpose of the Internet Assignments is to challenge you to find information on the Internet so that you can learn more about project management and can more effectively use Project 2000. The actual assignments are updated and maintained on the Course Technology Web site. Log on to the Internet, and use your Web browser to go to the Student Online Companion that accompanies this text at **www.Course.com/NewPerspectives/Project2000**. Click the link for Tutorial 4.

QUICK | CHECK ANSWERS

Session 4.1

1. The Resource Sheet view with the Entry Table columns is the view most commonly used to enter new resources.

2. To assign resources to tasks using the Resource Assignment dialog box, you can click the resource(s) that you want to assign and then click the Assign button, or you can drag the resource selector box for the appropriate resource to the task to which it should be assigned.

3. To display a split screen, click Window on the menu bar, and then click Split.

4. To change the form information in a split screen, right-click the form and then click the appropriate form choice from the shortcut menu.

5. The benefit of assigning resources to tasks using the Resource Work form is that more information about the assignment is displayed, including work fields.

6. Initial total work is calculated in hours and is defined as the task duration (converted to hours) multiplied by the number of resources initially assigned.

Session 4.2

1. The general formula to determine work is Work = Duration * Units.

2. Work for a task that does not yet have a resource assignment is calculated at 0 hours. Because units is zero, work is also zero. W=D*U.

3. If a task has two resources assigned to it that have different work values, the duration is calculated based on the resource assignment that has the highest work value. For example, if one resource was assigned eight hours of work and another four hours, the duration of the task would be one day to balance the formula W =D*U based on the resource with eight hours of work.

4. With effort-driven scheduling, work is held constant and duration is decreased in the W=D*U formula when new resources are added.

5. In fixed-duration scheduling, duration is held constant and work is increased in the W=D*U formula when new resources are added.

6. The default task type is Fixed Units.

7. Resource overallocations happen when you assign more hours of work on a day for a resource than are allowed by that resource's calendar. Therefore, overallocations usually occur when you assign more than eight hours of work in any given day to a resource.

8. Filtering refers to showing a subset of resources that meet a certain criteria. Sorting refers to reordering the resources in an ascending or descending sort order based on the values of a resource fields.

9. The Resource Usage view shows each resource with assigned tasks indented within that resource on the left and the number of hours each resource is assigned to that task on the right in a day-by-day format. The Task Usage view shows tasks with assigned resources indented within each task on the left and the number of hours that each resource is assigned to each task in a day-by-day format on the right.

Session 4.3

1. An overallocation occurs if a resource is assigned more work in a given time period than it has working hours. Leveling is the process of correcting overallocations.

2. To level overallocations, you can assign a different resource, assign overtime, add additional resources, or directly shorten task durations or hours of work assigned to a task. Project 2000 levels tasks by delaying them and splitting them so that work occurs on days when the resource has free working hours.

3. The techniques that Project 2000 uses to level overallocations generally result in a longer project. This is sometimes unacceptable to the project manager or to management.

4. The Leveling Gantt Chart shows both preleveled and leveled Gantt bars, as well as delay and free slack bars.

5. Material costs are those associated with consumable items, such as cabling, supplies, or computers. Fixed costs are costs inherent to the task itself and are not driven by the number of resource assignments made, such as a room charge, a convention entry fee, or a fixed travel expense.

6. To add a project summary bar, click Tools on the menu bar and then click Options. On the View tab, click the Project summary task check box and then click OK. To view project properties, click File on the menu bar and then click Properties.

7. Total slack is the amount of time that a task can be delayed without the delay's delaying the project's Finish Date. Free slack is the amount of time that a task can be delayed without its delaying any successor tasks. Total slack is used to determine if a task is critical.

8. The following situations will make a task critical.
   - The task has 0 slack.
   - The task has a Must Start On or Must Finish On date constraint.
   - The task has an As Late As Possible constraint in a project scheduled from a Start Date.
   - The task has an As Soon As Possible constraint in a project scheduled from a Finish Date.
   - The task has a scheduled finish date that is the same or beyond its deadline date.

9. You can crash the critical path using resources by assigning more resources to effort-driven critical tasks or by assigning overtime to resources assigned to critical tasks.

10. The Task Usage and Workload Usage reports are found in the Workload category.

TRACKING PROGRESS AND CLOSING THE PROJECT

Implementing the LAN

CASE

JLB Partners

You have created a Project 2000 file that contains the tasks, durations, dependencies, resources, costs, and assignments necessary to install a local area network (LAN) for the CPA firm, JLB Partners. Emily Kelsey, the managing partner, has evaluated the plan and approved the currently scheduled project Finish Date of November 4, 2002 and total project cost of $57,130. Now that the planning phase is finished and management approvals are obtained, it is time to start the project and track actual progress.

SESSION 5.1

In this session, you will create a project baseline and then practice how to track actual date, work, and duration progress of a project. You'll enter actual start and finish dates, work hours, and resource assignment information, as well as use the Tracking toolbar to track actual progress so that "planned" versus "actual" statistics can be analyzed.

Working with a Baseline

Now that the LAN project file is completely developed, you should *save a baseline* before you start recording actual progress on the first task of the project. A **baseline** is a record of the scheduled dates and costs for each task of a project *at a particular point in time*. Therefore, when the baseline is first saved, the baseline dates and costs and the scheduled dates and costs are the same. As you start implementing the project and record what has actually happened, baseline data and actual data will begin to differ (unless of course your project is implemented *exactly* as it was planned). This difference is called **variance**. Analyzing the variance within a project gives the project manager a great deal of information regarding how well the project was originally planned, how the original plan differs from reality, and how any variances will affect the final project Finish Date and costs. An **interim plan** is a portion of a baseline for a selected time period or group of tasks. Interim plans save projected start and finish dates for the chosen tasks, but not cost information.

REFERENCE   WINDOW   **RW**

Saving a Baseline or Interim Plan
- Click Tools on the menu bar, point to Tracking, and then click Save Baseline.
- Choose the appropriate options in the Save Baseline dialog box to save an entire baseline or an interim plan, and then click the button.

To save a baseline and check statistics:

1. Start Project 2000 and open the **LAN-5.mpp** file stored in the Tutorial folder of your Data Disk for Tutorial 5, then save the file with the name **LAN-5-Your Initials** without a baseline to the Tutorial folder for Tutorial 5.

2. Click the **Resource Sheet** button 📊 on the View bar, change **Your Name** to your name, change **YN** to your initials, and then click the **Gantt Chart** button 📊 on the View Bar.

3. Click **Project** on the menu bar, and then click **Project Information**.

   The currently scheduled Finish Date is 11/4/02. You can find more overall project information in the Statistics dialog box, accessible through the Project Information dialog box.

4. Click the **Statistics** button in the Project Information dialog box. Note that the current project cost is $57,130.00, the current work is calculated as 1,104 hours, and the current duration is calculated as 61 days. Because you have not saved this project with a baseline, all baseline data is either zero or N/A.

5. Click the **Close** button in the Statistics dialog box.

Satisfied with the overall statistics for this project, you will save a baseline.

6. Click **Tools** on the menu bar, point to **Tracking**, and then click **Save Baseline**.

The Save Baseline dialog box opens, as shown in Figure 5-1. In this dialog box, you can save a baseline for the entire project or an interim baseline for selected tasks or dates.

Figure 5-1	SAVE BASELINE DIALOG BOX

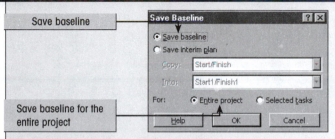

Save baseline

Save baseline for the
entire project

TROUBLE? When you previously saved or closed the project, Project 2000 might have prompted you to save a baseline. Had you previously saved a baseline, the new baseline dates and costs would override the old ones.

7. Click the **OK** button to accept the defaults to save a baseline for the entire project.

With a baseline saved for the project, you want to take a look at the data. To view the baseline dates for individual tasks, apply the Variance table to the Task sheet.

To view baseline data:

1. Right-click the **Select All** button for the Task sheet, click **Variance**, and then drag the **split bar** to the right so that all of the columns of the Variance table are visible.

Pound signs (######) indicate that data is too wide for the column.

2. Double-click ↔ on the right edge of the **Start** column heading, and then double-click ↔ on the right edge of the **Finish column heading** to clearly display all information, as shown in Figure 5-2.

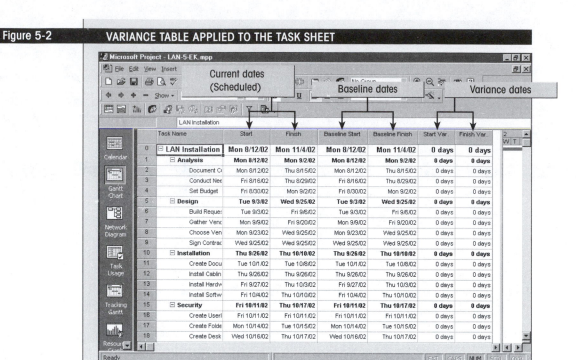

Figure 5-2   VARIANCE TABLE APPLIED TO THE TASK SHEET

Actual fields such as the Actual Start Date, record what really happened as the project is implemented. Since no actual dates, work, or cost entries have been made in this project, the scheduled start and finish dates and the baseline start and finish dates for each task are the same and variance is zero. Actual fields are found on the Tracking table and will be explored later.

You can track progress on a project without a baseline, but if you don't save a baseline, no variance information can be calculated. Baseline dates and costs are necessary for the variance calculation. It is therefore important that you save the baseline at the point at which the project is completely planned but has not yet been started. Now that the baseline is created, you will start tracking actual progress and view variance information.

Getting Ready to Track Progress

Project managers update the project with actual information in a variety of ways. Many set aside a specific day each week (such as Monday) to make all of the actual progress entries based on the progress documentation that they receive from the previous week. Therefore, it is important that you identify the **project Status Date**, the date for which the progress information that you are about to enter is up-to-date, before making update entries so that actual versus planned reports are accurate. If you do not enter a project Status Date, Project 2000 assumes that the Current Date is the project Status Date. If you do not enter a Current Date, it assumes that today's date is the Current Date.

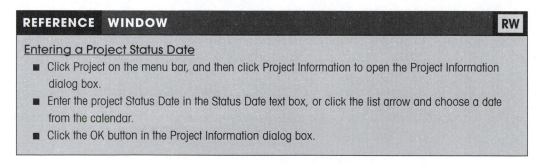

REFERENCE WINDOW   RW

Entering a Project Status Date
- Click Project on the menu bar, and then click Project Information to open the Project Information dialog box.
- Enter the project Status Date in the Status Date text box, or click the list arrow and choose a date from the calendar.
- Click the OK button in the Project Information dialog box.

The LAN project that you are working on has a Start Date of Monday, 8/12/02, and a scheduled Finish Date of Monday, 11/4/02. In this example, the LAN installation project has begun and you want to update progress as of Friday, 8/16/02. Because you are entering a specific project Status Date, the Current Date (today's date, unless you enter something else) won't be used in any tracking calculations.

If you were managing a real project, you wouldn't have to change the Current Date because the project would actually be happening during the curent time frame. In this book, the projects were intentionally engineered for a specific time frame.

To fully understand the implications of tracking a project and have your screens match the figures in this book, you must complete the exercises as though today's date is Monday, 8/19/02. This will put your project in the time frame of when the JLB LAN installation is occurring, as well as when the project manager would update actual progress on a project. The LAN installation was given a Start Date of 8/12/02, and therefore you will use the Current Date entry to place yourself in that time frame as well.

To enter a project Status Date:

1. Click **Project** on the menu bar, and then click **Project Information** to open the Project Information dialog box.

2. Double-click **NA** in the Status date text box, and then type **8/16/02**. You are updating the project's status as of Friday 8/16/02.

3. Click the **Current date** list arrow to display the calendar, click the **current year** to display the spin arrows, click the **spin arrows** to display the year **2002**, click the **current month**, click **August**, and then click **19** to specify that the Current Date is 8/19/02, as shown in Figure 5-3. Be sure that your screen shows the Status Date as 8/16/02 and the Current Date as 8/19/02.

   Remember that in a real project, you would not have to physically enter a Current Date because the real date would also be the Current Date. For this exercise, you are artificially placing yourself in this time frame.

4. Click the **OK** button in the Project Information dialog box.

Figure 5-3	PROJECT INFORMATION DIALOG BOX

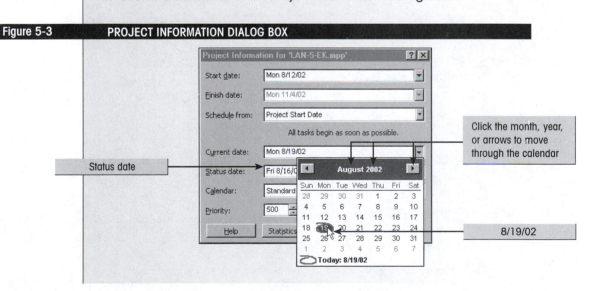

Understanding the various dates (both task dates and project dates) is essential to successfully tracking progress in a project. Figure 5-4 reviews the different types of project and task dates that you'll use in this tutorial.

Figure 5-4	SUMMARY OF PROJECT AND TASK DATES		
DATE	**DESCRIPTION**	**SPECIAL CONSIDERATIONS**	**WHERE CAN YOU VIEW THESE DATES?**
Project Start Date	The date that the entire project starts	If a project Start Date is entered, Project 2000 will schedule all tasks as soon as possible and will retain control over the project Finish Date.	Click Project on the menu bar, and then click Project Information.
Project Finish Date	The date that the entire project ends	If a project Finish Date is entered, Project 2000 will schedule all tasks as late as possible and will retain control over the project Start Date.	Click Project on the menu bar, and then click Project Information.
Project Current Date	Today's date or the date that you want the project to consider as today's date	This date determines the Current Date line on the Gantt Chart, as well as the default date from which new tasks are scheduled.	Click Project on the menu bar, and then click Project Information.
Project Status Date	The date that you use to measure project progress	This date helps determine how tasks are updated and rescheduled when you use the Update as Scheduled and Reschedule Work buttons on the Tracking toolbar.	Click Project on the menu bar, and then click Project Information.
Task Start and Finish Dates	The dates on which the individual task is currently scheduled to start and finish	The task's start and finish dates are calculated by Project 2000. These dates are also called the **current** or **scheduled** or **currently scheduled** start and finish dates for a task. These dates are constantly changed and recalculated as your project changes. *NOTE! If you manually enter a task start or finish date, you might create a constraint on that task, such as a "Start No Earlier Than" or "Finish No Earlier Than" that restricts Project 2000's ability to reschedule that task!*	Apply the Entry table to the Task sheet. The Start and Finish fields represent the scheduled start and finish dates for individual tasks.
Task Baseline Start and Baseline Finish Dates	The dates on which the individual task was scheduled to start and finish when the baseline was saved	These dates are copied from the currently scheduled task start and finish dates at the point in time at which the baseline is saved. They do not change unless the baseline is saved again.	Save a baseline by clicking Tools, on the menu bar, pointing to Tracking, and then clicking Save Baseline. View the baseline dates by applying the Variance table to the Task sheet.
Task Actual Start and Actual Finish Dates	The dates on which the individual task actually started and actually finished	These dates are either manually entered or automatically entered by using the buttons on the Tracking toolbar. In either case, these dates are based on actual progress information periodically collected by the project manager throughout the life of the project.	View the actual dates by applying the Tracking table to the Task sheet.
Task Interim Start and Interim Finish Dates	The dates on which the individual task was scheduled to start and finish when the interim plan was saved	These dates are copied from the currently scheduled task start and finish dates at the point in time at which the interim plan was saved. They do not change. You can establish up to ten different interim plans for a project.	Create a custom table, and insert the Interim start and finish fields (Start1 through Start10 and Finish1 through Finish10 fields).

Using the Tracking Toolbar

Now that you've established the project Status Date, you are ready to track progress. The **Tracking toolbar** provides quick access to many of the features that you'll need to use for this task.

To display the Tracking toolbar:

1. Right-click any **toolbar**, and then click **Tracking** on the shortcut menu. The Tracking toolbar is added to the Project 2000 window. You can display or hide toolbars as needed. Right now, you need to display the Standard, Formatting, and Tracking toolbars.

2. Right-click any **toolbar**. The shortcut menu shows the list of available toolbars. Toolbars that are displayed have a check mark next to them.

3. Click any toolbar name other than Standard, Formatting, or Tracking (such as **Resource Management**) that has a check mark next to it to hide that toolbar.

   Most users will leave the Standard and Formatting toolbars displayed at all times and display one or perhaps two other toolbars that are needed for the job at hand. Displaying more toolbars than needed clutters the screen. You want to change the Project Summary task name to a more descriptive name.

4. Double-click **LAN-5** (Task 0) to open the Summary Task Information dialog box, type **LAN Installation** in the Name text box, then click the **OK** button.

   Your toolbars should be positioned as shown in Figure 5-5.

Figure 5-5	THE TRACKING TOOLBAR IS DISPLAYED

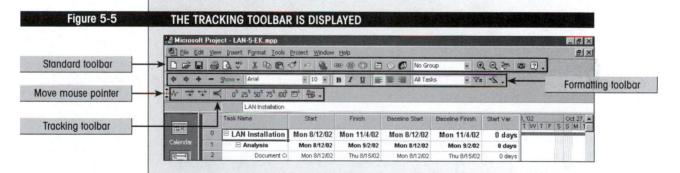

TROUBLE? If your toolbars are not aligned as shown in the figure, point to the left edge of any toolbar that needs to be repositioned and then drag the toolbar as needed.

You use the buttons on the Tracking toolbar to access some of the tracking features that Project 2000 provides to track a project. The buttons are described in Figure 5-6.

Figure 5-6		BUTTONS ON THE TRACKING TOOLBAR
BUTTON	**NAME**	**DESCRIPTION**
⌁	Project Statistics	Provides summary information about the project baseline, the actual project Start and Finish Dates, and overall project duration, costs, and work.
⇥	Update as Scheduled	Updates the selected tasks to indicate that actual dates, costs, and work match the scheduled dates, costs, and work.
⇥	Reschedule Work	Schedules the remaining duration for a task that is behind schedule so that it will continue from the Status Date.
📢	Add Progress Line	Displays a progress line on the Gantt Chart from a date that you select on the timescale.
0%	0% Complete	Marks the selected tasks as 0% complete as of the Status Date. (Actual date, work, and duration data is updated.)
25%	25% Complete	Marks the selected tasks as 25% complete as of the Status Date. (Actual date, work, and duration data is updated.)
50%	50% Complete	Marks the selected tasks as 50% complete as of the Status Date. (Actual date, work, and duration data is updated.)
75%	75% Complete	Marks the selected tasks as 75% complete as of the Status Date. (Actual date, work, and duration data is updated.)
100%	100% Complete	Marks the selected tasks as 100% complete as of the Status Date. (Actual date, work, and duration data is updated.)
▦	Update Tasks	Displays the Update Tasks dialog box for the selected tasks so that you can enter their percentages completed, actual durations, remaining durations, or actual start or finish dates.
▣	Workgroup Toolbar	Toggles on and off the Workgroup Toolbar, which displays buttons that enable you to share parts of the project with others. (Some features require Microsoft Exchange for e-mail or Web Server connectivity. Refer to the appendices for more information on Project Central and Project 2000's Web-based workgroup features.)

Project Statistics

The Project Statistics dialog box is a valuable overall summary of the date, duration, work, and cost information for a project in progress. You had a brief look at it earlier, but now that you have saved a baseline, you want to reexamine it.

To display project statistics:

1. Click the **Project Statistics** button ⌁ on the Tracking toolbar.

   The Project Statistics dialog box opens, as shown in Figure 5-7. You can see how the baseline data has been entered. Because no actual progress has yet been recorded for this project, the variance between the current (scheduled) and baseline dates for the overall project is zero.

Figure 5-7	PROJECT STATISTICS DIALOG BOX

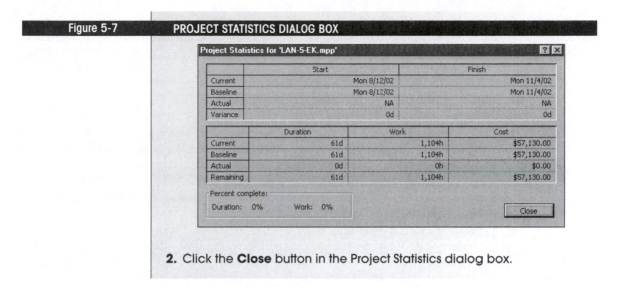

2. Click the **Close** button in the Project Statistics dialog box.

Understanding Variance

Because the JLB Partners LAN installation project has been scheduled from a Start Date of 8/12/02, Project 2000 retains control of the project's current (scheduled) Finish Date and will recalculate the project's current Finish Date and variance as actual start and finish dates for individual tasks are entered. The initially scheduled Finish Date was 11/4/02, so the baseline Finish Date will be 11/4/02 until a new baseline is saved. The formula for calculating variance is **Variance = Current (date) – Baseline (date)**. Projects *ahead* of schedule have a *negative* variance, and projects *behind* schedule have a *positive* variance.

Figure 5-8 shows the relationship between current and baseline dates for three hypothetical cases and how they calculate variance. In the first case (rows 1 and 2), the tasks are still on schedule. Therefore, the current dates and baseline dates are the same and variance is zero. In the second case (rows 4 and 5), the current finish date for the second task is *earlier* than the baseline finish date, thereby causing negative variance. In the third case (rows 7 and 8), the current finish date for the second task is *later* than the baseline finish date, thereby causing positive variance.

Figure 5-8	THE RELATIONSHIP BETWEEN CURRENT AND BASELINE DATES AND VARIANCE

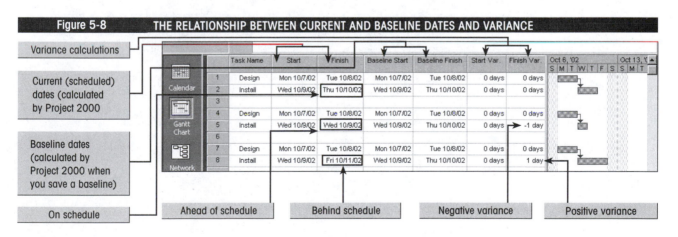

Currently, the Start Var. and Finish Var. fields for the LAN project are zero because no actual progress has been tracked and the project is neither ahead of nor behind schedule.

Understanding the Tracking Table

Many different ways are available to enter actual progress data into a project by using sheet, form, and graphical views. Also available are many different types of actual progress data that can be entered, including actual date, actual duration, actual cost, and actual work. Most project managers enter actual start and finish dates for individual tasks and allow Project 2000 to automatically update the actual duration, cost, and work fields based on default formulas. Others prefer to enter actual work hours while leaving the cost calculations to Project 2000.

When you enter actual start and finish dates for a task, many other actual fields of information are updated. For example, the actual start and finish dates of a task determine the actual duration (actual finish date – actual start date), which in turn determines the actual work (Work = Duration × Units) which calculates the actual cost (Cost = Work Hours × Cost/Hr/Resource). To enter the actual start and finish dates and observe the effect on other actual fields, use the **Tracking table** applied to the Task sheet because it provides all of the actual fields (actual date, actual duration, actual work, and actual cost) in one sheet view.

To apply the Tracking table to the Task sheet:

1. Right-click the **Select All** button for the Variance table, and then click **Tracking**. Currently, the value of the Rem. Dur. (remaining duration) field equals the Duration value from the Entry table because no progress has yet been applied to this project.

   If you see an error in the scheduled duration, you can change the duration in the Tracking table.

   For example, while working on the LAN installation, Adrian Creighton, one of the partners, located a binder of information on all of the current equipment and software at JLB Partners. Having this documentation will dramatically decrease the amount of time required to document the current environment.

2. Click the **Rem. Dur.** cell for row 2 (Document Current Environment), type **1**, press the **Enter** key, and then click the **LAN Installation** task name in row 0. The Tracking table should look like Figure 5-9. The remaining duration is now 58 days.

Figure 5-9   **TRACKING TABLE APPLIED TO THE TASK SHEET**

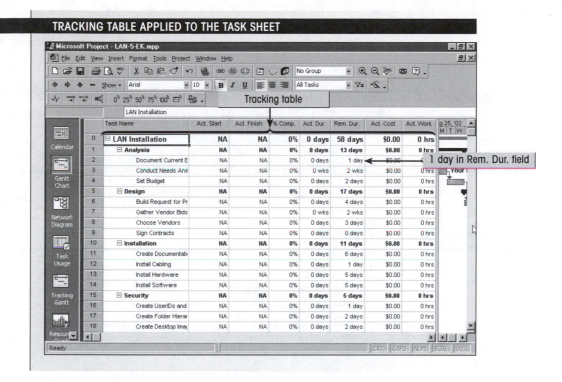

Even though you can directly type actual values into each field displayed by the Tracking table, you will want to use the buttons on the Tracking toolbar whenever possible. The buttons on the Tracking toolbar help you to productively update several actual fields (dates, duration, work, and costs) simultaneously by marking tasks complete as scheduled or at various percentage completed levels as of the project Status Date.

The specific tasks that you update are obviously driven by the progress information that you have collected. In a small project, you might simply *know* what tasks need to be updated because you are involved in the completion of each task in the project. In larger projects, you'll want to establish some sort of regular status reporting system with others so that the status information is productively collected and accurately entered.

Project 2000 provides a shared communication system called **Project Central** that allows you to implement Web-based workgroup features so that many people can view and update various parts of the project simultaneously. A **workgroup** is a subset of resources that exchanges status information about various parts of a project through a network. More information on Project 2000 workgroups and Project Central is in the appendices.

Updating Tasks That Are on Schedule

If your project is being completed according to schedule, you can quickly report its progress by using the Tracking toolbar. The LAN installation is progressing smoothly. You need to update those tasks that are on schedule as of the Current Date.

To update tasks that are on schedule as of the Current Date:

1. Click **Document Current Environment** (row 2), and then click the **Update as Scheduled** button ⬛ on the Tracking toolbar. Because Adrian Creighton found the documentation, you were able to complete this task in one day, as scheduled, on time.

2. Double-click ↔ on the right edge of each **column heading** (except the Task Name column) to adjust the columns of the Tracking table so that all of the information is visible, as shown in Figure 5-10.

Figure 5-10	UPDATING A TASK THAT IS ON SCHEDULE

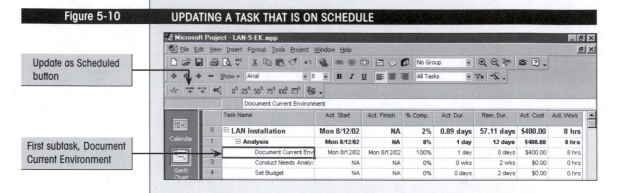

Clicking the Update as Scheduled button copies the dates in the current (scheduled) start and finish date fields and automatically enters them in the Act. Start (actual start) and Act. Finish (actual finish) date fields. In turn, the Act. Dur. (actual duration), Act. Cost (actual cost), and Act. Work (actual work) fields also are updated. You can monitor the progress of the project by looking at the information for the LAN installation project summary task bar. Updating a task automatically updates affected fields in the summary tasks to which it belongs. You can update more than one task at a time.

3. Click **Conduct Needs Analysis**, drag ➕ to **Set Budget** to select the two tasks, and then click the **Update as Scheduled** button ⊞ on the Tracking toolbar.

In this case, Conduct Needs Analysis was partially updated with actual values, but Set Budget was not updated at all. Remember that the Status Date entered in the Project Information dialog box is 8/16/02. Because the scheduled start date of the Conduct Needs Analysis is 8/13/02, "updating it as scheduled" indicates that it actually started on its scheduled start date of 8/13/02. And because the scheduled finish date for this task is 8/26/02, "updating it as scheduled" means that it is not finished. The scheduled finish date of 8/26/02 is after the Status Date for which you are updating progress. The scheduled start date for the Set Budget task is 8/27/02, so this task would not be updated using the Update as Scheduled button.

Using the Update as Scheduled button records only actual data for tasks scheduled *before* the Status Date. In other words, you can't update actual values for a task "as scheduled" that is scheduled in the future!

Updating Tasks That Are Ahead of Schedule

If a task is being completed *ahead* of schedule, you can use the Percent Complete buttons on the Tracking toolbar to indicate progress even if the task is scheduled for the future. Or, you can enter the specific progress dates, duration, cost, or work data directly into the Tracking table. Emily Kelsey has just informed you that she has completed 25% of the work for the Set Budget task ahead of schedule.

To update tasks that are ahead of schedule:

1. Click **Set Budget** (row 4), and then click the **25% Complete** button 25⁺ on the Tracking toolbar.

   This action updates the Set Budget task to be 25% complete in the areas of duration, cost, and work. It also copies the scheduled start date into the Act. Start field.

2. Click the **% Comp. cell** for the Build Request for Proposal task (row 6), type **10%**, and then press the **Enter** key. The Tracking table should look like Figure 5-11. Even though this task is not scheduled to start until 8/29, you have already completed 10% of the work.

Figure 5-11	UPDATING TASKS THAT ARE AHEAD OF SCHEDULE

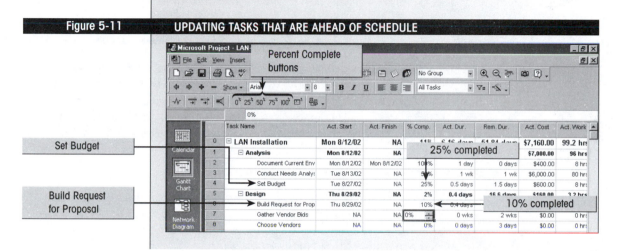

You can enter any percentage in the % Comp. field for any subtask or summary task. As you update tasks using either the Percent Complete buttons or % Comp. field, the currently scheduled start date will be copied into the Act. Start date field.

Conflicts and the Planning Wizard

The installation team has been making tremendous progress. The current scheduled start date for the Installation task is 9/23/02; but it actually started on 9/19/02. You can also update tasks ahead of schedule by entering the actual date that they started.

To enter an actual start date:

1. Click the **Act. Start** cell for the Create Documentation task (row 11), type **9/19/02**, and then press the **Enter** key.

   The Planning Wizard dialog box opens. It warns that this action will cause a scheduling conflict, as shown in Figure 5-12.

| Figure 5-12 | PLANNING WIZARD DIALOG BOX |

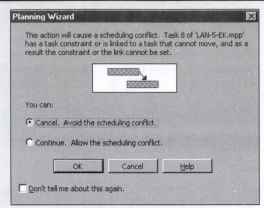

In other words, you have indicated that work has started on a successor task that has a finish-to-start relationship with a predecessor task that hasn't yet been finished! You can cancel the action or allow the scheduling conflict. Project 2000 allows actual entries to override logic easily but does not retain this information or track logic errors. If you override the Planning Wizard warning, you will not be reminded of the conflict in logic again.

2. Click the **OK** button to cancel the scheduling conflict.

Rather than move the Act. Start date, you decide to enter eight hours of work on this task to reflect what has been done and let Project 2000 calculate the other numbers. Project 2000 allows you to enter actual work for a task even though it is scheduled for the future and a predecessor task with a finish-to-start relationship with that task has not yet been completed.

3. Click the **Act. Work** cell for the Create Documentation task (row 11), type **8**, and then press the **Enter** key.

Notice how the scheduled start date of 9/23/02 was entered as the Act. Start date for the Create Documentation task and the task is calculated at 17% complete. Project 2000 does not warn you about entering progress on a day beyond the Status Date.

4. Click the **Save** button 🖫 on the Standard toolbar. You were not prompted whether you want to save a baseline (as you might have been prompted when saving previous projects) because you already saved a baseline for this project.

Recall the formula Work = Duration × Units. Because only one resource is assigned to the Create Documentation task, entering eight hours in the Act. Work cell calculated Act. Dur. (actual duration) as one day. The Rem. Dur. (remaining duration) is the difference between the current duration (six days for this task) and the actual duration and is therefore calculated as five days.

Updating Tasks That Are Behind Schedule

If a task is behind schedule, you can use the Percent complete buttons on the Tracking toolbar to indicate progress just as you did for tasks that are ahead of schedule. Or, you can enter the specific progress dates or duration, cost, or work data directly into the Tracking table. For example, you might have completed only 25% of the work for the Gather Vendor Bids task by 9/17/02, even though it was scheduled to be finished on that date.

Almost another month has passed and the LAN installation is progressing at JLB Partners. Usually, you wouldn't wait an entire month before updating a project's progress (as implied by changing both the Current and Status Date to a month forward in time). The needs of your business and the availability of the progress information determine how often you update progress. Some executives will want the project manager to enter and report progress information daily, whereas others require only weekly or monthly reports.

A few tasks are running a little behind schedule. You will set a new Current Date as well as a new Status Date and continue to update the **LAN-5-Your Initials.mpp file**.

To update tasks that are behind schedule:

1. Click **Project** on the menu bar, click **Project Information**, select **Mon 8/19/02**, type **9/16/02** as the new Current Date, select **Fri 8/16/02** in the Status date field, type **9/13/02** as the new Status Date, and then click the **OK** button.

2. Click **Build Request for Proposal** (row 6), and then click the **25% Complete** button [25%] on the Tracking toolbar, as shown in Figure 5-13.

| Figure 5-13 | UPDATING TASKS THAT ARE BEHIND SCHEDULE |

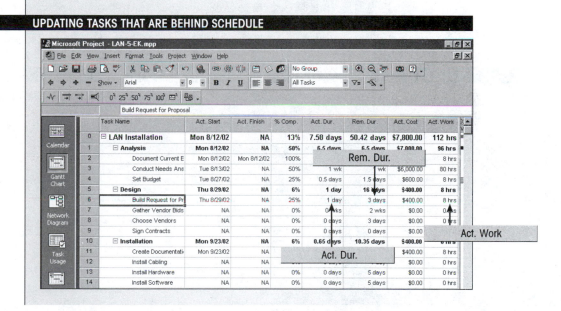

The Build Request for Proposal task was originally scheduled to be finished by 9/3/02, but your progress reports indicate that only 25% of the work was completed by that date. Notice that 25% of the duration (one day) is automatically entered in the Act. Dur. cell and 75% of the duration is displayed (three days) in the Rem. Dur. cell. The Act. Work cell is calculated at eight hours because one day of actual duration is equal to eight hours of work for the single resource that is assigned to this task. The Act. Cost field is calculated by multiplying the Act. Work hours by the resource's hourly rate (8 hours × $50/hr).

Rescheduling Tasks That Are Behind Schedule

Once a project has slipped behind schedule, you need a quick way to reschedule those tasks that *should* have been finished but are not completed. Project 2000 provides such a tool with the Reschedule Work 🔲 button. Using the Reschedule Work button, you can reschedule tasks that are behind schedule to start on the project's Status Date. The task that is most behind schedule is Conduct Needs Analysis (row 3).

To reschedule tasks that are behind schedule:

1. Double-click **Conduct Needs Analysis** (row 3) to open the Task Information dialog box, click the **General** tab if it is not already selected, and then observe the currently scheduled finish date for the task (8/26/02).

   Because this task has not had any more work completed between the last update and the Status Date (9/13/02), this task needs to be rescheduled.

2. Click the **OK** button in the Task Information dialog box.

   You want to use the Gantt Chart to help you understand the scheduling issues for the project. You reorganize the screen so that the Gantt Chart is visible.

3. Use the ◄║► pointer to drag the **split bar** to the left so that only the Task Name column is visible in the Tracking sheet, and then click the **Go To Selected Task** button 🔲 on the Standard toolbar. The Gantt Chart should look like Figure 5-14.

Figure 5-14	VIEWING THE GANTT CHART WITH TRACKING INFORMATION

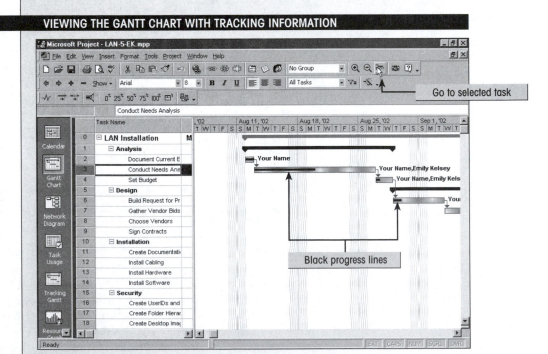

The **progress lines** within each task bar in the Gantt Chart indicate how much of that task has been completed. Conduct Needs Analysis (task 3) is approximately 50% completed, so the progress line is about half as long as that task's task bar. Tasks behind schedule are not *automatically* rescheduled. You must specifically indicate when a task that is behind schedule should be rescheduled.

4. Click **Conduct Needs Analysis** (row 3), click the **Reschedule Work** button on the Tracking toolbar, and then click the **Zoom Out** button on the Standard toolbar. Your screen should look like Figure 5-15.

| Figure 5-15 | RESCHEDULING TASKS THAT ARE BEHIND SCHEDULE |

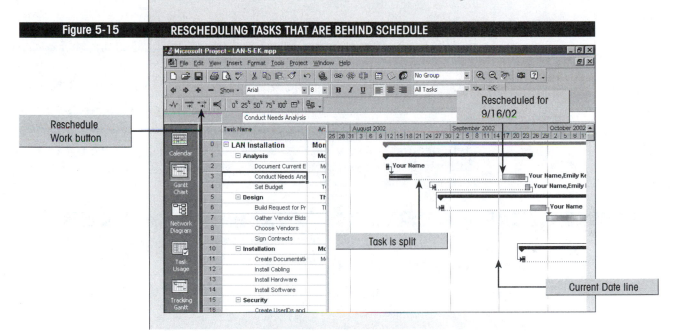

Because 50% of the work had already been completed on the Conduct Needs Analysis task, it was split and the remaining 50% of the work was rescheduled as of the Current Date (9/16/02). The Conduct Needs Analysis task has a finish-to-start relationship with Set Budget (and so forth), so several other tasks were rescheduled as well. Those tasks with partial work already completed were split and rescheduled, as dictated by their relationships with other tasks.

If you want to specify a split date other than the current date, click the task to select it, and then click the Split Task button on the standard toolbar. You will be prompted to enter the specific information needed to split the task.

Updating Progress By Using the Update Tasks Dialog Box

Some project managers would prefer viewing the graphical Gantt Chart rather than use the Tracking table. You can also update progress on a task using either the Gantt Chart or the Update Tasks dialog box. Another month has passed at JLB Partners, and you have to update progress for the next month's work on the LAN installation project.

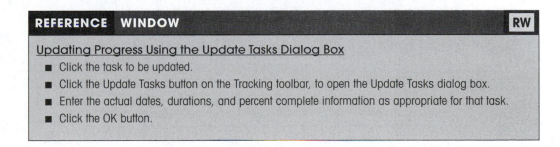

REFERENCE WINDOW **RW**

Updating Progress Using the Update Tasks Dialog Box
- Click the task to be updated.
- Click the Update Tasks button on the Tracking toolbar, to open the Update Tasks dialog box.
- Enter the actual dates, durations, and percent complete information as appropriate for that task.
- Click the OK button.

To update tasks using the Update Tasks dialog box:

1. Click **Project** on the menu bar, click **Project Information**, select **Mon 9/16/02**, type **10/28/02** as the new Current Date, select **Fri 9/13/02** in the Status date field, type **10/25/02** as the new Status Date, and then click the **OK** button.

   The Conduct Needs Analysis task was completed on September 25, and you have to update the project file.

2. Click **Conduct Needs Analysis** (row 3) if it is not already selected, and then click the **Update Tasks** button 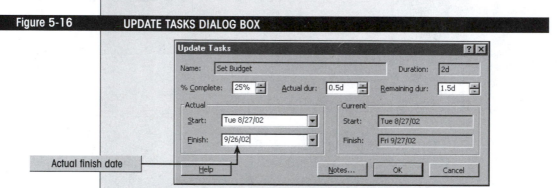 on the Tracking toolbar. The Update Tasks dialog box opens.

3. Double-click **NA** in the Finish field, type **9/25/02**, and then click the **OK** button.

   You can enter any actual dates, durations, and percentages completed in the Update Tasks dialog box.

4. Click **Set Budget** (row 4), click the **Update Tasks** button 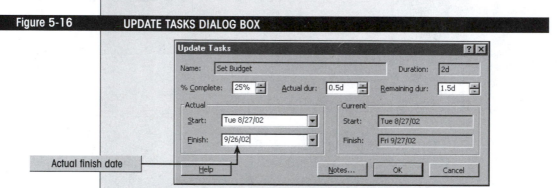 on the Tracking toolbar to open the Update Tasks dialog box, double-click **NA** in the Finish field, and then type **9/26/02**, as shown in Figure 5-16.

Figure 5-16	UPDATE TASKS DIALOG BOX

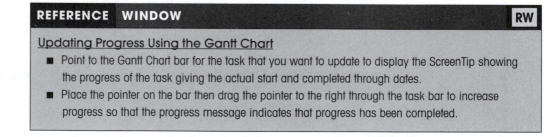

Actual finish date

Many project managers like to use the Update Tasks dialog box to update progress because it also shows the currently scheduled task start and finish dates (the default Tracking table does not show the scheduled start and finish dates).

5. Click the **OK** button. The Set Budget progress bar is updated to show that the task is completed.

REFERENCE WINDOW   **RW**

Updating Progress Using the Gantt Chart
- Point to the Gantt Chart bar for the task that you want to update to display the ScreenTip showing the progress of the task giving the actual start and completed through dates.
- Place the pointer on the bar then drag the pointer to the right through the task bar to increase progress so that the progress message indicates that progress has been completed.

Updating Progress By Using the Gantt Chart

Yet a third way to update actual progress on a project is by using the Gantt Chart itself. Dragging the 🔳 to the right through a task bar increases progress.

To update progress using the Gantt Chart:

1. Point to the first part of the bar for the **Build Request for Proposal** task (row 6). A Progress ScreenTip displays that indicates the progress of the task and gives its actual start and completed through dates.

2. Place the pointer on the bar so that it changes to 🔳, and then drag the 🔳 pointer to the right until the progress message indicates that progress has been completed through 10/1/02, as shown in Figure 5-17.

Figure 5-17   **UPDATING PROGRESS USING THE GANTT CHART**

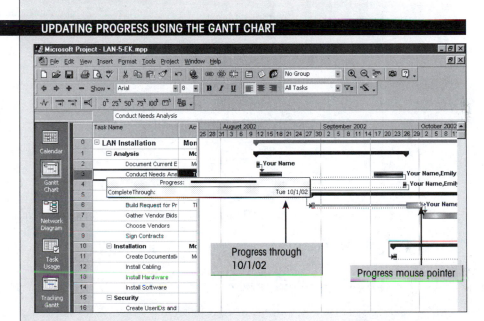

3. Point to the left side of the bar for the **Gather Vendor Bids** task (row 7), and then drag the 🔳 pointer to the right until the Progress ScreenTip indicates that progress has been completed through 10/14/02, as shown in Figure 5-18.

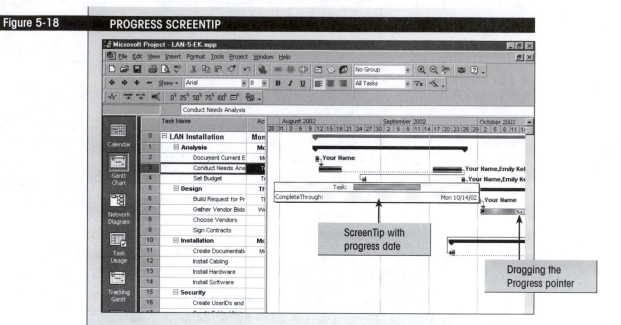

Figure 5-18   PROGRESS SCREENTIP

4. Point to the progress bar in the **Gather Vendor Bids** task to show the Progress ScreenTip.

When you point to a bar in the Gantt Chart, many different mouse pointers might appear, including ✥, ◀┃, and %▶, that move, reduce the duration, or extend the duration of the task, respectively. When you point to the Gantt Chart task bars, you also can point to the progress bar to display the Progress ScreenTip, which includes information about the progress of the task, or point to the task bar to display the Task ScreenTip with task information.

Entering Actual Costs

Actual costs are automatically calculated by multiplying the actual duration by the cost/hour for each resource applied to the task. You can also enter actual fixed costs. Recall from Tutorial 4 that **fixed costs** are costs associated with the task but are neither specific nor driven by any particular resource. They are costs inherent to the task itself. Examples of fixed costs are a room charge, a convention entry fee, and a fixed travel expense. You enter fixed costs into a task's Fixed Cost field. The easiest way to find the Fixed Cost field is to view a Task sheet with the Cost table applied. The Fixed Cost field is the second column in the sheet. JLB Partners incurred some one-time legal fees that fall into this category.

To enter actual fixed costs:

1. Right-click the **Select All** button for the Task sheet, and then click **Cost**.

2. Drag the **split bar** to the right to view the Fixed Cost column (if it is not already visible), click the **Fixed Cost** cell for Sign Contracts (row 9), type **2000**, and then press the **Enter** key.

Two thousand dollars represents the fixed fee that the attorney will charge to read and review the contracts. You can change this amount later if the estimate is too high or too low, but there is no baseline Fixed Cost field, so you cannot track variance in the Fixed Cost field over time.

3. Click the **Save** button ▣ on the Standard toolbar, click the **Print Preview** button ▣ on the Standard toolbar, click the **Page Setup** button on the Print Preview toolbar, replace Emily's name with your name in the left section of the header, and then print the Gantt Chart.

4. Click **File** on the menu bar, and click **Close**, then save your changes if prompted. The Planning Wizard dialog box opens, informing you that you have some tasks and resources for which there is no baseline information. You have three options.

5. Click the **OK** button to update the baseline for only the tasks and resources without baseline information in the **LAN-5-Your Initials.mpp** file. The file closes with the additional information saved.

Updating progress on a project is not difficult, but understanding how the many dates and actual data fields interact can be a challenge. This session was organized to show you that it is possible to update tasks that are on schedule, ahead of schedule, in conflict with the schedule, and behind schedule. In addition, it also showed you how to reschedule work that was behind schedule and how to mark progress using the Update Tasks dialog box and the Gantt Chart.

In a real project, however, you would most likely use some sort of tracking form that recorded each resource's actual progress for each task in the project. If you had planned your project so well that tasks were actually completed exactly as they were scheduled, you could use the buttons on the Tracking toolbar to mark tasks as "Updated as Scheduled" or a "Percentage Complete" as of the Status Date. In reality, however, you would probably enter actual values (such as the Actual Start, Actual Finish, and Actual Work) on a regular (perhaps a weekly) basis and let Project 2000 take care of determining whether those actual values put your schedule ahead of or behind schedule.

Session 5.1 QUICK CHECK

1. What are the steps to save a baseline?

2. How are baseline dates calculated?

3. What is variance, and how is it calculated?

4. Explain how positive and negative variance are calculated.

5. What table do you apply to the Task sheet to see baseline dates? What table do you apply to see actual dates?

6. Identify three ways that you can update progress on a task.

7. When you update tasks that are on schedule or reschedule tasks that are behind schedule, what date is used to determine which tasks should be updated or rescheduled?

8. Which table do you apply to enter actual fixed costs?

SESSION 5.2

In this session, you'll use a variety of Project 2000 progress tracking features to create a custom table and view, use interim plans, and work with variance reports. You'll use a copy of your LAN project file that was saved before any progress was reported in order to clarify what you are learning.

Inserting or Hiding a Column in a Table

When you are tracking progress, it is difficult to get all of the information that you want to see at one time on the screen because you are working with several sets of dates for each task (current, baseline, actual, and potentially interim dates). By default, the baseline dates are shown in the Variance table and the Actual dates are shown in the Tracking table. The currently scheduled task start and finish dates are shown in several tables (and are labeled Start and Finish). Therefore, it's important that you know how to create a table with the columns of information that you want to see. You can easily insert or hide a column in any table.

REFERENCE WINDOW   RW

Inserting a Column in a Table

- Right-click the column heading where you want to insert the new column.
- Click Insert Column in the shortcut menu.
- In the Column Definition dialog box, specify the new field name, title, alignment, and width that you want the new column to display, and then click the OK button.

To insert a column in a table:

1. Start Project 2000 (if not already running), and open the **LAN-5-2.mpp** file stored in the Tutorial folder of your Data Disk for Tutorial 5.

2. Save the file without a baseline with the name **LAN-5-2-Your Initials** to the Tutorial folder of your Data Disk for Tutorial 5, change task 0 to LAN Installation, click the **Resource Sheet** button 🖳 on the View bar, change **Your Name** to your name, change **YN** to your initials, and then click the Gantt Chart button 📊 on the View Bar.

   This file is a copy of your LAN project file before the baseline was saved and before any progress was reported.

3. Click **Tools** on the menu bar, point to **Tracking**, and then click **Save Baseline**.

   Remember, you must save the baseline before you start tracking progress so that variance reports can be created from the currently scheduled task start and finish dates. As soon as you enter progress that is ahead or behind schedule, those start and finish dates are recalculated.

4. Click the **OK** button in the Save Baseline dialog box to save the baseline for the entire project.

5. Right-click the **Select All** button for the Task sheet, click **Variance** to apply the Variance table to the Task sheet, and then drag the **split bar** to the right so that all of the columns of the Variance table are visible.

You might want to display the actual dates, scheduled dates, and baseline dates on one table. The second and third columns in this table show the scheduled start and finish dates for each task. You want to insert the Act. Start and Act. Finish columns in this table.

6. Right-click the **Start** column heading, and then click **Insert Column**.

The Column Definition dialog box opens in which you can choose a new field to insert as a new column. The Field name list includes all of the fields of data that are available in the project file that are appropriate to add for the current sheet.

7. Click the **Field name** list arrow, press the **A** key to quickly scroll to the entries that start with the letter A, and then click **Actual Start**, as shown in Figure 5-19.

Figure 5-19	COLUMN DEFINITION DIALOG BOX

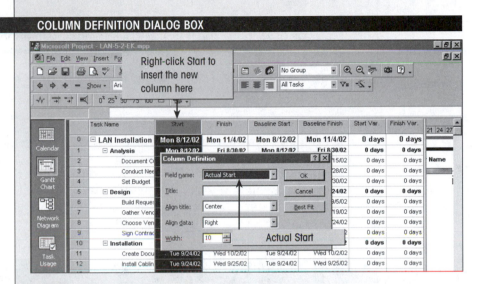

8. Click the **OK** button to insert the Actual Start column in the table.

9. Right-click the **Start** column heading, click **Insert Column**, click the **Field name** list arrow, press the **A** key to quickly scroll to the field names that begin with the letter A, click **Actual Finish**, and then click the **OK** button.

10. Resize the columns as necessary so that your screen looks like Figure 5-20.

Figure 5-20	INSERTING COLUMNS IN AN EXISTING TABLE

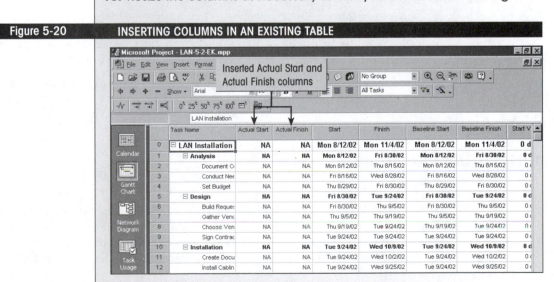

11. Click the **Actual Start** cell for the Document Current Environment task (row 2), type **8/14/02**, and then press the **Enter** key.

TROUBLE? If the columns display (####) signs, double-click ↔ on the right edge of the column heading to widen the columns to fully display all of the data.

Because 8/14/02 was two days later than originally planned, the start and finish dates for *every other task* dependent on the Document Current Environment task were automatically recalculated. Note that the Baseline Start date for this task remained at 8/12/02.

12. Press **Tab** several times to view the Start Var. (start variance) and Finish Var. (finish variance) fields.

The first task of the project started two days later than planned, so a positive two days of variance (both start and finish) rippled throughout most tasks in the project. This is because most have a finish-to-start relationship with the next task.

13. Press and hold the **Ctrl** key, and then press the **Home** key to return to the first column of the first row.

When you insert columns in an existing table, you redefine the columns for that table. In other words, now your Variance table will *always* display the Actual Start and Actual Finish columns for this project. (New projects would display the default Variance table.) Therefore, you might want to reestablish the default Variance table by hiding the Actual Start and Actual Finish columns and creating an entirely new table with the extra columns that you want to display.

REFERENCE WINDOW   **RW**

Hiding a Column in a Table
- Right-click the column heading that you want to hide.
- Click Hide Column on the shortcut menu.

To hide columns in a table:

1. Right-click the **Actual Start** column heading, and then click **Hide Column**. The Actual Start column table is no longer visible in the Variance table.

2. Right-click the **Actual Finish** column heading, and then click **Hide Column**. The columns in the Variance table are now set back to the default columns.

Creating a Custom Table

You can create a custom table containing the fields that you want and then give the new table a descriptive name. In this way, you can preserve the default tables that Project 2000 provides, while developing as many unique tables as you need to communicate the information during the project. You can create either task or resource tables. As you would suspect, task tables can be applied only to Task sheets and resource tables can be applied only to Resource sheets.

Emily Kelsey has asked to see how the project schedule is affected by the minor delays that have occurred in the LAN installation. You decide to create a new table called 3 Dates that contains the actual, current, and baseline start and finish dates that you were previously viewing in the modified Variance table.

REFERENCE   WINDOW   **RW**

To Create a New Table
- Right-click the Select All button for the current table.
- Click More Tables from the shortcut menu.
- Click New to create a new table in the More Tables dialog box, or click an existing table that you want to copy and then click Copy to create a copy of that table.
- In the Table Definition dialog box, identify the new table's name, specify each field (column) that should appear in the table, specify the other characteristics of each column, including alignment, width, and title, and then click the OK button to create the table.

To create a custom table:

1. Right-click the **Select All** button for the Variance table, and then click **More Tables** from the shortcut menu.

   The More Tables dialog box opens showing all of the current task tables that Project 2000 provides. If you click the Resource option button, you will see a list of the resource tables. You can use the More Tables dialog box to create a new table, edit any of the existing tables, or create a copy of an existing table. Since the Variance table already contains many of the fields that you want to display, you'll build your custom table based on a copy of the Variance table. Variance should be selected in the list.

2. Verify that **Variance** is the selected table in the Tables list, and then click the **Copy** button in the More Tables dialog box.

   TROUBLE? If Variance isn't selected in the Tables list in the More Tables dialog box, be sure that the Task option button is selected, scroll, and then click Variance.

   The Table Definition dialog box opens, as shown in Figure 5-21.

Figure 5-21 | TABLE DEFINITION DIALOG BOX

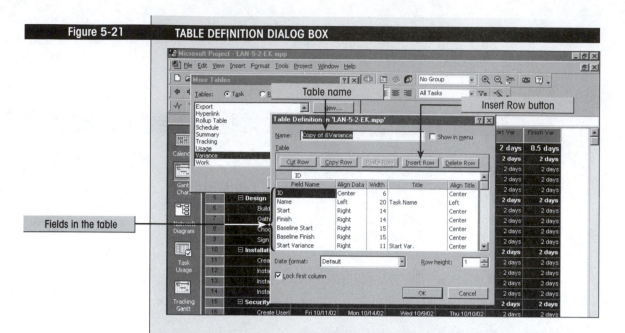

The new table should have a descriptive name so that you can identify it in a list.

3. Select **Copy of &Variance** (if it isn't currently selected), type **3 Dates** in the Name text box, and then click the **Show in menu** check box so that this table appears in the shortcut menu when you right-click the Select All button for a table.

Each column of the table is represented by a row in the Table Definition dialog box that describes the characteristics of that column. The order of the rows in the dialog box is the order from left to right that the columns will display in the table. You need to add two more fields, Actual Start and Actual Finish, to the table.

4. Click **Start** in the Field Name list, and then click the **Insert Row** button in the Table Definition dialog box. A new row is inserted above the Start Field Name. The field that you enter in this row will display to the left of the Start field in the new table. The new row Field Name cell is selected.

5. Click the blank selected Field Name cell **list arrow** to display the list of available fields, click **Actual Start**, and then press the **Enter** key. The new field is inserted with default settings for alignment and width. The Start field is selected.

6. Click the **Insert Row** button to add a blank row. The new blank row is between the new Actual Start field and the current Start field.

7. Click the blank selected Field Name cell **list arrow**, click **Actual Finish**, and then press the **Enter** key.

Your Table Definition dialog box should look like Figure 5-22.

Figure 5-22   **TABLE DEFINITION DIALOG BOX WITH NEW FIELDS**

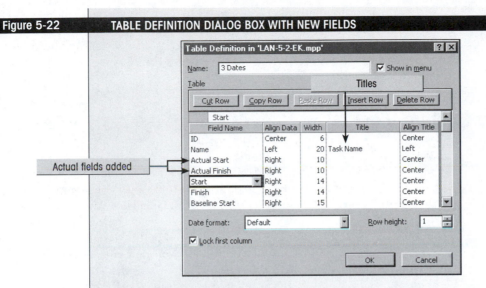

Actual fields added

You can also use the Table Definition dialog box to give the fields (columns) more descriptive names. For example, the Start and Finish fields can be somewhat confusing unless you understand that they represent the currently scheduled start and finish dates for a task. Use the Title field to clarify those fields.

8. Click the **Title** cell for the Start field, type **Sched. Start**, press the **Enter** key to move to the **Title** cell for the Finish field, type **Sched. Finish**, and then click the **OK** button in the Table Definition dialog box. The 3 Dates table is added to the list of tables in the More Tables dialog box and is the currently selected table.

   TROUBLE? If you press the Delete key or use the Cut command within the Table Definition dialog box, then you will delete or cut the entire row, not the individual cell within the current row.

9. Click the **Apply** button in the More Tables dialog box to apply the 3 Dates table to the Task sheet, and then resize the columns as necessary, as shown in Figure 5-23.

   The 3 Dates table is applied to the Task sheet. The 3 Dates table also appears in the list when you right-click the Select All button for any Task sheet.

Figure 5-23   **APPLYING A CUSTOM TABLE**

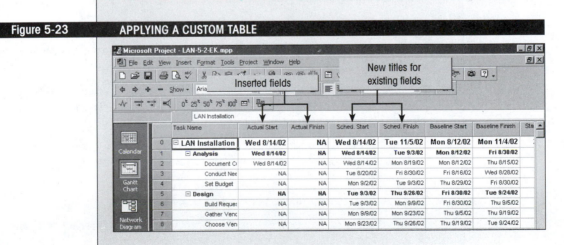

You can put any combination of task fields together to create a unique task table or any combination of resource fields to create a resource table. An estimated 200 different fields of information are available for each task and resource, so you'll want the flexibility of creating your own tables of information. You can also title any of the fields to be more descriptive or meaningful for your business.

Creating a Custom View

After you have used Project 2000 for a while, you'll develop your own favorite techniques for viewing, entering, updating, and analyzing data. Just as you created, named, and saved a custom table, you can create, name, and save a custom view. A **custom view** is any view that is saved with a name and that differs from the default views that Project 2000 provides. Custom views can contain a set of fields in a particular view (sheet/table, form, graphical, or a combination of these), **grouping** (tasks sorted and outlined together that meet a common criteria), and/or a filter. You can add a button for your new custom view in the View Bar.

During your last meeting with Emily, she asked if there was a way to view the project that highlights actual, scheduled, and baseline date information for critical tasks. To satisfy this request, you will develop a custom view called Critical Dates that include these characteristics:

- View: Resource Sheet with Gantt Chart
- Table: 3 Dates
- Grouping: Complete and Incomplete Tasks
- Filter: Critical

REFERENCE WINDOW   RW

To Create a Custom View
- Click View on the menu bar, and then click More Views.
- Click the view that most closely represents the custom view that you want to create, and then click Copy.
- In the View Definition dialog box, identify the desired view name, table, group, and filter characteristics, and then click the OK button.

To create a custom view:

1. Drag the **split bar** to the left so that the last visible column is the Sched. Finish column.

2. Click **Document Current Environment** (row 2), drag ✚ through **Set Budget** (row 4) to select the three tasks that comprise the Analysis phase, and then click the **100% Complete** button [100°] on the Tracking toolbar.

   The progress bars show that these three tasks are marked 100% complete. Marking them as being 100% complete will help you to see whether the grouping that you intend to apply for this view works properly.

3. Click **View** on the menu bar, and then click **More Views**.

   The More Views dialog box opens. The Gantt Chart view is the view that most closely resembles the custom view that you need to create, so start by making a copy of it that you can modify. Gantt Chart should be the currently selected view.

4. Click **Gantt Chart** in the Views list if it is not already selected, and then click the **Copy** button in the More Views dialog box.

The View Definition dialog box appears, as shown in Figure 5-24. The dialog box indicates that the current table that is applied to the Task sheet is 3 Dates, there is no group, and the filter is set to All Tasks. The current name, by default is Copy of &Gantt Chart. Descriptive names help identify views.

| Figure 5-24 | VIEW DEFINITION DIALOG BOX |

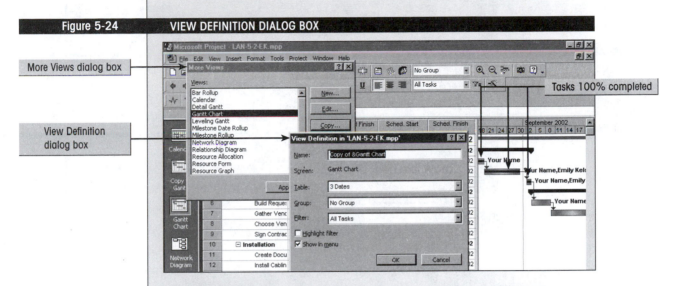

5. Type **Critical Dates** in the Name text box, click the **Group** list arrow, click **Complete and Incomplete Tasks**, click the **Filter** list arrow, click **Critical**, and then click the **Highlight filter** check box.

Your View Definition dialog box should look like Figure 5-25. The View name is Critical Dates, the table is 3 Dates, the group is Complete and Incomplete Tasks, and the filter is Critical.

| Figure 5-25 | DEFINING THE CRITICAL DATES VIEW IN THE VIEW DEFINITION DIALOG BOX |

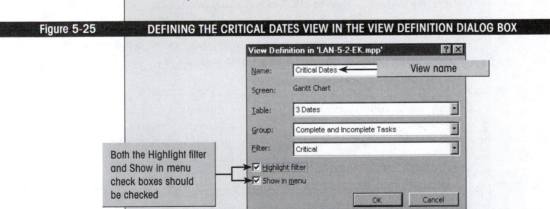

6. Click the **OK** button. The **Critical Dates** view should be selected in the More Views dialog box.

7. Click the **Apply** button in the More Views dialog box. The view that you just defined is applied to the Task sheet.

8. Drag the **split bar** to the right, press and hold the **Ctrl** key, and then press the **Home** key, as shown in Figure 5-26 so that you can see more fields and tasks in the Task sheet of the Critical Dates view.

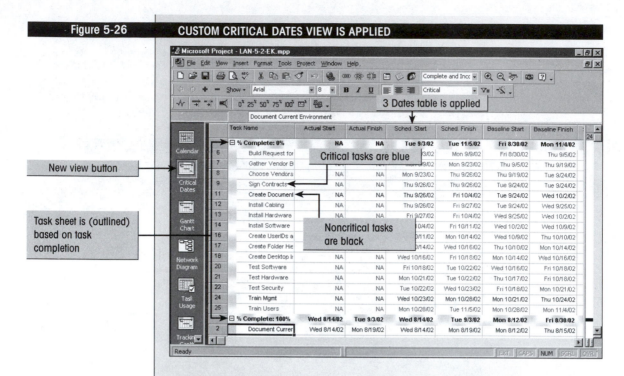

Figure 5-26   CUSTOM CRITICAL DATES VIEW IS APPLIED

9. Click the **Gantt Chart** button ▣ on the View Bar. The familiar Task sheet is applied.

10. Click the **Critical Dates** button on the View Bar to quickly reapply the custom view, and then scroll the sheet to view all of the tasks in the Critical Dates view.

    The tasks are not only shown in blue text (critical) and black text (noncritical); they are further outlined by percentage completed. Those with 0% completion are in the first group, and those with 100% completion are in the second group. Notice that tasks that are 100% are no longer critical.

11. Save the **LAN-5-2-Your Initials.mpp** file, preview the Critical Dates view of the project, replace Emily Kelsey's name with your name in the left section of the header, and then print the Critical Dates view.

You can edit or copy a custom view just as you edit or copy a Project 2000 view. In addition, by using the Organizer dialog box you can delete a custom view, copy a view to another project, or make a view available for every project. To open the organizer dialog box, you would click View on the menu bar, click More Views, and then click the Organizer button. To delete the custom view that you just created, you would click the view in the list of project views within the current project, and then click Delete. In the next tutorial, you'll learn how to work with the other features of the Organizer window, including the global template.

Using the Detail Gantt Chart to Examine Slack and Slippage

The **Detail Gantt Chart** is a Gantt Chart with extra bars that show total slack and slippage. Recall from the last tutorial that total slack (also called total float) is the amount of time that a task can be delayed without the delay's affecting the entire project. **Free slack** is the amount of time that a task can be delayed without affecting another task. When project managers speak of "slack," they are generally referring to total slack.

Slippage, or simply **slip**, is the difference between a task's scheduled start or finish date and its baseline start or finish date. A noncritical task can slip without affecting the project Finish Date. Recall that a noncritical task is one that has some slip—a task whose start date or finish date can change and the change will not affect the project Start Date or Finish Date. If a noncritical task slips too much, however, it can become critical and therefore change the critical path and extend the length of the project. So you need to track slippage on all tasks to see whether the project's noncritical tasks were planned properly, as well as to anticipate and deal with potential changes in the critical path.

As a project progresses, project managers use the Detail Gantt Chart to evaluate total slack and slippage to determine where to focus their efforts. After dealing with the critical path, they generally deal with tasks that have the least amount of slippage as the next highest priority, if they hope to keep their projects on schedule.

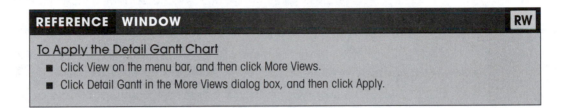

REFERENCE WINDOW	RW

To Apply the Detail Gantt Chart
- Click View on the menu bar, and then click More Views.
- Click Detail Gantt in the More Views dialog box, and then click Apply.

To use the Detail Gantt Chart:

1. Click **View** on the menu bar, click **More Views**, click **Detail Gantt** in the More Views dialog box, and then click the **Apply** button. The Detailed Gantt Chart is applied.

2. Click **Create Documentation** (row 11), and then click the **Go To Selected Task** button on the Standard toolbar.

   The Detail Gantt Chart appears as shown in Figure 5-27.

Figure 5-27   DETAIL GANTT CHART

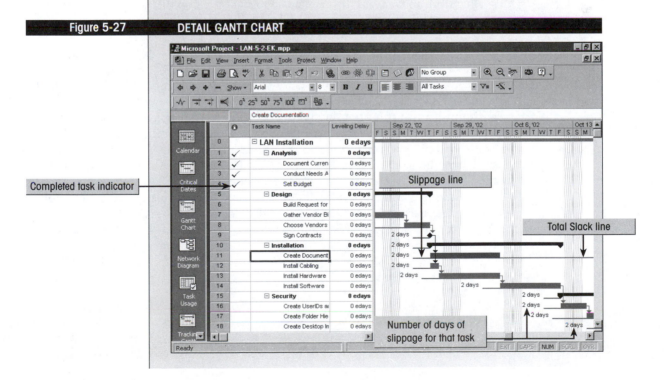

On the Detail Gantt Chart, the bars for the critical tasks are formatted in red and the bars for the noncritical tasks are blue. Because Create Documentation is a noncritical task, it shows a total slack line. Further, because it is dependent on a task that has already slipped, it also displays a slippage line.

3. Point to the **slippage line** before the **Create Documentation** task bar in the Gantt Chart. The Slippage ScreenTip identifies both the Baseline start date and the currently scheduled start date for that task.

4. Point to the **slack line** after the **Create Documentation** task bar in the Gantt Chart. The Slack ScreenTip displays information about the line.

The slack line represents total slack, the amount of time a task can be delayed without the delay's affecting the Finish Date for the entire project. The ScreenTip indicates that the task is currently scheduled to finish on 10/4/02 but that its free slack finish date (the last possible date that the task could finish without the delay's affecting the project) is 11/5/02.

5. Scroll down the Gantt Chart so that row 24 is visible, click **Train Mgmt** (row 24), and then click the **Go To Selected Task** button 🐿 on the Standard toolbar.

The Detail Gantt Chart shows the total number of days of free slack after the slack bar and the total number of days of slippage before the slippage bar. It shows that there are 22 days of total slack for the Create Documentation task and 6 days of total slack for the Train Mgmt task.

Tracking Gantt Chart

Another valuable Gantt Chart is the Tracking Gantt Chart. For each task, the Tracking Gantt Chart displays two task bars. The bars are placed one on top of the other. The lower bar shows baseline start and finish dates, and the upper bar shows scheduled start and finish dates. This view allows you to compare the baseline and actual dates so that you can see the difference between your plan and the current schedule.

Slack and Deadline Dates

As the LAN installation project currently stands, the 22 days of total slack on the Create Documentation task might be misleading. For example, you might not want to explicitly create a finish-to-start relationship between the Create Documentation task and any other tasks in the project, and yet you certainly don't want to wait until the very end of the project to have the documentation completed. You could apply any of a variety of constraints to the task, such as "Finish No Later Than" or "Must Finish On," to ensure that the task is done in a timely manner. Of special note is the **deadline** constraint.

The deadline constraint is a **flexible constraint**. It is flexible in that it does not dictate the scheduled start and finish dates of a task as does an inflexible constraint such as the "Must Start On" or "Must Finish On" constraint. Therefore, it is used more as a guideline than as a fact that your project must obey. The deadline constraint works well when you are trying to realistically display total slack values and yet maintain task scheduling flexibility.

To Set a Deadline Constraint
- Click the task that you want to set the deadline for, and then click the Task Information button on the Standard toolbar to open the task's Task Information dialog box.
- Click the Advanced tab, enter the deadline constraint date, and then click the OK button.

To set a deadline constraint:

1. Click the **Create Documentation** task (row 11), and then click the **Task Information** button on the Standard toolbar to open the Task Information dialog box.

2. Click the **General** tab (if it is not already selected) to observe that the currently scheduled finish date is 10/4/02.

3. Click the **Advanced** tab, double-click **NA** in the Deadline text box in the Constraint task section, type **10/11/02**, click the **OK** button, and then click the **Go To Selected Task** button to quickly view Create Documentation in the Detail Gantt Chart.

   The Detail Gantt Chart with the deadline date applied to the Create Documentation task is shown in Figure 5-28.

Figure 5-28	DETAIL GANTT CHART WITH A DEADLINE DATE

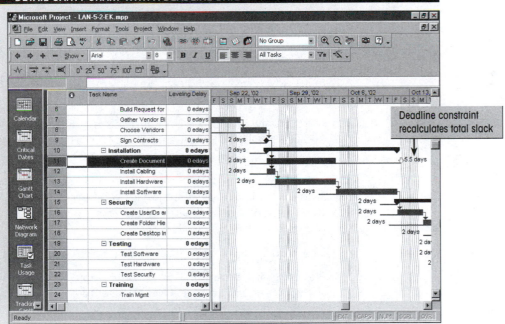

The new slack value for the Create Documentation task is 5.5 days, which is much more realistic than the previous 22 day calculation. In all Gantt Charts, a deadline constraint appears as a green outlined white arrow that points down at the deadline date.

4. Save the project, and then preview and print the Detail Gantt Chart with your name in the left section of the header.

Creating an Interim Plan

An **interim plan** is a portion of a baseline for a group of tasks in a project. While you hope that your initial baseline plan remains a realistic yardstick throughout the project, it is common to save an interim plan at various stages in the project (such as after each major phase or at the beginning of each month) so as to compare interim dates to the initial baseline dates. Unlike a baseline, the interim plan does not save duration, work, or cost values, but rather only start and finish dates. You can save up to ten interim plans for a project.

You decide to save an interim plan after completing each major phase of the project so that you can compare the interim plans to the baseline and more easily determine how accurate the initial planning was for each phase.

REFERENCE WINDOW   **RW**

To Save an Interim Plan

- Select the tasks for which you want to create the interim plan (or select no tasks if you want to save an interim plan for the entire project).
- Click Tools on the menu bar, point to Tracking, and then click Save Baseline.
- In the Save Baseline dialog box, click the Save interim plan option button, determine which fields you want to copy into which interim start and finish date fields by using the Copy and Into list arrows, click the appropriate option button to determine whether the interim plan is for the entire project or for selected tasks, and then click the OK button.

To save an interim plan:

1. Click **Tools** on the menu bar, point to **Tracking**, and then click **Save Baseline**.

2. In the Save Baseline dialog box, click the **Save interim plan** option button, and then click the **OK** button.

   The currently scheduled start and finish fields for the entire project are copied into the Start1 and Finish1 fields. To view the interim dates, you must add them to the Task sheet. You decide to use the 3 Dates custom table that you created earlier.

3. Right-click the **Select All** button for your Task sheet, click **3 Dates**, and then drag the **split bar** to the far right so that all of the columns of the 3 Dates table are visible.

   Now add the Start1 and Finish1 interim date fields to this table.

4. Right-click the **Baseline Start** column heading, click **Insert Column** in the shortcut menu to open the Column Definition dialog box, click the **Field name** list arrow, press the **S** key, click **Start1**, and then click the **OK** button.

5. Right-click the **Baseline Start** column heading, click **Insert Column** in the shortcut menu, click the **Field name** list arrow, press the **F** key, click **Finish1**, and then click the **OK** button.

6. Press and hold the **CTRL** key, press the **Home** key to select **LAN Installation** in row 0, and then resize the columns so that all data is visible, as shown in Figure 5-29.

Figure 5-29	DISPLAYING INTERIM DATES IN THE TASK SHEET WITH THE 3 DATES TABLE APPLIED

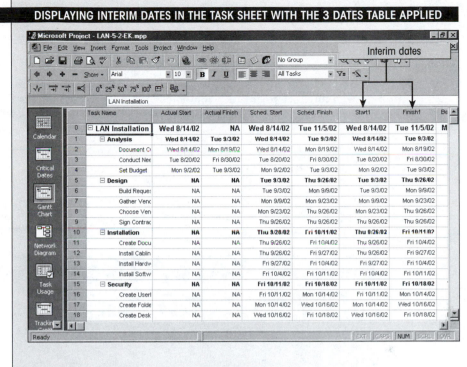

7. Save the file **LAN-5-2-Your Initials.mpp**.

Saving an interim plan allows you to compare the baseline or scheduled dates to interim dates saved at a particular point during the progression of the project. This type of detailed analysis helps project managers more clearly determine which phases or time periods were realistically scheduled, and which were not. However, no predeveloped tables, views, or reports are available that provide information based on the dates stored in the interim fields. Therefore, if you want to work extensively with interim plans, you should define custom tables and views that contain these fields so that you can quickly view and report on this information.

Using Project Progress Reports

Recall that in addition to the many sheet and graphical views that you can print at any time, Project 2000 also provides predeveloped reports that summarize information and focus on various areas of your project. The Project 2000 predeveloped report categories are shown in Figure 5-30.

Figure 5-30	PROJECT 2000 REPORT CATEGORIES

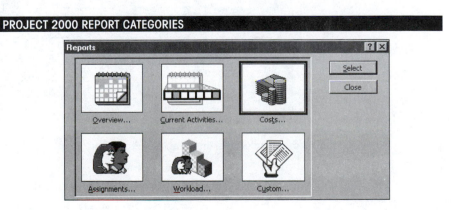

Reports used during the progression of the project help you to manage and prioritize work in progress to best meet the competing goals of finishing the project on time and within budget. The Current Activities reports focus on current project date progress. The reports that most directly focus on current project cost progress are in the Costs category.

As you might expect, you can edit each predeveloped report to show and summarize the specific fields of information on which you choose to report. In addition, you can use the Custom category to create a completely new report or to copy any existing report and modify it to meet your individual needs. If you have saved custom tables, filters, or views, you can use those definitions to create custom reports as well.

Current Activity Reports

The reports in the Current Activities category help you to analyze progress on your project. Use these reports to highlight various types of progress on the LAN installation project.

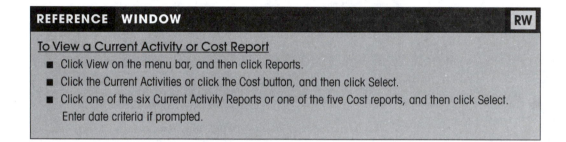

REFERENCE   WINDOW   **RW**

To View a Current Activity or Cost Report
- Click View on the menu bar, and then click Reports.
- Click the Current Activities or click the Cost button, and then click Select.
- Click one of the six Current Activity Reports or one of the five Cost reports, and then click Select. Enter date criteria if prompted.

To view a Current Activity report:

1. Click **View** on the menu bar, and then click **Reports**. The Reports dialog box opens with six large buttons that show each of the six report categories.

2. Click the **Current Activities** button, and then click the **Select** button.

   The Current Activities Reports dialog box provides access to six predeveloped reports that summarize task progress, as shown in Figure 5-31.

Figure 5-31   **CURRENT ACTIVITIES REPORTS DIALOG BOX**

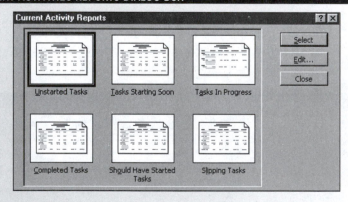

3. Click the **Tasks Starting Soon** button, and then click the **Select** button.

The Date Range dialog box opens. The Tasks Starting Soon report prompts you for a date range, which it uses to determine which tasks to display on the report. You want to see what's coming up the last two weeks in September.

4. Type **9/15/02**, click the **OK** button, type **9/30/02**, and then click the **OK** button.

The two-page report appears in preview mode.

5. Click the **Page Setup** button, type **your name** in the left section of the header, click the **Print** button, edit the print range to print only the first page of the report, and then click the **OK** button.

The report gives a detailed listing of all of the tasks that fall within the range that you specified, as well as a listing of the resources assigned to that task and the status of the work for each task. Task costs are not listed on this report, however, so you decide to print a Cost report, too.

To view a Cost report:

1. Double-click the **Costs** button in the Reports dialog box.

The Cost Reports dialog box opens, as shown in Figure 5-32.

| Figure 5-32 | COST REPORTS DIALOG BOX |

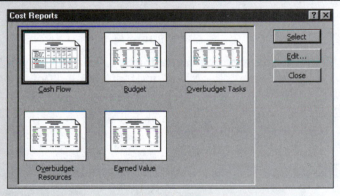

2. Click the **Cash Flow** button (if it is not already selected), and then click the **Select** button.

The two-page Cash Flow report appears in preview mode.

3. Click the **Page Setup** button, type **your name** in the left section of the header, click the **Print** button, and then print both pages of the report.

4. Click the **Close** button to close the Reports dialog box.

The Cash Flow report gives you a detailed analysis of how money is being spent by task for each day of the project.

Developing a Custom Report

Sometimes you will want either to customize an existing report or to create an entirely new report based on the custom tables, filters, and views that you have developed. Project 2000 allows you to edit any of its predeveloped reports or to create an entirely new report, by using the Custom report category.

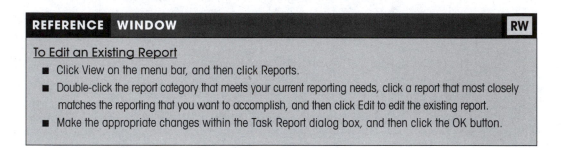

REFERENCE WINDOW   **RW**

To Edit an Existing Report

- Click View on the menu bar, and then click Reports.
- Double-click the report category that meets your current reporting needs, click a report that most closely matches the reporting that you want to accomplish, and then click Edit to edit the existing report.
- Make the appropriate changes within the Task Report dialog box, and then click the OK button.

In working with Emily at JLB Partners, some specific reporting requirements have been developed. You can meet these needs by editing the Current Activities report and adding the required additional fields.

To edit an existing report:

1. Click **View** on the menu bar, and then click **Reports**. The Reports dialog box opens.

2. Double-click the **Current Activities** button.

3. Click the **Tasks Starting Soon** button, click the **Edit** button to open the Task Report dialog box, and then click the **Definition** tab (if it isn't already selected).

   The Task Report dialog box is shown in Figure 5-33. You can use this dialog box to edit many different elements of the report.

Figure 5-33   **TASK REPORT DIALOG BOX**

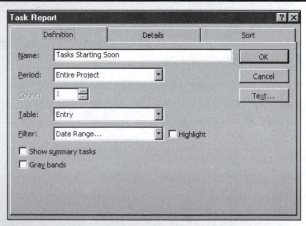

4. Click the **Table** list arrow, press the **3** key, and then click **3 Dates**. The 3 Dates table has the fields that you need for this custom report.

5. Click the **Details** tab. You can customize the details that appear for each task. For this report, you want Task notes and the Assignment schedule as specified in the tab. Additional formatting options such as borders and gridlines as well as totals are also available.

6. Click the **Border around details** check box, then click the **Gridlines between details** check box.

7. Click the **Sort** tab. You can sort by three fields and determine either ascending or descending order for each field. You accept the default sorting options that make the Start field the primary sort field and the ID field the secondary sort field. Both sort orders are ascending.

8. Click the **OK** button to accept the settings.

9. Double-click **Tasks Starting Soon** to open the Date Range dialog box. You want the report to cover the first two weeks of October.

10. Type **10/01/02**, click the **OK** button, type **10/15/02**, and then press the **Enter** key.

    The two-page report appears in preview mode.

11. Click the **Page Setup** button, enter **your name** in the left section of the header, and then print the report. You can see how formatting enhances a report.

12. Click the **Close** button in the Reports dialog box.

Review the report and notice the fields and details that it contains. This is an excellent communication tool for the staff and management at JLB Partners. However, the problem with editing existing reports is that your editing changes override the report choices originally provided by Project 2000 for this project. Therefore, if your changes are extensive, you might want to create an entirely new report to preserve the default settings for the Project 2000-supplied reports. You can copy new report definitions to other projects using the Organizer tool.

REFERENCE WINDOW | **RW**

__To Create a New Report__
- Click View on the menu bar, and then click Reports.
- Double-click the Custom report category, and then click New to create an entirely new report.
- Choose between a task, resource, monthly calendar, or crosstab report type, and then click OK.
- Make the appropriate changes and additions in the report definition dialog box, including a descriptive name for the new report, and then click the OK button.

To create a new report:

1. Click **View** on the menu bar, and then click **Reports**.

2. Double-click the **Custom** button in the Reports dialog box. The Custom Reports dialog box opens, containing a list of all of the Reports available. Rather than copying any of these reports and modifying them, you'll create an entirely new report.

3. Click the **New** button in the Custom Reports dialog box. The Define New Report dialog box opens. You can choose between four different types of custom reports: Task, Resource, Monthly Calendar, and Crosstab. You want to see information summarized in a column and row format, so you'll choose a Crosstab report.

4. Click **Crosstab**, and then click the **OK** button.

The Crosstab Report dialog box opens, as shown in Figure 5-34.

Figure 5-34   CROSSTAB REPORT DIALOG BOX

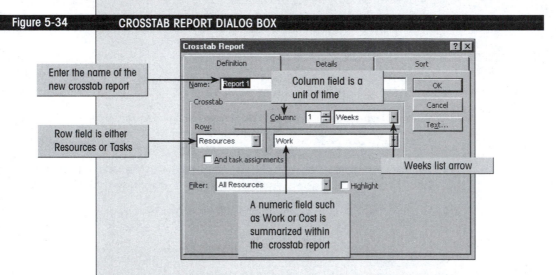

A **crosstab** report summarizes a numeric field for a resource or task over time. The numeric field is usually work or cost. The unit of time is usually days or weeks. The structure of the report is that the resource or task values form the column headings. The unit of time measurement forms the row headings. The numeric field is summarized within the intersection of the column and row. You must name the new report as well as determine which fields will serve as the row, column, and summarized positions within the crosstab report.

5. Select **Report 1** in the Name text box (if it is not already selected), and then type **Monthly Resource Work Crosstab** as the descriptive title for the report.

6. Click the **Weeks** list arrow, and then click **Months**. Now Months is specified for the column position, Resources is specified for the row position, and Work (hours) is chosen as the summarized field within the crosstab report. The other tabs of the dialog box allow you to further customize the report.

7. Click the **Details** tab, click the **Row totals** check box, click the **Column totals** check box, and then click the **OK** button. The Monthly Resource Work Crosstab report is added to the Reports list in the Custom Reports dialog box.

8. Click **Monthly Resource Work Crosstab** (if it is not already selected) in the Custom Reports dialog box, and then click the **Preview** button to display the new custom report.

9. Print the Monthly Resource Work Crosstab report with your name in the left section of the header.

10. Click the **Close** button in the Reports dialog box.

11. Save the changes to the **LAN-5-2-Your Initials.mpp** file, and then close the file.

The report provides the information that you need at JLB Partners. As you update and continue to track the progress of the LAN installation, you can access this report at any time from the Custom Reports dialog box.

Closing a Project

Closing a project (as opposed to saving and closing a project file) means finalizing the data that is stored in the project file. "Closing a project" is not a feature of Project 2000, but rather, a point in time or announcement that you as the project manager declare in order to clarify that the project is finished and the reports are final.

Once all tasks have been completed and no additional progress information will be reported on the LAN project, you will establish a date on which the project is officially "closed" and schedule a meeting with Emily Kelsey to review final cost and variance reports. Figure 5-35 summarizes several reports provided by Project 2000 that are used after the project is closed to analyze a project's overall success. Many of these reports can be used to evaluate progress during the project as well.

Figure 5-35	PROJECT 2000 REPORTS USED TO ANALYZE A CLOSED PROJECT		
TYPE OF INFORMATION	**REPORT CATEGORY**	**REPORT NAME**	**REPORT DESCRIPTION**
Summary	Overview	Project Summary	A summary of the project information, including date, duration, work, and cost values for the scheduled versus baseline values.
Summary	Overview	Top-Level Tasks	A summary of the major phases showing start, finish, cost, and work values for each phase.
Summary	Overview	Milestones	A summary of the milestones showing start, finish, cost, and work values for each milestone.
Task Information	Current Activity	Completed Tasks	Shows duration, start, finish, cost, and work information for each completed task.
Cost	Costs	Budget	Shows fixed costs, total costs, baseline costs, variance, actual costs, and remaining costs for all tasks.
Work	Workload	Task Usage	Crosstab report of summarized work. Resources within tasks are displayed in the row area. The columns are organized by weeks.
Work	Workload	Resource Usage	Crosstab report of summarized work. Tasks within resources are displayed in the row area. The columns are organized by weeks.

To print final reports:

1. Open the **LAN-5-2B.mpp** file in the Tutorial folder of your Data Disk for Tutorial 5.

2. Click **File** on the menu bar, click **Save As**, and then save the file with the name **LAN-5-2B-Your Initials** to the Tutorial folder of your Data Disk for Tutorial 5.

3. Change task 0 to LAN Installation, click the **Resource Sheet** button on the View Bar, change **Your Name** to your name, change **YN** to your initials, and then click the Gantt Chart button on the View Bar.

   The check marks in each row of the Indicators column show that you, the project manager, have updated the actual dates for each task and that each task has been completed.

4. Press the **Page Down** key to view the last tasks in the project.

5. Point to the **check mark indicator** for Train Users (row 25).

The ScreenTip indicates that this task was completed on 11/6/02. You need to print two reports for a final meeting of the management. You need one Project Summary report and one Cost report.

6. Click **View** on the menu bar, click **Reports**, double-click **Costs**, double-click **Budget**, and then print the two-page report with your name in the left section of the report header. The report shows fixed costs, total costs (fixed costs plus any costs incurred by resources assigned to the task), baseline costs, and variance. Next, you want a Project Summary report. The Reports dialog box is open.

7. Double-click **Overview**, double-click **Project Summary**, and then print the two-page report. You review the project summary report and see that your overall project cost variance was $2,000 and that your overall project finish variance was two days. You've done a great job managing your first project!

8. Close the Reports dialog box. Save and close **LAN-5-2B-Your Initials**, update the baseline information, and then exit Project 2000.

Session 5.2 QUICK CHECK

1. What are the steps to insert a new field (column) into an existing table?

2. What can you specify when creating a new view?

3. Why is the Detail Gantt Chart such a valuable tool for a project manager during the progression of the project?

4. What is an interim plan, and why would you use one?

5. What categories of predeveloped reports does Project 2000 provide?

REVIEW ASSIGNMENTS

Part of the LAN installation will involve training the users. In this assignment, you will open the Training project file with the final project plan. You'll save a baseline, track progress, analyze variance, and print several reports that highlight important progress and variance information.

1. Start Project 2000 and make sure that your Data Disk is in the appropriate disk drive. Open the **Training-5.mpp** file in the Review folder for Tutorial 5.

2. Use the Save As command to save the project as **Training-5-Your Initials** to the Review folder in your Data Disk folder for Tutorial 5 without a baseline.

3. This project is currently scheduled to start on 8/5/02 and finish on 9/16/02. You are working on the project, the planning is complete, and you want to save a baseline. Click Tools on the menu bar, point to Tracking, and then click Save Baseline. In the Save Baseline dialog box, click the OK button to save a baseline for the entire project.

4. Click Project on the menu bar, and then click Project Information. You are now in the middle of this project and need to update its progress. Enter 9/2/02 as the Current Date and 8/30/02 as the Status Date, and then click the OK button in the Project Information dialog box.

5. Use the Updated as Scheduled button on the Tracking toolbar to mark Identify existing skills (row 2) and Identify needed skills (row 3) as updated as scheduled.

6. Use the Tracking toolbar to mark Develop training documentation (row 4) as 50% Complete.

7. Use the Tracking toolbar to Reschedule Work for Develop training documentation (row 4) so that the remaining work is moved after the Current Date.

Explore 8. Read the ScreenTips available for Develop training documentation in the Gantt Chart by pointing to the progress, split, and task lines.

9. Use the Tracking toolbar to mark Hire Trainers (task 7) as 25% Complete.

10. Click the Project Statistics button on the Tracking toolbar. The Current Finish date should now be 9/26/02. The Finish Variance is 8.63 days.

Explore 11. Based on the values in the Project Statistics dialog box, determine which two values were used in the calculation of the Finish Variance. Write the formula (with the specific values labeled appropriately) on a piece of paper.

12. Close the Project Statistics dialog box.

13. Apply the Tracking table to the Task sheet, drag the split bar to the right to view all of the columns, and resize the columns so that all of the data is visible.

14. More time has passed, and the project has been progressing nicely. Open the Project Information dialog box and enter 10/7/02 as the Current Date and 10/4/02 as the Status Date, and then click the OK button in the Project Information dialog box.

15. Enter an Actual Start Date of 9/12/02 for Develop contract (row 6), and an Actual Finish Date of 9/16/02.

Explore 16. The Develop contract task (row 6) was originally scheduled to be completed in two working days, but the actual entries indicate that the actual duration is three working days. On a piece of paper, explain how this affects the project. (*Hint:* Apply the Variance table and look at the difference between the Start Var. and Finish Var. for this task.) Explain how this affects dependent tasks.

17. Reapply the Tracking table (if you switched to the Variance table in Step 16), and then enter 90% in the % Comp. cell for Develop training documentation (row 4).

18. Mark Secure lab space (row 9) as 100% Complete, and enter 32 (hours) into the Act. Work cell.

19. Print the Tracking table applied to the Task sheet replacing Emily's name with your name in the left section of the header.

20. Apply the Variance table to the Task sheet, right-click the Start column heading, and then insert the Actual Start and Actual Finish fields between Task Name and the Start column.

21. Adjust all columns so that all data is visible, and drag the split bar as far to the right as possible so that none of the Gantt Chart is visible.

22. Print the Variance table with your name in the left section of the header. (*Note:* It should print on one page without the Gantt Chart.)

Explore 23. On the Variance table printout, identify how the Start Var. and Finish Var. fields are calculated. Also on the printout, identify which sets of dates are automatically calculated once, which are constantly recalculated as project progress is entered, and which you enter directly as tasks are completed.

24. Apply the Cost table to the Task sheet, drag the split bar to the far right so that none of the Gantt Chart (resize the columns as necessary) is visible, and then enter $2,000 as a fixed cost for Secure lab space (row 9) because you just found out you had to spend $2,000 on a deposit.

25. Mark rows 4 through 11 as "Update as Scheduled," which records all final progress on the project, and then print the Cost table with your name in the left section of the header. (*Note:* The printout should be one page without the Gantt Chart.)

26. Click the Project Statistics button on the Tracking toolbar to determine how far over budget this project was. Write the answer on a piece of paper, and then close the Project Statistics dialog box.

Explore 27. On your printout identify which tasks contributed to this problem of being over budget. (*Hint:* Look at the Variance column.) Write a phrase explaining why each task was over budget. (*Hint:* One reason is that a task required more hours of work than initially anticipated in the baseline. You can view work variance by applying the Work table. Another reason is that a task had unanticipated fixed costs.)

28. Right-click the Select All button for the Task sheet, click More Tables, click New, and create a new table called Variance-Your Initials with the following fields in the following order: ID, Name, Duration Variance, Work Variance, and Cost Variance. Accept all of the default formatting by clicking OK in the Table Definition dialog box.

29. Apply the new table to the Task sheet, drag the split bar to the far right to hide the Gantt Chart, resize all columns to view all data, and then preview and print the Variance-Your Initials table with your name in the left section of the header and the words FINAL VARIANCE DATA in the center of the header.

30. Click View on the menu bar, click Reports, double-click the Workload button, click the Task Usage button, click the Select button, and then preview and print the report with your name rather than Emily Kelsey's in the left section of the header. On the printout, highlight which week had the most hours of work assigned.

31. Double-click the Workload button in the Reports dialog box, click the Task Usage button, and then click the Edit button. Select the Definition tab in the Crosstab Report dialog box, change the Work field that is summarized within this crosstab report to Cost, and then click the OK button. Click the Task Usage button, click the Select button, and then preview and print the report with your name in the left section of the header. On the printout, highlight which week had the highest cost.

32. Close the Reports dialog box.

33. Click View on the menu bar, click More Views, and then apply the Detail Gantt Chart. Go to the selected task for row 0. Preview and then print the Detail Gantt Chart with your name in the left section of the header. On the Detail Gantt Chart printout, identify the longest slippage line(s). Also on the paper, write down the definition for total slack and slippage.

34. Save **Training-5-Your Initials.mpp**, and then close the project file and exit Project 2000.

CASE PROBLEMS

Case 1. Building a House   You have a part-time job working for BJB Development, a general contracting company that manages residential construction projects. The manager has asked you to use Project 2000 to track progress on an actual project. In this assignment, you will open a project file with the final project plan. You'll save a baseline, track progress, and print various reports to highlight progress and final project information.

1. Start Project 2000 and make sure that your Data Disk is in the appropriate disk drive. Open the **House-5.mpp** file in the Cases folder for Tutorial 5 on your Data Disk.

2. Use the Save As command to save the project as **House-5-Your Initials** in your Cases folder for Tutorial 5 on your Data Disk without a baseline. Click File on the menu bar, click Properties, and then enter your name in the Title field on the Summary tab.

3. Using the Resource Sheet, change the resource "Your Name" to your actual name, and your actual initials.

4. This project is currently scheduled to start on 8/5/02 and finish on 10/8/02. For the purposes of this exercise, change the entry so that the Current Date is 8/1/02. The planning is complete, and you want to save a baseline. Click Tools on the menu bar, point to Tracking, and then click Save Baseline. Save a baseline for the entire project.

5. You are now in the middle of this project and need to update its progress. Click Project on the menu bar, and then click Project Information. Enter 9/2/02 as the Current Date and 8/30/02 as the Status Date, and then click the OK button in the Project Information dialog box.

Explore   6. Use the Update as Scheduled button on the Tracking toolbar to mark Secure Financing (row 2) and Purchase Lot (row 3) as updated as scheduled.

7. You have had good weather, so your project is a little ahead of schedule. Use the tracking toolbar to mark Foundation (row 4) as 100% complete. On a piece of paper, write down what happens to subtasks when a summary task is marked 100% complete.

8. Apply the Tracking table to the Task sheet, and then manually enter 8/22/02 as the Act. Start date for the Frame House task (row 8) and 8/23/02 as the Act. Finish date.

9. Enter 8/26/02 as the Act. Start date for the Roof house task (row 9) and 8/29/02 as the Act. Finish date.

10. Click View on the menu bar, and then click More Views. Apply the Detail Gantt Chart. Click Install insulation, and then click the Go to the Selected Task button. Which tasks have slack? How many days of slack? (Zoom out as necessary.)

11. Double-click the Brick Exterior task (row 11), click the Advanced tab in the Task Information dialog box, and then enter 9/20/02 as the Deadline date.

Explore

12. Preview and then print the Detail Gantt chart with your name in the left section of the header. On your paper, identify the longest slack line. Preview and then print the Tracking Gantt Chart with your name in the left section of the header. On the printout, identify the actual and baseline bars.

13. Click Project on the menu bar, and then click Project Information. The house is finished, and you need to update the project's progress. Enter 10/7/02 as the Current Date and 10/4/02 as the Status Date. (Note also that the currently scheduled project Finish Date is 10/3/02.)

14. Mark rows 10 through 15 as updated as scheduled.

15. Right-click the Task sheet Select All button, and then click Variance. Drag the split bar to the far right so that the Gantt Chart is not visible and resize the columns so that all data is visible. Preview and then print the Variance sheet with your name in the left section of the header.

16. On your paper, indicate what the –3 day variance means.

17. On your paper, identify which tasks created the –3 days of variance. (*Hint:* Look for changes in the Start Var. and Finish Var. fields to determine if that task changed the variance.)

18. Apply the Work table to the Task sheet, and then insert the Fixed Cost and Cost fields between the Task Name and Work fields. Resize the columns so that all of the data is visible.

Explore

19. Click View on the menu bar, click More Views, and then click the New button. Click Single view in the Define New View dialog box to indicate that the new view consists only of a Task sheet and not a Task sheet and Gantt Chart, and then click the OK button.

20. In the View Definition dialog box, enter the name Cost and Work – Your Initials as the view name. Click the Screen list arrow, and choose Task sheet. Click the Table list arrow, and choose Work. Click the Group list arrow, and choose No Group. Click the Filter list arrow, and choose All Tasks. Check the Show in menu check box, and then click the OK button.

21. In the More Views dialog box, the Cost and Work – Your Initials view should be selected. If it is not already selected, click the Cost and Work – Your Initials new view, and then click the Apply button. Preview and then print the view in landscape orientation with your name in the left section of the header.

22. Click View on the menu bar, click Reports, double-click the Workload button, click the Resource Usage button, and then click the Select button. Print the Resource Usage report with your name in the left section of the header.

23. In the Reports dialog box, double-click the Workload button, click the Resource Usage button, and then click the Edit button. Change the Column heading from Weeks to Days and the Work field to Cost, and then click the OK button.

24. Click the Resource Usage button in the Workload Reports dialog box, and then click the Select button.

25. Print only the last two pages of the new report with your name in the left section of the header.

26. Close the Reports dialog box. Save the file **House-5-Your Initials.mpp**, and then close the project file and exit Project 2000.

Case 2. Finding a Job   You are currently pursuing a new job that utilizes technical skills that you have recently acquired. In this assignment, you will open a project file with the final project plan. You'll save a baseline, track progress, and print various reports to highlight progress and track the project information.

1. Start Project 2000 and make sure that your Data Disk is in the appropriate disk drive. Open the **Job-5.mpp** file in the Cases folder for Tutorial 5 on your Data Disk.

2. Use the Save As command to save the project as **Job-5-Your Initials** in the Cases folder for Tutorial 5 on your Data Disk without a baseline. Click File, click Properties, and then enter your name in the Title field on the Summary tab.

3. This project is currently scheduled to start on 8/5/02 and finish on 8/28/02. For purposes of this exercise, change the Current Date to 8/1/02, the planning is complete, and you want to save a baseline. Click Tools on the menu bar, point to Tracking, and then click Save Baseline. In the Save Baseline dialog box, click the OK button to save a baseline for the entire project.

4. Using the Resource sheet, change the Your Name resource to your actual name and initials and the Your Friend resource to the name and initials of one of your friends.

5. Click Project on the menu bar, and then click Project Information. Now you are in the middle of this project and need to update its progress. Enter 8/19/02 as the Current Date and 8/16/02 as the Status Date, and then click the OK button in the Project Information dialog box.

6. Use the Tracking toolbar to mark tasks 1, 2, and 3 as "updated as scheduled."

7. Use the Tracking toolbar to mark tasks 4 and 5 as 50% complete.

Explore 8. Use the Tracking toolbar to reschedule work for task 4. Use the Split Tasks button to reschedule work for tasks on the current date.

Explore 9. Click the Add Progress Line button on the Tracking toolbar, position the mouse pointer on Friday, 8/16/02, on the timescale in the Gantt Chart (the Progress Line ScreenTip will indicate 8/16/02 as the Progress Date), and then click 8/16/02 to add the line to the Gantt Chart. This line indicates that progress was entered as of 8/16/02.

10. Click View on the menu bar, click More Views, and then apply the Detail Gantt Chart.

11. Preview and then print the Detail Gantt Chart with your name in the left section of the header. On your printout, identify the total slack for Call References (task 7).

Explore ▶ 12. Double-click Call references (task 7), and change the Constraint type to "As Late As Possible." On your printout, explain what happened to the total slack value.

13. Click View on the menu bar, and then click Reports. Double-click the Custom Reports button, and then click the New button.

14. Click the Crosstab Report type, and then click the OK button.

15. Name the report Weekly Job Hunt Hours, and then change the rest of the defaults on the Definition tab to calculate hours for each resource and week. (*Hint:* Work is measured in hours.) Don't close the Crosstab Report dialog box.

16. Click the Details tab in the Crosstab Report dialog box, check the Row totals and Column totals check boxes, and then click the OK button.

17. Preview and then print the Weekly Job Hunt Hours report with your name in the left section of the header, and then close the Reports dialog box.

Explore ▶ 18. Add a note to the Meet with Uncle Ralph task to take extra copies of your resume.[1]

19. Save the file **Job-5-Your Initials.mpp**, and then close the project file and exit Project 2000.

Case 3. Planning a Convention In your new job at Future Technology, Inc., you have been asked to help organize the company's annual convention, at which the company will unveil its new product ideas for customers. Because the convention *must* occur December 4, 5, and 6 of the year 2002, you scheduled the project from a Finish Date and let Project 2000 determine the project Start Date. In this assignment, you will open a project file with the final project plan. You'll save a baseline, track progress, and print various reports to highlight progress and final project information.

1. Start Project 2000 and make sure that your Data Disk is in the appropriate disk drive. Open the **Convention-5.mpp** file in the Cases folder for Tutorial 5 on your Data Disk.

2. Use the Save As command to save the workbook as **Convention-5-Your Initials** in the Cases folder for Tutorial 5 on your Data Disk. Do not save a baseline.

3. In the Resource sheet, change the Your Name resource to your name and initials.

4. This project is currently scheduled to start on 11/1/02 and finish on 12/4/02. It is scheduled from a project Finish Date. You have been working steadily on the convention. Change the Current Date to 10/1/02, the planning is complete, and you want to save a baseline. Click Tools on the menu bar, point to Tracking, and then click Save Baseline. In the Save Baseline dialog box, click the OK button to save a baseline for the project.

5. You now are in the middle of this project and need to update progress. Click Project on the menu bar, and then click Project Information. Enter 11/11/02 as the Current Date and 11/8/02 as the Status Date, and then click the OK button in the Project Information dialog box.

6. Use the Tracking toolbar to mark Survey customers (row 1) as "updated as scheduled."

7. Use the Tracking toolbar to mark Determine convention goals (row 2) as 50% Complete. Note on the Gantt Chart that the Determine convention goals task was automatically split.

[1]Add a deadline for the task, meet with Uncle Ralph for a date one week after it's currently scheduled to finish.

Explore

8. Preview and then print the Gantt Chart with your name in the left section of the header. Zoom out as necessary so that the printout fits on one page. On the printout, write an explanation for the automatic split for the Determine convention goals task. (*Hint:* Remember that this project is scheduled from a project Finish Date. What default constraint is placed on tasks in this situation? What would that mean if part of a task was finished ahead of schedule?)

9. Two more weeks have passed. Click Project on the menu bar, and then click Project Information. Enter 11/25/02 as the Current Date and 11/22/02 as the Status Date, and then click the OK button in the Project Information dialog box.

10. Use the Tracking toolbar to mark Determine convention goals (row 2) as 100% Complete.

11. Apply the Tracking table, and then enter 11/18/02 as the Act. Start date for the Determine number of attendees task (row 3). (*Note:* This is one working day later than it is currently scheduled.) When the Planning Wizard appears indicating that there is a scheduling conflict, click Continue and then click OK. When managing a project from a Finish Date and a task runs behind schedule, you have to use creative ways to get the project back on schedule, since you often can't move the Finish Date of the project.

12. Click Window on the menu bar and then click Split to split the screen and apply a form view to the bottom half of the screen. Right-click the form, and then click the Resource Work form.

13. With Determine number of attendees still the selected task, click in the blank Resource Name cell below your name, click the list arrow, and then click Joe Biel.

14. You have to redistribute half of the work (8h) to Joe Biel to change the duration of the task from two days to one day in order to make up for starting the task one day late. Click in the Work cell for Your Name, type 8, click the Work cell for Joe Biel, type 8, and then click the OK button. This action should cause the duration for this task to shorten from two days to one, thus clearing the scheduling conflict.

15. Click Window on the menu bar and then click Remove Split to remove the form view in the lower part of the screen. Then click the Go To Selected task to view the changes to the Gantt Chart.

16. Click Project on the menu bar, and then click Project Information. Another two weeks have passed. You are finished with this project and need to update its progress. Enter 12/9/02 as the Current Date and 12/6/02 as the Status Date, and then click the OK button in the Project Information dialog box.

17. Use the Tracking toolbar to practice a variety of task updating skills.
   - Click Determine number of attendees (row 3), and then click the Update as Scheduled button.
   - Click Set budget (row 4), and then click the 100% Complete button.
   - Click Set agenda (row 5), click the Update Tasks button, and then enter 4d as the actual duration.

18. Click the Book entertainment task (row 6), and then drag the Percent Completion mouse pointer through the bar in the Gantt Chart to indicate that the task is completed through 11/29/02. (*Hint:* You might want to Zoom In on the Gantt Chart to give yourself more room to drag the mouse pointer.)

19. View the columns of the Tracking table to view the Rem. Dur. column for the last two tasks, rows 7 and 8. Write down on a sheet of paper the Rem. Dur. for both tasks.

20. Use the columns of the Tracking table to update the Determine menu task (row 7) to indicate that the task has an actual duration (Act. Dur.) of two days and a remaining duration (Rem. Dur.) of zero days.

21. Use the columns of the Tracking table to update the Develop promotional materials task (row 8) to indicate that the task has an actual duration (Act. Dur.) of two days and a remaining duration (Rem. Dur.) of zero days.

22. What assumptions does Project 2000 make when you enter an actual duration value that is less than the remaining duration? Write your answer on a piece of paper.

23. Click the File menu, and then click Properties. Click the Summary tab, and then enter your own name in the Title text box (this will appear on the report that you are about to print). Click the OK button in the Properties dialog box.

24. Click View on the menu bar, and then click Reports. Double-click the Overview button, and then double-click the Project Summary button.

25. Preview the Project Summary report. (Your name should be in the title of the report because of the change that you made in the Properties dialog box.) Click the Page Setup button and note that this report doesn't support a header or footer. Click OK in the Page Setup dialog box, and then print the Project Summary report.

26. Close the Reports dialog box.

27. Save the **Convention-5-Your Initials.mpp** file, and then close the project file and exit Project 2000.

Case 4. Organizing a Fund-Raiser   You have volunteered to lead your neighborhood elementary school's major fund-raising effort to purchase new playground equipment. The equipment must be ready by school's start on September 16, 2002, so you scheduled the project from a Finish Date and let Project 2000 establish the project Start Date. In this assignment, you will open a project file with the final project plan. You'll save a baseline, track progress, and print various reports to highlight progress and final project information.

1. Start Project 2000 and make sure that your Data Disk is in the appropriate disk drive. Open the **Fund-5.mpp** file in the Cases folder for Tutorial 5 on your Data Disk.

2. Use the Save As command to save the file as **Fund-5-Your Initials** in the Cases folder for Tutorial 5 on your Data Disk without a baseline.

3. In the Resource sheet, change the Your Name resource to your actual name and initials.

4. This project is currently scheduled to start on 7/9/02 and finish on 9/16/02. It is scheduled from a project Finish Date. The project planning has been moving along nicely. Change the Current Date to 7/1/02, the planning is complete, and you want to save a baseline. Click Tools on the menu bar, point to Tracking, and then click Save Baseline. In the Save Baseline dialog box, click the OK button to save a baseline for the entire project.

5. Click Project on the menu bar, and then click Project Information. A few weeks have passed, and you are in the middle of this project and need to update its progress. Enter 8/5/02 as the Current Date and 8/2/02 as the Status Date, and then click the OK button in the Project Information dialog box.

6. Use the Tracking toolbar to mark Planning (row 1) as 100% complete.

7. Use the Tracking toolbar to mark Fund Raising (row 4) as 50% complete.

8. Apply the Tracking table to the Task sheet, and then drag the split bar to the far right so that you can view the Act. Work column.

9. Preview and then print the Tracking table with your name in the left section of the header.

Explore   10. On the printout, determine why the Send informational flyers task was marked as 60% complete when the Fund Raising phase was marked 50% complete. (*Hint:* Look at the total duration for all of the tasks as determined by the Act. Dur. and Rem. Dur. fields for this phase. Total the duration for all three tasks, and then calculate 50% of that total duration.)

11. Click Project on the menu bar, and then click Project Information. Now another two months have passed. You are finished with this project and need to update progress. Enter 10/7/02 as the Current Date and 10/4/02 as the Status Date, and then click the OK button in the Project Information dialog box.

12. Click Fund Raising (row 4), and then click the 100% Complete button on the Tracking toolbar.

13. Click Building (row 8), and then click the 100% Complete button on the Tracking toolbar.

14. Some tasks had additional fixed costs that were not anticipated in the original budget. Apply the Cost table to the Task sheet to record these costs.

15. Enter 3000 in the Fixed Cost cell for the Building phase (row 8) to cover the costs of inspections, contracts, and construction insurance.

16. Click View on the menu bar, and then click Reports. Double-click the Workload button, double-click Resource Usage, and then print the report with your name in the left section of the header. You'll take this report to the next PTO board meeting to summarize the number of hours that each resource on the project has dedicated to the new playground.

17. Close the Reports dialog box. Save and close **Fund-5-Your Initials.mpp**, and then exit Project 2000.

INTERNET ASSIGNMENTS

The purpose of the Internet Assignments is to challenge you to find information on the Internet so that you can learn more about project management and can more effectively use Microsoft Project 2000. The actual assignments are updated and maintained on the Course Technology Web site. Log on to the Internet, and use your Web browser to go to the Student Online Companion that accompanies this text at **www.course.com/NewPerspectives/Project2000**. Click the link for Tutorial 5.

QUICK CHECK ANSWERS

Session 5.1

1. Click Tools on the menu bar, point to Tracking, and then click Save Baseline.

2. Baseline dates are copied from the currently scheduled start and finish dates for each task at that particular point in time.

3. Variance is the difference between the baseline date and the currently scheduled date. It is calculated in days with the following formula: Variance = Baseline (date) – Current (date).

4. Projects ahead of schedule have a negative variance, and projects behind schedule have a positive variance.

5. Variance (to see baseline dates), Tracking (to see actual dates)

6. You can enter tracking information by entering actual dates into the Tracking table applied to the Task sheet, using the buttons on the Tracking toolbar, using the Update Tasks dialog box, or dragging the progress bar in the Gantt Chart.

7. The Status Date in the Project Information dialog box is used to determine which tasks are on schedule and which should be rescheduled.

8. Cost

Session 5.2

1. Right-click the column heading where you want to insert the new column.
   - Click Insert Column.
   - In the Column Definition dialog box, specify the new field name, title, alignment, and width that you want the new column to display, and then click OK.

2. A custom view specifies a particular view (sheet, chart, form, or a combination of these), grouping (tasks sorted and outlined together that meet a common criteria), and filter.

3. The Detail Gantt Chart is a Gantt Chart with extra bars that show total slack and slippage. Total slack is the amount of time that a task can be delayed without affecting the entire project and is also called total float. Slippage is the difference between a task's scheduled start or finish date and its baseline start or finish date when the project falls behind schedule. Project managers analyze total slack and slippage to determine where to focus their resources during the project so as to complete the project on time and within budget.

4. An interim plan is a set of start and finish dates for selected tasks in a project. It is common to save an interim plan at various stages in the project (such as after each major phase or at the beginning of each month) so as to compare interim dates to the initial baseline dates.

5. Overview, Current Activities, Costs, Assignments, Workload, and Custom

SHARING
PROJECT INFORMATION WITH OTHER PEOPLE AND APPLICATIONS

Making LAN Project Information Available to Others

CASE

JLB Partners

First, you effectively created a Project 2000 file that was used to plan the installation of the LAN at JLB Partners. Then, you used the file to successfully manage the actual project. Now, Emily Kelsey and others at JLB Partners want you to integrate segments of the project data with other software tools. You will use the completed LAN installation and training project files to share and analyze information in various ways. You'll also learn about some of the advanced features of Project 2000 so that the next time that you manage a project, you'll be able to use Project 2000 even more effectively.

SESSION 6.1

In this session, you will learn how to export and import information between Project 2000 and Excel. You'll also learn about some of the advanced features of Project 2000 that help you build and manage multiple project files, including templates, the Organizer tool, and master files.

Sharing Project Data with Other Applications

Project 2000 provides many capabilities to manage, analyze, and report project information. However, other people in your company might want to use your Project 2000 file information in other applications, such as Microsoft Office Excel, Word, or Access. For example, an Excel user might want to copy some of the cost data into an Excel spreadsheet (also called a **workbook**) to incorporate into a future budget or graph. You can exchange data between Project 2000 and other files in several ways, as described in Figure 6-1.

Figure 6-1   **TECHNIQUES TO SHARE PROJECT 2000 INFORMATION WITH OTHER APPLICATIONS**

TECHNIQUE	DESCRIPTION	STEPS	EXAMPLE
Copy and paste	**Copying** means to duplicate selected information and place it on the Clipboard. **Pasting** means to take a copy of the information that is on the Clipboard and insert it at a specified location.	Select the information that you want to copy (cells within a sheet view, for example), and then click the Copy button. Click where you want the information to be pasted, and then click the Paste button.	You might want to copy data from a Cost sheet in Project 2000 to an Excel spreadsheet. Or you might want to copy resource data from an Excel spreadsheet and paste it into a Resource sheet within Project 2000.
Import or export	**Importing** and **exporting** are the process of converting data from one file format to another. They differ in the direction of the data conversion. Import means to bring in, and export means to send out. Project 2000 uses **data maps** to define how the data will be imported and exported.	Import data by clicking the Open button and then choosing the file that you want to import into Project 2000. To export data, click File and then click Save As. Choose the appropriate file type to export.	You might want to export Project 2000 data to other project databases, to ODBC-compliant databases such as Microsoft SQL Server, to an HTML file, to a text file, to Excel for special numeric analysis, or to Excel as a pivot table. You might want to import information such as resource data into a project file that is already stored in other Project 2000 databases, ODBC-databases, or Excel speadsheets.
Earned value analysis	**Earned value data** allows you to measure project performance against a budget. When earned value data is exported to Excel for further analysis, project managers call the resulting spreadsheet an **earned value analysis**.	Right-click the Select All button for the Task Sheet, click More Tables, click Earned Value in the More Tables dialog box, and then click Apply. Export the data to Excel.	Earned value analysis indicates how much of the budget should have been spent, in view of the amount of work done so far, and the baseline cost for the task, assignment, or resource. Earned value is also referred to as budgeted cost of work performed (BCWP).
Linking	**Linking** means to copy data from one file (source) to another (destination) so that only one physical copy of the data exists in the original, source location. In addition, changes to the data can be made in either the source or destination, with changes in that location automatically made in the other.	Select the information that you want to link (cells within a sheet view, for example), and then click the Copy button. Click where you want the information to be linked, click the Edit menu option, click Paste Special, and then click Paste Link.	You might want to link an entire Microsoft Excel file into your Project 2000 file so that changes made to the original Excel data are dynamically updated in Project 2000.
Embedding	**Embedding** is a way to copy or insert data from one file in another. Embedded data can be edited using the features of the data's native application even though it is physically stored in another application file. Changes made to the embedded data are not automatically made to the original copy.	Select the information that you want to embed elsewhere (a graph within Excel, for example), and then click the Copy button. Click where you want the information to be embedded, click the Edit menu option, click Paste Special, and then click Paste.	You can embed an Excel graph in a Project 2000 file so that you can store the actual graph in the Project 2000 file.

Copying **Sheet Data from Project 2000 to Excel**

Excel is the spreadsheet software program in the Microsoft Office Suite. It is an excellent tool for analyzing and graphing numbers. Many people already use Excel to track expenses and budgetary information, so you want to be able to quickly copy Project 2000 information and paste it into an Excel spreadsheet to satisfy the many requests that Excel users will have for Project 2000 data. If you already know how to copy and paste in Microsoft Office products, copying data from Project 2000 and pasting it into Excel will be easy. If you are not familiar with copying and pasting, gaining this valuable skill is important.

JLB Partners is an accounting firm, and its partners use Excel extensively in their practices. Emily Kelsey wants to analyze the cost of the Training Lab by using Excel, the software tool that she is most familiar with.

REFERENCE   WINDOW   **RW**

Copying Project 2000 Data into an Excel Spreadsheet
- View the project in a sheet view that contains the data that you want to copy.
- Select the rows and fields that you want to copy.
- Click the Copy button on the Project 2000 Standard toolbar.
- Open the Excel spreadsheet and click where you want to paste the data.
- Click the Paste button on the Excel Standard toolbar.

To copy Project 2000 data into an Excel spreadsheet:

1. Start Project 2000 and open the **TrainingLab-6.mpp** file stored in the Tutorial folder of your Data Disk for Tutorial 6.

   Although the Training Lab project is already completed, you have been asked to further analyze what happened because many of the costs ran over base-line budget values. Excel can help highlight and analyze this cost data.

2. Change the task name for task 0 to **Training for JLB**, click **File** on the menu bar, click **Save As**, click the **Save in** list arrow to find your Data Disk, and then save the file with the name **TrainingLab-6-Your Initials** to the Tutorial folder for Tutorial 6.

3. Right-click the **Select All** button for the Task Sheet, and then click **Cost** to apply the Cost table. The Cost table displays several fields that contain cost information including actual, baseline, and scheduled costs.

4. Drag the **split bar** to the far right side of the screen so that the Remaining column is the last field in the Cost table.

   TROUBLE? If you cannot see all eight columns of information in the Cost table, resize the columns so that all of the data is visible. You might have to resize the Task Name column so that some of the task names are not fully displayed.

5. Click the **Show** button Show ▾ on the Formatting toolbar, and then click **Outline Level 1** to show only the summary tasks. Tasks 0, 1, 5, and 8 should be visible.

You can copy any level of detail from Project 2000 to Excel. You want to analyze the summary tasks.

TROUBLE? If Microsoft Excel is not installed on the computer that you are using, your screens will not match the figures in Session 6.1. You might be able to use other spreadsheet products such as Lotus 1-2-3 or Quattro Pro.

6. Click the **Select All** button for the Task Sheet, and then click the **Copy** button 📋 on the Standard toolbar.

    Clicking the Select All button is a fast and easy way to select all of the rows and columns for the displayed sheet. To select only certain rows, columns, or cells, however, you can click and drag through just the specific items that you want to copy. Only selected data is copied to the Clipboard when you click the Copy button.

7. Click the **Start** button on the taskbar, point to **Programs**, and then click **Microsoft Excel**.

    A new, blank spreadsheet entitled Book1 should open in a new Microsoft Excel window on your screen, and cell A1 (column A, row 1) should be selected.

    TROUBLE? If you can't find Microsoft Excel on the Programs menu, it might also be in a group under Microsoft Office.

8. Maximize the **Excel window** if it is not filling the screen, click the **Paste** button 📋 on the Excel Standard toolbar, double-click the right edge of each lettered column header using ↔ to adjust the columns, and then click cell **A1**, as shown in Figure 6-2.

    Each of the four rows from the Cost table is now a row in the spreadsheet. Each of the eight columns from the Cost table is now a column in the spreadsheet.

Figure 6-2	PROJECT 2000 DATA COPIED INTO AN EXCEL SPREADSHEET

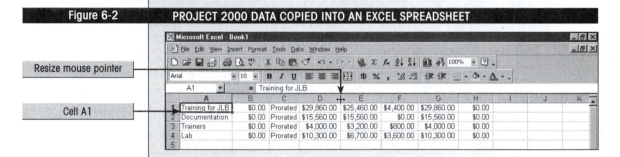

Resize mouse pointer

Cell A1

Now that data is copied into Excel, you can use some of the powerful features within Excel, such as graphing, to analyze the data.

Graphing in Excel

One of the most common reasons for copying numeric data to Excel is to be able to use Excel's powerful graphing tools. For example, you might want to graph the baseline and actual costs for each of the three major summary tasks—Documentation, Trainers, and Lab—that were required for the JLB Partners training for the LAN installation. Displaying numeric information as a graph often communicates data in a much more powerful and effective way than can standard reports. You use Excel's **Chart Wizard** tool to create a graph.

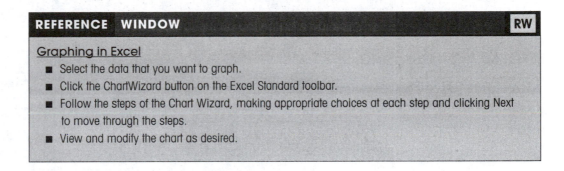

REFERENCE WINDOW   RW

Graphing in Excel

- Select the data that you want to graph.
- Click the ChartWizard button on the Excel Standard toolbar.
- Follow the steps of the Chart Wizard, making appropriate choices at each step and clicking Next to move through the steps.
- View and modify the chart as desired.

You can use many of the skills that you mastered when working in the sheet views in Project 2000 as you work in Excel. A group of cells in Excel is called a **range**. To select a range, click the first cell in the proposed range and then drag the pointer to the last cell in the range. Each cell is identified by a unique cell address. The **cell address** is the column letter and row number for the intersection of the column and row for that cell. Ranges are defined by the first cell address in the upper-left corner of the block or group of cells and the last cell address in the lower-right corner of the range, for example A2 and G3.

To graph in Excel:

1. Click cell **A2**, and then drag ✛ to cell **A4** to select the range of cells that includes cells **A2**, **A3**, and **A4**.

2. Press and hold the **Ctrl** key, select cells **E2**, **E3**, and **E4**, continue to press and hold the **Ctrl** key, select cells **G2**, **G3**, and **G4**, and then release the **Ctrl** key. You have selected three noncontiguous (not touching) ranges, as shown in Figure 6-3. Column E has the baseline costs, and column G has the actual costs for each task named in column A.

Figure 6-3	SELECTING CELLS TO GRAPH IN EXCEL

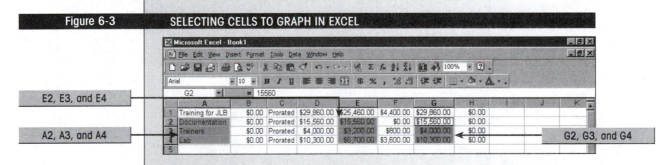

3. Click the **ChartWizard** button 📊 on the Excel Standard toolbar, click the **Next** button to accept the Column Chart type (Clustered Column Chart), click the **Series** tab, click the **Name** text box, type **Baseline**, click **Series2** in the Series list, click in the **Name** text box, type **Actual**, and then click the **Next** button.

The Chart Wizard should look like Figure 6-4.

Figure 6-4   **CHART WIZARD STEP 3 OF 4**

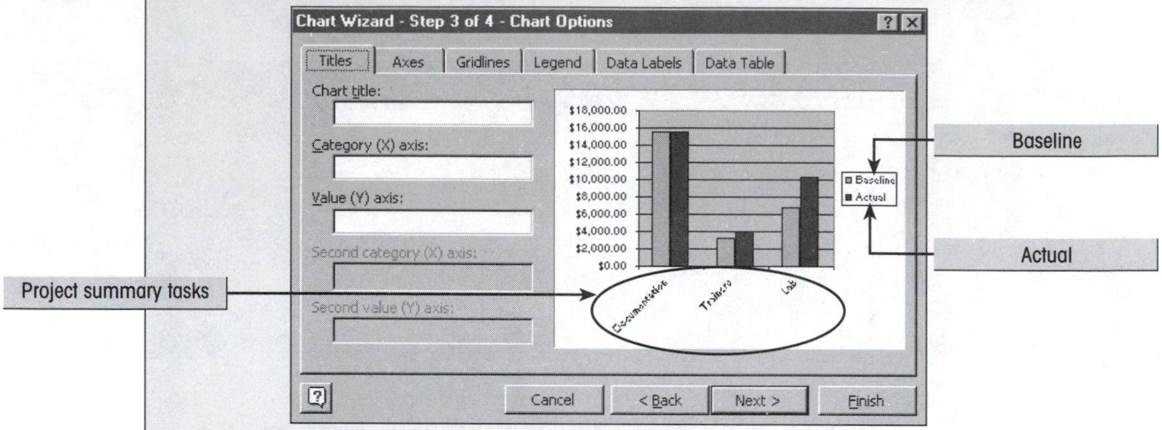

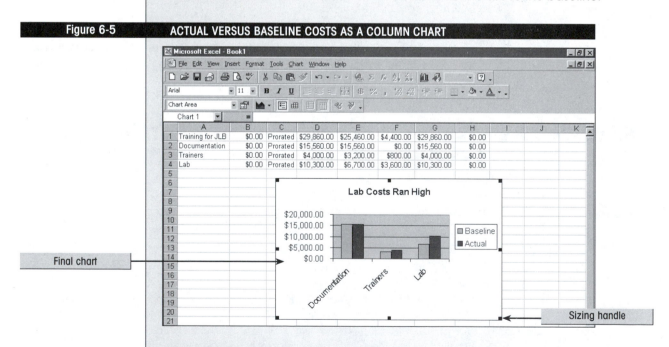

TROUBLE? If your Chart Wizard Step 3 of 4 doesn't match Figure 6-4, click the Back button and redo step 3.

4. Click the **Chart title** text box, type **Lab Costs Ran High**, and then click the **Next** button. The final Chart Wizard dialog box determines the chart location.

5. Click the **Finish** button to place the chart as an object in Sheet1.

   Your worksheet with the chart should resemble Figure 6-5. The graph highlights the fact that the Actual Lab costs were much higher than the baseline, whereas the Trainers and Documentation actual costs were close to the baseline.

Figure 6-5   **ACTUAL VERSUS BASELINE COSTS AS A COLUMN CHART**

TROUBLE? If the labels on the x-axis are not easy to read, resize the chart by dragging a corner sizing handle on the chart until you are satisfied with the way the information is positioned.

6. Click in cell **A6**, type **Your Name**, and then press the **Enter** key.

7. Click the **Print Preview** button 🔍 on the Standard toolbar, click the **Setup** button on the Print Preview toolbar, click the **Landscape** option button in the Orientation section of the Page Setup dialog box, click the **OK** button, click the **Print** button, verify the settings in the Print dialog box, and then click the **OK** button.

   The printout highlights the facts that you need to convey to management.

8. Close the spreadsheet without saving the file that you created, and then exit Excel.

Copying **the Gantt Chart as a Picture**

Project 2000 allows you to copy almost any view of a project as a picture. Once copied, the picture can be pasted in another Microsoft Office application file, such as a Word document or a PowerPoint presentation, by using the **Copy Picture** feature. The Project 2000 Copy Picture feature also allows you to save a view as a **GIF** (graphics interchange format, a common form of image for a Web page) image file that can be inserted on a Web page. You might want to place a picture of the Gantt Chart into a Word document as a part of a larger proposal that is being written in Word. Or you might want to save a picture of the Gantt Chart as a Web page to be shared over the Internet.

REFERENCE WINDOW   **RW**

Copying a Picture
- Display the view that you want to copy as a picture.
- Click the Copy Picture button on the Standard toolbar.
- Make the appropriate choices in the Copy Picture dialog box to save the image in the desired format.
- Open the file (such as a Word document or PowerPoint presentation) in which you want to paste the image, and then click the Paste button on that application's Standard toolbar. If you saved the Project view as a GIF image, insert the image into the new document using the Insert menu.

To copy a picture of the Gantt Chart view and paste it in a Word document:

1. Click the **Microsoft Project-TrainingLab-6-Your Initials.mpp** button in the taskbar if the window is not displayed on your screen, click **task 0**, click the **Go To Selected Task** button 🔖 on the Standard toolbar, click the **Show** button on the Formatting toolbar, click **All Subtasks**, and then drag the **split bar** toward the left edge so that the Project Summary Bar total cost is displayed, and only the Task Name column is visible on the sheet. The Gantt Chart should begin at 7/31/02.

   TROUBLE? If you cannot see all of the subtasks and Gantt bars on your screen, you might need to adjust the width of the Task Name column, use the scroll bar, and adjust the split bar to best fit the dates on the timescale.

2. Click the **Copy Picture** button 📷 on the Standard toolbar.

The Copy Picture dialog box opens, as shown in Figure 6-6.

TROUBLE? The Copy Picture dialog box might display different dates than those in the figure. The dates do not have to be exactly the same. However, you can click the From and To list arrows in the Timescale section of the Copy Picture dialog box and select the exact dates from the calendar.

Figure 6-6   COPY PICTURE DIALOG BOX

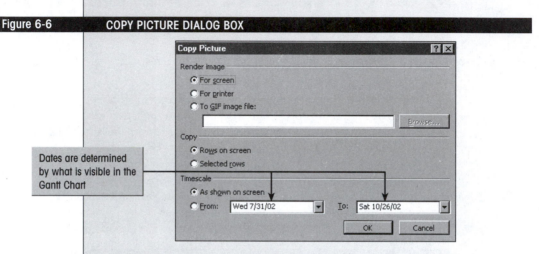

Dates are determined by what is visible in the Gantt Chart

The Copy Picture dialog box allows you to copy the current view in three different ways. The For screen option copies the information on the screen with all color formatting intact. The For printer option copies the view as it would be printed on a black and white printer. The To GIF image file option allows you to create a GIF file (for use in a Web page or other programs) from the copy. If you specify the GIF file option, you also must identify a filename and location for the file.

3. Click the **OK** button to accept the For screen option.

4. Click the **Start** button on the taskbar, point to **Programs**, and then click **Microsoft Word**.

TROUBLE? If Microsoft Word is not installed on your system, you can use another word processor such as WordPad to complete this exercise. WordPad is located under Accessories on the Programs menu.

5. Click the **Paste** button 📋 on the Standard toolbar, press the **Enter** key twice, and then type **This Gantt Chart represents actual progress on the finished project**, as shown in Figure 6-7.

Figure 6-7	PASTING THE GANTT CHART PICTURE INTO A WORD DOCUMENT

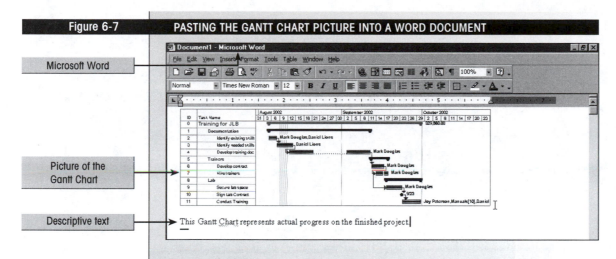

Microsoft Word

Picture of the Gantt Chart

Descriptive text

6. Press the **Enter** key, type **Your Name**, print the Word document, close the Word document without saving it, and then exit Word.

If you had been using Word to write an extensive business proposal for a new product, pasting an image of the Gantt Chart of the product rollout into the Word document would have helped illustrate the phases, milestones, and time span of the project.

Copying the Gantt Chart as a GIF or HTML file

Next, save a copy of the Gantt Chart as a GIF file.

To copy a picture of the Gantt Chart view as a GIF file:

1. Click the **Copy Picture** button 📷 on the Standard toolbar.

2. Click the **To GIF Image file** option button, click the **Browse** button, click the **Save in** list arrow to navigate to your Data Disk, open the Tutorial folder for Tutorial 6, select **Tutorial** in the File name text box, type **Final Training Gantt Chart**, click the **OK** button in the Browse dialog box, and then click the **OK** button in the **Copy Picture** dialog box.

   The Gantt Chart is saved as a GIF file on your Data Disk. You can view GIF files in many different programs.

3. Right-click the **Start** button, and then click **Explore**.

4. Locate and then expand the **Tutorial.06** folder, and then select the **Tutorial** folder on your Data Disk.

5. Double-click the **Final Training Gantt Chart** file to open it in the program associated with GIF files on your computer, as shown in Figure 6-8.

   The GIF file in the figure was opened in Microsoft Photo Editor, a program that can be used to edit and modify images.

A different program might open the GIF file depending on which software program is associated with the GIF file type on your computer.

| Figure 6-8 | FINAL TRAINING GANTT CHART GIF FILE |

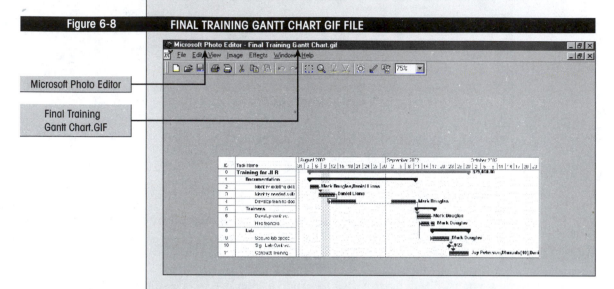

Microsoft Photo Editor

Final Training Gantt Chart.GIF

6. Close the program that is currently displaying the GIF image.

Once you have saved the image as a GIF file, you can insert it on a Web page by using a Web page editing package such as Microsoft FrontPage, Netscape Composer, or any other product that creates **HTML** (hypertext markup language) codes, the file format for Web pages. You can also create a Web page directly from a Project 2000 file.

To create a Web page directly from Project 2000:

1. Click the **Microsoft Project TrainingLab-6-Your Initials.mpp** button on the taskbar, if the Project 2000 window isn't already displayed.

2. Click **File** on the menu bar, and then click **Save As**.

3. Click the **Save in** list arrow, navigate to the tutorial folder in your Data Disk for Tutorial 6, click the **Save as type** list arrow, click **Web Page (*.html; *.htm)**, and then click the **Save** button.

The Export Mapping dialog box opens, listing the predefined import/export maps that you can use. Each map is designed with a special purpose in mind. Later, you might want to use the Project 2000 Help system to learn how to use each map.

You select Export to HTML using standard template because you want to export the following task information: ID, name, durations, resources, start and finish dates, units assignments, and % complete.

4. Click **Export to HTML using standard template** in the Export Mapping dialog box, and then click the **Save** button.

You have created a Web page from the **TrainingLab-6-Your initials.mpp** project file Gantt Chart.

5. Click the **Exploring** button on the taskbar to open Explorer.

TROUBLE? If your Data Disk is not in the right pane of Explorer, navigate to your Data Disk, expand the **Tutorial.06** folder, and then click the Tutorial folder.

6. Double-click the **TrainingLab-6-Your Initials** HTML file to open it in the program associated with HTML files on your computer, as shown in Figure 6-9.

Figure 6-9	WEB PAGE CREATED DIRECTLY FROM THE PROJECT 2000 FILE

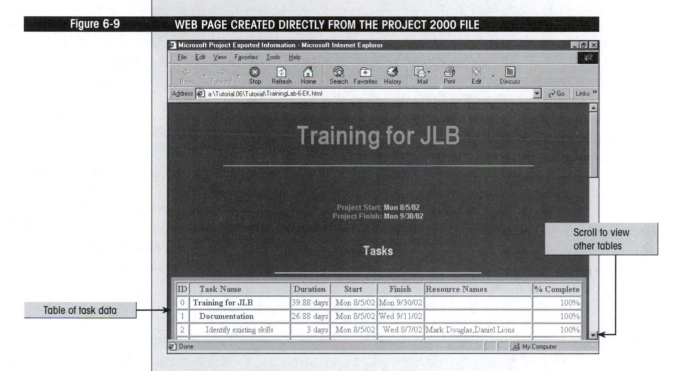

In this case, the Web page file was opened by Internet Explorer, but on your computer, HTML files might be associated with Netscape Navigator or another browser program. Notice that the template created a heading from the project summary task. The project Start and Finish Dates are formatted below the heading, and the task information is displayed in a formatted table. The template also created a table of information for the Resources and Assignments for each task ID.

7. Scroll the **Web page** to view all of the tables in the Web page.

8. Click the **Print** button on the browser toolbar.

TROUBLE? To identify your page in a large print queue, look at the footer of the printed Web page. Most browsers are configured to print the URL in the footer of a printed Web page. In this case, the URL will include the filename that includes your initials.

9. Close the browser window, and then click the **Microsoft Project TrainingLab-6-Your Initials.mpp** button on the taskbar to return to the project window.

10. Close the **Project TrainingLab-6-Your Initials.mpp** file, and do not save the changes.

Exporting Earned Value Data to Excel

Analyzing financial data using Excel is common, so Project 2000 provides a way to show project costs as a budget and then to compare expected progress with actual progress. This process is called **earned value analysis**. Earned value analysis uses budget values for each task to calculate useful variance values. These budget values can be easily exported to Excel to show useful ratios. You have been asked to further analyze the costs within the Training Lab project file. You will open a project file that was used during the actual Training phase to record actual versus baseline data so as to examine earned value analysis.

Applying the Earned Value Table

To apply the Earned Value table to a Task Sheet:

1. Open the **TrainingLab-6-2.mpp** file in the Tutorial folder on your Data Disk for Tutorial 6.

2. Click **File** on the menu bar, click **Save As**, and then save the file with the name **TrainingLab-6-2-Your Initials** to the Tutorial folder for Tutorial 6 on your Data Disk.

3. Right-click the **Select All** button for the Task Sheet, click **More Tables**, click **Earned Value** in the More Tables dialog box, and then click the **Apply** button.

4. Drag the **split bar** all of the way to the right, and then resize the columns so that as much data as possible is visible, as shown in Figure 6-10.

| Figure 6-10 | EARNED VALUE TABLE APPLIED TO THE TASK SHEET |

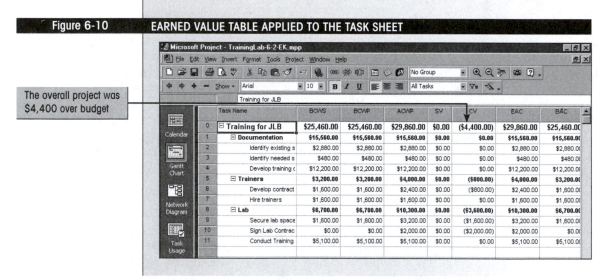

The overall project was $4,400 over budget

The fields of the Earned Value table are described in Figure 6-11. The variance values (CV, SV, VAC) can be either negative or positive. Negative variance indicates that you're behind schedule or over budget. Positive variance indicates that you're ahead of schedule or under budget. Therefore, when you apply the Earned Value table in the middle of a project, you get an idea of where you might be able to reallocate money and resources (from those with positive variances to those with negative variances) in order to keep the project on schedule and within budget. Because this project has already been completed, the BCWS and BCWP values are the same and the SV (schedule variance) is 0.

Like any other sheet table, you can apply the Earned Value table as often as you want. When you apply it after the project has been completed, the CV (completion variance) value for the project summary task shows in this case, that the overall project was $4,400 over budget.

Figure 6-11		FIELDS OF THE EARNED VALUE TABLE
FIELD	**NAME**	**DESCRIPTION**
BCWS	Budgeted cost of work scheduled	The portion of the cost that is planned to be spent on a task between the task's start date and the project Status Date
BCWP	Budgeted cost of work performed	The percentage of the budget that should have been spent for a given percentage of work performed on a task
ACWP	Actual cost of work performed	The total actual cost incurred while performing work on a task during a given time period
SV	Scheduled variance	The difference between the current progress and the scheduled progress of the task; SV = BCWP – BCWS
CV	Cost variance	The difference between a task's estimated cost and its actual cost; CV = BCWP – ACWP
EAC	Estimate at completion	Total scheduled cost for a field
BAC	Budget at completion	Total baseline cost for a field
VAC	Variance at completion	Difference between the baseline and scheduled cost for a field; VAC = BAC – EAC

You can export the data contained in this Earned Value Table to Excel to do further analysis. For example, it is common to want to calculate the cost performance index (**CPI**): BCWP/ACWP or schedule performance index (**SPI**): BCWP/BCWS. Both of these values are calculated by creating a ratio from two other earned value indicator fields, so Excel's formula creation capabilities are the perfect tool to create these valuable ratios.

A value that's greater than 1 indicates that you're ahead of schedule or under budget. A value that's less than 1 indicates that you're behind schedule or over budget.

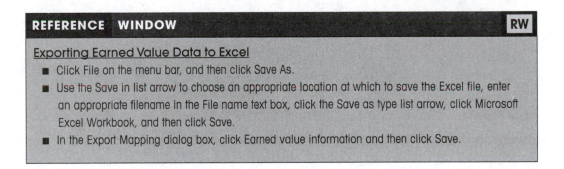

REFERENCE WINDOW   RW

Exporting Earned Value Data to Excel
- Click File on the menu bar, and then click Save As.
- Use the Save in list arrow to choose an appropriate location at which to save the Excel file, enter an appropriate filename in the File name text box, click the Save as type list arrow, click Microsoft Excel Workbook, and then click Save.
- In the Export Mapping dialog box, click Earned value information and then click Save.

Exporting Earned Value Data to Excel

To export earned value data to Excel:

1. Click **File** on the menu bar, and then click **Save As**. The Save As dialog box opens.

   It should be displaying the files in the Tutorial folder of your Data Disk for Tutorial 6. You work in the Save As dialog box to specify the Excel file type and to name the file appropriately.

2. Click to the right of your initials in the File name text box, and then type **-earned value**. Excel files have an .xls file extension.

3. Click the **Save as type** list arrow, scroll to and then click **Microsoft Excel Workbook**, and then click the **Save** button.

The Export Mapping dialog box opens, as shown in Figure 6-12. This is the same dialog box that you used to export the data to an HTML file.

Figure 6-12   **EXPORT MAPPING DIALOG BOX**

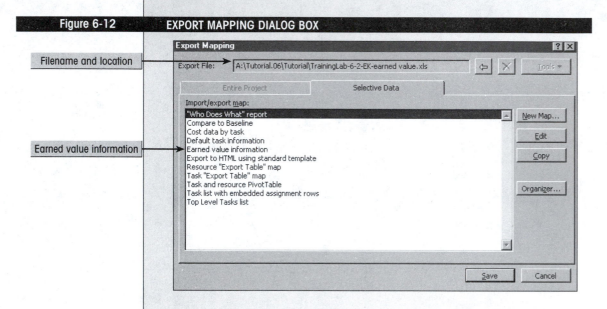

Filename and location

Earned value information

4. Click **Earned value information**.

The Export Mapping dialog box helps you to determine exactly which fields of data to export in the new file format. The fields of a project revolve around three major subjects: tasks, resources, and assignments. By using the Export Mapping dialog box, you can quickly export all of the fields for a given subject. You can further examine the specific information that you are exporting by clicking the Edit button in the Export Mapping dialog box. Exporting data is probably faster than creating a sheet view with the specific fields that you need and then copying and pasting them into an Excel spreadsheet, although the results of both actions are essentially equivalent.

5. Click the **Save** button.

The earned value data is now saved as an Excel spreadsheet. You can use the power of Excel to develop formulas for further analysis of the data and to create charts to display the data.

Using Excel

To work with the exported earned value data in the Excel spreadsheet:

1. Click the **Exploring** button on the taskbar to open the Explorer window, and then expand the folders within the Data Disk to find the **TrainingLab-6-2-Your Initials-earned value** Excel file.

2. Double-click the **TrainingLab-6-2-Your Initials-earned value** Microsoft Excel file.

The **TrainingLab-6-2-Your Initials-earned value** Excel file automatically opens in Excel, as shown in Figure 6-13. Not only is exporting data often faster than copying and pasting it, but the export process also preserves the field names and enters them in row 1. This is a benefit over the copy and paste method. Now, however, many of the field values are too wide to be displayed within the default width of an Excel column.

| Figure 6-13 | FILE OPENED IN EXCEL |

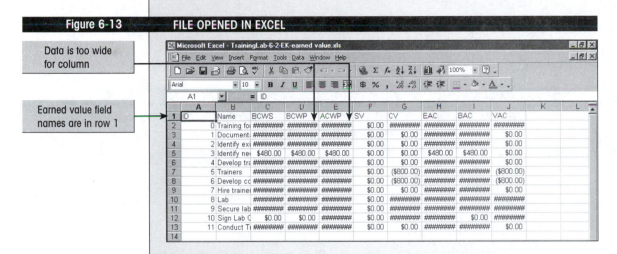

Data is too wide for column

Earned value field names are in row 1

3. Click the **Select All** button for the Excel spreadsheet (to the left of column A and above row 1) to select the entire sheet.

4. Double-click ↔ between the column A and column B headings to adjust the width of all columns automatically, and then click in cell **A1**.

Your screen should look like Figure 6-14.

| Figure 6-14 | EARNED VALUE DATA EXPORTED TO EXCEL |

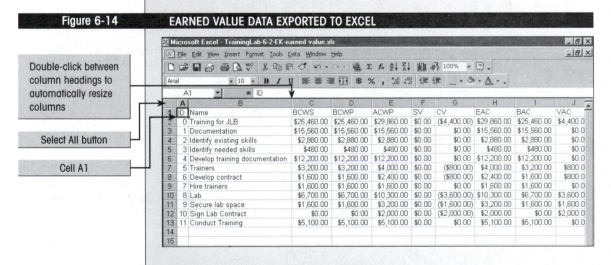

Double-click between column headings to automatically resize columns

Select All button

Cell A1

5. Press the **End** key, press the → key, and then press the → key again to make **cell K1** (column K row 1) the active cell.

6. Type **CPI**, and then press the **Enter** key to move to cell K2.

The CPI column will calculate the cost performance index ratio. Be sure that you are in cell K2 before you enter the formula in Step 7.

7. Type **=d2/e2**, and then press the **Enter** key.

This formula divides the BCWP (budgeted cost of work performed) value by the ACWP (actual cost of work performed). A ratio that is less than 1 indicates that you're over budget; a ratio greater than 1 indicates that you're under budget. You want to use Excel to calculate this ratio for all tasks.

8. Drag ✛ to select cells **K2** through **K13**, click **Edit** on the menu bar, point to **Fill**, click **Down**, and then click cell **K2**.

Your screen should resemble Figure 6-15.

| Figure 6-15 | CALCULATING THE CPI IN EXCEL |

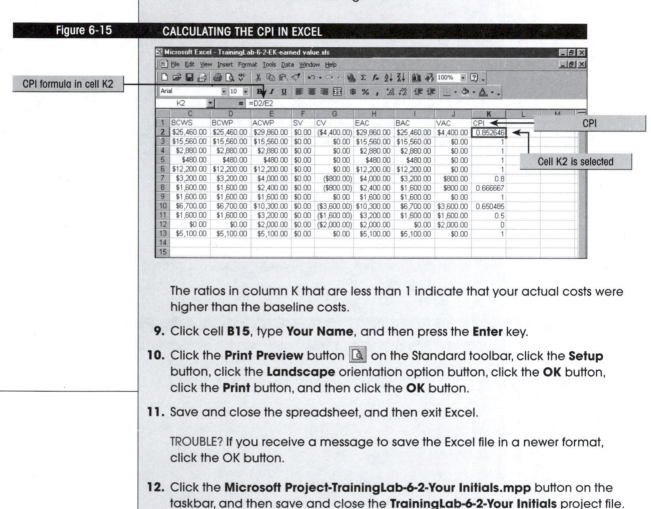

CPI formula in cell K2

CPI

Cell K2 is selected

The ratios in column K that are less than 1 indicate that your actual costs were higher than the baseline costs.

9. Click cell **B15**, type **Your Name**, and then press the **Enter** key.

10. Click the **Print Preview** button 🔍 on the Standard toolbar, click the **Setup** button, click the **Landscape** orientation option button, click the **OK** button, click the **Print** button, and then click the **OK** button.

11. Save and close the spreadsheet, and then exit Excel.

TROUBLE? If you receive a message to save the Excel file in a newer format, click the OK button.

12. Click the **Microsoft Project-TrainingLab-6-2-Your Initials.mpp** button on the taskbar, and then save and close the **TrainingLab-6-2-Your Initials** project file.

Importing Excel Data into Project 2000

Importing data into a Project 2000 file means to convert it from a non-Project 2000 file format into a Project 2000 file format. Copying can accomplish the same task under certain conditions. If the information that you want to import is in an Excel file and the structure of the spreadsheet columns match the structure of the sheet fields within Project 2000, you can copy the data from the Excel spreadsheet and directly paste it into a Project 2000 sheet. The import process, however, is more powerful and flexible because Project 2000 allows you to map how the columns of the Excel spreadsheet will match the fields in the Project 2000 file.

A technician who helped install the LAN at JLB Partners developed a task list using an Excel spreadsheet. This list describes the computer configuration process, including durations and notes. The list is shown in Figure 6-16. You want to import it into Project 2000.

| Figure 6-16 | CONFIGURATION TASKS EXCEL FILE |

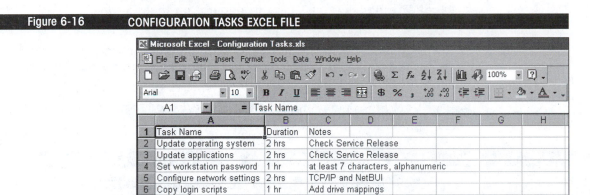

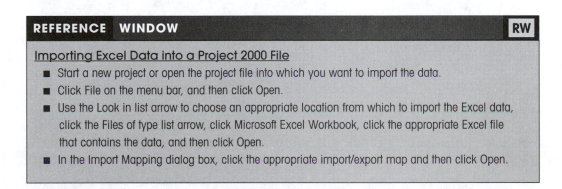

REFERENCE WINDOW RW

Importing Excel Data into a Project 2000 File

- Start a new project or open the project file into which you want to import the data.
- Click File on the menu bar, and then click Open.
- Use the Look in list arrow to choose an appropriate location from which to import the Excel data, click the Files of type list arrow, click Microsoft Excel Workbook, click the appropriate Excel file that contains the data, and then click Open.
- In the Import Mapping dialog box, click the appropriate import/export map and then click Open.

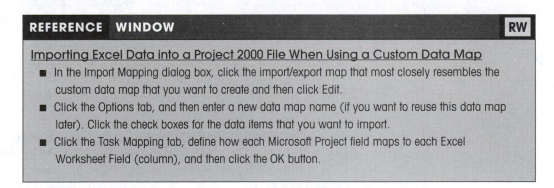

REFERENCE WINDOW RW

Importing Excel Data into a Project 2000 File When Using a Custom Data Map

- In the Import Mapping dialog box, click the import/export map that most closely resembles the custom data map that you want to create and then click Edit.
- Click the Options tab, and then enter a new data map name (if you want to reuse this data map later). Click the check boxes for the data items that you want to import.
- Click the Task Mapping tab, define how each Microsoft Project field maps to each Excel Worksheet Field (column), and then click the OK button.

To import task data into Excel using a custom data map:

1. Click the **New** button 🗋 on the Standard toolbar to start a new project file. The Project Information dialog box opens. Accept all of the defaults.

2. Click the **OK** button in the Project Information dialog box.

3. Click the **Open** button 🖼 on the Standard toolbar.

The Open dialog box opens. You need to locate the file that the technician created and saved.

4. Click the **Look in** list arrow, navigate to your Data Disk, open the Tutorial folder, click the **Files of type** list arrow, scroll to and then click **Microsoft Excel Workbooks (*.xls)**, click **Configuration Tasks.xls** in the file list window, and then click the **Open** button.

To import the Excel file with the existing data into the new Project 2000 file, you work through the Import Mapping dialog box and define how you want the fields and data to be imported.

5. Click **Default task information** in the Import/Export map list, as shown in Figure 6-17.

Figure 6-17	IMPORTING EXCEL DATA INTO PROJECT 2000

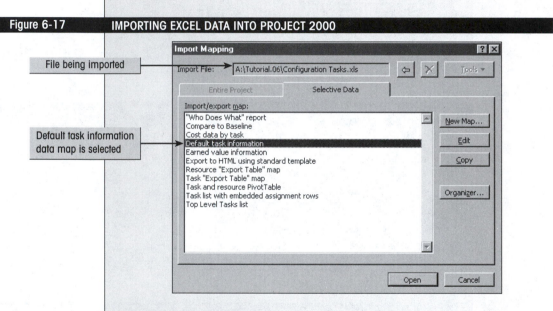

6. Click the **Copy** button.

The Define Import/Export Map dialog box opens. You can create and name a new data map or check the settings on an existing data map. You decide to give this map a descriptive name based on the three columns of data in the Excel file that the technician created.

7. Type **Task Duration Note Your Initials** in the Import/Export map name text box. Because you created a new name, you can save the map that you are about to create and use it later.

8. Click the **Task Mapping** tab, click the **Source worksheet name** list arrow, and then click **Sheet1**, as shown in Figure 6-18.

Figure 6-18   **DEFINE IMPORT/EXPORT MAP DIALOG BOX**

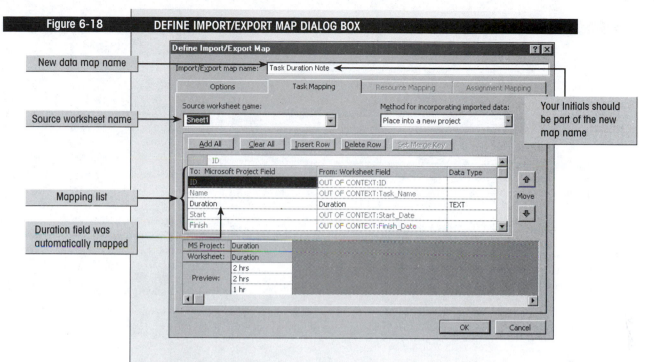

New data map name

Source worksheet name

Mapping list

Duration field was
automatically mapped

The Duration field in the Excel spreadsheet has the same spelling as the Duration field for the Project file, so that field is automatically mapped. Then scroll down the list to see how the other two columns were automatically mapped.

9. Click the **down scroll arrow** to the right of the Data Type column to scroll down to the end of the mapping list.

Notice that the Notes field was also correctly mapped, but that there is a (not mapped) entry in the To: Microsoft Project field list for the Task Name in the From: Worksheet field column. You must manually map the Task Name column between the Excel spreadsheet and the Project 2000 file because the names of the column differ slightly between the two files. The field is called "Name" in Project 2000 and "Task Name" in the Excel file.

10. Click the **(not mapped)** cell in the To: Microsoft Project field, and then click the **Delete Row** button.

With that row eliminated, you are free to use that Excel column in another place in the mapping list.

11. Scroll to the top of the mapping list, click the **OUT OF CONTEXT: Task_Name** cell in the From Worksheet field column, click the **list arrow**, click **Task Name**, and then click the Data Type cell in the Start Date row, as shown in Figure 6-19.

Figure 6-19   CREATING A CUSTOM IMPORT MAP

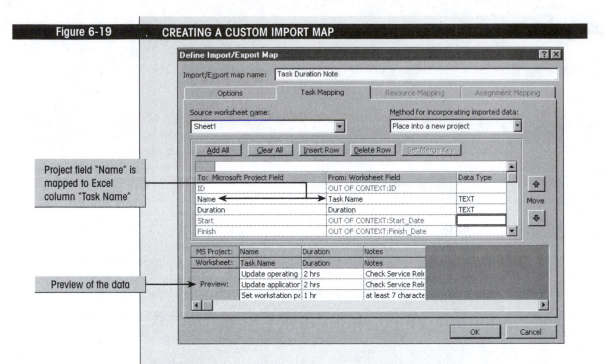

Project field "Name" is mapped to Excel column "Task Name"

Preview of the data

The bottom part of the Define Import/Export Map dialog box shows a preview of how the data in the Excel columns will be mapped to the Project 2000 fields.

12. Click the **OK** button.

The Task Duration Note Your Initials mapping definition appears selected in the Import/Export map list in the Import Mapping dialog box. The file that you are importing is identified in the Import File text box.

13. Click the **Open** button.

The configuration tasks appear in the Task Sheet.

14. Click **Project** on the menu bar, click **Project Information**, type **11/11/02** in the Start Date text box, and then click the **OK** button.

The Excel data is imported into the Project 2000 file successfully, as shown in Figure 6-20.

Figure 6-20   EXCEL CONFIGURATION TASKS IMPORTED INTO PROJECT 2000

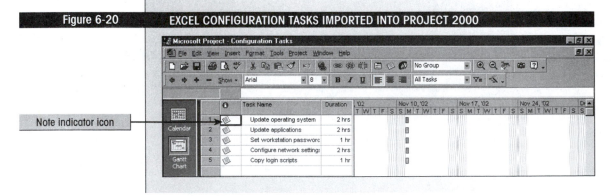

Note indicator icon

Linking Excel Data to a Project 2000 File

Sometimes you should link rather than copy and paste or import or export data. The major benefit of linking data is that the linking process *does not* create a duplicate copy of data in the destination file. For example, if you link Excel data (the *source file*) to a Project 2000 file (the *destination file*), the data will only be physically stored in the Excel file. Changes made to the data from the source automatically update the data in the destination file and vice versa.

The major disadvantage of linking data is that it is not as powerful as the import process. You cannot map linked data like you can map imported and exported data. Also, if you link data from an external file into a Project 2000 file, you must ensure that the two files travel together if they are copied or moved; otherwise, you will "break a link" and get an error message in the destination file. Because both the copy and paste process and the import process create a separate copy of the data in the Project 2000 file, you don't have to worry about "breaking a link" to the source file if the Project 2000 file is moved or copied.

Data that is linked to a Project 2000 file is not physically stored in the project. This means that if you copy or move the Project 2000 file, you also must copy or move the data file that contains the linked information.

REFERENCE WINDOW   **RW**

Linking Excel Data to a Project 2000 File

- Select the data that you want to link in Excel, and then click the Copy button on the Excel Standard toolbar.
- Open the Project 2000 file, click where you want to paste the data, and then click Edit on the menu bar.
- Click Paste Special, click the Paste Link option button in the Paste Special dialog box, and then click the OK button.

To link resource data from Excel into a Project 2000 file:

1. Right-click the **Start** button, click **Explore**, locate your Data Disk, and then open the **Tutorial** folder within the **Tutorial.06** folder.

2. Double-click the **New Resources** Excel file to open it, as shown in Figure 6-21.

| Figure 6-21 | NEW RESOURCES EXCEL FILE |

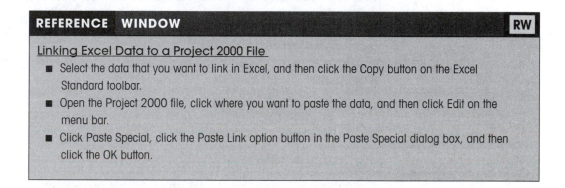

The arrangement of the columns in the New Resources Excel file matches how the fields are organized for the Resource Sheet when the Entry table is applied.

3. Click **cell A1**, press and hold the **Shift** key, press and hold the **Ctrl** key, and then press the **End** key to select the entire range of cells A1:L5 (cells A1 through L5) in the spreadsheet.

4. Click the **Copy** button 📑 on the Excel Standard toolbar, click the **Microsoft Project-Configuration Tasks** button on the taskbar, scroll in the View Bar, and then click the **Resource Sheet** button 📄.

You want to link the resources from the Excel worksheet to the Project 2000 file.

5. Click the **Indicators** cell for row 1, click **Edit** on the menu bar, click the **Paste Special**, click the **Paste Link** option button in the Paste Special dialog box, and then click the **OK** button.

The data from Excel is linked to the Project Resource Sheet, as shown in Figure 6-22. Linked data has a special symbol in the lower right-hand corner of the cell to indicate that it is linked from an outside source.

| Figure 6-22 | LINKED RESOURCE DATA |

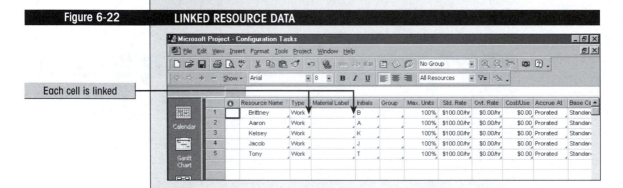

Each cell is linked

6. Click the **Microsoft Excel-New Resources.xls** button on the taskbar to open the Excel window, click cell **H1** (the Std. Rate cell for Brittney), type **120/hr**, and then press the **Enter** key.

7. Click the **Microsoft Project-Configuration Tasks Project.mpp** button on the taskbar to open the Project 2000 window.

The Std. Rate for Brittney changes to $120/hr because the information is linked.

8. Click the **Save** button 💾 on the Standard toolbar, type **Configuration Tasks-Your Initials** in the File name text box, click the **Save** button, and then save the project file without a baseline.

9. Click the **Microsoft Excel-New Resources.xls** button in the taskbar, save and close the New Resources spreadsheet, and then exit Excel.

Embedding Information in Project

Embedding differs from linking in that the destination file contains a separate copy of the data so that changes to the data in either the source or destination file are *not* automatically updated in the other location. Embedded data differs from copied and pasted data in that it retains the ability to be modified with its native application. For example, if you embed an

Excel graph in a Project 2000 file, you will retain Excel's ability to modify the graph even though the graph is completely contained in the Project 2000 file.

Embedding also refers to the ability of a program such as Project 2000 to insert data created by shared Office programs, such as Microsoft Draw or the Organization Chart program. When you insert embedded data directly into the Project 2000 file (instead of copying it from an external source), it exists only within the Project 2000 file.

Using the Drawing Tool

The Drawing tool is a special program within Project 2000 that allows you to add drawn shapes, lines, and text boxes to a Gantt Chart. It is commonly used to annotate or draw attention to key information.

REFERENCE WINDOW RW

Using the Drawing tool

- Click the View menu, point to Toolbars, and then click Drawing to display the Drawing toolbar.
- Click the shape that you want to create on the Drawing toolbar, and then drag on the Gantt Chart where you want the shape to appear.

To use the Drawing tool:

1. Confirm that the **Configuration Tasks-Your Intials.mpp** project file is open on your screen, and then click the **Gantt Chart** button 🖩 in the View Bar.

2. Drag ✛ to select all of the task names from **Update operating system** (row 1) to **Copy login scripts** (row 5), and then click the **Link Tasks** button 🔗 on the Standard toolbar.

3. Click the **Zoom In** button 🔍 on the Standard toolbar as necessary to change the minor timescale to two-hour intervals, click **Update operating system** (row 1), and then click the **Go To Selected Task** button 🔁 to expand and reposition the screen so that you can better analyze the tasks in this project.

4. Click **View** on the menu bar, point to **Toolbars**, and then click **Drawing**. The Drawing toolbar opens.

   Adding graphical effects to the Gantt Chart helps you to communicate information. If you have previous experience with drawing objects in other applications, you will find the buttons and functions to be similar in Project 2000.

   TROUBLE? If your toolbar is floating, you can dock it below the Formatting toolbar. The only toolbars that you need for this session are Standard, Formatting, and Drawing. To give yourself more room on the screen, right-click any toolbar and click the name of other open toolbars to close them.

5. Click the **Text Box** button 🖺 on the Drawing toolbar, click and drag a box within the white working time area and below the blue bars in the Gantt Chart, and then type **Configuring a PC takes 1 full day**, as shown in Figure 6-23.

Figure 6-23   DRAWING A TEXT BOX

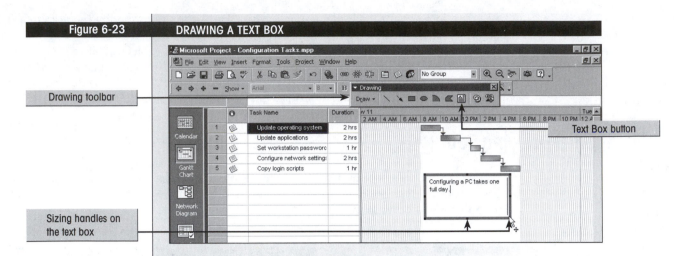

Once the drawn object is on the Gantt Chart, you can move, resize, or format it.

6. Click the edge of the **text box**. The selected text box will have a thick dark border. An object must be selected so that it can be moved, resized, or formatted.

7. Drag the corner and middle sizing handles as necessary so that all of the text fits on one line, as shown in Figure 6-24.

   TROUBLE? If you moved the text box instead of resizing it, drag it back to where you want it to be on the Gantt Chart.

Figure 6-24   RESIZED TEXT BOX

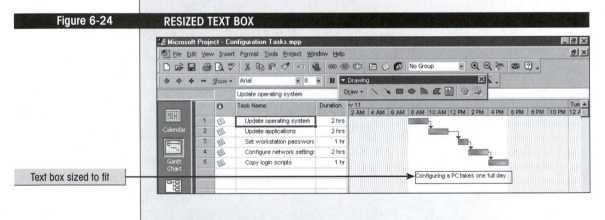

8. Close the Drawing toolbar.

9. Click the **Print Preview** button on the Standard toolbar, click the **Page Setup** button, click the **Header** tab, type **Your Name** in the left section of the header, and then print the Gantt Chart.

You can embed text boxes, shapes, arrows, and lines from the Drawing Tool onto a Gantt Chart. These graphical objects are very useful for pointing out trends, important dates, and significant events.

Saving a Project 2000 File as a Project 98 File

You've seen how Project 2000 data can be copied, pasted, linked, imported, and exported to various file formats. You've also worked with some of the powerful tools such as the data map that simplifies the export and import conversion. You likely will often want to save a Project 2000 file to a Project 98 file format so as to share data with a person who is still using Project 98, so this export process is worth special mention. Project 2000 has new features that are not available in Project 98, so it is important that you know exactly what data you might lose during this file conversion process.

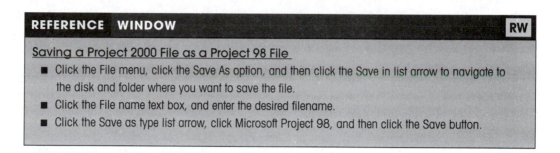

To save a Project 2000 File as a Project 98 File:

1. Click **File** on the menu bar, and then click **Save As**.

   The Save As dialog box should display the files on your Data Disk. Note that both Project 2000 and Project 98 files have the same file extension (.mpp).

2. Click to the right of the word **Tasks** but before **your initials** in the File name text box, and then type **-98**.

   This will help to identify the file as a Project 98 file, since you cannot differentiate between the two file types simply by looking at the file extensions.

3. Click the **Save as type** list arrow, click **Microsoft Project 98 (*.mpp)**, and then click the **Save** button.

   Depending on how your system is set up, you will see either the Planning Wizard dialog box or the Saving to Microsoft Project 98 dialog box.

4. Click **Save Configuration Tasks-98-Your Initials.mpp without a baseline**, and then click **OK**. Depending on how your system is set up, you will see either a dialog box that looks like the one shown in Figure 6-25 or a Planning Wizard that helps you save the file.

Figure 6-25	SAVING TO MICROSOFT PROJECT 98 FORMAT DIALOG BOX

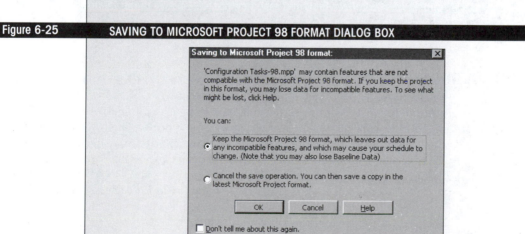

> The dialog box warns you that the file might contain some data or features that are not compatible with the Project 98 file format. To learn more about the differences between Project 2000 and Project 98 file formats, refer to the Microsoft Project Web site.
>
> 5. Click **OK** to keep the Project 98 file format.
>
> 6. Close the **Configuration Tasks-98-Your Initials.mpp** project file, and then exit Project 2000.

Many ways are available to share and save Project 2000 information in other file formats. Now that you have an overview of the different techniques and Project 2000 tools for sharing data, you can evaluate each situation to determine the best way to satisfy the data needs of various users.

Session 6.1 QUICK CHECK

1. Give an example of the type of data that you would copy from Project 2000 and paste into Excel.

2. List the file formats into which you can export Project 2000 data.

3. What menu and menu option do you use to export Project 2000 data?

4. How does Project 2000 help you create Web pages?

5. What is the purpose of the earned value analysis?

6. What is the purpose of a data map?

7. What is the main advantage of linked data?

8. What type of data is created with the Drawing tool?

SESSION 6.2

Emily Kelsey has determined that Project 2000 will be the standard project management tool for all projects at JLB Partners. In this session, you'll become more familiar with templates, the Organizer tool, and resource pools. Each of these features helps you to become more productive as you standardize Project files across your organization.

Using Templates

A **template** is a special Project 2000 file that contains sample data such as task, resource, cost, and baseline data on which you can create a new project file. Project 2000 provides several templates. You also can create your own. You use templates to help you build a project faster, as well as to standardize projects. For example, if you manage many projects that are very similar and each project you build contains the same basic tasks, you should build a template so that you don't need to remember and reenter the common tasks for each new project. A project file created from a template can be edited and modified like a project file created from scratch. You decide to explore the templates provided by Project 2000.

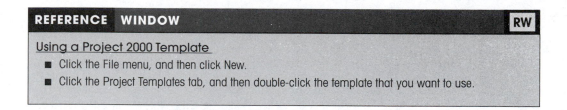

REFERENCE   WINDOW   RW

Using a Project 2000 Template

- Click the File menu, and then click New.
- Click the Project Templates tab, and then double-click the template that you want to use.

To use a Project 2000 template:

1. Start Project 2000, and then click the **Close Window** button in the upper-right corner to close the current project file and leave Project 2000 running.

   The Project 2000 window is open, but there are no current projects. You aren't going to use the blank project file that automatically loads when you start Project 2000.

2. Click **File** on the menu bar, and then click **New**. The New dialog box opens. This dialog box has two tabs: General and Project Templates. It also has buttons for three views: List, Details, and Large Icons. If a Preview is available for the selected project, it will display in the Preview pane.

3. Click the **Project Templates** tab to display the Project 2000 templates, as shown in Figure 6-26.

   Project 2000 provides 12 templates from which you can choose to build a new project file.

Figure 6-26   NEW DIALOG BOX SHOWING PROJECT 2000 TEMPLATES

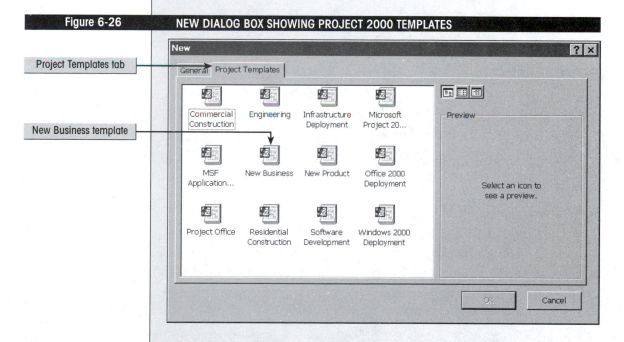

4. Double-click **New Business**, and then click the **OK** button to accept the given project Start Date and close the Project Information for the 'New Business' dialog box.

   TROUBLE? You may have to insert your Project 2000 CD if this is the first time the template is used on your computer system.

   Your screen displays a New Business project file that has many tasks organized into phases. Each task has durations, and the tasks are linked with appropriate dependencies. Sample resources also have been entered.

5. Click the **Show** button [Show] on the Formatting toolbar, and then click **Outline Level 1**.

   The four phases of developing a new business are shown as summary tasks.

6. Click the **Show** button [Show] on the Formatting toolbar, click **Outline Level 3**, and then press the **Page Down** key several times to move through the tasks of the project.

   A fourth level of indenting exists in Phase 4, but most of the project's 101 rows are now displayed. Notice that this template organizes all of the common tasks of starting a new business. Using your Project 2000 skills, you can choose to keep or change any of the tasks and durations to meet the specific needs of your project.

7. Click the **View** menu bar, and then click **Resource Sheet**.

   Nine resources have been entered as samples; two are already overallocated. As you use this template to manage your project, you will enter the resources, units, and rates for your specific project.

8. Click **File** on the menu bar, click **Close**, and then close the New Business project without saving any changes.

You could have edited this project file. You would have added your own tasks and resources, formatted the file, and saved the file with a unique name, just as you can with any other project file. The purpose of basing a project on a template file is simply to give you a fast start in developing a new project and to help you organize and remember the many details of a project.

You also can create your own templates. Although JLB Partners is a small company, its employees still discuss major projects using terms from the traditional **systems development lifecycle (SDLC)** model. This model is commonly used to manage the development of a new information system, but it can be modified and applied to almost any project. The model has six stages that roughly equate to the phases or summary tasks within a project:

1. project definition
2. evaluation of current process
3. design
4. construction
5. installation
6. evaluation

You decide to create a template that has these six phases so that you can use the template over and over again without having to reenter these summary tasks.

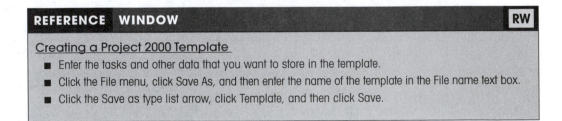

REFERENCE WINDOW   **RW**

Creating a Project 2000 Template
- Enter the tasks and other data that you want to store in the template.
- Click the File menu, click Save As, and then enter the name of the template in the File name text box.
- Click the Save as type list arrow, click Template, and then click Save.

To create a Project 2000 template:

1. Click the **New** button on the Standard toolbar, type **11/18/02** as the Start Date in the Project Information dialog box, and then click the **OK** button.

    A new template starts as a regular Project 2000 file. The first step is to enter the tasks and other data that you want to store in the template.

2. Enter the six phases of the SDLC model, as shown in Figure 6-27.

Figure 6-27	SIX PHASES OF THE SDLC MODEL

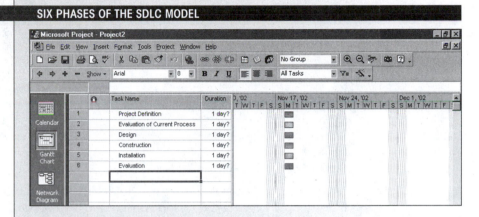

3. Click **File** on the menu, click **Save As**, and then type **SDLC-Your Initials** in the File name text box.

4. Click the **Save as type** list arrow, and then click **Template**.

    The Save As dialog box navigates to a Templates folder. This is typically located in the Program Files\Microsoft Office\Templates folder on the hard disk drive.

5. Click the **Save** button.

    The Save As Template dialog box opens, prompting you to check the type of data that you do *not* want saved in the template. You have not entered any baseline, actual, resource, or fixed cost data into this file, so you do not need to worry about these check boxes for this template. Had you decided to save a *finished* project as a template, however, it would be important to ask yourself whether you really wanted to save baseline and actual costs in the template too, or whether you wanted to delete this data for the template.

6. Click the **Save** button. Note that template files have the **.mpt** extension.

    Now that the template is saved, you should close it. Note that when you build a new project on a template, you don't *open* the template. Rather, you *use* the template by accessing it in the New dialog box.

7. Click **File** on the menu bar, and then click **Close** to close the template.

    To make sure that the template is working properly, start a new project based on it.

8. Click **File** on the menu bar, and then click **New**.

    The new template that you created should appear on the General tab along with the Blank Project template, as shown in Figure 6-28. The **Blank Project template** is the default template that all projects are created from unless you choose a different template in the New dialog box. It is the template on which new projects are based when you click the New button on the Standard toolbar.

| Figure 6-28 | NEW SDLC TEMPLATE THAT YOU CREATED |

New SDLC template that you created

9. Double-click **SDLC-Your Initials**.

A new project file is started, and the Project Information dialog box automatically opens, prompting you to check the options in it.

10. Click the **OK** button.

You will now add the unique tasks for this project to the summary tasks provided by the template.

11. Click **Evaluation of Current Process** (row 2), press the **Insert** key, type **Schedule Kickoff Meeting**, press the **Enter** key, click **Schedule Kickoff Meeting**, click the **Indent** button ⇨ on the Formatting toolbar, and then click the **Save** button 💾 on the Standard toolbar.

The Save As dialog box opens, prompting you for a location and name for the current project file.

12. Preview and then print the new project, with your name in the left section of the header.

13. Click the **Save in** list arrow, navigate to your Data Disk, click to the right of **SDLC-Your Initials** in the File name text box, type **-1**, click the **Save** button and then save the file without a baseline.

14. Close the **SDLC-Your Initials-1.mpp** project.

A template is a wonderful tool for storing standard data on which multiple projects will be based. It is very important to realize that you *create* a template by using the Save As option on the File menu and that you *use* a template by using the New option on the File menu. The only time that you *open* a template is when you want to modify the template itself, an action that would change every file based on that template from that point on.

To delete a Project 2000 template:

1. Click **File** on the menu bar, click **New**, right-click **SDLC-Your Initials**, click **Delete**, and then click **yes** when asked to verify the action.

2. Click **Cancel** in the New dialog box.

Creating Data Templates

You can create a special type of template called a data template. A **data template**, also called a box template, defines how the boxes in the Network Diagram are formatted. Once created, you can share a data template with other projects.

The default data template is called **Standard**, but projects that were migrated from Project 98 may use the **Microsoft Project 98 upgrade template** as the default data template. You can switch between these data templates in the Network Diagram View by clicking the Format menu, choosing the Box Styles option, and choosing the appropriate data template from the drop-down list. You can also create new data templates that can be shared with other projects.

You want to create a custom format for the Network Diagram that shows baseline and actual costs in the box. You also want to be able to copy this data template to another project file.

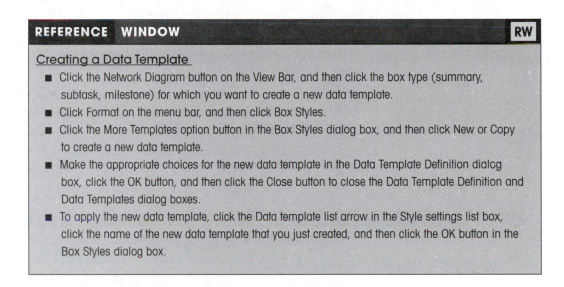

REFERENCE WINDOW   **RW**

Creating a Data Template

- Click the Network Diagram button on the View Bar, and then click the box type (summary, subtask, milestone) for which you want to create a new data template.
- Click Format on the menu bar, and then click Box Styles.
- Click the More Templates option button in the Box Styles dialog box, and then click New or Copy to create a new data template.
- Make the appropriate choices for the new data template in the Data Template Definition dialog box, click the OK button, and then click the Close button to close the Data Template Definition and Data Templates dialog boxes.
- To apply the new data template, click the Data template list arrow in the Style settings list box, click the name of the new data template that you just created, and then click the OK button in the Box Styles dialog box.

To create a new data template:

1. Click the **Open** button [icon] on the Standard toolbar, click the **Look in** list arrow, navigate to your Data Disk, and then double-click the **LAN-6.mpp** file stored in the Tutorial folder of your Data Disk for Tutorial 6.

2. Change task 0 to **Lan Installation**, click **File** on the menu bar, click **Save As**, click the **Save in** list arrow to find your Data Disk, and then save the file with the name **LAN-6-Your Initials**.

3. Click the **Network Diagram** button [icon] on the View Bar, and then click the **Analysis box**, as shown in Figure 6-29.

| Figure 6-29 | NETWORK DIAGRAM |

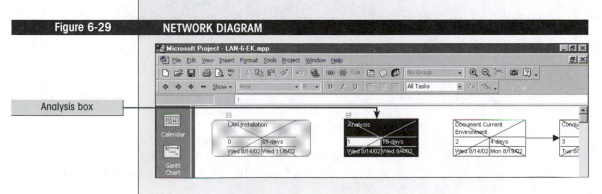

The default formatting choices for the Network Diagram include Xs on tasks that are complete. You want to create a new data template that displays baseline and actual costs in the project summary box instead of scheduled start and scheduled finish dates. You can also specify new borders, shapes, and colors for new data templates.

4. Click **Format** on the menu bar, and then click **Box Styles**. The Box Styles dialog box opens.

   You can format style settings for various types of tasks, as listed in the Style settings for list. You are not simply changing the format for a specific box at this time; you want to create a new data template based on the Standard template.

5. Click the **More Templates** button, click **Standard** in the Templates in "Network Diagram" list, and then click the **Copy** button.

   The Data Template Definition dialog box opens. The default template name is Copy of Standard; you will rename the template later. You define the box by identifying the cells, formatting, and font in the box using this dialog box.

6. Type **Cost Info** in the Template name text box, click **Start** in the Choose cell(s) section, click the **list arrow**, press the **b** key to scroll to Baseline Cost, and then click **Baseline Cost**.

7. Click **Finish** in the Choose cell(s) section, click the **list arrow**, press the **a** key to scroll to Actual Cost, click **Actual Cost**, and then press the **Enter** key, as shown in Figure 6-30.

Figure 6-30	DATA TEMPLATE DEFINITION DIALOG BOX

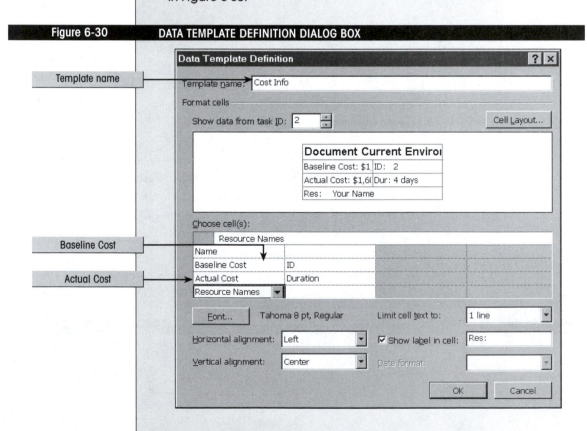

8. Click the **OK** button in the Data Template Definition dialog box, click the **Close** button in the Data Templates dialog box, click the **Data Template** list arrow in the Box Styles dialog box, click **Cost info**, and then click the **OK** button.

The new data template is applied to the Network Diagram to the summary-level tasks.

9. Click the **Show** button [Show ▾] on the Formatting toolbar, click **Outline Level 1**, and then Zoom Out.

All summary tasks should display baseline and actual costs, as shown in Figure 6-31. You can view detail information by placing the pointer on each box.

Figure 6-31   **UPDATED NETWORK DIAGRAM**

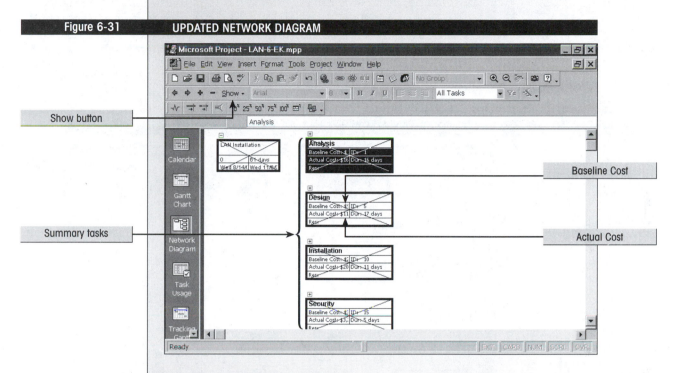

10. Preview and then print the Network Diagram, with your name in the left section of the header.

You can use your new data template with other projects. If you are working at a company and want to present a standard format for all network diagrams across all projects, this is a good way to guarantee that all printouts have the same format. Next you'll create a sample project to learn how to share the custom Cost Info data template from the **LAN-6-Your Initials.mpp** project.

Sharing Data Templates

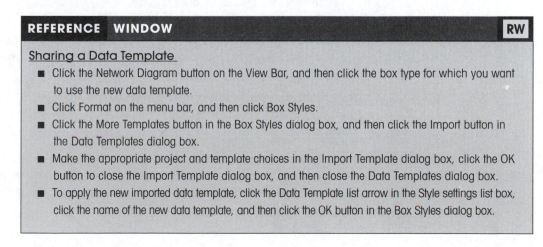

REFERENCE WINDOW   **RW**

Sharing a Data Template
- Click the Network Diagram button on the View Bar, and then click the box type for which you want to use the new data template.
- Click Format on the menu bar, and then click Box Styles.
- Click the More Templates button in the Box Styles dialog box, and then click the Import button in the Data Templates dialog box.
- Make the appropriate project and template choices in the Import Template dialog box, click the OK button to close the Import Template dialog box, and then close the Data Templates dialog box.
- To apply the new imported data template, click the Data Template list arrow in the Style settings list box, click the name of the new data template, and then click the OK button in the Box Styles dialog box.

To share a new data template with another project:

1. Click the **Open** button 📂 on the Standard toolbar. The Open dialog box should display the files in the Tutorial folder for Tutorial 6 on your Data Disk.

2. Double-click **Software.mpp** in the filename list, and then save the file as **Software-Your Initials** to the Tutorial folder on your Data Disk for Tutorial 6.

   This is the beginning of a project used to manage a new software installation. Currently, the project has two summary tasks and a few resource assignments. A baseline has been saved, but no progress has been recorded on the project, so the baseline and scheduled costs are the same.

3. Click the **Network Diagram** button 🖼 on the View Bar to view the default Network Diagram, as shown in Figure 6-32.

Figure 6-32	DEFAULT NETWORK DIAGRAM FOR SOFTWARE.MPP

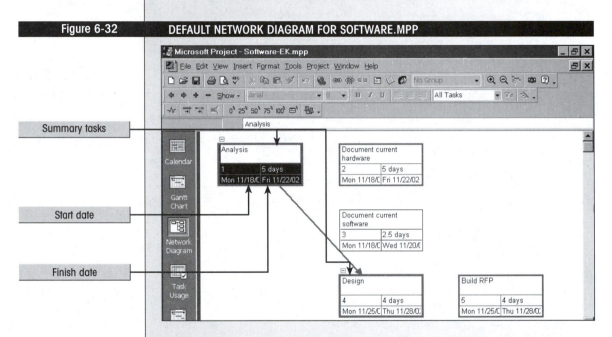

The summary tasks display scheduled start and finish dates in the box. To make this Network Diagram match the one in the LAN-6.mpp file, you apply the Cost Info data template.

4. Click the **Analysis box**, click **Format** on the menu bar, and then click **Box Styles**.

5. Click the **More Templates** button in the Box Styles dialog box, and then click the **Import** button in the Data Templates dialog box.

   The Import Template dialog box opens. Currently, the Cost Info data template is only in the LAN-6-Your Initials file. You need to import it into this file.

6. Click the **Project** list arrow in the Import Template dialog box, click **LAN-6-Your Initials.mpp**, click the **Template** list arrow, and then click **Cost Info**, as shown in Figure 6-33.

Figure 6-33   **IMPORTING A DATA TEMPLATE**

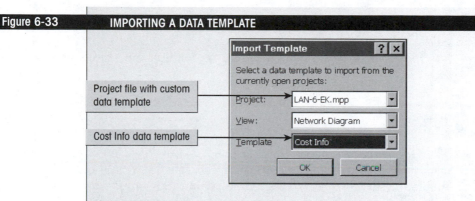

Project file with custom data template

Cost Info data template

7. Click the **OK** button. The Cost Info data template is imported into the Software.mpp file.

   The lower Preview section in the Data Templates dialog box shows you the information that the selected Cost Info data template will display.

8. Click the **Close** button.

   Now that the data template has been imported into this project, you need to select it for the Network Diagram.

   Critical Summary should still be selected in the Style settings for list.

9. Click the **Data Template** list arrow in the Bar Styles dialog box, click **Cost Info**, and then click the **OK** button.

   The Cost Info template is applied. The final Network Diagram is shown in Figure 6-34. You can see how the Baseline and Actual Costs are displayed in the Critical Summary task boxes. You can place the pointer over any part of the box to expand the detail information.

Figure 6-34   **FINAL NETWORK DIAGRAM**

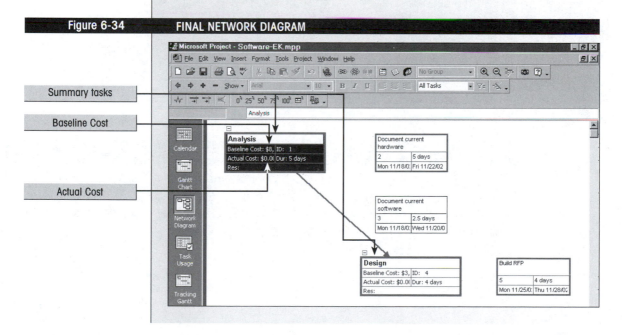

Summary tasks

Baseline Cost

Actual Cost

10. Preview and then print the Network Diagram, with your name in the left section of the header.

11. Save and then close the **Software-Your Initials.mpp** project file.

Using the Organizer

The **Organizer** is a special tool that allows you to copy custom views, tables, filters, data maps, forms, calendars, macros, toolbars, and other customizations from one project file to another. It also gives you access to **Global.mpt**, the global template that stores all of the views, tables, filters, and so forth that are available for each new project. Each new file that you create (regardless of the template that you use from the New dialog box) has access to all of the items in the Global.mpt template as well. Therefore, if you have created a custom view or report and want it to be available to every project, you should copy it to the Global.mpt template using the Organizer. The Organizer, shown in Figure 6-35, is accessed by clicking Tools on the menu bar and then clicking Organizer.

Figure 6-35	ORGANIZER DIALOG BOX

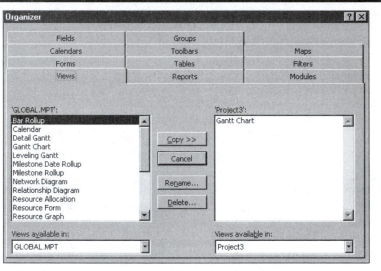

REFERENCE WINDOW   **RW**

Using the Organizer to Change the Global.mpt File
- Click Tools on the menu bar, and then click Organizer.
- Click the element that you want to copy from the Global.mpt file to the project file or vice versa, and then click Copy.

To use the Organizer:

1. Click the **Microsoft Project LAN-6-Your Initials.mpp** button on the taskbar (if that project is not the current window), and then click the **Gantt Chart** button 📰 on the View Bar.

   You want to create a custom table that contains the Entry table fields plus the Fixed Cost field.

2. Right-click the **Select All** button for the Task Sheet, click **More Tables**, click **Entry** in the Tables list, and then click **Copy**.

   The Table Definition dialog box opens, allowing you to name and edit the fields in the table.

3. Type **Entry and Fixed Cost** in the Name text box, click the **Duration** field name, click the **Insert Row** button, click the **list arrow** in the new Field Name cell, type **Fix** to quickly scroll to the Fixed Cost field, click **Fixed Cost**, and then press the **Enter** key.

   The Table Definition dialog box should look like Figure 6-36.

Figure 6-36	TABLE DEFINITION DIALOG BOX

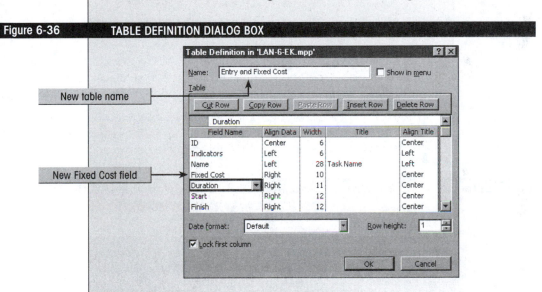

4. Click the **OK** button, click the **Apply** button to apply the Entry and Fixed Cost table, and then drag the **split bar** to the right to view the fields.

   At this point, the new Entry and Fixed Cost table exists only in the **LAN-6-Your Initials.mpp** project, but you can use the Organizer to copy it to the Global.mpt template so that you can use it in any project.

5. Click **Tools** on the menu bar, and then click **Organizer**.

   The Organizer dialog box opens.

6. Click the **Tables** tab, click **Entry and Fixed Cost** in the **LAN-6-Your Initials.mpp** list, and then click the **Copy** button. The new table is copied to the Global.mpt template, as shown in Figure 6-37.

Figure 6-37   USING THE ORGANIZER TO COPY A CUSTOM TABLE TO THE GLOBAL.MPT TEMPLATE

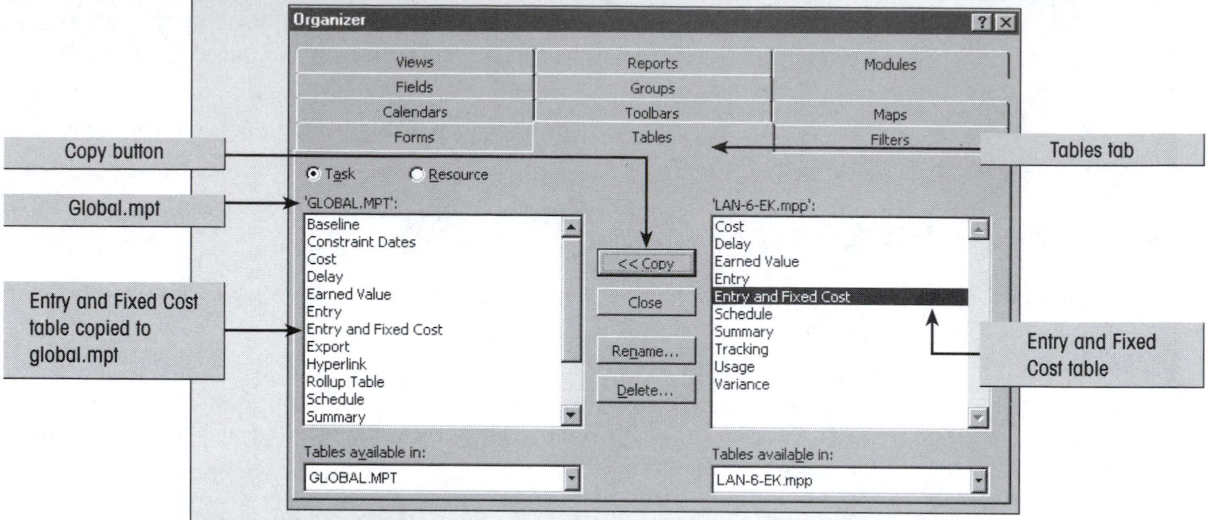

Now test the Global.mpt file by applying the new Entry and Fixed Cost table to a new project.

7. Click the **Close** button to close the Organizer dialog box, click the **New** button on the Standard toolbar, click the **OK** button in the Project Information dialog box, right-click the **Select All** button on the Task Sheet, and then click **More Tables**.

The More Tables dialog box opens, as shown in Figure 6-38. The Entry and Fixed Cost table that you created in the **LAN-6-Your Initials.mpp** file is included in the list because it was copied to the Global.mpt template using the Organizer.

Figure 6-38   MORE TABLES DIALOG BOX

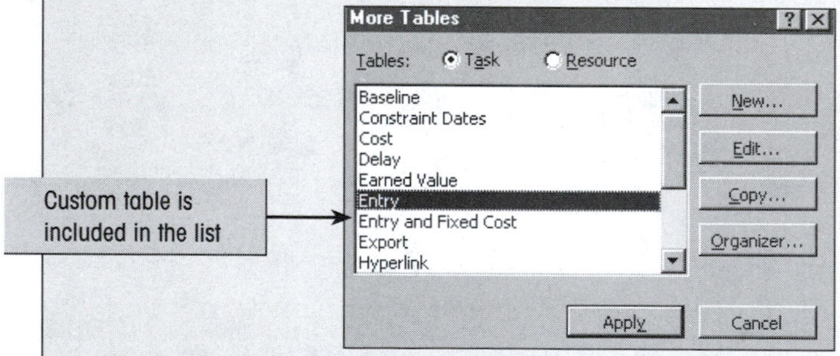

8. Click the **Entry and Fixed Cost** table in the list, and then click the **Apply** button.

9. Drag the **split bar** to the right to make sure that the Fixed Cost field, as well as all of the other fields in the Entry table, have been applied to the Task sheet.

10. Click the **Close Window** button to close the new project, and then click **No** when prompted to save the changes.

11. If you were not returned to the **LAN-6-Your Initials** project window, click the **Microsoft Project LAN-6-Your Initials Project.mpp** button in the taskbar and then close **LAN-6-Your Initials.mpp** without updating baseline information.

TROUBLE? If you are working on a shared computer in a lab you may want to use the organizer to delete the Entry and Fixed Cost table from the global.mpt file.

Another way to access the Organizer dialog box is by clicking the Organizer button in other dialog boxes that define custom elements, such as the More Tables, the More Views, and the Custom Reports dialog boxes.

Using **Resource Pools**

A **resource pool** is a project file that usually contains only data associated with resources, such as resource name, costs, units, and calendar information. A resource pool file is linked to other project files in a way that allows you to share the resources in the pool. The benefits of using a resource pool include the ability to do the following:

- Enter shared resources only once.
- Schedule resources with consideration to resource allocations made in other projects.
- Identify conflicts among assignments in different projects.
- Manage resource units, costs, and calendars in only one place.

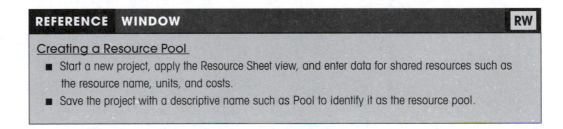

REFERENCE WINDOW   **RW**

Creating a Resource Pool

- Start a new project, apply the Resource Sheet view, and enter data for shared resources such as the resource name, units, and costs.
- Save the project with a descriptive name such as Pool to identify it as the resource pool.

To create a resource pool:

1. Click the **New** button 🗋 on the Standard toolbar, type **8/5/02** as the Start Date for the new project in the Project Information dialog box, and then click the **OK** button.

2. Scroll the **View Bar**, and then click the **Resource Sheet** 🔲 button.

3. Enter the following three resources, as shown in Figure 6-39: Conference Room, Ben Lee, and CPA Temps.

Figure 6-39	THE FIRST THREE RESOURCES IN THE RESOURCE POOL

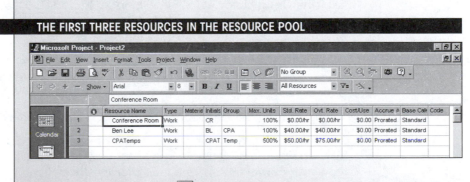

4. Click the **Save** button 🔲 on the Standard toolbar, click the **Save in** list arrow, navigate to the Tutorial folder for Tutorial 6 on your Data Disk, type **Pool** in the File name text box, and then click the **Save** button.

The three resources that you want to include in the shared resource pool now exist as a project file. Even though you can use any other existing project file as a resource pool, you should create a project file just for resource information to make it easier to manage resource information between multiple files. You will share these resources with the LAN installation project.

Shifting Existing Resources to a Resource Pool

If you already have resources in other projects that you want to add to the resource pool, you can shift all of a project's resource information to the resource pool so that other projects can also use those resources. When you shift a project's resource information to the resource pool, you need to determine which file should take precedence if conflicts between the two files arise. **Precedence** determines which file's resources and resource information will be used if conflicts between the two files arise when they are merged (for example, if two resources with the same name have different cost values). The Pool takes precedence option means that the resource pool file will overwrite conflicting information from the sharing file. The Sharer takes precedence option allows the sharing file to overwrite information in the resource pool and any other sharing files. You can shift and share resources from as many project files to the resource pool file as you want.

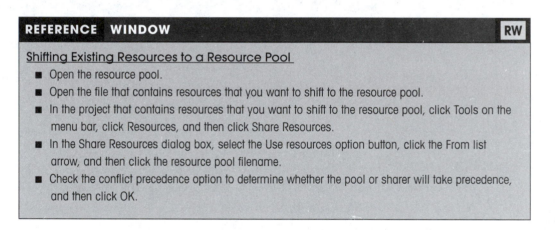

REFERENCE WINDOW   **RW**

Shifting Existing Resources to a Resource Pool
- Open the resource pool.
- Open the file that contains resources that you want to shift to the resource pool.
- In the project that contains resources that you want to shift to the resource pool, click Tools on the menu bar, click Resources, and then click Share Resources.
- In the Share Resources dialog box, select the Use resources option button, click the From list arrow, and then click the resource pool filename.
- Check the conflict precedence option to determine whether the pool or sharer will take precedence, and then click OK.

To shift existing resources to a resource pool:

1. Click the **Open** button 📂 on the Standard toolbar. The files in the Tutorial folder for Tutorial 6 on your Data Disk should be displayed in the Open dialog box. Then double-click **LAN-6-Your Initials**.

2. Scroll in the **View Bar**, and then click the **Resource Sheet** ▦ button to observe the 13 resources that are currently contained in the LAN-6-Your Initials project file.

    You need to change the second resource to your name as one of the resources.

3. Double-click the **Your Name** resource to open the Resource Information dialog box, type **Your actual Name** in the Resource name text box, double-click **YN**, type **Your actual Initials**, and then click the **OK** button.

    You want to shift these resources to the existing resource pool so that they can be available for other projects. The **LAN-6-Your Initials.mpp** file will become a sharing file.

4. Click **Tools** on the menu bar, point to **Resources**, and then click **Share Resources**.

   The Share Resources dialog box opens. You set the preferences for sharing the resources and creating the resource pool.

5. Click the **Use resources** option button, click the **From** list arrow, click **Pool.mpp**, and ensure that the **Pool takes precedence** option button is selected as shown in Figure 6-40.

Figure 6-40   **SHARE RESOURCES DIALOG BOX**

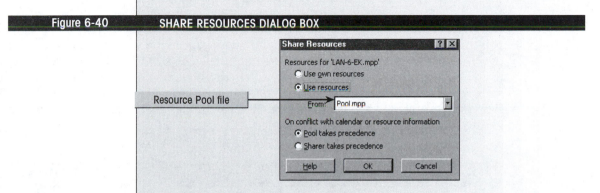

Resource Pool file

6. Click the **OK** button.

   The three resources from the **Pool.mpp** file are now being shared by the **LAN-6-Your Initials.mpp** file, and the 13 resources from the **LAN-6-Your Initials.mpp** file have been shifted to the Pool file.

7. Click the **Project Pool.mpp** button on the taskbar.

   All 16 resources are now visible in the Pool.mpp file, as shown in Figure 6-41.

Figure 6-41   **POOL FILE AFTER RESOURCES ARE SHIFTED**

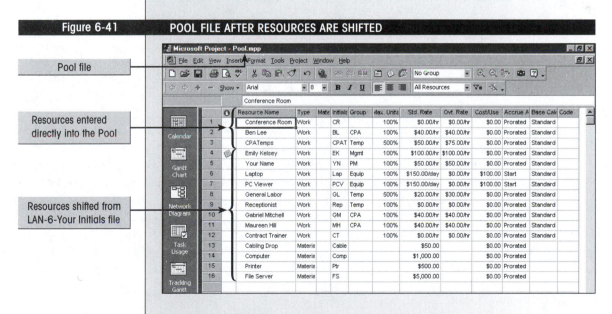

Pool file

Resources entered directly into the Pool

Resources shifted from LAN-6-Your Initials file

8. Click the **Save** button [icon] on the Standard toolbar.

Updating and Refreshing the Pool

When both the sharing and resource pool files are open on your computer, as resource information is entered in one file, the other file will be automatically updated. If many different users need access to the resource pool file, however, the situation becomes a little more complex. Only one person can have **read-write access** (the ability to both open the file—read it—and edit the file—write to it) to the resource pool file. (All others will have only read access.)

If you are working with a resource pool file and do *not* have read-write access to it (or if the resource pool file is not currently open on your computer), you can still update the resource pool manually with changes made in *your* project. Click Tools on the menu bar, point to Resources, and then click Update Resource Pool. To make sure that the resource pool is updated with changes made to *other* projects that share that pool, click the Tools menu, point to Resources, and then click Refresh Resource Pool. When you have read-write access to both the sharing and resource pool files, both the Update Resource Pool and Refresh Resource Pool menu options are dimmed out because resources are automatically updated and these menu options are not needed.

REFERENCE · WINDOW   **RW**

<u>Updating a Resource Pool (with read-write access to the pool file)</u>
- Open the resource pool and sharing project files.
- Make resource changes in either file. The changes will be automatically updated in the other file.

To update a resource pool (with read-write access to the pool file):

1. Click the **Std. Rate** cell for the Cabling Drop resource (row 13), type **60**, and then press the **Enter** key.

2. Click in the blank **Resource Name** cell (row 17), type **PC Lab**, click in the **Std. Rate** cell for row 17, type **100**, click in the **Cost/Use** cell for row 17, type **200**, and then press the **Enter** key.

   The two resource changes are entered in the shared pool file.

3. Click the **Microsoft Project LAN-6-Your Initials.mpp** button in the taskbar.

   The new resource in row 17 as well as the change to the Cabling Drop resource in row 13 should be automatically updated in this sharing file, as shown in Figure 6-42.

| Figure 6-42 | LAN-6-YOUR INITIALS.MPP RESOURCE SHEET IS AUTOMATICALLY UPDATED |

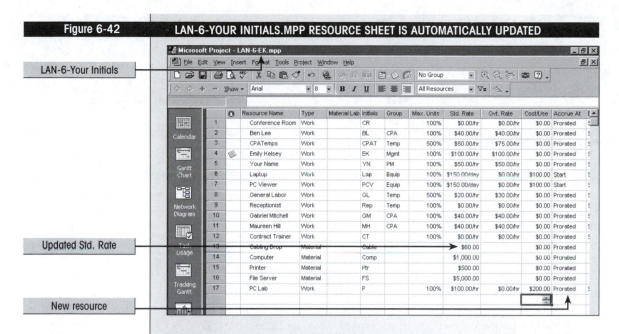

LAN-6-Your Initials

Updated Std. Rate

New resource

4. Preview and then print the Resource Sheet for the **LAN-6-Your Initials.mpp** file in landscape mode, with your name in the left section of the header.

5. Save and close the **LAN-6-Your Initials.mpp** file, and leave the baseline unchanged.

6. Save and close the **Pool.mpp** file.

You can see the power of a shared resource pool. It helps ensure that changes are accurately reflected across all projects that share resources.

Session 6.2 QUICK | CHECK

1. What types of Project 2000 templates are available?

2. What menu options do you click when you want to use an existing template?

3. What is the purpose of a data template?

4. What types of items do you copy and manage with the Organizer tool?

5. What is the name of the template that stores all of the views, tables, and filters that are available for each new project?

6. What are the benefits of using a resource pool?

7. What does resource precedence mean?

8. What do you do to keep the sharing and resource files updated when you have both open and read-write access to them?

SESSION 6.3

You have been charged with learning about many of the advanced features that are available in Project 2000. In this session, you'll learn about using master projects, inserting hyperlinks in project files, working with multiple critical paths, creating and tracking custom fields of information, creating macros, using work contours, and setting advanced options.

Using a Master Project

A **master project** is a project file that contains subprojects. It is also called a **consolidated** project. A **subproject** is a project file that is inserted into a master project. By organizing an entire project into a master project and one or more subprojects, you can delegate separate parts of the projects, through multiple Project 2000 files, to various people for data entry and update purposes. A Project 2000 file is not inherently multiuser—that is, only one person can have read-write access to a Project 2000 file at any time. Breaking a project into multiple files through the master-subproject organization allows more than one person to enter, edit, and update tasks simultaneously in separate subproject files that are linked to a master project. Viewing or printing the master project displays or prints the latest updates in any subprojects contained therein. Furthermore, by using a master project you can create views and printouts based on information from multiple projects (whether or not the projects are related).

You'll create a new master file that represents the tasks involved in documenting a LAN installation. Then you'll build two subproject files that list the tasks involved in hardware and software documentation. Breaking the tasks into two files enables two people to simultaneously update the subprojects. The scope of the entire project can be viewed from the master project.

REFERENCE WINDOW   **RW**

Creating a Master Project

- Create a new or open an existing project file that you will use as the master project.
- In Task Sheet view, click the row where you want the subproject to be linked.
- Click the Insert menu, and then click Project.
- In the Insert Project dialog box, click the Look in list arrow, navigate to the folder with the subproject, and then double-click the project name to insert it as a subproject into the master project.

To create a master project:

1. If needed, start Project 2000, and then start a new, blank project scheduled from a Start Date of today's date.

2. Click the **Save** button 🖫 on the Standard toolbar, click the **Save in** list arrow, navigate to the Tutorial folder for Tutorial 6 on your Data Disk, type **Master-6-Your Initials** as the filename, and then click the **Save** button.

   A master file can itself contain tasks or can serve only as the container into which subprojects are linked. Next, create the two subprojects that will be linked to the master project.

3. Click the **New** button on the Standard toolbar, click the **OK** button to accept today's date as the project's Start Date and Current Date in the Project Information dialog box, and then save the file as **Document Hardware-6-Your Initials** to the Tutorial folder on your Data Disk.

This new project is the first of the two subprojects.

4. Enter the tasks, durations, and relationships, as shown in Figure 6-43. To create the relationships, select the three tasks and then click the **Link Tasks** button on the Standard toolbar.

| Figure 6-43 | CREATING THE HARDWARE SUBPROJECT |

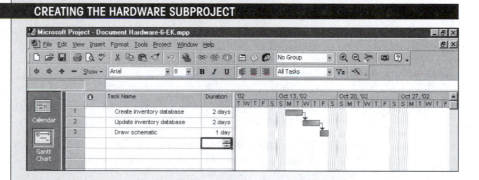

5. Click the **Save** button on the Standard toolbar, and then save your work without a baseline.

6. Click the **New** button on the Standard toolbar, click the **OK** button to accept today's date as the project's Start Date and Current Date in the Project Information dialog box, and then save the file as **Document Software-6-Your Initials** to your Data Disk without a baseline.

This new project is the second of the two subprojects.

7. Enter the tasks, durations, and relationships, as shown in Figure 6-44. To create the relationships, select the three tasks and then click the **Link Tasks** button on the Standard toolbar.

| Figure 6-44 | CREATING THE SOFTWARE SUBPROJECT |

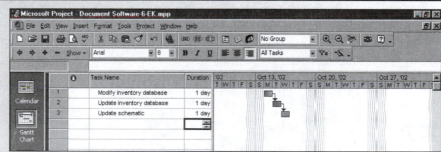

8. Click the **Save** button on the Standard toolbar, and then save your work without a baseline.

You now have the three files that you need: a master project file and two subproject files.

You must be careful how you name and save your task names and your project filenames. When you create master projects and subprojects, you want to be able to easily identify the files that you are working with.

To insert subprojects into a master project:

1. Click **Window** on the menu bar. You will see the three files listed on the menu.

2. Click **Master-6-Your Initials.mpp**.

   The blank master project file is now the active window and should fill your screen.

   Next, insert the first subproject in the first blank row of the project.

3. Click the **Task Name** cell for row 1, click **Insert** on the menu bar, and then click **Project**.

   The Insert Project dialog box opens. It resembles the Open and Save dialog boxes. The files in the Tutorial folder for Tutorial 6 should be listed in the dialog box. If you click the Insert button's list arrow, you will see that Insert has two options: Insert and Insert Read-only.

4. Click **Document Hardware-6-Your Initials.mpp**, and then click the **Insert** button. Document Hardware is inserted as the first task in the master project file. Notice the icon in the Indicator column.

5. Point to the **Indicator for Document Hardware** in row 1.

   The ScreenTip tells you that this is an inserted project and displays its path.

   Next, insert the second subproject in the second blank row of the project.

6. Click the **Task Name** cell for row 2, click **Insert** on the menu bar, click **Project** to open the Insert Project dialog box, and then double-click **Document Software-6-Your Initials**.

   The Document Software project is now inserted as the second subproject in the master project file.

7. Click the **Expand** button ➕ for both subprojects, as shown in Figure 6-45.

| Figure 6-45 | MASTER PROJECT WITH TWO SUBPROJECTS |

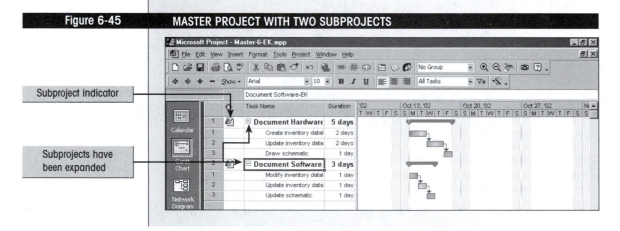

Note the row numbers for the tasks in the master project. The master project sequentially numbers the subprojects but not the tasks in each. Each subproject's tasks have their own row numbering system that starts with 1.

Updating a Master Project

Updating a master project is very similar to updating any other project. For example, you can add tasks, resources, and relationships at the master project level. The master project can save a baseline and can record actual progress. The differences between working with a master project and with a regular project file include the following.

- Any changes to subprojects are automatically updated in the master project.
- You can add tasks to both the subprojects and the master project from within the master project file.
- If you expand a subproject and insert a new row in or below the tasks of that subproject, you are adding a task directly to that subproject.
- To make sure that you are working at the master project level (when you add or move tasks, for example), collapse all of the inserted subprojects.

Next, you want to add a final task to the master project and also save a baseline.

To modify the master project:

1. Click the **Document Hardware** task, press and hold the **Ctrl** key, click the **Document Software** task, release the **Ctrl** key, and then click the **Link Tasks** button 🔗 on the Standard toolbar.

   A dependency created between subprojects is a **cross-project link**. You can also create an external cross-project link for a task using the Predecessor tab of the task's Task Information dialog box.

2. Click the **Document Hardware** task, press the **Insert** key to insert a new row, type **Present report to mgmt**, press the → key to move into the Duration cell, type **0**, and then press the **Enter** key.

   This task is a milestone and is entered directly into the master project file, as shown in Figure 6-46.

| Figure 6-46 | ADDING A TASK DIRECTLY INTO THE MASTER PROJECT FILE |

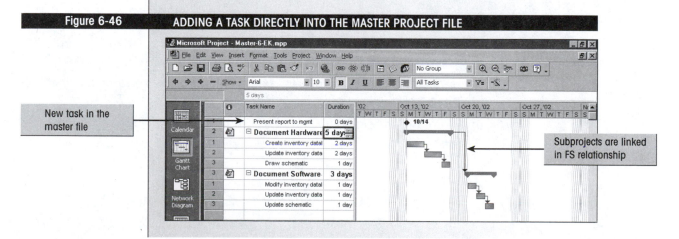

New task in the master file

Subprojects are linked in FS relationship

Next, move the new task in the master project to the end of the project.

3. Click the **Collapse** button ⊟ to the left of the **Document Hardware** task, click the **Collapse** button ⊟ to the left of the **Document Software** task, click the **row selector** for row 1, and then drag **row 1** to below row 3, as shown in Figure 6-47.

TROUBLE? If you resize the row or move it too far, click the Undo button ⟲ on the Standard toolbar and try again.

| Figure 6-47 | MOVING A ROW IN A MASTER FILE |

Drag row 1 to below row 3

Hatched line indicates row is being moved

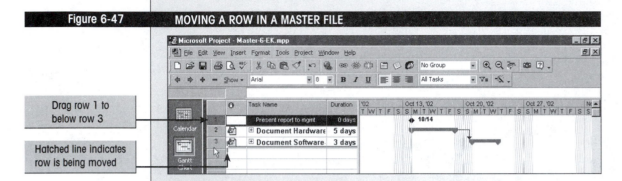

By default, a subproject acts as a summary task in the master project file. Any summary task calculation that you are already familiar with, such as for summary task duration or cost, now represents that subproject. You can change the way that the master file calculates the subproject. Do this by changing the Calculation features in the Options dialog box. Now link the milestone to the second subproject.

4. Click the **Document Software** task, press and hold the **Ctrl** key, click the **Present report to mgmt** task, release the **Ctrl** key, and then click the **Link Tasks** button ⊕ on the Standard toolbar.

Project 2000 allows you to create dependencies between subprojects as well as between subprojects and tasks in the master project.

5. Click the **Expand** button ⊞ to the left of the **Document Hardware** task, and then click the **Expand** button ⊞ to the left of the **Document Software** task to view the expanded master project.

Next, add a task to a subproject from within the master project file.

6. Click **Create inventory database** (the first task in the Document Hardware subproject), and then press the **Insert** key.

7. Type **Design inventory database**, press the **Right arrow** key, type **2** in the Duration cell, and then press the **Enter** key.

The new task is added to the Document Hardware subproject. Link the task in a finish-to-start relationship.

8. Drag ✛ to select **Design inventory database** and **Create inventory database**, and then click the **Link Tasks** button 🔗 on the Standard toolbar so that your master project looks like Figure 6-48.

| Figure 6-48 | **UPDATED MASTER PROJECT** |

New task added to the Document Hardware subproject

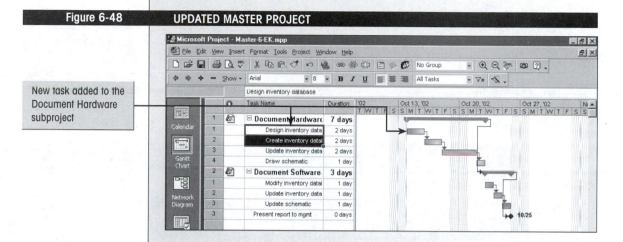

9. Click **Window** on the menu bar, click **Document Hardware-6-Your Initials.mpp** to confirm that it now contains four tasks instead of three, click **Window** on the menu bar, and then click **Master-6-Your Initials.mpp** to make it active.

You can also click the appropriate Project 2000 buttons in the taskbar to switch among open projects.

10. Click the **Save** button 💾 on the Standard toolbar, click **Yes to All** when prompted to save changes to the subprojects, and then click the **OK to All** button to save each of the three files without a baseline.

11. Preview and then print the **Master-6-Your Initials** Gantt Chart view, with your name in the left section of the header.

When you are finished planning your master project, you will probably want to set a baseline so that you can track actual progress against your initial plan.

To set a baseline for a master project:

1. Click **Tools** on the menu bar, point to **Tracking**, and then click **Save Baseline**.

2. Click **OK** in the Save Baseline dialog box to save the baseline for the entire project.

When you set a baseline for the master project, baseline fields are calculated for the master project tasks only and not for the subproject tasks. In other words, each task inserted at the master project level, as well as every summary task that represents the subproject, is updated with baseline field values. The baseline start and baseline finish fields for the individual tasks of each subproject are still driven by the baselines for those individual subprojects.

Adding **Hyperlinks to a Project File**

Another type of Project 2000 link is a hyperlink. Within Project 2000, a **hyperlink** connects files and Web pages to a Project 2000 file. For example, you might have a Word document, an Excel spreadsheet, a PowerPoint presentation, or a Web page that relates to a particular task or resource. By using a hyperlink, you can keep track of this external information, and access it quickly, through the Project 2000 file. You can also use a hyperlink to link to another view in the Project 2000 file.

You have started a Word document that will summarize the documentation information that you have collected for the LAN installation. You will add a hyperlink to the last task of your master project to link to this document.

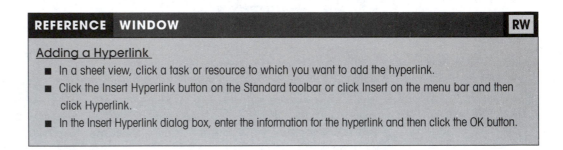

REFERENCE WINDOW   **RW**

Adding a Hyperlink

■ In a sheet view, click a task or resource to which you want to add the hyperlink.

■ Click the Insert Hyperlink button on the Standard toolbar or click Insert on the menu bar and then click Hyperlink.

■ In the Insert Hyperlink dialog box, enter the information for the hyperlink and then click the OK button.

To add a hyperlink:

1. Click the **Present report to mgmt** task in the **Master-6-Your Initials.mpp** file, and then click the **Insert Hyperlink** button 🖳 on the Standard toolbar.

   The Insert Hyperlink dialog box shows the options when the Existing File or Web Page link and the Browsed pages buttons are selected. See Figure 6-49. The browsed pages in the dialog box on your screen will differ from the links shown in Figure 6-49. You want to browse for an existing Word file called **JLB LAN Documentation.doc**, which is in the Tutorial folder for Tutorial 6 on your Data Disk.

Figure 6-49	INSERT HYPERLINK DIALOG BOX

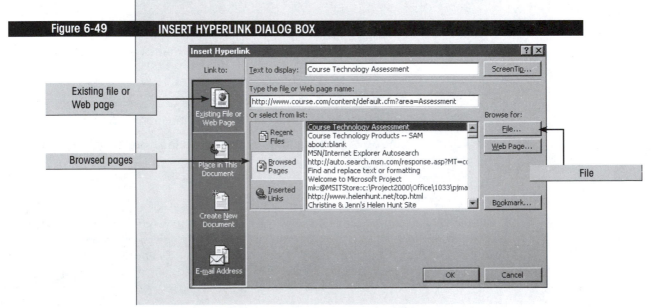

2. Click the **File** button, click the **Look in** list arrow in the Link to File dialog box, navigate to the Tutorial folder for Tutorial 6 on your Data Disk, and then double-click **JLB LAN Documentation.doc**.

The file name appears in the Type the file or Web page name text box.

3. Click the **OK** button in the Insert Hyperlink dialog box, and then point to the **hyperlink icon** 🖼 in the Indicator column for the Present report to mgmt task. Note that the mouse pointer changes to a pointing hand 👆 when you are pointing to a hyperlink.

4. Click the **hyperlink indicator** 🖼 .

The JLB LAN Documentation Word document opens, as shown in Figure 6-50.

Figure 6-50	JLB LAN DOCUMENTATION WORD DOCUMENT

JLB LAN Documentation
Word document

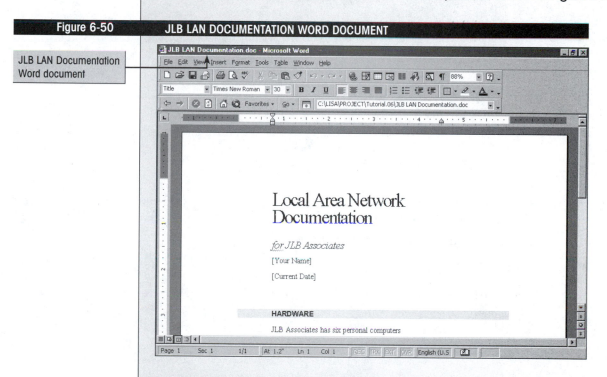

5. Select **Your Name** in the Word document, type **Your Actual Name**, select **(Current Date)**, type **Today's Actual Date**, and then click the **Print** button 🖨 on the Standard toolbar.

6. Close the Word document, saving the changes, and then click the **Microsoft Project Master-6-Your Initials Project** button in the taskbar to return to Project 2000 (if it isn't the current window).

The Web toolbar appears because you clicked a hyperlink. If you won't be working with hyperlinks any longer, you should toggle off that toolbar.

7. Right-click any **toolbar**, and then click **Web** to toggle off the Web toolbar.

Many other types of information can be linked through the Insert Hyperlink dialog box. Figure 6-51 summarizes them.

Figure 6-51	HYPERLINK OPTIONS	
LINK TO OPTION	**SUBOPTION**	**CREATES A HYPERLINK TO**
Existing File or Web Page	Recent Files	An existing file on your computer. You can enter a filename or choose from a list of the files that you have recently used.
	Browsed Pages	A Web page. You can enter a Web page address (a URL) or choose from a list of Web pages that you have recently browsed.
	Inserted Links	A file or Web page. You can enter a file or Web page address or choose from a list of Web page URLs that you have recently entered into your browser Address bar.
Place in This Document	Views	One of 22 Project 2000 views.
Create New Document	Name of new document	A new document of any type (that your computer supports) stored in any folder on your computer.
E-mail Address	Recently used e-mail addresses	An e-mail address. You can enter an e-mail address or choose from a list of e-mail addresses that you have recently used.

Working with Multiple Critical Paths

Although there is only one critical path for the entire master project, each subproject has a separate, critical path. Project 2000 allows you to show those critical paths by changing a default setting in the Options dialog box.

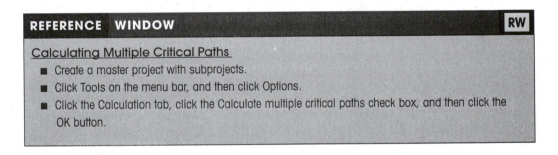

REFERENCE WINDOW   RW

Calculating Multiple Critical Paths
- Create a master project with subprojects.
- Click Tools on the menu bar, and then click Options.
- Click the Calculation tab, click the Calculate multiple critical paths check box, and then click the OK button.

To calculate multiple critical paths:

1. In the **Master-6-Your Initials.mpp** project file, click **Document Hardware**, press and hold the **Ctrl** key, click **Document Software**, release the **Ctrl** key, and then click the **Unlink Tasks** button 🔗 on the Standard toolbar.

   With the subprojects unlinked, the critical path for the master project is the same as the critical path for the Document Hardware subproject, since that subproject has a longer duration. Next, you'll prove this by filtering for critical tasks.

2. Click the **Filter** list arrow, and then click **Critical**.

   Currently, the critical path for the Master-6-Your Initials file is driven by the critical path for the Document Hardware-6 subproject.

3. Click **Tools** on the menu bar, click **Options**, and then click the **Calculation** tab to display the dialog box, as shown in Figure 6-52.

Figure 6-52	CALCULATION OPTIONS IN THE OPTIONS DIALOG BOX

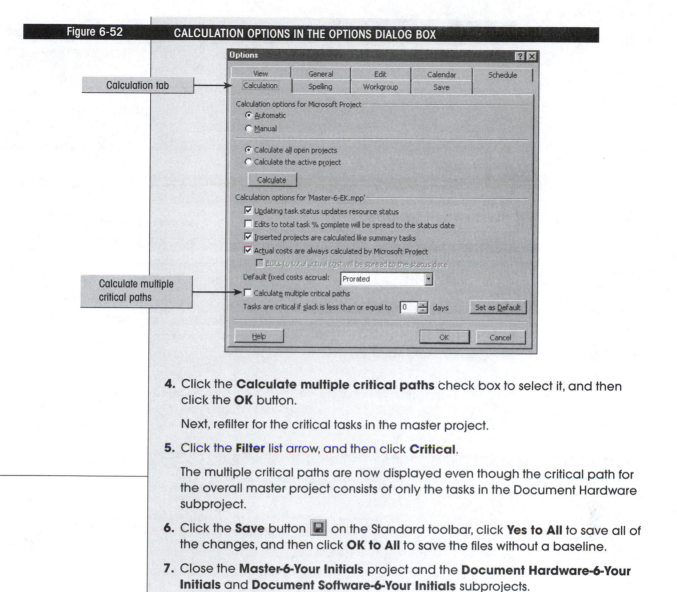

4. Click the **Calculate multiple critical paths** check box to select it, and then click the **OK** button.

   Next, refilter for the critical tasks in the master project.

5. Click the **Filter** list arrow, and then click **Critical**.

   The multiple critical paths are now displayed even though the critical path for the overall master project consists of only the tasks in the Document Hardware subproject.

6. Click the **Save** button 🖫 on the Standard toolbar, click **Yes to All** to save all of the changes, and then click **OK to All** to save the files without a baseline.

7. Close the **Master-6-Your Initials** project and the **Document Hardware-6-Your Initials** and **Document Software-6-Your Initials** subprojects.

You can also calculate multiple critical paths in a single project file.

Tracking **Custom Fields of Information**

There are 20 **flag** fields (Flag1 through Flag20) provided for each task, resource, and assignment. By default, all flag fields are set to No, but they can be set to Yes to mark an item for special identification. For example, you might want to use the resource Flag1 field to identify resources that are being used for the first time (for example, subcontractors, consultants, or other outsourced resources). By filtering for the resource Flag1 field set to Yes, you can find the new resources and more easily examine their performances. In this way, you can use flag fields to create any type of custom grouping of resources or tasks that you desire.

REFERENCE   WINDOW   **RW**

<u>Using a Flag Field on a Sheet View</u>
- Apply the sheet view where you want to add the flag field.
- Right-click the column heading where you want to insert the flag field, and then click Insert Column.
- In the Insert Column dialog box, choose a flag field from the Field name list, enter a descriptive title or other changes if desired, and then click the OK button.

To use a flag field on a sheet view:

1. Click the **Open** button �) on the Standard toolbar. The Open dialog box should open to the Tutorial folder for Tutorial 6 on your Data Disk. Then double-click **TrainingLab-6-Your Initials**.

2. Right-click the **Select All** button for the Task Sheet, click **Entry**, and then drag the **split bar** so that the Duration field is the last one visible on the Task Sheet.

   Although this project has been finished, you want to set the task Flag1 field to Yes for those tasks that you want to further review with Adrian Creighton, the tasks in rows 4 and 7.

3. Right-click the **Duration** column heading, click **Insert Column** from the short-cut menu, click the **Field name** list arrow, type **fl** to quickly scroll to the Flag fields, click **Flag1**, click in the **Title** text box, and then type **Review**, as shown in Figure 6-53.

Figure 6-53   **INSERT COLUMN DIALOG BOX**

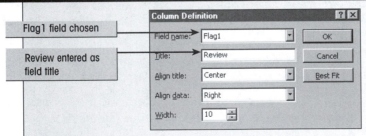

Flag1 field chosen

Review entered as field title

4. Click the **OK** button.

   By default all values in a flag field are set to No. The only other option for a flag field is Yes. The title Review is used as the field name even though the field still functions as a flag field. You can name the field anything to identify its purpose in the file.

5. Click **No** in the Review cell for the **Develop training documentation** task (row 4), click the **list arrow**, click **Yes**, click **No** in the Review cell for the **Hire trainers** task (row 7), click the **list arrow**, click **Yes**, and then press the **Enter** key, as shown in Figure 6-54.

Figure 6-54	TASK SHEET WITH FLAG1 FIELD ENTITLED REVIEW

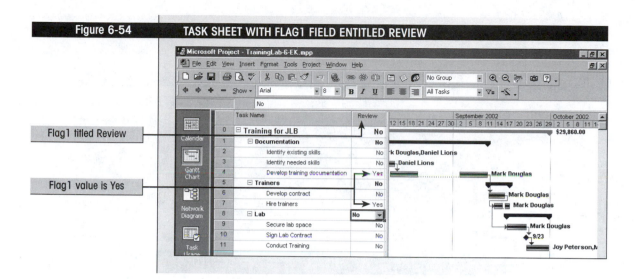

Flag1 titled Review

Flag1 value is Yes

Once you have determined a need for a flag field, you might also want to view the field on a form. Project 2000 allows you to create custom and new tables and forms that contain the flag fields. You copy custom forms to other projects by using the Organizer dialog box, just as you copy and manage other custom elements of a project.

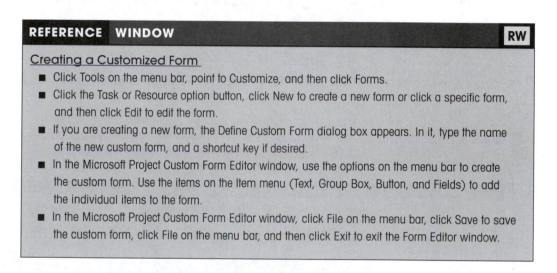

REFERENCE WINDOW   **RW**

Creating a Customized Form

- Click Tools on the menu bar, point to Customize, and then click Forms.
- Click the Task or Resource option button, click New to create a new form or click a specific form, and then click Edit to edit the form.
- If you are creating a new form, the Define Custom Form dialog box appears. In it, type the name of the new custom form, and a shortcut key if desired.
- In the Microsoft Project Custom Form Editor window, use the options on the menu bar to create the custom form. Use the items on the Item menu (Text, Group Box, Button, and Fields) to add the individual items to the form.
- In the Microsoft Project Custom Form Editor window, click File on the menu bar, click Save to save the custom form, click File on the menu bar, and then click Exit to exit the Form Editor window.

To create a customized form:

1. Click **Develop training documentation** (row 4), click **Tools** on the menu bar, point to **Customize**, and then click **Forms**.

   The Customize Forms dialog box opens, in which you can edit existing forms or create new ones.

2. Make sure that the **Task** option button is selected, click the **New** button, type **Task Review** in the Name text box of the Define Custom Form dialog box, and then click the **OK** button.

The Microsoft Project Custom Form Editor window opens with a blank Task Review form, as shown in Figure 6-55.

| Figure 6-55 | MICROSOFT PROJECT CUSTOM FORM EDITOR WINDOW |

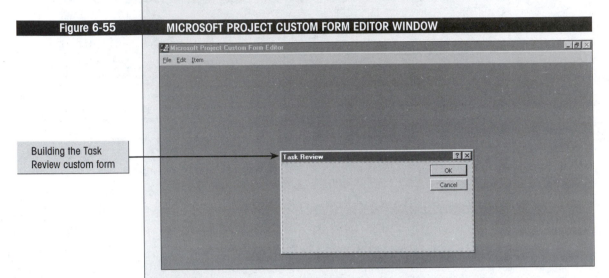

Building the Task Review custom form

Use the Item menu (Text, Group Box, Button, and Fields) to add the individual items to the form. You want to show two fields on this form: Name (of the task) and Flag1.

3. Click **Item** on the menu bar, and then click **Fields**. The Item Information dialog box opens, in which you define each item.

4. Click the **Field** list arrow, type **n** to scroll to the fields that start with "n," click **Name**, and then click the **OK** button.

5. Click **Item** on the menu bar, click **Fields**, click the **Field** list arrow, type **fl** to scroll to the fields that start with "fl," click **Flag1**, double-click **Flag1**, type **Review** in the Text box, as shown in Figure 6-56, and then click the **OK** button.

| Figure 6-56 | ADDING FIELDS TO A CUSTOM FORM |

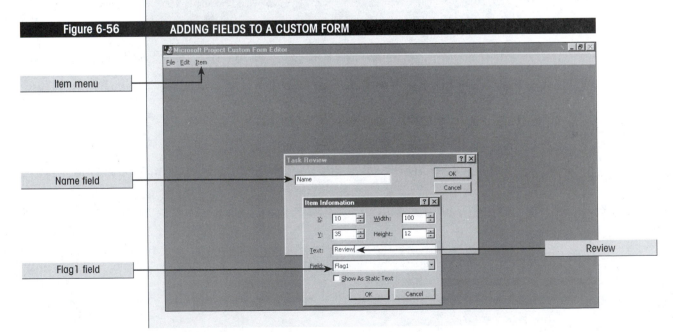

Item menu

Name field

Flag1 field

Review

Since the flag fields can hold only two values, Yes or No, the Flag1 field appears as a check box.

6. Click **File** on the menu bar, click **Save** to save the custom form, click **File** on the menu bar, click **Exit** to exit the Form Editor window, click **Task Review** in the Customize Forms dialog box, and then click the **Apply** button.

The Task Review dialog box opens, as shown in Figure 6-57. The Flag1 field for the currently selected task (row 4) is Yes, so the Review check box appears checked.

Figure 6-57

USING THE CUSTOM TASK REVIEW FORM

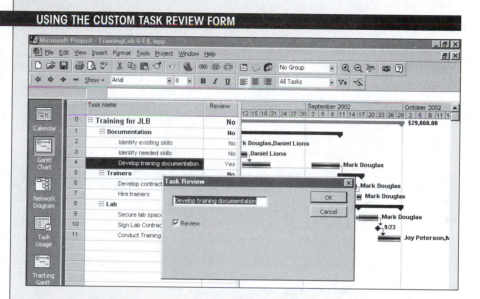

7. Click the **Review** check box on the Task Review form, and then click the **OK** button.

The Flag1 field in the Review column on the sheet is set to No because you removed the check mark from the Flag1 field on the Task Review form.

8. Click the **Save** button on the Standard toolbar.

TROUBLE? If the Task Review form is displaying a task other than Develop training documentation (row 4), click Cancel in the Task Review form, click the Develop training documentation task and then reapply the custom Task Review form. Click the Tools menu, point to Customize, click Forms, click Task Review in the list, and then click Apply.

A custom form shows information for only one task at a time, but you can make the form as elaborate as you want by continuing to add custom items (fields, group boxes, buttons, and text). If you plan to use the custom form often, you'll probably want to create a way to open it quickly. A **macro** can automate almost any repetitive steps. Opening a custom form for a particular task is an excellent candidate for a macro.

Creating Macros

A **macro** is a stored set of actions that can be executed over and over. Macro instructions are stored in a Visual Basic (VB) module. Any time that you find yourself repeating a series of keystrokes or mouse clicks many times (such as opening a custom form), ask yourself if the process can be automated by using a macro. You can create a macro either with the macro recorder or by directly entering code in a Visual Basic module. The **macro recorder** works much like a tape recorder in that it "listens" to the actions that you perform and records them for you to "replay" later.

The macro recorder translates your Project 2000 commands into Visual Basic programming code so that you don't need to be a VB programmer in order to create a macro. VB is a robust programming language, so most new users will use the macro recorder to create their macros. As your experience with macros and programming knowledge increase, however, you will find that directly coding your macros in VB will allow you to create a wider variety of, as well as more powerful, macros than those created via the macro recorder. Also, you might want to use the Visual Basic Editor for macro maintenance tasks such as editing, deleting, copying, and renaming of macros.

REFERENCE WINDOW   **RW**

Creating a Macro Using the Macro Recorder
- Click Tools on the menu bar, point to Macro, and then click Record New Macro.
- Enter a macro name in the Macro name box, set other options such as a shortcut key, description, and where the macro should be stored, and then click the OK button.
- Carefully complete the steps that you want the macro recorder to record. If you make a mistake, simply fix the mistake and go on. The recorder will record not only the mistake, but also the fact that you fixed it.
- To stop recording, click Tools on the menu bar, point to Macro, and then click Stop Recorder.

Your work with the Training Lab file has become very involved. You find that using the Task Review form helps you to organize your tasks and to track what you have to do on the project. You want to create a macro that quickly opens the custom Task Review form for the selected task.

To create a macro using the macro recorder:

1. Click **Develop contract** (row 6), click **Tools** on the menu bar, point to **Macro**, and then click **Record New Macro**. The Record Macro dialog box opens.

   A macro name cannot include spaces (VB rules), but you can use underscores to simulate spaces if you want.

2. Type **OpenTaskReviewForm** in the Macro name box, click the **Shortcut key box**, type **t** to assign this shortcut keystroke to the macro, click the **Store macro in** list arrow, and then click **This Project**.

   Notice that Project 2000 enters the current date and your name (the name of the registered user) in the Description text box, as shown in Figure 6-58. Also, many shortcut keystrokes such as Ctrl+C (copy) or Ctrl+P (print) are already reserved by Project 2000 and cannot be assigned to macros.

TROUBLE? If your name and the current date are not in the Description text box, select the text and edit it appropriately.

Figure 6-58	RECORD MACRO DIALOG BOX

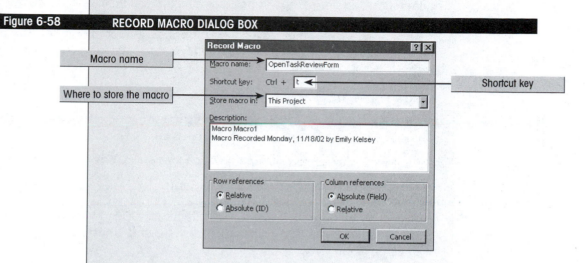

3. Click the **OK** button.

The macro recorder will now record each keystroke and mouse click that you make. You want the macro to automate the opening of the custom Task Review form.

TROUBLE? If the OpenTaskReviewForm was already created and stored in the global file instead of the project file, you will not be able to create a new macro that has this name. First, you need to delete the existing OpenTaskReviewForm macro. Click Tools on the menu bar, point to Macro, and then click Macros. In the Macros dialog box, click OpenTaskReviewForm, and then click Delete. Repeat steps 1, 2, and 3 to create the macro again.

4. Click **Tools** on the menu bar, point to **Customize**, click **Forms**, click **Task Review** in the list, click the **Apply** button, and then click the **OK** button to close the custom Task Review form.

The keystrokes that you performed in step 4 are recorded. Next, turn off the macro recorder.

5. Click **Tools** on the menu bar, point to **Macro**, and then click **Stop Recorder**.

Next, test the macro to see if it works.

6. Press and hold the **Ctrl** key, and then press the **t** key.

The Task Review dialog box should open for the Develop contract task. The Flag1 field (Review) should not be checked.

7. Click the **OK** button to close the Task Review dialog box.

TROUBLE? If the macro doesn't work as intended, you can delete it and record it again. To delete a macro, click Tools on the menu bar, point to Macro, and then click Macros. In the Macros dialog box, click the macro name that you want to delete in the list, and then click Delete. If OpenTaskReviewForm doesn't appear in the list of macros, you are probably still recording it and need to turn off the macro recorder by clicking the Tools menu, pointing to Macro, and then clicking Stop Recorder.

Now, test the macro again, this time in a different view.

8. Click the **Calendar** button ▦ on the View Bar, click the **Hire trainers** task, press and hold the **Ctrl** key, and then press the **t** key.

The Task Review dialog box should open for the Hire trainers task. In this instance, the Flag1 field was set to Yes, so the Review check box should be checked.

9. Click the **Review** check box to indicate that the Flag1 field should be reset to No, click the **OK** button, and then click the **Gantt Chart** button ▦ to return to Gantt Chart view.

Look in the Review field for the Hire trainers task. It is set to No in the Review field because you changed it through the form in Calendar view.

10. Save and then close the **TrainingLab-6-Your Initials.mpp** file; leave the baseline unchanged for now.

Macros can be used in any view in a project file. You also can copy macros to other projects or to the Global.mpt template by using the Organizer tool.

Exploring **Advanced Project Customizations**

In addition to the customizations discussed in this tutorial, such as data maps, file and task templates, macros, and custom forms, many other Project 2000 customizations are available that deal with work and default file options. These customizations, discussed in this section, are not as commonly used as templates, macros, or forms, but they nevertheless are very powerful and useful for certain situations. This section, therefore, presents a handful of advanced customizations to expand your awareness of the extensive power and flexibility of Project 2000.

Work Contouring

Work contouring is a customization applied to a resource assignment that adjusts the amount of effort (hours) that a resource devotes to a task over its duration. For example, if you have assigned a senior employee to oversee a five-day task, you could use a work contour to determine how the employee spent his or her time. You might want the employee to devote more time to the first part of the task and taper off toward the end, or you may want to increase the senior employee's involvement as the task progresses.

The default contour is Flat, meaning that the resource work is assigned evenly over the length of the task duration at a 100% level. The 100% level means that eight hours of work will be applied to each day during the task's duration. A 50% level will assign four hours of work for a one-day duration. Project 2000 offers ten preexisting resource contours, listed in Figure 6-59. The segments represent ten divisions of a task's duration. For a ten-day task, each segment represents one day. For a five-day task, each segment represents half of a day, and so forth. Each value shown in the table represents the percentage of the assigned resource's work on the task in a day, assuming 100% of the resource is available for that task.

Figure 6-59   WORK CONTOURS

WORK CONTOUR NAME	SEGMENT 1	SEGMENT 2	SEGMENT 3	SEGMENT 4	SEGMENT 5	SEGMENT 6	SEGMENT 7	SEGMENT 8	SEGMENT 9	SEGMENT 10
Flat (default)	100	100	100	100	100	100	100	100	100	100
Back Loaded	10	15	25	50	50	75	75	100	100	100
Front Loaded	100	100	100	75	75	50	50	25	15	10
Double Peak	25	50	100	50	25	25	50	100	50	25
Early Peak	25	50	100	100	75	50	50	25	15	10
Late Peak	10	15	25	50	50	75	100	100	50	25
Bell	10	20	40	80	100	100	80	40	20	10
Turtle	25	50	75	100	100	100	100	75	50	25

REFERENCE WINDOW   RW

Using Work Contours

- Apply a sheet view to your project in which you can see resource assignments, such as the Task Usage or Resource Usage view.
- Right-click the column heading where you want to insert the Work Contour field, and then click Insert Column.
- In the Insert Column dialog box, choose the Work Contour field from the Field name list, and then click the OK button.

You decide to build a project with one task and one resource to explore work contours.

To use work contours:

1. Click the **New** button ☐ on the Standard toolbar, and then click the **OK** button in the Project Information dialog box to accept the current date as the project Start Date.

2. Click the first **Task Name** cell, type **Hire new employee**, press the → key, type **10**, and then press the **Enter** key.

   Hiring is the type of task whose work can greatly fluctuate over its duration depending on whether ads need to be written, interviews need to be conducted, and other work-intensive activities need to be done. A work contour divides the task duration into ten segments, regardless of the duration. Because you gave this task a ten-day duration, the ten contour segments will be very clear.

3. Click **View** on the menu bar, click **Resource Sheet**, click the first **Resource Name** cell, type **Your Name**, and then press the **Enter** key.

   For this exercise, you won't bother with costs or other resource data.

4. Click the **Task Usage** button 🖩 on the View Bar.

   This view shows all tasks and indents the resources assigned to them on the left. The right side of the view shows a timescale, with the number of hours that resource is assigned to that task for the given time period. You can zoom in and zoom out of the timescale on the right in the Task Usage view, just as you can in many other views. To explore work contouring, you must first make a resource assignment.

5. Click **Hire new employee**, and then click the **Assign Resources** button 🖪 on the Standard toolbar.

6. Click **Your Name** in the Assign Resources dialog box, click the **Assign** button, and then click the **Close** button.

   By default, the resource was assigned to eight hours of work for each day. Now add the Work Contour field to the Assignment Sheet.

7. Drag the **split bar** to the right edge of the Start field, right-click the **Start** field column heading, click **Insert Column**, click the **Field name** list arrow, press the **w** key to quickly scroll to the fields that start with "w," click **Work Contour**, and then click the **OK** button.

   The Work Contour field shows that the Flat contour was automatically applied to the assignment. Eighty hours of work is automatically calculated for this task, since one resource supplies eight hours of work per day and the duration of the task is ten days.

8. Click **Flat** in the Work Contour field for Your Name, click the **list arrow**, click **Back Loaded**, and then press the **Enter** key.

   Your screen should resemble Figure 6-60.

Figure 6-60	A BACK LOADED WORK CONTOUR ASSIGNMENT

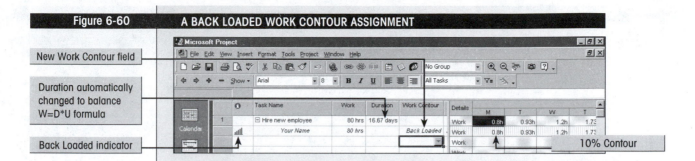

New Work Contour field

Duration automatically changed to balance W=D*U formula

Back Loaded indicator

10% Contour

The Back Loaded contour dictates that 10% of a normal day's work will be completed in the first segment (in this case, the first day), which equals 0.8 hours (10% * 8 hours). However, in effort-driven scheduling, work cannot simply "disappear." The Work = Duration * Units formula helps you to understand how Project 2000 will handle this contour. Because work remained at 80 hours and the number of units remained at 100% of one person, the duration changed to balance the formula. Notice that the current duration for the task is now 16.67 days.

9. Click the **Work Contour** list arrow for your name, click **Front Loaded**, and then press the **Enter** key. Review the changes to the task's duration and the timescale grid.

10. Click the **Work Contour** list arrow for your name, click **Bell**, and then press the **Enter** key. Review the changes to the task's duration and the timescale grid.

11. Experiment with other work contour choices for this assignment. Watch how the task duration changes when you make a new work contour choice and how the actual work is distributed in the timescale grid on the right.

Advanced **Default Options**

You have already used some of the default settings found in the Options dialog box. These settings control many powerful features in Project 2000. It is difficult to appreciate them without first using Project 2000 for several projects.

You open the Options dialog box by clicking Tools on the menu bar and then clicking Options. The Options dialog box organizes Project 2000 default settings on nine tabs: View, General, Edit, Calendar, Schedule, Calculation, Spelling, Workgroup, and Save. Some of the most important default settings are summarized in Figure 6-61.

Figure 6-61	OPTIONS DIALOG BOX SETTINGS
TAB	**SETTINGS**
View	■ Which default view appears when you start a new project? ■ What default date format will be used throughout the project? ■ Which screen elements will be shown or hidden, such as scroll bars, the Entry bar, and the Project 2000 summary task bar? ■ How will external links be displayed? ■ How will currency be displayed? ■ How will outline information be displayed?
General	■ Will Help load at startup? ■ What is the user name? ■ How will the Planning Wizards work? ■ What are the default standard and overtime rates?
Edit	■ What special options control the mouse and keyboard? ■ What are the abbreviations for time units? ■ How will hyperlinks appear?
Calendar	■ When does the project's week and fiscal year begin? ■ When converting durations to work, what are the default start and end times, hours in a day, hours in a month, and days in a month?
Calculation	■ Should calculation be automatic or manual? ■ How should actual status updates be applied to the task and resource status? ■ Will inserted projects be handled as summary tasks? ■ What is the default cost accrual method? ■ Should the project calculate multiple critical paths? ■ How is slack used when critical tasks are calculated?
Spelling	■ Which fields should the spell checker check? ■ What types of items should the spell checker ignore? ■ What types of suggestions should the spell checker suggest?
Workgroup	■ What is the default workgroup communication method? ■ What are the Web server and Project Central settings for the project?
Save	■ What is the default file format for saved projects? ■ What is the default location for projects, templates, and databases? ■ How should AutoSave be handled? ■ Do you want to save expanded time-phased data?
Schedule	■ Will assignment units be displayed as percentages or units? ■ What are the default scheduling options for new tasks, work, duration, and task types? ■ Are new tasks effort driven? ■ Will tasks honor their constraint dates? ■ Do new tasks have and show estimated durations?

An **accessibility option** is an option that determines how accessible the product will be for people who have some level of disability. Some of the options available in the Options dialog box and elsewhere in the product are especially useful for those people who have poor vision or limited dexterity and could affect their ability to use the product easily. Changes include setting the proper magnification level and default view, providing one-key shortcuts for common abbreviations, and specifying correct default locations for saved projects. For more information on accessibility options, search for the word "accessibility" in any Microsoft product Help manual and then link to the appropriate subject area for your question. Microsoft Help manuals are linked to the World Wide Web, so if your computer is currently connected to the Web, you can expand your search for information beyond the local Help manual.

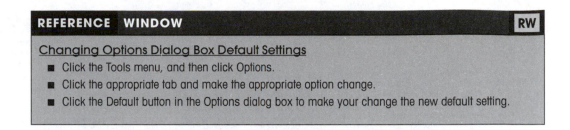

REFERENCE   WINDOW   **RW**

Changing Options Dialog Box Default Settings

■ Click the Tools menu, and then click Options.

■ Click the appropriate tab and make the appropriate option change.

■ Click the Default button in the Options dialog box to make your change the new default setting.

Next, you explore the default settings found in the Options dialog box.

To explore Options dialog box default settings:

1. Click **Tools** on the menu bar, click **Options** to open the Options dialog box, and then click the **Save** tab.

   The Projects in the File types list is selected, as shown in Figure 6-62.

Figure 6-62   **SAVE TAB OF THE OPTIONS DIALOG BOX**

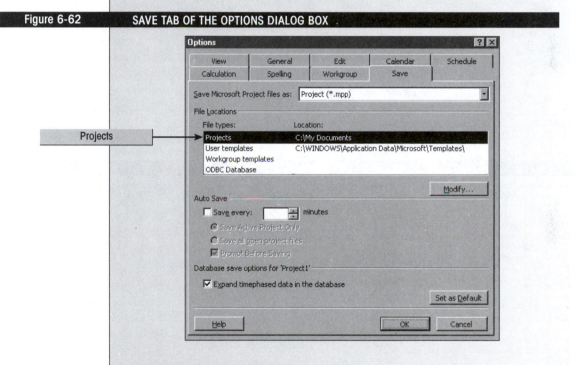

2. Click the **Modify** button.

   The Modify Location dialog box opens in which you can set a default location for all saved projects. If you are working on a big project and have organized your files in a specific folder on your hard disk, you might want to set this default so that when you click Save or Open the dialog boxes automatically default to that location.

3. Click the **Cancel** button in the Modify Location dialog box, and then click the **Schedule** tab, as shown in Figure 6-63.

Figure 6-63   SCHEDULE TAB OF THE OPTIONS DIALOG BOX

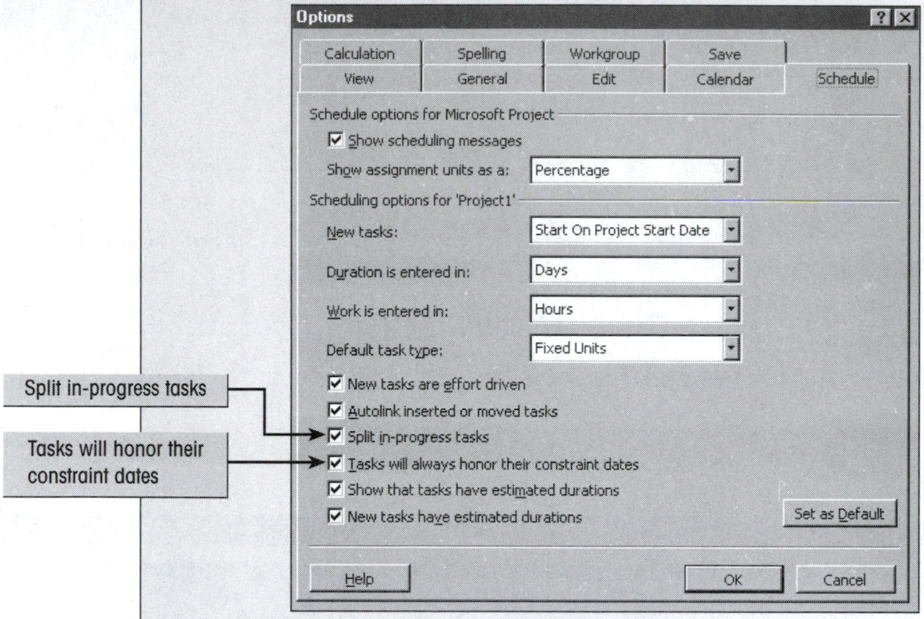

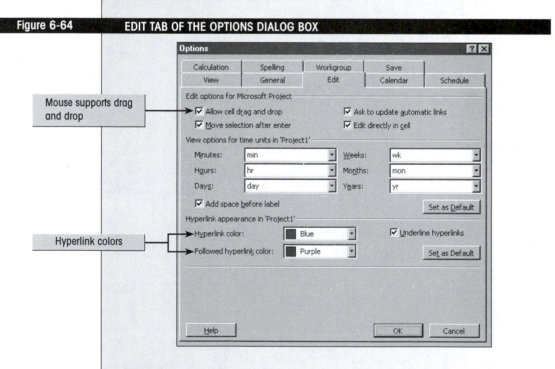

This tab shows some important options, such as whether you are allowed to split the work of a task in progress or whether you can override task constraint dates.

4. Click the **Edit** tab, as shown in Figure 6-64.

Figure 6-64   EDIT TAB OF THE OPTIONS DIALOG BOX

Someone with diminished dexterity to control a mouse might not want to allow the mouse to drag and drop information inadvertently. Someone who is color-blind might not be able to see or read the default hyperlink colors and could change those colors so as to better distinguish hyperlinks.

5. Click the other tabs of the Options dialog box to explore the choices, and then click the **Cancel** button to close the dialog box.

Changing the settings in the Options dialog box changes the settings for only that project file. Clicking the Set as Default button in the Options dialog box changes the setting for each project file created after the change was made.

6. Close the project without saving changes, and exit Project 2000.

Project 2000 offers many powerful tools to help you manage a project. You have had the opportunity to explore many of them. You will probably not use all of them as you manage a project, but you will have the experience to know which tools are appropriate for the task at hand to help you work as an effective project manager.

Session 6.3 QUICK | CHECK

1. Why would you create a master file with subprojects?

2. Why would you use a hyperlink?

3. What types of information can a flag field contain?

4. What are the two ways that you can create a macro?

5. What is the purpose of work contouring?

6. How do you access the Options dialog box?

7. What are the categories within the Options dialog box?

REVIEW ASSIGNMENTS

Part of the LAN installation involved training the users. In this assignment, you will open a project file that documents training tasks that were completed. You will use Project 2000's powerful data-sharing capabilities to share data with Excel, Word, and Web page files. You'll explore templates, the Organizer, resource pools, master files, macros, and advanced customizations.

1. Start Project 2000 and make sure that your Data Disk is in the appropriate disk drive. Open the **Training-6** file in the Review folder for Tutorial 6. Change task 0 to Training for JLB.

2. Use the Save As command to save the project as **Training-6-Your Initials** on your Data Disk. Some printouts will show the resource names. In the Resource Sheet view, change Mark Douglas to Your Name and the initials MD to Your Initials so that you will be automatically identified on those printouts.

3. You want to copy and paste the cost data for the summary tasks to Excel and use Excel's graphing tools to create a bar chart of actual versus baseline cost data. Click the Gantt Chart view button, apply the Cost table to the Task Sheet, and then drag the split bar to the far right to see the columns of the Cost table.

4. Click the Show Subtasks button on the Formatting toolbar, and then click Outline Level 1.

5. Click the Select All button for the Task Sheet, and then click the Copy button on the Standard toolbar.

6. Start Excel so that a blank workbook opens. Click cell A2 so that when you paste information into the workbook, it starts in that cell.

7. In Excel, click the Paste button on the Standard toolbar to paste the Cost table data into the range of cells A2:H5. Resize the columns so that all of the data clearly displays.

8. To clarify the data in Excel, click cell D1 and type "Actual." Click cell E1 and type "Baseline."

9. In Excel, you want to graph the three phases as well as their total and baseline costs. In all, you want to graph nine cells. To select all nine cells, drag to select cells A3, A4, and A5, press and hold the Ctrl key, drag to select cells D3, D4, and D5, drag to select cells E3, E4, and E5, release the Ctrl key, and then click the ChartWizard button.

10. In Step 1 of 4, choose a Column chart type and a Clustered Column subtype, the default choice. In Step 2 of 4, the Data Range tab should display your graph correctly, but the information in the Legend is unclear. Click the Series tab, click Series1 in the Series list, click in the Name text box, and then click cell D1 on the workbook. (*Hint:* You might have to drag the title bar of the Chart Wizard dialog box in order to click D1 on the workbook.) Similarly, click Series2 in the Series list, click the Name text box, click cell E1 on the workbook, and then click Next.

11. In Step 3 of 4, click in the Chart title text box and type "Total Baseline was $9K Higher Than Actual Costs." Click the Next button, click the As new sheet option button in Step 4 of 4, and then click the Finish button. The chart opens on the Chart1 sheet tab of the workbook.

12. Click the Print Preview button on the Standard toolbar to preview the chart, click the Setup button, click the Header/Footer tab, click the Custom Footer button, click the Right section, and then type Your Name. Click the OK button in the Footer dialog box, click the OK button in the Page Setup dialog box to return to preview, and then print the chart. Close the workbook without saving changes.

Explore 13. Return to the **Training-6-Your Initials.mpp** project file, apply the Variance table to the Task Sheet, and then drag the split bar to the left so that the last column visible in the table is the Actual Finish field. Click View on the menu bar, click More Views, and then apply the Tracking Gantt Chart view. Click the Training for JLB task name in row 0, click the Go To Selected Task button, and then adjust and zoom the Gantt Chart as necessary so that all of the bars are clearly visible.

14. Click the Copy Picture button, click the To GIF image file option button, and then click the Browse button to locate your Data Disk. Save the GIF file, with the name Tracking Gantt, to the Review folder for Tutorial 6, and then click the OK button to close the Copy Picture dialog box.

15. Start Word so that a blank document opens. Click Insert on the menu bar, point to Picture, and then click From File. In the Insert Picture dialog box, click the Look in list arrow and locate your Data Disk to find the **Tracking Gantt.gif** file. Double-click the **Tracking Gantt.gif** file to insert it into the Word document. Press the Enter key two times to enter a blank line below the picture, type Your Name, press the Enter key, and then type the current date.

Explore 16. In Word, press the Enter key two times and then type a short explanation as to what the percentages on the right edge of the bars in the Tracking Gantt Chart represent, as well as what the blue and gray bars for a subtask represent. (*Hint:* In Project 2000, point to the bar in the Gantt Chart to display a ScreenTip of the bar name as well as information about the bar. Or click Format on the menu bar, and then click Bar

Styles. Scroll through the bar styles until you see the new ones that appear on the Tracking Gantt Chart.) Preview and print the document, and then close the document without saving it.

17. Click the **Project Training-6-Your Initials.mpp** button on the taskbar. Right-click the Select All button for the Task Sheet, click More Tables, apply the Earned Value table to the Task Sheet, drag the split bar to the far right, and then resize the columns so that all of the data in each field is visible.

18. Preview and then print the Earned Value Table, with your name in the left section of the header. On the printout, write down what each field represents. For example, BCWS means Budgeted Cost of Work Scheduled. For those fields that are also calculated formulas, write down the formula that creates the calculation.

19. Apply the Gantt Chart view with the Entry table, click File on the menu bar, click Save as, click the Save as type list arrow in the Save As dialog box, and choose Web Page to save the view as a Web Page with the filename **Training Data** to the Review folder on your Data Disk.

20. In the Export Mapping dialog box, click Export to HTML using standard template, and then click the Save button.

21. Right-click the Start button, and then click Explore. Locate the Review folder for Tutorial 6 on your Data Disk, and then double-click the **Training Data.html** file to open the Training Data Web page.

22. The Training Data Web page should automatically open in the default browser for your computer (Internet Explorer or Netscape Navigator). Your Name should be listed as a resource. Print the Web page, close the browser window, and return to the Training-6-Your Initials project window.

23. One trainer has developed an Excel spreadsheet called **Survey.xls** that lists three tasks and corresponding durations for another phase of the Training-6-Your Initials project. To import the Excel data into a new project, click the New button on the Standard toolbar, and then click the OK button to accept the default dates.

24. In the new project window, click File on the menu bar and then click Open. In the Open dialog box, locate the Review folder for Tutorial 6 on your Data Disk, use the Files of type list arrow to display Microsoft Excel Workbooks, and then double-click **Survey.xls**.

25. In the Import Mapping dialog box, click Default task information, and then click the Edit button. In the Define Import/Export Map dialog box, click the Task Mapping tab, click the Source worksheet name list arrow, and then click Sheet1. Sheet1 contains only two fields of information for the three tasks: Task Name and Duration. Scroll through the mapping fields to determine whether these two fields were mapped correctly. (*Hint*: Fields that are in the Excel 2000 spreadsheet will appear in black.) You should see that the Duration field was mapped automatically but the Task Name field in the worksheet was not.

26. The Task Name field in the Excel worksheet should be mapped to the Name field in Project 2000. Click the Current Name Microsoft Project Field (it is currently displayed in red and is located just above the black Duration field), and then click the Delete Row button. Scroll to the Task Name field (Worksheet Field), click the (not mapped) list arrow, click Name (Microsoft Project Field), click the Move Up arrow several times to move to the top of the list so that the Name (Microsoft Project Field) row rests just above the Duration (Microsoft Project Field) row. Click the OK button, and then click the Open button. The three tasks are entered in the new project file, which is now named **Survey.mpp**.

27. Select all three tasks in the **Survey.mpp** file, and link them with finish-to-start relationships by clicking the Link Tasks button on the Standard toolbar. Click the Save button on the Standard toolbar, and save the project as **Survey-Your Initials** to the Review folder for Tutorial 6 your Data Disk. Do not save a baseline for the project.

28. Click the **Microsoft Project Training-6-Your Initials.mpp** button on the taskbar. Click the first blank row below the Conduct Training (ID 10) task. Click Insert on the menu bar, and then click Project. Double-click **Survey-Your Initials.mpp** to insert the **Survey-Your Initials.mpp** project file into the **Training-6-Your Initials.mpp** file in a master-subproject relationship. Click the Outdent button on the Formatting tool-bar once to outdent the project to the same summary task level as Documentation, Trainers, and Lab.

29. Expand the Survey-Your Initials task, and then link Conduct Training (ID 10) and Create survey (ID 1 within Survey-Your Initials) with a finish-to-start relationship.

30. Enter a new subtask below Tally Results (ID 4 within Survey-Your Initials) with the task name of Discuss Findings, a duration of two hours, and a finish-to-start relationship with the prior task, Tally Results.

31. Click the Save button to save **Training-6-Your Initials.mpp**, and then save **Survey-Your Initials.mpp** with a baseline. Preview and then print the Gantt Chart view of both files, with your name in the left section of the header.

32. Make sure that **Training-6-Your Initials.mpp** is the active file, click the Task Usage button in the View Bar, press and hold the Ctrl key while pressing the Home key to quickly go to the first task, and then click the Go To Selected Task button on the Standard toolbar. Preview and then print just the first page of the Task Usage printout, with your name in the left section of the header.

Explore ▶ 33. On the Task Usage printout, identify how the information is grouped.

Explore ▶ 34. Use the Project 2000 Help file to read about sharing resources. Click the Learn More about Sharing Resources link in the Help screen, and read the Help screens.

35. Right-click the Select All button for the Task Sheet, click More Tables, click Usage in the More Tables dialog box if it isn't already selected, and then click the Copy button. In the Name text box, type the table name "Usage Facts" to create a new custom table with that name. Click Start Field Name, click the Insert Row button, click the list arrow for the blank Field Name cell, click Cost, and then click the OK button. In the More Tables dialog box, click Apply to apply the Usage Facts table. Adjust the split bar and columns so that all of the data in the Work, Duration, and Cost fields are visible, and then print the first page of the custom table.

36. Click Tools on the menu bar, and then click Organizer. Click the Tables tab in the Organizer dialog box, click Usage Facts in the **Training-6-Your Initials.mpp** list, and then click the Copy button to copy the table to the Global.mpt template. Now the custom table is available to all new projects. Close the Organizer.

37. Save and close both the **Training-6-Your Initials.mpp** as well as the **Survey-Your Initials.mpp** project files. Do not save baseline information.

38. Click File on the menu bar, and then click New. Click the Project Templates tab in the New dialog box, and then double-click Software Development. Click the OK button in the Project Information dialog box.

39. Click the Task Usage button in the View Bar, right-click the Select All button for the Task Sheet, and then click More Tables. Apply the Usage Facts table to this project, and then move the split bar to resize all of the columns so that the Work, Duration, and Cost fields are clearly visible.

Explore 40. Note that the cost value is $0.00 for each resource assignment. Do you know why? Click the Resource Sheet button in the View Bar, and then enter 100 in the Std. Rate cell for the Project Manager. Click the Task Usage button on the View Bar, and then preview and print the first page of the Task Usage view. In the margin of the paper, explain why some tasks have costs and others do not.

41. Click Tools on the menu bar, point to Macro, and then click Record New Macro. In the Macro Name box, type "MyNameinHeader," assign the shortcut key combination Ctrl+m, click the Store macro in list arrow, click This Project, and then click the OK button. Now you are recording the macro that inserts your name in the upper-left section of the printout. Follow these steps precisely:

   ■ Click the Preview button on the Standard toolbar.
   ■ Click the Page Setup button in the Preview window.
   ■ Click the Header tab in the Page Setup dialog box (even if it is already selected).
   ■ Click the Left tab in the Header section of the Page Setup dialog box.
   ■ Select any text in the Header section and type Your Name (even if your name already exists in that section, you must select it and retype it).
   ■ Click the OK button in the Page Setup dialog box.
   ■ Click the Close button in the Preview window.
   ■ Click Tools on the menu bar, point to Macro, and then click Stop Recorder.

42. Test the new macro by using a different view. Click the Calendar button on the View Bar, press and hold the Ctrl key, and then press the m key. The macro will stop when your name has been entered in the left section of the header and will preview the Calendar with the new header. Print one page of the Calendar view.

43. Close the Software Development project without saving changes.

Explore 44. Explore the options in the Options dialog box. With Project 2000 running but no active project file, click Tools on the menu bar and then click Options. View the different tabs. Change some of the view options on the Edit tab. Open a new project file to see how the changes affect that file.

Explore 45. Explore: Start Project 2000 Help, and use the Answer Wizard to find information about the flag fields. Read the information about Flag 1–20 for resource, task, and assignment fields, and then print the page for Task fields. Exit Help.

46. Close the Project file and then exit Project 2000.

CASE PROBLEMS

Case 1. Using Project 2000 Templates You have been hired at a project management consulting firm. Project consulting engagements range from traditional construction projects to information systems installations to new product deployments. The Project 2000 templates represent some of the most common types of project categories, so you'll explore these templates further to see if they can be applied to the jobs that you'll be working on at the firm.

1. Start Project 2000, click File on the menu bar, click New, click the Project Templates tab, and then double-click the Residential Construction template. Click the OK button in the Project Information dialog box.

2. Use the Outline levels to get a feel for the phases and lengths of the sample tasks in this project. Click the Show button on the Formatting toolbar, and then click Outline Level 2. Scroll through the project, display Outline Level 3, and then scroll through the project again. Click the Show button on the Formatting toolbar, and then click All Subtasks to display all of the tasks of the project again.

3. Click the Resource Usage button on the View Bar, enter Your Name in the Resource Name cell instead of the Owner entry (ID 7), and then print the first page of this report, with your name in the left section of the header.

4. Click the Task Usage button on the View Bar, and then print the first page of this report, with your name in the left section of the header.

Explore

5. In the margin of the Resource Usage and Task Usage printouts, identify how the information is grouped.

6. Click the Gantt Chart button, and observe the total number of days that the project is scheduled by viewing the Duration cell for the project summary task. On the back of the Task Usage printout, write the total number of days scheduled for the Residential Construction project. Press and hold the Ctrl key while pressing the End key and then press the Home key to go to the first cell in the last row of the project. On the back of the Resource Usage printout, write the total number of task rows that the template provides.

7. Close the Residential Construction file without saving changes.

8. Click File on the menu bar, click New, click the Project Templates tab, and then double-click the Commercial Construction template. Click the OK button in the Project Information dialog box.

9. Print the first page of the Gantt Chart, with your name in the left section of the header. Circle the value that represents the total duration for the project on the printout.

10. On the back of the Commercial Construction Gantt Chart printout, write the total number of task rows that the template provides. Close the project file.

11. Start a new project with the Infrastructure Deployment template, and then display, preview, and print the Outline Level 2 tasks of the Gantt Chart. Be sure that your name is in the left section of the header. On the back of the printout, identify three uses for this project template.

12. Close the Infrastructure Deployment project without saving the changes.

13. Start a new project for each of the three templates: Engineering, MSF (Microsoft) Application Development, and Software Development. Click Tools on the menu bar, click Options, click the View tab, and then check the project summary task check box for each project to add the summary task bar.

14. Display each project at Outline Level 1, and then print the first page of each project's Gantt Chart, with your name in the left section of the header. Based on the Level 1 tasks, determine the task name that most closely represents the Design phase in each project. Write your answer on the back of the Engineering Gantt Chart printout. Based on the Level 1 tasks, what task name most closely represents the Implementation phase in each project? Write your answer on the back of the MSF Application Development printout.

15. Close all three projects without saving them.

16. Start a new project by using the New Product template, display the Outline Level 2 tasks, zoom out so that Years are displayed in the upper portion and quarters are displayed in the lower portion of the timescale, and then print the Gantt Chart (it should be only one page). On the printout, identify which task is estimated to be almost one year long. On the back of the printout, write the total project duration as determined by the project summary task bar.

17. In Gantt Chart view, scroll to row 81, and then delete the last two major phases (Commercialization Stage and Post Commercialization Review). On the back of your printout, write the total project duration as determined by the project summary taskbar. Also write down the type of product that would be appropriate for the durations currently listed in this project. Write down one or two sentences to support your answer.

18. Close the New Product template without saving changes.

19. Start a new project by using the New Business template, click the Group By list arrow on the Standard toolbar, and then click Critical. Expand both the Critical and Noncritical groups, and zoom out so that months are on the upper portion of the Gantt Chart timescale and weeks are in the lower portion of the timescale. Print the first page of the Gantt Chart, with your name in the left section of the header.

20. Click Tools on the menu bar, click Options, click the Calculation tab, click the Calculate multiple critical paths check box, and then click the OK button.

21. Click the Group by list arrow on the Standard toolbar, and then regroup by Critical tasks. Print the first page of the Gantt Chart, with your name in the left section of the header. Write a sentence or two that explains what happened to the number of critical tasks when you calculated multiple critical paths.

22. Close the New Business template without saving changes, and then exit Project 2000.

Case 2. Integrating Project 2000 Data with Other Office 2000 Applications You are currently using Project 2000 to manage the upgrade to the latest version of Microsoft Office for your large business. You'll use the Infrastructure Deployment template to quickly create a project file to manage this large effort. Then you'll use this file to explore various ways to share the Project 2000 information with other Office 2000 applications. To complete this case you will need Word and Excel installed on your computer.

1. Start Project 2000, click File on the menu bar, click New, click the Project Templates tab, and then double-click the Infrastructure Deployment template. Change the Project Start date to 1/3/02, and then click the OK button in the Project Information dialog box.

2. In the Task Sheet of the Gantt Chart, edit the task name in row 1 to be Office Deployment. In the Resource Sheet, edit the first resource name to be Your Name.

3. In Gantt Chart view, click the Show button on the Formatting toolbar, click Outline Level 2, and then zoom out on the Gantt Chart so that the major scale of the timescale is measured in quarters and the minor scale is measured in months.

4. Position the Gantt Chart so that you can see all of the summary bars, and then click the Copy Picture button on the Standard toolbar. Click the To GIF image file option button, click the Browse button, click the Save in list arrow, and then navigate to the Cases folder for Tutorial 6 on your Data Disk. Change the filename to **Office Deployment**, click the OK button in the Browse dialog box, and then click the OK button in the Copy Picture dialog box. The image is saved as a GIF file to your Data Disk.

5. Start Word and in a new, blank document type the following.

To: Julia Asay, President

From: Your Name

Date: Today's Date

Re: Office Deployment

Project planning for the corporate update of the Microsoft Office suite is almost

complete. The following figure shows the major phases of the project, as well as the

overall Start Date of January 3, 2002 and Finish Date of July 19, 2002. I will continue to

provide information regarding the status of the deployment as the project progresses.

6. Press the Enter key twice to create a blank line at the end of the document, click Insert on the menu bar, point to Picture, and then click From File. Navigate to the Cases folder for Tutorial 6 on your Data Disk, and then double-click the Office Deployment file.

7. Proofread, preview, and then print the Word document. Save the Word document as **Office Deployment.doc** to the Cases folder for Tutorial 6 on your Data Disk, and then exit Word.[1]

8. Next, you want to save project information as a Web page. Click File on the menu bar, click Save As, click the Save as type list arrow, click Web Page, navigate to the cases folder for Tutorial 6, then click the Save button.

9. Click Task and resource PivotTable in the Export Mapping dialog box, and then click the Save button. A Web page is created with the name **Infrastructure Deployment.html**. Infrastructure Deployment is the entry in the Title field in the project file Properties dialog box and is used as the default name for saved Web pages. Web page files are automatically given an .html extension that represents the hypertext markup language code that they contain.

10. Right-click the Start button on the taskbar, click Explore, and then navigate to the Cases folder on your Data Disk. Double-click the **Infrastructure Deployment.html** file to open it in Internet Explorer or other browser on your computer system. Print the Web page, and then close Internet Explorer or other browser that you are using.

11. Finally, you want to graph the summary task costs. Return to the Infrastructure Deployment project window, and then click the Resource Sheet button on the View Bar. Enter the following hourly costs in the Std. Rate cell for each resource.

Your Name	$80/hour
Project management	$75/hour
Deployment resources	$40/hour
Procurement	$30/hour
Management	$100/hour

12. Click the Gantt Chart button on the View Bar, right-click the Duration column heading, and then click Insert Column. In the Column Definition dialog box, click the Field name list arrow, click Cost, and then click the OK button.

13. Select task name Scope (row 2) through the Post Implementation Review summary task cost (row 95). Important: Do not select the Indicators column, be sure to select only the two columns Task Name and Cost, and then click the Copy button on the Standard toolbar.

14. Start Excel 2000. In a new, blank workbook, click the Paste button to paste the task names and costs for the summary tasks into the first two columns. Double-click the column header for each column so that you can see all of the cost data in the workbook.

---

[1] Add a hyperlink from task 1 in the project file to the Office Deployment.doc Word document that you just created.

15. With cells A1 through B7 still selected, click the ChartWizard button on the Standard toolbar. Accept the default chart settings for both steps 1 and 2 of the Chart Wizard. In the Step 3 of 4 dialog box, enter Total Cost by Phase-Your Initials in the Chart title text box, click the Legend tab, uncheck the Show Legend check box, and then click the Next button.

16. In the Step 4 of 4 dialog box, click the As new sheet option button and then click the Finish button.

17. Preview and then print the chart.

18. Save the workbook **Total Cost by Phase-Your Initials.xls** to the Cases folder for Tutorial 6, exit Excel, save the project with a Project 98 file format and then exit Project 2000.

Case 3. *Using a Macro to Help Find Overallocations* In using the Project 2000-supplied templates, you have noticed that many of the resources are overallocated. To appreciate the problem of finding overallocated resources, you review the steps required to find them without using an automated macro. Your steps might be the following.

- Click the Resource Usage button in the View Bar.
- Display the Resource Tracking toolbar.
- Click the Go To Next Overallocation button in the Resource Tracking toolbar to move the focus to the work values for each overallocated day.

The Go To Next Overallocation button does exactly that—it goes to the *next* overallocation. If you start in the middle or end of your project, the Go To Next Overallocation button will not help you find the *first* overallocation. Therefore, it's important to remember always to start at the beginning of the Resource Sheet as well as the beginning of the project to find all overallocations. To return to the beginning of the project, use the Go To option on the Edit menu.

In this case, you'll create a macro that helps you to find a project's first overallocation.

1. Start Project 2000, click File on the menu bar, click New, click the Project Templates tab, and then double-click the Residential Construction template. Change the Project Start date to 1/3/02, and then click the OK button in the Project Information dialog box.

2. Click the Resource Sheet button in the View Bar, click the Filter list arrow on the Formatting toolbar, and then click Overallocated Resources. With so many overallocated resources, it is hard to have much confidence in project dates.

3. Display the Resource Management toolbar.

4. After studying the steps involved in finding the first allocation, you are ready to record your macro. Click the Gantt Chart button on the View Bar to start in a view other than the Resource Usage view. Click Tools on the menu bar, point to Macro, and then click Record New Macro.

5. In the Record Macro dialog box, type FindFirstOverallocation in the Macro Name text box, assign the shortcut key combination Ctrl+l (alphabetic lowercase L), click the Store macro in list arrow, click This Project, and then click the OK button. (Ctrl+1, f, or o might have been logical choices for a shortcut in this case, but they are reserved for Project 2000, so you selected Ctrl+1.)

6. Carefully record the following steps.

   a. Click the Resource Usage button in the View Bar.

   b. Click Edit on the menu bar, click Go To, type "1" in the ID text box, and then click the OK button. (*Note*: These steps position the Resource Usage view sheet portion (left side) at the first resource (ID1).)

   c. Click Edit on the menu bar, click Go To, press the Tab key, type 1/1/2002 in the Date text box, and then click the OK button. (*Note:* These steps position the Resource Usage view timescaled portion (right side) at the beginning of the project.)

   d. Click the Go To Next Overallocation button in the Resource Management toolbar to move the focus to the work values for the first overallocated day.

   e. Click Tools on the menu bar, point to Macro, and then click Stop Recorder.

7. Now test your macro. Click the Go To Next Overallocation button in the Resource Usage view five times to move to the middle of the project, and then press and hold the Ctrl key and press the l key. The first project overallocation, for the Framing Contractor on Tuesday, May 7, 2002, should be highlighted.

Explore   8. If your macro doesn't run correctly, you can edit or delete it. You delete an existing macro with the following instructions: Click Tools on the menu bar, point to Macros, and then click Macros. Click the ResidentialConstruction!FindFirstOverallocation macro, and then click Delete.

Explore

9. Rather than deleting a macro and starting from scratch, you can debug or edit it, especially if you have some familiarity with Visual Basic programming code, the language used to store recorded macro steps. To edit an existing macro, click Tools on the menu bar, point to Macros, and then click Macros. Click the Residential Construction!FindFirstOverallocation macro, and then click the Edit button. The Visual Basic programming code that should have been created for the ResidentialConstruction!FindFirstOverallocation macro is shown next.

```
Sub FindFirstOverallocation()
' Macro FindFirstOverallocation
' Macro Recorded (Today's Date) by (Your Name).
    ViewApply Name:="Resource Usage"
    GotoTaskDates
    EditGoTo ID:=1
    EditGoTo Date:="1/1/02 8:00 AM"
    GotoNextOverAllocation
End Sub
```

10. If you opened the Microsoft Visual Basic programming code window to view or edit your macro, close it.

Explore

11. If you forgot to assign the Ctrl + shortcut key or if you want to change the shortcut key, you can make this type of change without deleting and re-recording the macro. Click Tools on the menu bar, point to Macro, and then click Macros. Click the ResidentialConstruction!FindFirstOverallocation macro, and then click the Options button. Enter or change the shortcut key and the description in the Macro Options dialog box, and then click the OK button.

12. Close any open dialog boxes, and then save the project with the name **House-Macro-Your Initials.mpp** to the Cases folder for Tutorial 6 on your Data Disk, do not save a baseline.

13. Close **House-Macro-Your Initials.mpp**, and exit Project 2000.

Case 4. Organizing a Fund-Raiser You have volunteered to lead your neighborhood elementary school's major fund-raising effort to purchase new playground equipment. The equipment must be ready for school's start on September 16, 2002, so you'll schedule the project from a Finish Date and let Project 2000 establish the project Start Date. The project has three main phases: Planning, Fund-Raising, and Building. The Building Committee wants to be able to manage the Building phase in a separate Project 2000 file, so you'll break the Building phase tasks into their own project file and link that file back to the **Fund-6-Your Initials** project file, which will serve as the master file.

1. Start Project 2000 and make sure that your Data Disk is in the appropriate disk drive.

2. Open the file **Fund-6.mpp** in the Cases folder for Tutorial 6, click File on the menu bar, click Save As, save the project as **Fund-6-Your Initials** to the Cases folder for Tutorial 6, and then change the Your Name resource to your name.

3. Select rows 9 through 11 by dragging their ID numbers (choose Contractor through Build Playground), and then click the Cut Task button on the Standard toolbar. (*Hint:* Before you click the Cut button, be sure to drag across the ID numbers in the gray ID number area so that the entire task row is selected.

4. Click the New button on the Standard toolbar, click the Schedule from list arrow in the Project Information dialog box, click Project Finish Date, enter 9/16/02 in the Finish Date text box, and then click the OK button.

5. Click the first Task Name cell for the first row in the new project, and then click the Paste button on the Standard toolbar. The three subtasks for the Building summary task should appear in the new project.

6. Save the new project with the name **Building-Your Initials** to the Cases folder for Tutorial 6 on your Data Disk. Do not save a baseline.

7. Click the **Fund-6-Your Initials.mpp** button in the taskbar, and then delete the existing row 8 task. Inserting a subproject automatically adds a summary task to the master file, so you do not need to enter an extra summary task to organize the subtasks in the linked file.

8. Click the blank row 8 Task Name cell, click Insert on the menu bar, click Project, and then double-click **Building-Your Initials.mpp**. The **Building-Your Initials.mpp** file is inserted as a linked project in row 8, but it was inserted at the wrong level.

9. With the Building-Your Initials task selected, click the Outdent button on the Formatting toolbar so that the linked project appears at the same level as the Planning and Fund-Raising summary tasks.

10. Click the Fund-Raising summary task, press and hold the Ctrl key, click the Building-Your Initials summary task, release the Ctrl key, and then click the Link Tasks button on the Standard toolbar.

11. Print the first page of the Gantt Chart, with your name in the left section of the header.

Explore 12. Click the Resource Sheet button in the **Fund-6-Your Initials.mpp** file. Note that linking projects combines their resources (Your Name, School Sponsor, and Contractor are all listed twice because they are resources in both the Fund-6 and Building files) in the same way that a resource pool copies its resources to all project files that use it. Use the Answer Wizard in Project 2000 help to read about sharing resource pools and updating information for the pool of shared resources.

13. Add a milestone task as the last task of the project at the master project level.

14. Save and close the **Fund-6-Your Initials.mpp** and **Building-Your Initials.mpp** files, and then exit Project 2000. Do not save the baseline.

INTERNET ASSIGNMENTS

The purpose of the Internet Assignments is to challenge you to find information on the Internet so that you can learn more about project management and to use Microsoft Project 2000 more effectively. The actual assignments are updated and maintained on the Course Technology Web site. Log on to the Internet, and use your Web browser to go to the Student Online Companion that accompanies this text at **www.course.com/NewPerspectives/Project2000**. Click the link for Tutorial 6.

QUICK CHECK ANSWERS

Session 6.1

1. You could copy data from a Cost Sheet within Project 2000 and paste it into an Excel spreadsheet.

2. ODBC-compliant databases such as Microsoft SQL Server, Excel worksheets, Excel pivot tables, a text file, or an HTML file

3. Click the File menu, and then click Save As.

4. You can save a copy of a view as a GIF file that can be inserted in an HTML file, or you can use the Save As option on the File menu to directly save part of a Project 2000 file as an HTML file.

5. Earned value analysis allows you to measure project performance against a budget.

6. Project 2000 uses data maps to help you to define how the data will be imported and exported.

7. Changes made to linked data in either location update the single copy of data stored in the source location.

8. The Drawing tool allows you to add shapes, lines, arrows, and text boxes to a Gantt Chart.

Session 6.2

1. Commercial Construction, Engineering, Infrastructure Deployment, Application Development, New Business, New Product, Project Office, Residential Construction, Software Development

2. Click the File menu, and then click New to use an existing template.

3. A data template defines how the boxes in the Network Diagram are formatted.

4. The Organizer will help you to manage views, tables, filters, data maps, forms, calendars, macros, and toolbars.

5. Global.mpt

6. The benefits of using a resource pool include the ability to
   - enter shared resources only once
   - schedule resources with consideration to resource allocations made in other projects
   - identify conflicts between assignments in different projects
   - manage resource units, costs, and calendars in only one place

7. Resource precedence determines which file's resources and resource information will be used if conflicts between the two files arise when they are merged.

8. Nothing. If you have both the sharing and resource files open and you have read-write access to both, they will be automatically updated.

Session 6.3

1. One purpose of organizing a project into a master and one or more subprojects is to allow you to delegate separate parts of the projects, through multiple Project 2000 files, to various people for data entry and update purposes. Another reason to create a master project is to create views and printouts based on information from multiple projects (whether or not the projects are related).

2. A hyperlink connects non-Project 2000 generated files and Web pages to a Project 2000 file. For example, you might have a Word document, an Excel spreadsheet, a PowerPoint presentation, or a Web page that relates to a particular task or resource. By using a hyperlink, you can keep track of this external information, and access it quickly, through the Project 2000 file. You can also use a hyperlink to link to another view within the Project 2000 file.

3. By default, a flag field is set to No. The only other entry for a flag field is Yes.

4. You can use the macro recorder to record your mouse clicks and keystrokes, or you can write a macro using the Visual Basic programming language.

5. Work contouring is a customization applied to a resource assignment that adjusts the amount of effort (hours) that a resource devotes to a task over its duration.

6. The Options dialog box is opened by clicking the Tools menu and then clicking Options.

7. The Options dialog box organizes Project 2000 default settings on nine tabs: View, General, Edit, Calendar, Schedule, Calculation, Spelling, Workgroup, and Save.

OBJECTIVES

- Explore the Help Menu
- Understand how to use the Help system
- Get the most out of Getting Started
- Take advantage of available reference materials

THE MICROSOFT PROJECT 2000 HELP SYSTEM

As you work with Project 2000, you might need assistance on how to complete a specific task. Project 2000 provides several innovative features within the Help system that are extremely valuable to both new and experienced project managers. The Help manual is hyperlinked so that you can jump among various sections of the manual quickly. It includes dynamic help topics to support both novice and expert users. The Help system also provides an excellent introduction to project management concepts.

This appendix provides an overview of the various Help tools included as part of Project 2000.

Microsoft Project Help System: The Help Menu

Help is available by clicking Help on the menu bar, pressing the F1 key while working in Project 2000, or clicking the Help Topic links that appear in ScreenTips as you work with your project file.

Figure A-1 displays the options available within the Help menu when you click Help on the Project 2000 menu bar. Depending on how often the Help system is used, your Help menu options might appear in a different order than shown in Figure A-1.

| Figure A-1 | PROJECT 2000 HELP MENU OPTIONS |

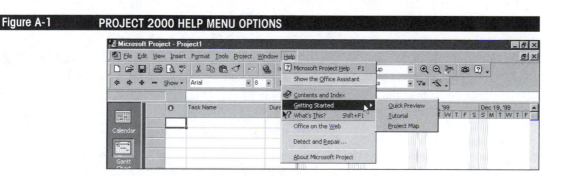

The Office Assistant

If you have used Microsoft Office, you might be familiar with the Office Assistant. The Office Assistant provides an interface to the Help system into which you type questions. You are presented with a list of options that best match the keywords in your question. It also automatically provides Help topics and tips on the current activity that you are performing. You access it by clicking the Help button ⌗ on the Standard toolbar. By default, the Office Assistant appears as an animated paperclip called Clippit, but you can change the appearance and behavior of the Office Assistant.

Project 2000 Help Menu Option Descriptions

When you click Help on the menu bar, you get several options for Help. Figure A-2 provides of short description of each menu option.

Figure A-2	HELP MENU OPTION DESCRIPTIONS
MENU OPTION	**DESCRIPTION**
Microsoft Project Help	Opens the Microsoft Project Help window. Depending on how your Office Assistant is configured, this menu option may open the Office Assistant.
Show the Office Assistant Hide the Office Assistant	Shows or hides the Office Assistant.
Contents and Index	Opens the Microsoft Project Help window. The Microsoft Project Help window is divided into three major sections organized by tabs: Contents, Answer Wizard, and Index. The Contents tab presents the Help manual in a table of contents format. The Answer Wizard allows you to search the entire Help manual by entering a search phrase or question. The Index provides an alphabetical listing of all reference words within the Help system.
Getting Started	Provides a special section of the Help system especially designed for the new user. Getting Started is divided into three sections: Quick Preview, Tutorial, and Project Map.
What's This?	Provides context-sensitive Help information. When you choose this command, the pointer changes to the Help pointer ▯?, which you can then use to click any object or option on the screen, including menu commands, to see a description of the item.
Office on the Web	If you are connected to the Internet, you can use this option on the Help menu to get up-to-the-minute information, news, and answers to common Project 2000 questions at the Microsoft Web site.
Detect and Repair	Automatically finds and fixes errors in the project.
About Microsoft Project	Provides product version, product identification, copyright, and system information, as well as technical support information, for your copy of Project 2000.

Microsoft Project Help System: Contents, Answer Wizard, and Index

Figure A-3 shows the Microsoft Project Help window for the main Help system when the Contents tab is chosen. To access this window, you click Help on the Project 2000 menu system, click Contents and Index, maximize the window, and then click the Contents tab. The Contents tab acts as the "table of contents" for the vast Help manual.

Figure A-3   **THE CONTENTS TAB OF THE MICROSOFT PROJECT HELP SYSTEM**

Microsoft Project Help System: Getting Started

The What's New section of the Help manual is a great resource for users who have used a previous version of Project and are upgrading to Project 2000. It is divided into New Scheduling features, Network Diagram improvements, Workgroup features, Administration, and Programmability.

The Getting Started sections are especially valuable for new users. To access the Quick Preview, click Help on the Project 2000 menu bar, point to Getting Started, and then click Quick Preview. Quick Preview provides an overview for building a project plan, managing a project, communicating project information, and getting assistance. Figure A-4 shows the first page of the Quick Preview section of the Help system.

Figure A-4   **THE QUICK PREVIEW SECTION OF THE HELP SYSTEM**

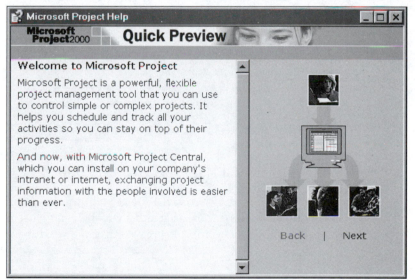

To access the Tutorial, click Help on the Project 2000 menu bar, point to Getting Started, and then click the Tutorial option. The Tutorial is an excellent place for a first-time user to start working with Project 2000. The first page of the Tutorial is shown in Figure A-5.

Figure A-5	THE TUTORIAL SECTION OF THE HELP SYSTEM

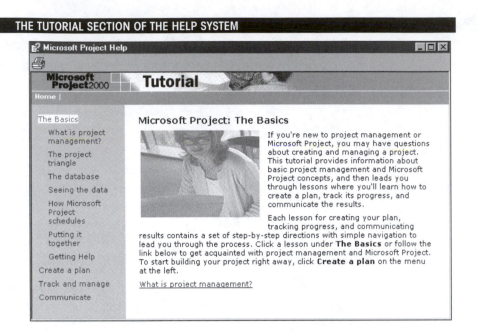

The Project Map describes common project management activities and is a useful review for project managers with all levels of experience. To access the Project Map, click Help on the Project 2000 menu system, point to Getting Started, and then click Project Map. Figure A-6 shows the opening screen of the Project Map.

Figure A-6	THE PROJECT MAP SECTION OF THE HELP SYSTEM

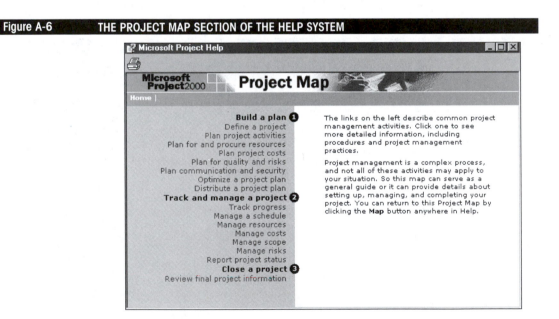

Microsoft Project Help System: Reference Material

The Reference page provides links to several valuable reference materials, such as project file limitations, mouse and keyboard shortcuts, descriptions of views, filters, and groups, a glossary, and troubleshooting tips. To access the Reference page, click Help on the Project 2000 menu bar, click Contents and Index, maximize the window, click the Contents tab, click the Expand button to the left of the Reference section, and then click Microsoft Project reference.

Figure A-7 shows the Microsoft Project Reference page in the Help system.

Figure A-7	THE REFERENCE PAGE IN THE HELP SYSTEM

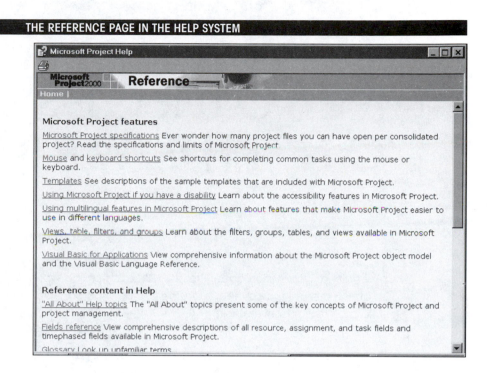

By scrolling down the Reference page to the bottom, you will find links for additional resources, as shown in Figure A-8.

Figure A-8	THE LOWER PORTION OF THE REFERENCE PAGE IN THE HELP SYSTEM

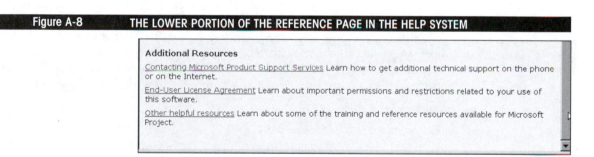

Getting the Most from the Glossary

Microsoft Project 2000 and project management in general involves learning many new terms. If you read about a word or phrase that you are not sure of, you can look it up using the comprehensive glossary that is part of the Help system. To access the glossary, click Help on the Project 2000 menu bar, click Contents and Index, maximize the window, click the Contents tab, click the Expand button to the left of the Reference section, and then click Microsoft Project glossary. Click the first letter of the word or phrase to find it in the list, and then click the word to open a window that includes the definition.

As you work with Project 2000, you will find the Help system to be a valuable partner in helping you to manage your project. Comprehensive and flexible, it is available at any time.

PROJECT 2000 RESOURCES ON THE WEB

A wealth of information about Project 2000 exists on the World Wide Web. If the computer that you are using is connected to the Internet, you can find the information provided by Microsoft through several links.

Office on the Web

Office on the Web offers a direct link to the most up-to-date information about Project 2000. To access this site, click Help on the Project 2000 menu bar and then click Office on the Web. This page includes all of the important updates for Project 2000. You should consider visiting this site periodically as you work with Project 2000 and manage your projects.

The Web page shown in Figure B-1 is the home page for Microsoft Project. The URL that will get you to this information is *www.microsoft.com/project*. Web pages change often as new and updated information is added to the site. At the time of this writing, however, the Microsoft Project home page offered several exciting features, including these.

- A tour of Microsoft Project
- Extensive product information
- Project 98 versus Project 2000 feature comparison and migration charts
- Pricing and ordering information
- Case studies
- Discussion groups
- Extensive FAQ and support documentation
- Third-party products, resources, and downloads
- Links to other project management sites
- Free 60-day trial versions of Project 98 and Project 2000
- A link to the premier Microsoft Project discussion group:
  - newsgroup server: *msnews.microsoft.com*
  - newsgroup: *microsoft.public.project*

Figure B-1   **PROJECT 2000 HOME PAGE**

PROJECT
MANAGEMENT
RESOURCES
ON THE WEB

A wealth of information and resources about general project management knowledge exists on the World Wide Web. You can find these by searching on the keywords "project management" with your favorite search engine.

The Project Management Institute

The Web page shown in Figure C-1 is the home page for the Project Management Institute, located at *www.pmi.org*. Web pages change often as new and updated information is added to the site. At the time of this writing, the site offered in-depth project management information in several areas such as these:

- *A Guide to the Project Management Body of Knowledge* (free download)
- Project management seminars
- Professional certification information
- Career information
- Research efforts and resource materials
- Project management forums, links, and vendor information

A Guide to the Project Management Body of Knowledge covers project management knowledge areas, terminology, and project plan development. Approximately 200 pages, it is also called the PMBOK® Guide. It is a basic reference for anyone interested in the profession. The Project Management Institute, Inc., as the author and owner of this guide, provides the PMBOK Guide through its Web site at no charge to users for personal noncommercial use.

Figure C-1   **PROJECT MANAGEMENT INSTITUTE HOME PAGE**

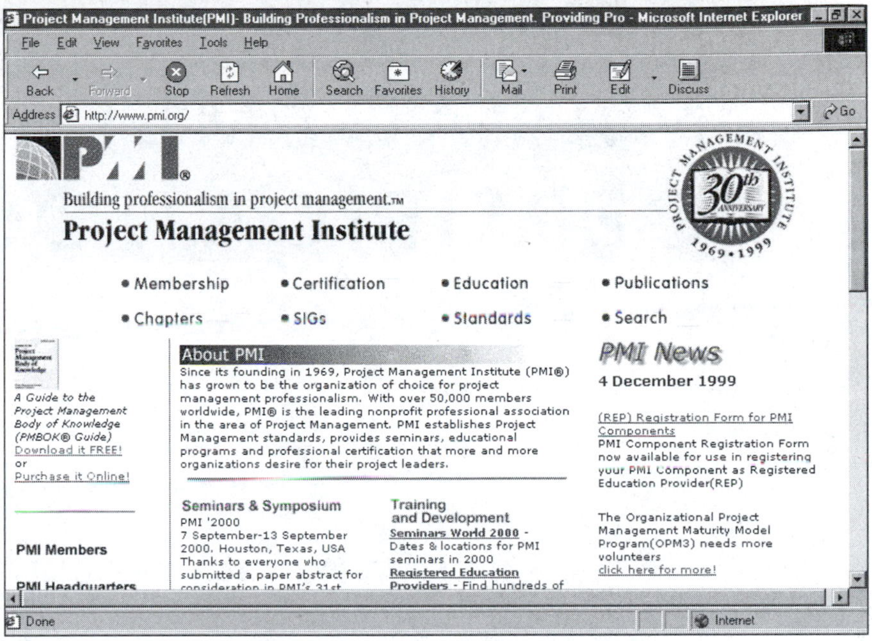

PROJECT
MANAGEMENT
CERTIFICATIONS

Currently two industry certifications are available that project managers might want to pursue:

- Project Management Professional
- Microsoft Office User Specialist in Project 2000

Project Management Professional

The Project Management Professional (PMP) certification is a professional credential somewhat analogous to the Certified Public Accountant certification for an accountant. It requires the achievement of rigorous education, experience, and examination requirements. It also involves agreement and adherence to a code of ethics. The Project Management Institute Web site, *www.pmi.org/certification*, provides excellent information and resources supporting this credential.

Microsoft Office User Specialist—Project 2000

Microsoft offers a series of certification exams for several products, including Word, Excel, Access, PowerPoint, Outlook, and Project. As of this writing, it had not finalized the Microsoft Office User Specialist (MOUS) certification tests for Project 2000. Check the official MOUS Web site, *www.mous.net*, for information on the availability of a MOUS certification test for Project 2000.

The authors of this book worked closely with Microsoft and the Project 2000 MOUS skill sets when writing this book. They took great care in covering not only the skills documented for the MOUS exams, but also the fundamental through advanced skills needed for true mastery of Project 2000 at an expert level.

WORKGROUPS AND PROJECT CENTRAL

One of the most important aspects of your job as a project manager is to communicate information to the members of your team. As computers have evolved and networking and connectivity among systems are now standard on most computer systems, the ability to take advantage of that connectivity is being built into many application software packages. Project 2000 is no exception. One of Project 2000's most significant enhancements is Project Central. **Project Central** is software that allows you to share project details and collaboratively update a single project with multiple people across a network.

Workgroups

A **workgroup** is a group of people who need to receive and send information about the status of a project. Each person within the workgroup is called a **workgroup member**. The person responsible for defining and managing a workgroup is called the **workgroup manager**. The workgroup manager is often the project manager. Together, the workgroups, workgroup members, and the workgroup manager(s) make up the **team**.

Microsoft **Project Central**

Although some Microsoft e-mail systems will support a simple workgroup messaging system for workgroup members, the most robust workgroup messaging system is Microsoft Project Central, or simply Project Central. A **workgroup messaging system** is a special communications system used to send and receive project information within the team. A workgroup messaging system requires that the workgroup members be electronically connected through a computer network. Depending on the physical location and other electronic communication needs of the workgroup members, this supporting computer network might consist of a simple **LAN** (local area network) or a corporate **WAN** (wide area network). Or the messages might be routed through the **Internet**, a worldwide network of computer networks.

Project Central is installed on a **Web server**, a computer dedicated to storing, routing, and managing information using Internet communication protocols and Web pages. Using **Web browser** software (the required browser is Internet Explorer, IE), a workgroup member can connect to the Project Central Web server to receive project updates, assignments, and messages from the project manager. Project Central supplies this information to the workgroup member in the form of Web pages that are downloaded and displayed in IE. Additionally, the workgroup member can accept or decline assignments, enter actual project updates, and respond to issues.

Collaborative Computing with Project Central

Once the workgroup members have responded to Project Central, the project manager may automatically accept their update information sent back from the workgroup members, set up rules to automatically update the project schedule based on various parameters, and use member feedback to manually update the project. Automatically sharing project information and keeping the project up-to-date by coordinating the efforts of multiple workgroup members is often called **collaborative computing**.

Figure E-1 illustrates the relationship between the key software components for the workgroup members, workgroup administrator, and Web server when Project Central is used. Project Central handles the tasks of routing information among the workgroup members and the workgroup administrator. It sets up the workgroups as well as presents project information as Web pages to the workgroup members. It also updates the actual project file located on the workgroup administrator's computer.

Figure E-1	MICROSOFT PROJECT CENTRAL INSTALLATION

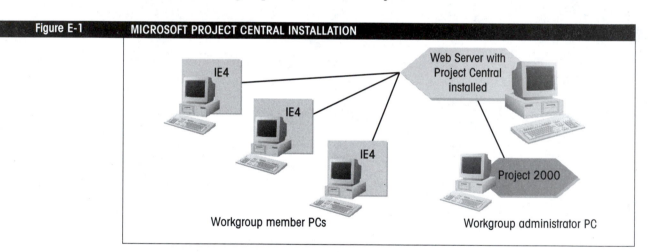

For the latest information about the Project 2000 collaborative computing features, including workgroups and Microsoft Project Central, consult the Microsoft Web site at *www.microsoft.com/project* and *www.microsoft.com/teammanager*.

Workgroup and Project Central Requirements

Requirements at the workgroup member level:

- Network access and identification (a user Id and password plus the associated network hardware and software that allow that user and computer to send and receive information across the network) must be installed.
- The Web server's network address URL (Uniform Resource Locator) in order to access Project Central must be known.
- Microsoft Internet Explorer 4.01 Service Pack 1 or later (or the Browser Module for Microsoft Project Central for Windows, which comes with Microsoft Project Central) in which to enter the URL and display the Web pages downloaded from Project Central must be installed.
- A Microsoft Project Central license to use Microsoft Project Central must be purchased for each workgroup member.

Requirements at the workgroup administrator level:

- All of the requirements of the workgroup member apply at the workgroup manager level.
- Microsoft Project must be installed on the workgroup administrator's computer (but not on the workgroup member's computer). Microsoft Project comes with one copy of the Microsoft Project Central license.

Requirements at the Web server level:

- Microsoft Windows NT Server 4.0 Service Pack 4 or later must be installed.
- Internet Information Server (IIS) 4.0 or later must be installed.
- Microsoft Project Central must be installed.

Using Workgroups and Project Central

Figure E-2 identifies many common tasks and the steps involved in setting up and using Project Central to handle those tasks.

Figure E-2	WORKGROUP AND PROJECT CENTRAL TASKS
TASK	**STEPS**
Create a workgroup (workgroup administrator task).	1. Install Microsoft Project Central (requires Microsoft Windows NT Version 4.0 Service Pack 4 or later) on the Web server. 2. Use the functionality within Microsoft Project Central to create workgroups with the user information and the security required to define each distinct workgroup.
Connect the workgroup administrator's PC to Microsoft Project Central (workgroup administrator task).	1. Start Project 2000 on the workgroup administrator's computer, click the Tools menu, click Options, and then click the Workgroup tab. 2. Click the Default workgroup messages list arrow, and then click Web. 3. In the Microsoft Project Central Server URL text box, type the URL for the Microsoft Project Central server. 4. Under the Identification for Microsoft Project Central Server section, enter the appropriate identification and security information. 5. To apply your workgroup choices to all new projects, click Set as Default.
Delegate tasks using Project Central (workgroup administrator task).	1. Enter tasks and resource assignments in the Project 2000.mpp file. Select the tasks that you want to delegate. To delegate all tasks, you do not need to select any tasks. 2. Click Tools on the menu bar, point to Workgroup, and then click TeamAssign. 3. In the Workgroup Mail dialog box, click the All tasks or Selected tasks option button, as appropriate. 4. In the TeamAssign dialog box, change the subject or body of the message or enter comments for each assignment as appropriate. 5. Click Send.
Communicate changes to tasks using Project Central (workgroup administrator task).	1. As part of your project manager responsibilities, update tasks and resource assignments in the Project 2000.mpp file as the project planning progresses. Select the tasks that you want to send to workgroup members. To send all tasks, do not select any tasks. 2. Click the Tools menu, point to Workgroup, and then click TeamUpdate. 3. In the TeamUpdate dialog box, change the subject or body of the message. 4. Click Send.
Monitor progress on a task using Project Central (workgroup administrator task).	1. Select the tasks for which you want to receive progress information from workgroup members in the Project 2000.mpp file. To update all tasks, do not select any tasks. 2. Click the Tools menu, point to Workgroup, and then click TeamStatus. 3. In the TeamStatus dialog box, change the subject or body of the message. 4. Click Send.
Accept or decline a TeamAssign, TeamUpdate, or TeamStatus request (workgroup member task).	1. Start Internet Explorer. 2. Enter the URL for the Project Central Web server. 3. Enter your username and password to identify yourself and your workgroup associations. 4. Click the links and enter the appropriate information to accept, respond, or update project data as it is presented by the Web page.
Set AutoAccept rules (workgroup administrator task).	1. Start Project 2000, click Tools on the menu bar, point to Workgroup, and then click TeamInBox. 2. Use the options and settings of the TeamInBox to determine which responses from which workgroup members you want to automatically update the project and which you want to update manually.
Format or modify a project (workgroup administrator task).	A project that is being updated through Project Central can be formatted (for example, formatting a Gantt Chart) or customized (for example, creating a new view or report) like any other project. The new capabilities provided by Project Central affect only the project manager's ability to quickly disseminate information and update status regarding the project.

Project 2000 Enhancements to Microsoft Project Central

Enhancements to the latest version of Project Central include the ability to create and display personal Gantt Charts and enhanced capabilities to filter, sort, group, and report. Other improvements are better AutoAccept rules (which allow you to automatically update status information), tighter integration with Microsoft Outlook, and more options when working offline.

SUCCESSFUL PROJECT MANAGEMENT

Obviously, there is more to successful project management than mastering the features of a software management tool. It requires organizational support such as a reasonable budget, access to the right resources, and a supportive corporate infrastructure that might involve extensive computer networks. Also, the personal characteristics of the project manager are very important, such as an overall understanding and commitment to the project, attention to detail, self-discipline, and an ability to manage many competing forces.

You will have to consider many general project management issues as you work through a project. Some of these will determine how you will use and document the details of the project in project management software. These decisions also have a large impact on the project's success. Following is a sampling of project management issues that you might want to explore further.

- To what level of detail should tasks be consolidated or separated in the project?
- What factors are used to determine a summary task?
- What is the policy for estimating task durations? Should risk factors be considered in the calculation of the duration?
- How should you deal with uncertainty as it relates to either the nature of a task or the resources assigned to it?
- What is the policy for scheduling noncritical tasks? Should duration, resources, predecessors, slack, or any other factor be used to prioritize such tasks?
- How will risk, cost, and quality be balanced when crashing the path?
- Who is responsible for updating progress on a project?
- What tools will be used to gather progress data? How often will progress be updated on a project?
- How will the work breakdown structure be set up? How will it interface with other accounting systems in your business?
- What reports and other communication tools should be provided to project members and management? How often should these reports be provided?

■ How can effort-driven scheduling be used with the huge number of details involved in variable work schedules, unpaid time, holiday and vacation schedules, and union contracts?

■ What actual values will you track? Which ones will provide the information needed so that you can appropriately adjust the project during its duration and objectively evaluate it at the end?

■ How will you address the multiuser issues concerning resource pools and consolidated projects? Do you have the LAN, WAN, and technical support infrastructure to use Project Central?

To learn more about the general world of project management, and specifically how it relates to managing information systems projects, read *Information Technology Project Management* by Kathy Schwalbe, published by Course Technology. More information about this book is available at Course Technology's Web site, *www.course.com*.

Also, be sure to visit the Project Management Institute's Web site at *www.pmi.org* for additional resources and reference materials on all aspects of project management.

A

Active cell

The cell that you are editing in a sheet view. It is surrounded by a dark border.

As late as possible

A default constraint for any task entered in a project that is scheduled from a given Finish Date.

As soon as possible

A default constraint for any task entered in a project that is scheduled from a given Start Date.

B

Baseline

An iteration of the project from which you want to track actual progress.

Bottom-up method

A method of planning a project by listing all of the individual tasks and then collecting them into logical phases.

Budget

The amount of money, based on estimated costs, that you have allocated for the project.

C

Cell reference

The name for a cell in Excel determined by the column letter and row number, such as A1 or B2.

Closing a project

The act of finalizing the data that is stored in the project file. "Closing a project" is not a feature of Project 2000, but rather a point in time or an announcement that the project manager declares in order to clarify that the project is finished and the reports are final. It is not the same as saving and closing a project file.

Collaborative computing

The process of automatically sharing project information and keeping the project up-to-date by coordinating the efforts of multiple workgroup members.

Context-sensitive

A phrase used to describe some parts of the Help system that are designed to offer information related to the task currently being worked on.

Cost

The expenditure paid or charged to accomplish a task.

Cost rate table

A grid of different hourly and per-use costs for a resource.

Crash the path

The process of cutting the amount of time that it takes to complete a project.

Critical path

The tasks that must be completed by the given schedule dates in order for the overall project to be completed in the shortest amount of time.

Critical task or **critical activity**

A task on the critical path.

Cross-project link

A dependency between different project files.

Crosstab report

A report that summarizes a numeric field (such as work or cost) by resource or task as the row heading and a unit of time (such as days or weeks) as the column heading.

Current date

Today's date as determined by your computer or network time server.

D

Data map

A tool that helps to define how data will be imported and exported.

Data template

A template that defines how the boxes in the Network Diagram are formatted. Once you create a template, you can share it with other projects. Also called a **box template**.

Deadline

A flexible date constraint. It is flexible in that it does not dictate the scheduled start and finish dates of a task like an inflexible constraint does, such as the "Must Start On" or "Must Finish On" constraint. Therefore, it is used more as a guideline than as a fact that your project must obey.

Default setting

A standard setting that is appropriate for most projects.

Detail Gantt Chart

A Gantt Chart with extra bars that show total slack and slippage.

Duration

The time it takes to complete a task.

E

Earned value analysis

An indication of how much of the budget should have been spent, in view of the amount of work done so far, and the baseline cost for the task, assignment, or resource. Earned value is also called **budgeted cost of work performed** (BCWP).

Efficient

Refers to doing tasks faster, with fewer resources or with lower costs.

Effort-driven scheduling

When a task is scheduled with the effort-driven scheduling field checked (set to yes, the default), work (effort) remains constant and determines (drives) the way that the $W=D*U$ formula will calculate when additional resources are assigned to a task. When a new resource is added to a task that has an existing resource assignment, total work (effort) remains constant and the duration is adjusted (shortened) to accommodate the redistribution of work across multiple resources.

Elapsed time

Clock time (rather than working time).

Embedding

A way to copy or insert data from one file to another. Embedded data can be edited using the features of the data's native application even though it is physically stored to another file. Changes made to the embedded data are not automatically made to the original copy.

Entry bar

A bar used to enter or edit an existing entry, such as a task name or duration. Located just below the Formatting toolbar and just above the project window.

Entry table

A spreadsheet-like display of project information, organized in rows and columns.

Estimated duration

An approximation of the time that it takes to complete a task. Appears with a question mark (?) after the duration.

F

Fill handle

A tool used to copy and paste cell entries within a sheet view.

Filtering

The process of showing a subset of resources or tasks that meet certain criteria.

Finish Date

The day that the project will finish. If a project is scheduled from a Start Date, the Finish Date is calculated by Project 2000. If a project is scheduled from a Finish Date, the Finish Date is entered.

Finish-to-finish (FF)

A dependency type that specifies that task 1 must finish before task 2 can finish.

Finish-to-start (FS)

A dependency type that specifies that task 1 must finish before task 2 can start.

Fixed cost

A cost inherent to the task itself and not driven by the number of resource assignments made, such as a room charge, a convention entry fee, or a fixed travel expense.

Flag field

A field that can be set to Yes to mark that item for special identification. There are 20 (Flag1 through Flag20) provided for each task, resource, and assignment. By default, all flag fields are set to No.

Float

When a project is scheduled from a Start Date, the amount of time that a task can be delayed from its planned start date without delaying the project Finish Date. Also called **slack**.

Form

A view that displays detailed information about one task or resource at a time.

Formatting toolbar

A toolbar that contains buttons that change the appearance of the project, such as the font or the text alignment.

Free slack

The amount of time that a task can be delayed without affecting another task. When project managers speak of "slack" they are generally referring to total slack, rather than free slack.

G

Gantt Chart

A view of a project that provides a graphical visualization of the project by displaying each task as a horizontal bar.

GIF (graphics interchange format)

A common form of graphical image, often used for Web pages.

Global.mpt

The default Project 2000 template that stores all of the views, tables, filters, and other elements that are available for each new project.

Grouping

The process of sorting and outlining tasks that meet a common criteria.

H

Heuristic

A rule of thumb.

Hyperlink

Connects a file or a Web page to a Project 2000 file.

I

Importing and **exporting**

The process of converting data from one file format to another. The difference between importing and exporting is the direction of the data conversion. **Import** means to bring in, and **Export** means to send out.

In-cell editing

Editing made directly in a cell of a sheet view, rather than via the Entry bar.

Indenting

The process of moving the task to the right (a lower level in the outline) in a task sheet.

Indicator column

A column in a sheet view that displays icons to indicate information about a task.

Interim plan

A portion of a baseline for a selected time period or group of tasks. Interim plans save projected start and finish dates for selected tasks in a project but not cost information.

Lag time

A period of time (either positive or negative) imposed on a relationship between tasks. In the most common scenario, positive lag time is applied to a finish-to-start relationship that moves the start of task 2 forward a certain amount of time after the finish of task 1.

Lead time

See negative lag time.

Legend

A section of a printout that provides information about bars or symbols used on the printout.

Leveling

The process of correcting overallocations so that no resource is assigned more work than is available in the given time period.

Linking

A way to copy data from one file (source) to another (destination) so that only one physical copy of the data exists, in the original, source location.

Macro

A stored set of actions that can be executed over and over. Macro instructions are stored in a Visual Basic module.

Macro recorder

A tool that translates Project 2000 commands into Visual Basic programming code so that a project manager doesn't need to be a Visual Basic programmer to create a macro. It works much like a tape recorder in that it "listens" to the actions you perform, and records them for you to "replay" at a later time.

Major scale

The upper row in the timescale on a Gantt Chart. By default, the major scale is measured in weeks and displays the date for the Sunday of that week.

Master project

A project file that contains subprojects. It is also called a **consolidated project**.

Material (consumable) resource

A resource such as building materials or supplies that are consumable.

Material cost

A cost associated with a consumable item, such as cabling, supplies, and computer(s).

Menu bar

A bar that contains the File, Edit, View, Insert, Format, Tools, Project, Window, and Help menus, which are used to issue commands in Project 2000.

Microsoft Project Central

A robust workgroup messaging system included with Project 2000 that supplies project information as Web pages to participating workgroup members.

Milestone

A task that has a zero duration. Milestones are symbolic tasks that are used to communicate progress or the end of a significant phase of the project.

Minor scale

The lower row in the timescale on the Gantt Chart. By default, the minor scale is measured in days and displays the first letter of the day of the week.

Negative lag time

When a project is scheduled from a Start Date, moves the second task of two related tasks backward in time. Negative lag time is called **lead time** in general project management discussions.

Network Diagram

A view of a project that graphically highlights the interdependencies and sequencing of tasks. Also called the **PERT Chart** (Program Evaluation Review Technique).

Nonworking time

The hours of a 24-hour day that are not specified as working time.

Note icon

An icon that appears in the Indicator column to the left of a task in Gantt Chart view to indicate that a note is attached to the task.

O

Office Assistant

An interactive guide to finding information on Microsoft Project.

Organizer

A special tool that allows you to copy custom views, tables, filters, data maps, forms, calendars, macros, toolbars, and other customizations from one project file to another. The Organizer also gives you access to the global template.

Outdenting

The process of moving a task to the left (a higher level in the outline) in a task sheet.

Overallocated

The condition of having assigned more work to a resource in a given time period than it has working hours. Usually this means that a resource has been assigned more than eight hours of work in a day.

Overallocation

The process of assigning a resource more work than it can complete in a given day.

Overtime hour

A work hour outside of those specified by the calendar.

P

Page Setup dialog box

A dialog box in which can be changed many of a printout's characteristics, including its orientation, margins, legend, header, and footer.

PERT Chart (program evaluation review technique)

See Network Diagram.

Phase

See summary task.

Planning Wizard

A special function of the Project 2000 Help system that suggests certain actions at various steps.

Positive lag time

When a project is scheduled from a Start Date, moves the second of two related tasks forward in time. Positive lag time is the traditional definition of lag time in general project management discussions.

Precedence

When two files are merged, determines which file's resources and resource information will be used if conflicts occur.

Predecessor task

The first task described in a dependency.

Predecessor

A task that must be completed before a given task.

Project calendar

See Standard calendar.

Project Central

A feature of Project 2000 that allows you to implement Web-based workgroup features so that many people can view and update various parts of a project simultaneously.

Project goal

The goal achieved when a series of tasks are completed that produce a desired outcome.

Project management

The process of defining, organizing, tracking, and communicating information about a project in order to meet a project goal.

Project manager

The central person who gathers project data and communicates progress.

Project status date

The date for which you enter the progress information.

Q

Quality

The degree to which something meets an objective standard.

R

Range

A group of cells in Excel. A range is defined by the first cell reference in the upper-left corner of the block or group of cells and the last cell reference in the lower-right corner of the range.

Recurring task

A task that repeats at a regular interval.

Report

Detailed or summarized information about a particular aspect of a project, such as task, resource, cost, date, or progress information.

Resource availability date

A date that determines when resource units grow or shrink.

Resource calendar

A special calendar created for each resource used when the resource does not follow the working and nonworking times specified by the project calendar.

Resource pool

A project file that contains resource information. A resource pool file may be linked to other project files in a way that allows the sharing of the resources in the pool among multiple projects.

Resource sheet

A sheet view that is commonly used to present information in an easy-to-use row and column format. Each row represents a different resource, and each column represents a field of information about the resource.

Resource

People, equipment, and facilities that need to be assigned to a task to complete it.

Risk

The probability that a task, resource, or cost is miscalculated in a way that creates a negative impact on the project.

S

Scope

The total amount of products and services that the project is supposed to provide.

Scope creep

A condition that occurs in projects that grow and change in unanticipated ways that increase costs, extend deadlines, or otherwise negatively affect the project goal.

ScreenTip

A small box that appears with the name of the item you are pointing to. The item can be a button, indicator, or bar and helps determine the item name or function.

Slack

The amount of time that a task may be delayed from its scheduled start date without delaying the entire project.

Slippage

The difference between a task's scheduled start or finish date and its baseline start or finish date when the project falls behind schedule.

Sorting

The process of reordering the resources or tasks in a sheet in an ascending or descending sort order based on the values of a field.

Split window

A view in which the screen is split into two parts (two views). The top part is often the Gantt Chart view. The bottom part is often a form view.

Standard calendar

The calendar used to schedule tasks within the project. By default, the Standard calendar specifies that Monday through Friday are working days with eight hours of work completed each day. Saturday and Sunday are designated as nonworking days.

Standard toolbar

A toolbar that contains buttons that are common to almost all applications, such as New, Open, Save, Print, Print Preview, Spell Check, Cut, Copy, and Paste.

Start Date

The day on which the project will start. If a project is scheduled from a Start Date, the Start Date is entered. If a project is scheduled from a Finish Date, the Start Date is calculated by Project 2000.

Start-to-finish (SF)

A dependency type that specifies that task 1 must start before task 2 can finish.

Start-to-start (SS)

A dependency type that specifies that task 1 must start before task 2 can start.

Status date

Refer to the project status date.

Subproject

A project file that is inserted as tasks into a master project.

Successor task

The second task described in a dependency.

Successor

A task that cannot be completed until after a given task.

Summary task

A grouping of tasks that logically belong together. Summary tasks are listed in bold text in the Task Entry table. Each displays a Collapse/Expand button to its left so that showing or hiding the task can easily be done within that phase. Also called a **phase**.

Systems development lifecycle model (SDLC)

A model that is commonly used to manage the development of a new information system but that can be modified and applied to almost any project. It has six stages that roughly equate to the phases within a project: project definition, evaluation of current process, design, construction, installation, and evaluation.

T

Task calendar

A special calendar that can be created for tasks that do not follow the working and nonworking times specified by the Standard calendar.

Task dependency

The relationship between two tasks in a project. The most common dependency is finish-to-start (FS).

Task type

The item (Units, Duration, or Work) that will remain constant when additional resources are added to a task. The task type field has three possible choices: Fixed Units, Fixed Duration, and Fixed Work. By default, the task type is Fixed Units.

Task usage

A view that shows tasks with assigned resources indented within each task on the left and the number of hours that each resource is assigned to each task in a day-by-day format on the right.

Task

A specific action that needs to be completed within the project.

Team

The workgroups, workgroup members, and workgroup manager(s).

Template

A special project file that contains sample data such as task, resource, cost, and baseline data on which a new project file can be based.

Timescale

A display of the unit of measurement that determines the length of each bar. Displayed along the top edge of the Gantt Chart. It has two rows, called a major scale (the upper scale) and minor scale (the lower scale).

Title bar

The top bar of any application software running on a Windows computer.

Toolbar

A toolbar that represents the most popular Project 2000 commands as little pictures or icons. By default, two toolbars should be at the top of the opening Project 2000 screen: Standard and Formatting.

Top-down method

A method of planning a project by starting with the summary tasks.

Total slack

The amount of time that a task can be delayed without the delay's affecting the entire project. It is also called **total float**.

Total work

The total work for a task. It is initially calculated as the task duration (converted to hours) multiplied by the number of resources assigned to that task.

Tracking table

When applied to the Task Sheet, provides all of the actual fields (actual date, actual duration, actual work, and actual cost) in one sheet view.

Variance

The difference between baseline data and actual data.

View bar

A bar that contains several buttons that enable switching between project views.

View

A way to display task, resource, and cost information with varying levels of detail.

Visual Basic

A robust programming language.

Web server

A computer dedicated to storing, routing, and managing information by using Internet communication protocols and Web pages.

What's this?

A command on the Help menu that provides context-sensitive Help information.

Work (hourly) resource

A resource, such as people, rooms, and equipment, that has an associated hourly cost.

Work breakdown structure (WBS)

A way to code each task to identify and group project tasks for communication, documentation, or accounting purposes.

Work contouring

A customization applied to a resource assignment that adjusts the amount of effort (hours) that a resource devotes to a task over its duration.

Workgroup

A subset of people that exchange status information about various parts of a project through a network.

Workgroup manager

The person responsible for defining and managing a workgroup. The workgroup manager is often the project manager.

Workgroup member

A person in the workgroup.

Workgroup messaging system

A special communication system used to send and receive project information to team members across a computer network.

Working time

The hours during which work can occur, by default 8:00 AM to 12:00 PM and 1:00 PM to 5:00 PM Monday through Friday.

INDEX

Go to *www.mous.net* for the most up-to-date information on MOUS certifications. Exam objectives, test availability, and testing center locations are subject to change.

Standardized Coding Number	Certification Skill Activity	Tutorial Pages	End-of-Tutorial Practice	
			Exercise	Step Number
Proj2000-1	**Create a Project Plan**			
Proj2000-1-1	Import a task list from Excel to Microsoft Project	6 (292–296)	T6 Review Assignment	25
Proj2000-1-2	Set default folder options and AutoSave	6 (341–343)		
Proj2000-1-3	Create recurring tasks	2 (80–81)	T2 Review Assignment	9
Proj2000-1-4	Split a task	5 (241)	T5 Case 3	7
Proj2000-1-5	Modify task duration	2 (70–71)	T2 Review Assignment	4–5
Proj2000-1-6	Modify calendar working time options	2 (63–65)	T2 Review Assignment	6
Proj2000-1-7	Apply a calendar to a task	2 (65–69)	T2 Review Assignment	7–8
Proj2000-1-8	Add material resources to a project	4 (199–200)	T4 Review Assignment	3
Proj2000-1-9	Enter costs on resources	4 (164–165) 4 (199–200)	T4 Review Assignment	3
Proj2000-1-10	Assign an additional resource to a task without increasing work on the task	4 (176–181)	T4 Review Assignment	14–15
Proj2000-1-11	Assign an additional resource to a task to increase work on the task	4 (181–183)	T4 Review Assignment	16–17
Proj2000-1-12	Create base calendars	2 (62–65)	T2 Review Assignment	6–7
Proj2000-1-13	Set task types (fixed work, fixed units, fixed duration)	4 (181–183)		
Proj2000-1-14	Create a summary task	2 (97–100)	T2 Review Assignment	15–17
Proj2000-1-15	Use deadlines and constraints	3 (148–149) (constraints) 5 (256–257) (deadlines)		
Proj2000-1-16	Create a milestone task	2 (81–82)	T2 Review Assignment	18
Proj2000-1-17	Create a new project	1 (10–12) (create a new project) 2 (58–59) (examine default settings for a new project)	T1 Case 4 T2 Case 4	T1, 1–3 (create a new project) T2, 1–3 (examine default settings for a new project)

MOUS CERTIFICATION GRID

Standardized Coding Number		Tutorial Pages	End-of-Tutorial Practice Exercise	Step Number
Proj2000-1-18	Assign initial resources to tasks	4 (169–171)	T4 Review Assignment	4
Proj2000-1-19	Enter task relationships	2 (83–91)	T2 Review Assignment	10–13
Proj2000-1-20	Enter task information	2 (69–70) (using the Entry table) 3 (142–149) (using the Task Information dialog box)	T2 Review Assignment (Entry table) T3 Review Assignment (Task Information dialog box)	T2, 4–5 (Entry table) T3, 23 (Task Information dialog box)
Proj2000-2	**Track a Project**			
Proj2000-2-1	Assign tasks using Project Central	Appendix E	Appendix E	Appendix E
Proj2000-2-2	Add a progress line to a Gantt chart for a given date	5 (240–241)		
Proj2000-2-3	Set reminders and send schedule note messages	Appendix E	Appendix E	Appendix E
Proj2000-2-4	Record task status in Microsoft Project and Project Central	Appendix E	Appendix E	Appendix E
Proj2000-2-5	Display resource allocations	4 (185-192)	T4 Case 1	13
Proj2000-2-6	Reschedule uncompleted work	5 (240–241)	T5 Case 2	8
Proj2000-2-7	Modify project duration	3 (142–149)		
Proj2000-2-8	Compare actuals with the project baseline	5 (246–247)	T5 Review Assignment	20–22
Proj2000-2-9	Record actual work on a task	5 (235–245)	T5 Review Assignment	5–8
Proj2000-2-10	Save a baseline for the entire project or selected tasks	5 (226–227)	T5 Review Assignment	3
Proj2000-2-11	Edit task relationship types and lag	2 (91–92) (edit task relationships) 2 (92–95) (lag)	T2 Review Assignment	14 (edit task relationships) 12 (lag)
Proj2000-3	**Communicating project information**			
Proj2000-3-1	Use the drawing tools	6 (299–300)		
Proj2000-3-2	Add a hyperlink to a task	6 (326–328)		
Proj2000-3-3	Identify lost elements when saving a project to Project 98	6 (301–302)		
Proj2000-3-4	Copy picture of a view and save as a Web page	6 (283–286)	T6 Review Assignment	19–21

Standardized Coding Number	Certification Skill Activity	Tutorial Pages	End-of-Tutorial Practice	
			Exercise	Step Number
Proj2000-3-5	Use Organizer to share custom views	6 (312–314) (Organizer) 5 (252–254) (custom views)	T6 Review Assignment T5 Case 1	T6, 36 (Organizer) T5, 19–21 (custom views)
Proj2000-3-6	Modify a standard report	5 (262–264)	T5 Review Assignment	30–31
Proj2000-3-7	Copy and paste Gantt chart into a Microsoft Word document	6 (283–285)	T6 Review Assignment	14–15
Proj2000-3-8	Copy and paste sheet information into a Microsoft Excel spreadsheet	6 (279–280)	T6 Review Assignment	5–7
Proj2000-3-9	Update server-based project information using Project Central	Appendix E	Appendix E	Appendix E
Proj2000-3-10	Set page setup options	1 (42–44)	T1 Review Assignment	12–14
Proj2000-3-11	Create a new custom report	5 (262–264)	T5 Case 2	13–16
Proj2000-4	**General Project Management Concepts**			
Proj2000-4-1	Display the critical path using filtering and formatting techniques	3 (115–117) (filtering for the critical path) 3 (120–122) (formatting the critical path)	T3 Review Assignment	5 (filter for critical tasks) 7 (format the critical tasks)
Proj2000-4-2	Differentiate work from duration	4 (176–182)	T4 Review Assignment	15–17
Proj2000-4-3	Apply WBS codes	2 (102–104)		
Proj2000-5	**Customizing a project**			
Proj2000-5-1	Reset table defaults	5 (246–249) (modifying) a table 6 (312) (using Organizer to reset defaults)	T5 Review Assignment (modifying an table)	T5, 20 (modifying an existing table)
Proj2000-5-2	Create custom filters	3 (119–120)	T3 Review Assignment	6
Proj2000-5-3	Define WBS codes	2 (102–104)		
Proj2000-5-4	Create and apply custom groupings	2 (97–100) (grouping tasks within an outline)	T2 Review Assignment	15–17
Proj2000-5-5	Format individual bars and bar styles	3 (120–124)	T3 Review Assignment	7–9

Standardized Coding Number	Certification Skill Activity	Tutorial Pages	End-of-Tutorial Practice	
			Exercise	Step Number
Proj2000-5-6	Sort a view	4 (186–187)		
Proj2000-5-7	Apply custom filters	3 (119–120)	T3 Review Assignment	6
Proj2000-5-8	Create a custom table	5 (246–249)	T5 Review Assignment	20
Proj2000-5-9	Create and apply a custom view	5 (252–254)	T5 Case 1	19–21
Proj2000-5-10	Format a time scale	3 (128)	T3 Review Assignment	11
Proj2000-5-11	Use outlining features	2 (97–101)	T2 Review Assignment	15–17
Proj2000-5-12	Apply a filter using AutoFilter	3 (118–120)	T3 Review Assignment	6
Proj2000-5-13	Insert a column in a table	5 (246–248)	T5 Review Assignment	20
Proj2000-6	**Multi-project management**			
Proj2000-6-1	Set baselines for a master project	6 (325)		
Proj2000-6-2	Add a task to a master project	6 (323)		
Proj2000-6-3	Create relationships between tasks in a master project and subproject files	6 (323–324)	T6 Review Assignment	29
Proj2000-6-4	Insert a subproject into a master project	6 (322)	T6 Review Assignment	28

Expert	Certification Skill Activity	Tutorial Pages	End-of-Tutorial Practice	
Standardized Coding Number			Exercise	Step Number
Proj2000E-1	**Resource Management**			
Proj2000E-1-1	Set an accrual option for a resource cost	4 (163–165)		
Proj2000E-1-2	Create and apply rate tables to resource assignments	4 (166–167)		
Proj2000E-1-3	Modify task priority values	4 (197–198)		
Proj2000E-1-4	Set precedence when linking to the resource pool	6 (317)		
Proj2000E-1-5	Use leveling options	4 (195–197)		
Proj2000E-1-6	Apply resource contours	6 (336–339)		
Proj2000E-1-7	Modify resource availability over time	4 (168–169)		
Proj2000E-1-8	Update/refresh the resource pool	6 (318–319)		
Proj2000E-1-9	Modify resource usage view	4 (185–186)	T4 Review Assignment	5–6
Proj2000E-1-10	Share resources using a resource pool	6 (316–317)		
Proj2000E-2	**Track a Project**			
Proj2000E-2-1	Disable Split-in project tasks	6 (342)		
Proj2000E-2-2	Enter overtime work	4 (210–211)	T6 Case 2	13
Proj2000E-2-3	Enable resources to delegate tasks using Project Central	Appendix E		
Proj2000E-2-4	Enter actual costs	5 (244–245)	T5 Review Assignment	24
Proj2000E-2-5	Create interim plans	5 (258–259)		
Proj2000E-2-6	Set project information dates	2 (58–61) (Start date and Finish date) 5 (228–229) (Current date and Status date)	T2 Review Assignment T5 Review Assignment	T2, 3 (Start date and Finish date) T5, 4) (Current date and Status date)
Proj2000E-2-7	Set options governing how tasks will honor constraint dates	6 (342)		
Proj2000E-2-8	Compress the overall duration of a project schedule	3 (142–149)	T3 Review Assignment	21–24
Proj2000E-2-9	Enter remaining work or remaining duration values	5 (241–244)	T5 Review Assignment	25

Expert Standardized Coding Number	Certification Skill Activity	Tutorial Pages	End-of-Tutorial Practice	
			Exercise	Step Number
Proj2000E-3	**Create a Project Plan**			
Proj2000E-3-1	Enter fixed costs	4 (201–202)	T4 Review Assignment	19
Proj2000E-3-2	Enter various costs for resources	4 (162–167)	T4 Review Assignment	3
Proj2000E-3-3	Create and use templates	6 (302–311)	T6 Case 1	1
Proj2000E-3-4	Modify task calendar options	2 (66–69)	T2 Review Assignment	6–8
Proj2000E-3-5	Assign resources with different units or hours of work to the same task	4 (178–179)	T4 Case 3	12–13
Proj2000E-3-6	Apply views which analyze slack and slip	5 (254–256)	T5 Review Assignment	33
Proj2000E-4	**Communicating project information**			
Proj2000E-4-1	Create and use a custom data map	6 (293–296)		
Proj2000E-4-2	Use flag and text fields	6 (329–331)		
Proj2000E-4-3	Use Organizer to customize a project file	6 (312–315)	T6 Review Assignment	T6, 36
Proj2000E-4-4	Create a new custom report incorporating custom tables and filters	5 (262–264)	T6 Review Assignment	28–29
Proj2000E-4-5	Display current, interim, and baseline plans in a Gantt chart	5 (258–259)		
Proj2000E-5	**General Project Management Concepts**			
Proj2000E-5-1	Set options to calculate multiple critical paths	6 (329)		
Proj2000E-5-2	Calculate cost of work performed (earned value analysis)	6 (288–292)	T6 Review Assignment	17–18
Proj2000E-5-3	Create activity reports to manage slack	5 (260–261)		
Proj2000E-6	**Customizing MS Project**			
Proj2000E-6-1	Set AutoAccept rules for resources in Project Central	Appendix E		
Proj2000E-6-2	Create and use custom forms	6 (331–333)		
Proj2000E-6-3	Set accessibility and user options	6 (340–342)		

Expert Standardized Coding Number	Certification Skill Activity	Tutorial Pages	End-of-Tutorial Practice	
			Exercise	Step Number
Proj2000E-6-4	Set Security options in Project Central	Appendix E	Appendix E	
Proj2000E-6-5	Create users and permissions in Project Central	Appendix E	Appendix E	
Proj2000E-6-6	Create and manage views and categories in Project Central	Appendix E	Appendix E	
Proj2000E-6-7	Format Gantt charts in Project Central	Appendix E		
Proj2000E-6-8	Set various Microsoft Project options in the Options dialog box	6 (339–342)		
Proj2000E-6-9	Customize the global template file	6 (307–309)	T6 Review Assignment	T6, 36
Proj2000E-7	**Customizing a project**			
Proj2000E-7-1	Create a custom box style in the network diagram	3 (139–141)	T3 Review Assignment	18–19
Proj2000E-7-2	Modify code mask	2 (102–104)		
Proj2000E-7-3	Record, assign, and play a macro	6 (334–336)	T6 Review Assignment	41
Proj2000E-7-4	Set calculation options	6 (339–342)		
Proj2000E-8	**Multi-project management**			
Proj2000E-8-1	View multiple critical paths in a consolidated project	6 (329)	T6 Case 1	20–21
Proj2000E-8-2	Modify inserted project information	6 (323–325)	T6 Review Assignment	28–30

File Finder

Location in Tutorial	Name and Location of Data File	Student Saves File As...*	Student Creates New File
Tutorial 1			
Session 1.1			
Session 1.2			LAN.mpp
Session 1.3	Tutorial.01\Tutorial\LAN-1.mpp	LAN-1-Your Initials.mpp	
Review Assignment	Tutorial.01\Review\Training-1.mpp	Training-1-Your Initials.mpp	
Case Problem 1	Tutorial.01\Cases\House-1.mpp	House-1-Your Initials.mpp	
Case Problem 2	Tutorial.01\Cases\Job-1.mpp	Job-1-Your Initials.mpp	
Case Problem 3	Tutorial.01\Cases\Convention-1.mpp	Convention-1-Your Initials.mpp	
Case Problem 4			Fund-1-Your Initials.mpp
Tutorial 2			
Session 2.1			LAN-2-Your Initials.mpp
Session 2.2	Tutorial.02\Tutorial\LAN-2-2.mpp	LAN-2-2-Your Initials.mpp	
Session 2.3	Tutorial.02\Tutorial\LAN-2-3.mpp	LAN-2-3-Your Initials.mpp	
Review Assignment	Tutorial.02\Review\Training-2.mpp	Training-2-Your Initials.mpp	
Case Problem 1	Tutorial.02\Cases\House-2.mpp	House-2-Your Initials.mpp	
Case Problem 2	Tutorial.02\Cases\Job-2.mpp	Job-2-Your Initials.mpp	
Case Problem 3	Tutorial.02\Cases\Convention-2.mpp	Convention-2-Your Initials.mpp	
Case Problem 4			Fund-2-Your Initials.mpp
Tutorial 3**			
Session 3.1	Tutorial.03\Tutorial\LAN-3.mpp	LAN-3-Your Initials.mpp	
Session 3.2	Tutorial.03\Tutorial\LAN-3-2.mpp	LAN-3-2-Your Initials.mpp	
Session 3.3	Tutorial.03\Tutorial\LAN-3-3.mpp	LAN-3-3-Your Initials.mpp	
Review Assignment	Tutorial.03\Review\Training-3.mpp	Training-3-Your Initials.mpp	
Case Problem 1	Tutorial.03\Cases\House-3.mpp	House-3-Your Initials.mpp	
Case Problem 2	Tutorial.03\Cases\Job-3.mpp	Job-3-Your Initials.mpp	
Case Problem 3	Tutorial.03\Cases\Convention-3.mpp	Convention-3-Your Initials.mpp	
Case Problem 4	Tutorial.03\Cases\Fund-3.mpp	Fund-3-Your Initials.mpp	
Tutorial 4**			
Session 4.1	Tutorial.04\Tutorial\LAN-4.mpp	LAN-4-Your Initials.mpp	
Session 4.2	Tutorial.04\Tutorial\LAN-4-2.mpp Tutorial.04\Tutorial\LAN-4-2B.mpp	LAN-4-2-Your Initials.mpp LAN-4-2B-Your Initials.mpp	
Session 4.3	Tutorial.04\Tutorial\LAN-4-3.mpp Tutorial.04\Tutorial\PCLab-4.mpp	LAN-4-3-Your Initials.mpp PCLab-4-Your Initials.mpp	
Review Assignment	Tutorial.04\Review\Training-4.mpp	Training-4-Your Initials.mpp	
Case Problem 1	Tutorial.04\Cases\House-4.mpp	House-4-Your Initials.mpp	
Case Problem 2	Tutorial.04\Cases\Job-4.mpp	Job-4-Your Initials.mpp	
Case Problem 3	Tutorial.04\Cases\Convention-4.mpp	Convention-4-Your Initials.mpp	
Case Problem 4	Tutorial.04\Cases\Fund-4.mpp	Fund-4-Your Initials.mpp	
Tutorial 5**			
Session 5.1	Tutorial.05\Tutorial\LAN-5.mpp	LAN-5-Your Initials.mpp	
Session 5.2	Tutorial.05\Tutorial\LAN-5-2.mpp Tutorial.05\Tutorial\LAN-5-2B.mpp	LAN-5-2-Your Initials.mpp LAN-5-2B-Your Initials.mpp	
Review Assignment	Tutorial.05\Review\Training-5.mpp	Training-5 Your Initials.mpp	
Case Problem 1	Tutorial.05\Cases\House-5.mpp	House-5-Your Initials.mpp	
Case Problem 2	Tutorial.05\Cases\Job-5.mpp	Job-5-Your Initials.mpp	
Case Problem 3	Tutorial.05\Cases\Convention-5.mpp	Convention-5-Your Initials.mpp	
Case Problem 4	Tutorial.05\Cases\Fund-5.mpp	Fund-5-Your Initials.mpp	

*(NOTE: Initials will vary for each student. EK is used for solution files)

**NOTE: Files for Tutorials 3, 4, and 5 do not fit on one floppy disk. If using floppies, we recommend one disk for each session, one disk for Review, and one disk for cases.

File Finder

Location in Tutorial	Name and Location of Data File	Student Saves File As...*	Student Creates New File
Tutorial 6**			
Session 6.1	Tutorial.06\Tutorial\TrainingLab-6.mpp Tutorial.06\Tutorial\Training Lab-6-2.mpp Tutorial.06\Tutorial\Configuration Tasks.xls Tutorial.06\Tutorial\New Resources.xls	TrainingLab-6-Your Initials.mpp TrainingLab-6-2-Your Initials.mpp Configuration Tasks-Your Initials.xls Documentation.doc (with changes)	Final Training Gantt Chart.gif TrainingLab-6-2-Your Initials-earned value TrainingLab-6-Your Initials.htm Configuration Tasks-Your Initials.mpp Configuration Tasks-98-Your Initials.mpp JLB LAN Work contour file.mpp
Session 6.2	Tutorial.06\Tutorial\LAN-6.mpp Tutorial.06\Tutorial\Software.mpp	LAN-6-Your Initials.mpp Software-Your Initials.mpp Pool.mpp	SDLC-Your Initials.mpp SDLC-Your Initials–1.mpp
Session 6.3	Tutorial.06\Tutorial\JLB LAN Documentation.doc Tutorial.06\Tutorial\TrainingLab-6-Your Initials.mpp (created in session 6.1)		Master-6-Your Initials.mpp Document Hardware-6-Your Initials.mpp Document Software-6-Your Initials.mpp
Review Assignment	Tutorial.06\Review\Training-6.mpp Tutorial.06\Review\Survey.xls	Training-6-Your Initials.mpp Tutorial.06\Review\Survey-Your Initials.mpp	Tracking Gantt.gif Training Data.htm
Case Problem 1	Project file created using template	CASE 1: No files saved, all printouts for solutions	
Case Problem 2	Project file created using template		Office Deployment.gif Office Deployment.doc Infrastructure Deployment.html Total Cost by Phase-Your Initials.xls
Case Problem 3	Project file created using template		House-Macro-Your Initials.mpp
Case Problem 4	Tutorial.06\Cases\Fund-6.mpp	Fund-6-Your Initials.mpp	Building-Your Initials.mpp

****NOTE:** Files for Tutorial 6 do not fit on one floppy disk. Tutorial 6 must be completed from the hard drive or from a large, removable storage device.